Teach Your Child to Read in 100 Easy Lessons

Teach Your Child to Read in 100 Easy Lessons

Siegfried Engelmann
Phyllis Haddox
Elaine Bruner

A FIRESIDE BOOK
Published by Simon & Schuster
New York London Toronto Sydney

First Fireside Edition, 1986
Published by Simon & Schuster, Inc.

Rockefeller Center
1230 Avenue of the Americas
New York, New York 10020

Teach Your Child to Read in 100 Easy Lessons is adapted from *Distar® Reading II*, Second Edition
by Siegfried Engelmann and Elaine C. Bruner, © 1975, 1969, Science Research Associates, Inc.
Adapted by permission of the publisher.

Illustrations for lesson 17 and lessons 77–100 are by Susan Jerde

Manufactured in the United States of America

35 Pbk.

Library of Congress Cataloging in Publication Data
Engelmann, Siegfried.
Teach your child to read in 100 easy lessons.
1. Reading (Preschool) I. Haddox, Phyllis.
II. Bruner, Elaine. III. Title.
LB1140.5.R4E53 372.4'1 81-21245
AACR2

ISBN 0-346-12557-X

ISBN: 0-671-63198-5 Pbk.

Book design H. Roberts Design

Acknowledgments
The authors are very grateful to Science Research Associates (SRA) for generously providing us with permission to adapt the **Distar** Fast Cycle® for *Teach Your Child to Read in 100 Easy Lessons*.

INTRODUCTION

In 1955 Rudolph Flesch rocked the educational community with his book *Why Johnny Can't Read.* The theme of the book was that phonics methods are more effective than the look-say methods used in schools, but phonics methods are not used in schools. Twenty-five years later, Flesch's follow-up book came out—*Why Johnny Still Can't Read.* The title says it all. Although words and epithets flew during those years, very little changed. According to Flesch, the look-say, or whole-word, method is still being used in three out of four schools.

The bad news is further explained by Robert Benjamin in his book *Making Schools Work.* Benjamin, a newspaper reporter commissioned by the Ford Foundation to identify educational programs that work, says, "Teaching children to read well from the start is the most important task of elementary schools. But relying on education to approach this correctly can be a great mistake. Many schools continue to employ instructional methods that have been proven ineffective. The staying power of the look-say or whole-word method of teaching beginning reading is perhaps the most flagrant example of this failure to instruct effectively."[1]

So much for the bad news. The first part of the good news is that there is a program that works. This program—**Distar,** published by Science Research Associates, Inc. (SRA)—involves no snappy motivational tricks and no instructional magic. It is simply a very, very careful program, and research consistently shows that **Distar** does the best job of all commercial programs in teaching reading. Benjamin writes:

> The program bears almost nothing in common with the way students are taught in most of America's public schools. But DISTAR works. It consistently has delivered what other programs usually just promise. . . . In the largest, most expensive, most ambitious social experiment ever conducted in the United States—in which nine different instructional programs representing the major educational theories of the 1970's were pitted against each other to find out what works best with low-income children—DISTAR far and away came out on top.[2]
>
> Research on DISTAR shows it has had dramatic effects with almost every kind of child. . . . DISTAR is particularly effective with young children.[3]

The second part of the good news is that the hundred-day program presented in this book is an adaptation of the **Distar** Fast Cycle Reading Program. The program has been streamlined somewhat and modified for home use. If you follow the program, you will teach your child to read quite well in one hundred days.

[1]Robert Benjamin, *Making Schools Work* (New York: Continuum, 1981), pp. 94–96.
[2]Benjamin, *Making Schools Work,* p. 71.
[3]Benjamin, *Making Schools Work,* p. 79.

The hundred-day program is appropriate for preschool children (bright three-and-a-half-year-olds, average four- and five-year-olds).

The hundred-day program is also appropriate for children who have been in school but who have not learned to read.

The program is *not* recommended for "poor readers" who have been taught how to read but who make frequent mistakes.

The only materials that you'll need to teach reading are this book and some paper (or a chalkboard)—no flash cards, lesson plans, special books, or machines.

The instructions for each lesson are complete, telling you exactly what to say and do. Each lesson is designed so that it takes only about half an hour each day. That time includes all preparation time and the time that you spend presenting the lesson to your child.

After you complete the program, you'll know more about teaching reading than most public-school teachers, because you will have carefully observed and participated in the step-by-step development of your child's reading skills. And because the program works, something very nice happens: perhaps not on the first lesson or on the fifth, but long before Lesson 100 your child will turn on to reading. The child's surroundings are full of written words that the child will read with great pride. Your life will be enriched as you watch your child grow in a wonderful way.

THE COMPLEX SKILL OF READING

The sophisticated reading that adults do is analogous to playing a concerto on the piano. The ultimate goal of reading instruction is to prepare children for the concerto of reading—reading complicated material silently, at a reasonably fast rate, and understanding the details of the message the author presents.

The program that prepares the child should be a careful one, just as good instruction in playing the piano starts with simple skills that are modified and expanded to create more complicated ones. A piano-playing program is poor if it requires the naive student to play a concerto. The student will not be able to perform and will understandably become frustrated. A more reasonable program would build toward the concerto one step at a time, designed so that the student achieves mastery of each step before moving to a more difficult one.

So it is with reading instruction. A reasonable program begins *at the beginning* and builds. The skills that are needed for more complicated tasks are first taught in their simplest form. Once the child has mastered these skills, the program presents more complicated variations.

The following are the four most important points about *an effective sequence for teaching reading:*

1. The beginning exercises are simple and do not resemble later exercises (just as beginning piano exercises do not look much like advanced ones).
2. The program provides teaching for every single skill that the child is expected to use when performing even the simplest reading exercises.
3. The exercises change form slowly, and the changes are relatively small, so that the exercises are always relatively easy for the child.
4. At every step, the program provides for very clear and unambiguous communications with the child.

THE DISTAR® READING PROGRAM

The major force that has determined the design and content of the **Distar** program is feedback about specific, detailed problems that children experience. When **Distar** was developed, the authors assumed that if students had problems with any of the exercises presented, the program—not the students—was at fault. So the program was changed, and tried out with new students, and changed again until it was smooth and manageable. In its final form it has the potential to teach virtually any child who goes through it. Note that it has only the *potential.* For this potential to be realized, the "teacher" must present the various exercises as specified and must make sure that the child is able to perform every task presented in each lesson.

Research Involving Distar

Distar has been involved in more than a dozen comparative studies. The results are fairly uniform: children taught with **Distar** outperform their peers who receive instruction in other programs. These results hold after one year of instruction, after two, after three, and after four. The largest single study in which **Distar** was involved was the comparison of U.S. Office of Education Follow Through sites—the largest educational experiment ever conducted. Various geographic sites in the United States selected a specific educational program from those made available. Each site agreed to implement the chosen program for teaching poverty children in kindergarten through grade three. The University of Oregon Follow Through model, which used **Distar** instruction in all grades and for all major subjects (reading, language, math), consistently outperformed all the other sponsored programs in reading achievement, arithmetic achievement, language performance, and measures of self-esteem. The more than ten thousand children in the University of Oregon model came from various cities and counties in the United States—some from Indian reservations; others from poverty neighborhoods in cities like New York and Washington, D.C.; still others from rural places like DeKalb County, Tennessee, and Williamsburg County, South Carolina. The **Distar** programs worked better than any other program in the cities, better in rural areas, better with whites, with blacks, and with brown, better with poverty children and with middle-class children.

The **Distar** programs are more effective than other programs because they control more of the details that are important to successful teaching. Some beginning reading programs control the reading vocabulary that is presented to the child. **Distar** goes far beyond this. It controls vocabulary, the specific tasks that are presented, the type of example, the number of times the example appears, and even the teacher's wording—including specifications about how to effectively correct different types of errors that may occur. The control involves all the details that might make a difference in how the child receives the communication. Some things that **Distar** controls may seem quite reasonable and necessary to a person not familiar with educational practices, (for instance, the control of how to correct the child's mistakes.) Yet the "basal reading" programs that are most widely used in schools do not provide teachers with this type of information. We analyzed the four most widely used basal reading programs in grades four through six and discovered that none of them contains any specific correction procedures. The teacher's guides simply provide general suggestions cautioning the teacher to work longer with the children who learn more slowly than others.

COMMUNICATING CLEARLY WITH THE CHILD

Traditional reading programs are poor devices for teaching *all* children because they do not have provisions for communicating clearly. To appreciate the pitfalls that are involved in clear communication, we have to put ourselves in the place of the child who is trying to learn to read. This child may not understand exactly what reading is or precisely how one goes about doing it. Adults may have a clear idea of what they are trying to tell the child, but things may look quite different from the child's perspective. Let's say that we teach the child to look at the first letter of words and identify those words (an activity common in poor reading programs). We might begin by presenting words that are easy to distinguish by looking at the first letter. Here's a possible list of such words:

he go fat run with

Although the naive child might quickly "read" those words by looking at the first letter, the child may later encounter a serious problem. As soon as we introduce a new word that begins with the same letter that one of those first words begins with, we will probably discover that the child confuses the new word with the familiar word. For example, when we introduce the word **him,** we will probably discover that the child calls the word **he,** because both words begin with **h.**

This example points out a very important feature of poor communication in a teaching sequence. *The problem that the communication creates is not evident at the time the teaching occurs.* The child in the example reads the initial set of words without a hitch. Everything seems to be fine. Only later, when we introduce examples that call for more difficult discriminations, does the problem emerge.

If we examine the communication involved in early instruction, we can identify the kind of confusion that it may create and predict the kind of problem the child may later encounter. One of the more popular (but less effective) techniques for teaching initial reading skills is called the language experience method. This method involves doing something with the children, then talking about the experience, then writing sentences on the board that tell about the experience, then pointing to the words in the sentences and showing the children how to "read" them. The most obvious problem with the method is that it is far easier for the children to *remember* the sentences than it is for them to identify the individual words. Remember, these children do not know anything about reading. The teacher stands up, makes some squiggles on the board, points to them, and talks slowly. While pointing to the different squiggles, the teacher then requires the children to repeat what was said. Although it is possible for some children to extract the intended meaning from this communication, the communication is very poor. Some children predictably come away from it with the idea that when you read, you simply point to the squiggles and talk slowly as you recite one of the familiar sentences. If we were to put up one of the charts the children worked on earlier without first cueing them about the content, some children would point to the words in order and say sentences for *another chart* with great fidelity.

Another communication problem occurs if we try to teach too much during the initial reading exercises. This problem is characteristic of most of the basal reading programs that are used in schools. These programs are extremely poor at communicating the difference between decoding and understanding. Decoding is the simple act of identifying the words in a sentence. Decoding does not necessarily imply understanding. To decode the sentence **Ruf unter glop splee,** you simply say the words. This illustration points out that you may be able to decode without understanding what the sentence means. Traditional reading programs typically confuse the beginning reader about whether the teacher is trying to teach decoding or understanding. These programs typically begin with the teacher discussing details of a picture. If the picture shows a girl named Jan, the teacher talks about Jan—what she is wearing, the color of her hair, and so forth. After discussing Jan, the teacher points to the word below the picture. The word, of course, is **Jan.**

It might seem that this communication is effective because it promotes interest and gives the children the motivation for both reading and understanding the written message. However, this communication may prompt the child to formulate a serious misconception about how to read. If the teacher always talks about the picture before reading the word, and if the word is always predictable by referring to the picture, the child may reasonably assume that:

- You read words by referring to a picture.
- You must understand the word that is to be decoded before you can read it.

Unfortunately, most children who fail to learn to read in school learn either one or a combination of these misconceptions. The typical poor reader in the upper elementary grades, for instance, reads some words by saying a *synonym* that bears no resemblance to the word on the page. The word may be **fine** and the reader calls it **good.** Consider the machinations that must occur in the reader's confused mind for this type of mistake to occur. The reader must approach the task of decoding with the idea that before reading a word, you must understand that word. The child looks at the word and seems to understand it, but when the child tries to say the word, a synonym comes out. (After all, the synonym and the word have the same meaning.)

A careless teaching communication permits the child to succeed for the moment, only to experience a serious setback later. To avoid these pitfalls, we must use a program that proceeds very carefully, tiptoeing around the pitfalls without taking costly shortcuts. The communications make it very clear when the child is simply to figure out the word and when the child is supposed to attend to the meaning. The communication arranges the order of these events so that the child *first* decodes, *then* discovers the meaning. The communication further shows the child a workable set of procedures for decoding or figuring out the word. At first this procedure is directed, a step at a time. As the child becomes adept at linking the steps, the directions shrink and the child assumes increasing responsibility.

Decoding—is the central skill in initial reading. Most of the other skills are nothing more than language skills. Once a sentence has been decoded, it is like a spoken sentence that may have been presented slowly. If the child has the language skills necessary to understand the spoken sentence, the child has the skills necessary to *understand* the decoded sentence. The central issue is not that of teaching the child to understand, but of teaching the child how to decode the sentences that *are to be understood.* (We should not require the child to read sentences that are beyond the child's understanding, any more than we would require somebody to read a Spanish text if the person had no understanding of Spanish. But if we have met this obvious language requirement, the central thrust of initial reading becomes the emphasis on decoding.)

MAKING TEACHING EASIER

Just as some of the control measures used in **Distar** may seem reasonable, others may initially seem contraintuitive or simply unnatural. An example of this control is the script that the teacher is to present verbatim when teaching the lessons. A typical response to the scripted presentations is "Why would a program have to choreograph what the teacher says?" The answer becomes apparent only if you observe teachers trying to teach without carefully controlled scripts, particularly when the presentation is delicate (which is the case when trying to teach a naive five-year-old to read). We know about these problems because before designing **Distar** we ran a master's training program at the University of Illinois. We provided our interns with detailed instruction in how to present tasks to children—the rate at which to pace them, procedures for stressing different words, and procedures for reinforcing and correcting the children. Unless you are a teacher who has had a great deal of training, the amount of information that you must attend to when carrying out an effective presentation of this type to a group of eight fidgety five-year-olds is overwhelming. If you add the requirement that the teacher must also supply the wording for each example that is presented, the overwhelming becomes impossible. Typically, the interns attended either to the content they presented or to the behavior of the children they were trying to teach. When they attended to the behavior, they frequently became verbose, repetitive, and often bumbled. When they talked too much (which they frequently did), their delivery suffered because their pacing became poor. The children became confused and lost interest. The solution was to remove some of the variables from the teacher by scripting what the teacher was to say. The teacher was left with plenty to do because the material still had to be presented in a way that was both effective and dynamic. But the teacher could now concentrate primarily on delivering the content, not on trying to create it or design ways to "get it across." After all, sitting in front of a group of children, each of whom may produce an incredible variety of responses at any moment, is not the best place to create smooth presentations.

Effective communication is the sum of many *details*. Unless all these details are controlled, the child will receive poor communication from the teacher, and the teacher will receive poor information about the child. The naive child fails to perform very well unless all details are carefully controlled. The information that the teacher receives is that the child cannot perform and therefore must be slow, must have some sort of visual perception problem or emotional problem. This information is categorically wrong. Each author of this book has worked with thousands of children, from gifted to "severely retarded." The authors have never seen a child four years old or older with an IQ above 70 who could not be taught to read, and read well, within a reasonable period of time. We have seen hundreds of children who have not been taught to read in school. We have worked with children at preschool to college levels who could not read and whose parents probably believed in the finality of the labels with which the school had adorned these students: dyslexic, perceptually handicapped, learning-disabled. These labels are nonsense. Almost without exception, the "disabled" students that we have worked with had two obvious problems. The first was that they had not been taught properly. Their confusion suggested that the malfunctions existed in the teachers' techniques, not in the children's minds. The second problem was that these students seemed to *believe* the labels. They hated reading (or trying to read). But the cure for these problems did not involve neurosurgery or wonder drugs. It involved nothing more than starting over and teaching carefully. The children soon discovered that they could learn, that their progress impressed their teacher, and that reading (or learning) was not so bad after all. A child's self-image goes through a remarkable growth spurt when the child receives powerful demonstrations of success.

Distar ORTHOGRAPHY: WHY THE "FUNNY" PRINT?

Orthography is a fancy word that refers to the letters that make up words, or how words are spelled. One problem with reading from the kind of orthography that occurs in everyday reading is that the spelling is sometimes outrageous. The word **said** is not spelled the way it sounds: "sed." Many of the simplest words that we would use to make up even the simplest sentence are also irregular—**the, off, of, what, to, do, where, who** . . . An interesting exercise for beginning reading teachers is to try to make up simple sentences in which the orthographic code is perfectly regular. For it to be perfectly regular, each letter would make exactly the same sound each time it appeared in the sentence. **Pam had ham** is a perfectly regular sentence. The letter **m** occurs twice, but it makes the same sound each time it occurs: "m." The letter **a** occurs in all words. Each time it occurs, it makes the same short-vowel sound. Although it is possible to use conventional symbols and conventional spelling to make up sentences in which all words have a regular spelling, as soon as we move from Pam and her ham, the task becomes much more difficult. If we try to express the idea that a girl and a boy went to a lake, we may encounter a great deal of difficulty in creating sentences in which all the letters make one and only one sound. Consider the sentence **He and she go to the lake.** The letter **e** has the same function in the words **he** and **she.** In the words **the** and **lake,** however, the letter takes on two different roles. First it makes an "uh" sound (in **the**), and then it becomes silent (in **lake**). The letter **o** has different sound roles in the word **go** and the word **to.** The letter **h** takes on some bizarre roles. First it makes the common **"h"** sound (in the word **he**). Then it becomes combined with **s** to make the **"sh"** sound (in the word **she**). Then it combines with **t** for the **th** sound (in the word **the**).

English, clearly, is not a regularly spelled language. It is an amalgam of contributions from Latin, Greek, and French. But there are ways to simplify it for the beginning reader.

Distar solves the problem by introducing an altered orthography. This orthography does two things. It presents variations of some symbols so that we can create a larger number of words that are spelled regularly (each symbol having only a single sound function). At the same time, the orthography permits us to spell words the way they are spelled in traditional orthography. Here is the **Distar** alphabet:

a ā b c ch d e ē f g h i ī I j k l m n

o ō oo p qu r s sh t th u ū v w wh x y ȳ z

Notice that there are two variations for the letter **a** and for the letter **e.** By using these letters we can make the word **he** and **went** regular. The word **he** is presented as **hē** and the word **went** as **went.** Now both words are clearly the sum of their letters. Stated differently: if you say the sound value for each letter, you will say the word.

The orthography also provides joined letters. We can use these to make the word **she** regular: **shē.** The clue that **s** and **h** are joined is very important to the beginning reader. We can also make the word **the** sort of regular: **thē.** (We do not normally pronounce the word that way, unless we are making a speech or trying to be super-proper; however, the beginning of the word is now regular.)

One more convention in **Distar** orthography that permits us to spell words correctly and yet make them regular involves *small letters.* The rule about small letters is this: you don't say them. Silent letters are presented in small type. With the small letters we can now make the word **lake** regular: **lāke.** You do not read the final **e,** but the letter is present and the word is spelled as it should be: **l-a-k-e.**

Here's the entire sentence about **he** and **she,** with all the **Distar** conventions:

hē and shē went to the lāke.

Everything is now regular (one symbol making one and only one sound) except for the word **the** and the word **to.** Your first impulse might be to think, "Isn't that a shame," and then start trying to figure out ways to make these words perfectly regular. Hold the impulse. When we first began working with the modified alphabet, we used one that was completely regular. We discovered that when we attempted to provide a transition to traditional orthography, some children had a lot of trouble. Their trouble was created by our poor communication. By making the code completely regular, we had implied that reading involves nothing more than looking at the sounds for each word and adding them up. We failed to alert them to the fact that some words are different and that a different strategy is needed to approach these words. Later, we discovered that when we introduced some irregularly spelled words early in the program, the transition was much easier because we had provided practice in dealing with the kind of strategy needed for irregularly spelled words like **to, was,** and **said.**

But **Distar** orthography permits us to do a lot of nice things. We can make potentially difficult words like **where** and **were** perfectly regular:

(where were)

Notice that the word **were** has the joined **er,** which makes the sound "ur." The **e** is silent, so if you say the sounds for **w** and **er,** you will say **were. Where** is also regular now. It has the short **e** (as in **end**). By saying the sounds for **wh, e,** and **r,** you will say **where.**

The alphabet does not provide for all possible sounds. The goal in using this alphabet is not to replace traditional orthography but rather to create a variation of it that facilitates initial instruction. Once the child has learned to read words written in this modified orthography, we make the transition to traditional orthography. **Distar** orthography does not have to be exhaustive (presenting symbols for every sound) because we do not have to teach all words or all sound combinations at the beginning of reading instruction. We can teach many skills after we have made the transition to traditional orthography. By then the child has many reading skills, which means that the communications do not have to be as careful as those for the initial skills. The most careful part of the program must be the first part, because it develops the most basic skills that are later expanded and made more precise. If poor communications occur in the first part, the later parts cannot build successfully on skills that had been taught. These parts may then have to include the unpleasant job of reteaching the basics.

TEACHING FIRST THINGS FIRST

A good reading program should introduce actual reading as soon as possible. But before the child is able to perform the simple act of decoding words such as **mat** and **if,** the child must have some important prereading skills. We can figure out what most of those skills are by determining what a child would have to do to read a simple, regularly spelled word like **mat.**

The most obvious skill the child needs is knowledge of the sounds that each letter makes. This fact suggests some preteaching in sound identification. **Distar** does not initially teach letter names, because letter names play no direct role in reading words. The simplest way to demonstrate this fact is to say the letter names "em," "ay," and "tee" very fast and see if they add up to the word **mat.** They do not. They generate something like "emmaytee." It may not be a dirty word, but it certainly is not **mat.**

Sounds are functional in reading. So we preteach the sounds before we present them in words. Before reading the word **mat** and other words composed of these letters, the child would learn to identify **m** as "mmm." The repeated letters do not mean that you say the sound again and again. They signal you to hold the sound. Take a deep breath and say "mmmmmm" for a couple of seconds.

Not all sounds can be held for a long time. The sounds that can be held are called continuous sounds. They include **f, s, n, l, z, w,** and all the vowels. The sounds that cannot be held are noncontinuous. This group includes **b, d, ch, g, h, p, j,** and **t.** To say these sounds, you pronounce them very fast and add no "uh" sound to the end of them. The sound at the end of the word **mat** is unvoiced, which means that it is whispered. It is not "tuh." It is a whispered little "t." That is how it occurs in the word, and that is how it is pretaught. When the child has mastered the sounds that will occur in various words, the child has mastered the most obvious skill that is needed to read.

But other skills are quite important. Blending skills are verbal, not visual, skills. A child who does not have them will have difficulty linking the sounds of a word. To teach the blending skills called for by the word **mat,** we get rid of the written word **mat** but require the verbal behavior that the child would use in reading that word. First the child says the word very slowly, holding each sound but not stopping between the sounds: "mmmaaat." Next the child says it fast: "mat."

Here's how we might present the task:
"Say **mmmaaat.**"(Child says:) "mmmaaat."
"Say it fast." (Child says:) "mat."

For the blending task, the teacher does not stop between the sounds. (Learning this skill is sometimes difficult for children; however, it is usually much more difficult for teachers.) The reason for presenting the sounding out without stopping between the sounds is that it creates a much cleaner communication than one created by stopping between the sounds: "mmm—aaa—t." When the child says the sounds without pausing, the child is actually saying the word slowly. To say the word at a regular speaking rate, the child simply speeds up the word. The child does not first have to put the parts together and then say it fast.

When we add the written word to the blending exercise, we have an initial word-reading exercise.

You point to the word **mat** and touch under the letters **m, a,** and **t** as the child says "mmmaaat."

You say, "Say it fast." Child says, "mat."

We've identified two important skills that are called for by the simple word-reading task. There are others, the most important of which is rhyming. Rhyming points out the relationship of one word to words that are similar. If we start with the ending **op** and add different beginnings (by putting different consonants in front of **op**), we create a series of related words. If the child has basic rhyming skills, the relationship between the words becomes very clear. They rhyme. This understanding promotes important generalizations about word families (which are based on common endings). This understanding helps the child see that a word like **hop** is not an island but is part of a network of words that includes **top, pop,** and **drop.**

To summarize, you are going to teach your child the sounds the different letters make. You do not teach the letters all at once. You present them one at a time and give your child plenty of practice with each new letter. While you are teaching the letters, you also work on blending skills. The child practices saying a variety of simple words slowly and then saying each word fast. Also, you work on rhyming and other skills related to the task of sequencing the different sound parts of words. During the initial lessons, your child will work on these skills, not on reading words. After your child has learned the sounds for the letters that will appear in the first words presented in the program, and learned the other necessary skills, you introduce the simplest form of word reading. At this time your child will have practiced all the verbal components called for by the complex task of decoding. Your child will have made rhymes for the words that are to be read and will have blended them. Now simply put the parts together, add the written word, and presto: your child can read.

The sequence is designed so that the child who takes the first steps can take the next step and the steps that follow that step. Furthermore, all the skills that are needed are pretaught, which means that you should always be able to correct mistakes in more complicated tasks by referring to the specific skills that were pretaught.

Irregulars and Comprehension

Initial decoding is certainly not the end of reading instruction; however, it is the major stumbling block. After you guide the child past the initial decoding, you must still teach a great deal. You must introduce different groups of irregularly spelled words (such as the group that contains **ar,** like **part, smart, bark,** and so on). And you must switch emphasis from the reading of isolated words to sentence reading and sentence comprehension. To make reading the key to the discovery of meaning, you first direct the child to read a sentence, then answer questions about the sentence. If the sentence the child has just read is **We went home,** you would ask questions such as "What did we do? . . . Who went home?" This type of comprehension is simple, literal understanding, but like initial decoding, it is the simplest and most basic form that can be presented. In addition to the strictly literal questions about the sentences the child reads, you also introduce comprehension activities to promote the idea that the sentences may tell about pictures, and that these pictures show what the sentence tells. If the sentence is **It is on,** you tell your child, "You're going to see a picture. And what do you know about the thing you'll see in the picture?" (Child says, "It is on.") You present the picture showing a child who has just turned on a light. You now ask questions that relate the text to the picture. "What is on?" You also ask questions that serve as rewards.

As your child becomes more proficient at handling the simpler forms of comprehension activities, more elaborate ones are introduced. One type is the prediction question. After the child reads a sentence that tells what somebody wants to do, tries to do, or starts to do, you ask, "What do you think will happen?" The next sentence in the text answers the question. Prediction questions help the child develop the skill of "anticipating" what will happen next. These questions help the reader form a tie between the skills used in listening to a story and those involved in the more active role of reading it.

So your child starts the program with presumably very few reading-related skills. Within one hundred teaching days—about two-thirds of a school year—your child reads, although not as well as an adult. But through the course of the lessons your child has learned to read words without first sounding them out—and therefore has learned to read at a rate much faster than that at which the child read during the first lessons that presented word reading. Your child has learned to read from traditional orthography and now reads simple stories that are more than 250 words long (through a transition that begins in Lesson 74). The child has learned basic sentence-comprehension skills (literal comprehension and prediction skills).

And the program provides for teaching you. As you read the description of the various comprehension skills, you may have wondered, "How will I know which questions to present and when to present them?" It's easy. All the questions that you are to present are written in the program. All tasks and activities that you are to present are written in the program. In fact, all the correct responses that your child should make for the various tasks are indicated. If you follow the program religiously the first time you present it, the outcome is guaranteed. Your child will read, and you will be an effective reading teacher. When you present the program a second or third time to other children, you will understand where each type of exercise is going. You will be able to free-lance more, add, change, possibly streamline. If you try to become too fancy the first time you present it, however, you will probably find out later in the program that you should not have modified some of the things you did earlier. Our discussion of the program was very general. A host of mini-skills is taught along the way, and unless you know how each of these skills relates to others that are to be taught, you may change an exercise from the way it is specified and in so doing fail to teach one of these skills.

GETTING READY

Before you start teaching your child, you should do four things:

- Learn the sounds that are introduced in the program, particularly the first ten.
- Make up a teaching schedule.
- Practice some corrections.
- Practice presenting the first couple of lessons in the program.

The sounds. The following list presents the sounds in the order of their appearance. Accompanying each sound is a brief description of it, indicating whether it is *continuous* or *noncontinuous* and whether it is *voiced* or *whispered.*

Before you present any sounds in the program, make sure that you can pronounce each sound properly. First make sure that you can produce an individual sound in isolation (apart from a word) in a way that is not distorted. The sound will be distorted if you add a funny sound to the end of it.

The simplest procedure is to start with a word that ends in the sound you are interested in. Say the word slowly and loudly, as you would say it to a person who is hard of hearing. For example, to figure out how to say the sound **nnn** in isolation, say the word **fan** very slowly, holding each sound for at least one second. The way you say the **nnn** sound in that word is the way you would say the sound **nnn** in isolation. Note that you do not say "fffaaannn*uh*" or "fffaaannn*ih*." So when you say the **nnn** sound in isolation, you would not say "nnnuh" or "nnnih." You would say a pure **nnn** with no additional sound tacked onto the end.

To figure out how to say the **t** sound, say the word **fat** slowly and loudly. Note that you cannot hold the **t** sound. It occurs quickly no matter how long you hold the **fff** sound and the **aaa** sound (both of which can be held a long time). Note also that you do not add a funny sound to the end. You do not say "fffaaat*uh*" or "fffaaat*ih*." So you would not say "tuh" or "tih" when you present the **t** sound in isolation.

Remember, the simplest procedure for figuring out how to say sounds in isolation is to say a word that ends in that sound. Say the word slowly and loudly, but not in a way that distorts the sounds. The sound that you say at the end of the word is the sound you would produce when presenting that sound in isolation.

A sound is whispered if your voice is not turned on when you say the sound. Place your hand on your throat and *whisper* the entire word **fuss.**

PRONUNCIATION GUIDE

Symbol	Pronounced	As in	Voiced or Whispered	Introduced in Lesson
m	mmm	ram	v	1
s	sss	bus	w	1
a	aaa	and	v	3
ē	ēēē	eat	v	5
t	t	cat	w	7
r	rrr	bar	v	9
d	d	mad	v	12
i	iii	if	v	14
th	ththth	this and bathe (not thing)	v	16
c	c	tack	w	19
o	ooo	ox	v	21
n	nnn	pan	v	23
f	fff	stuff	w	25
u	uuu	under	v	27
l	lll	pal	v	29
w	www	wow	v	31
g	g	tag	v	33
I	(the word *I*)		v	34
sh	shshsh	wish	w	35
ā	āāā	ate	v	37
h	h	hat	w	39
k	k	tack	w	41
ō	ōōō	over	v	43
v	vvv	love	v	45
p	p	sap	w	48
ar	ŏrrr	car	v	49
ch	ch	touch	w	50
e	ĕĕĕ	end(ed)	v	52
b	b	grab	v	54
ing	iiing	sing	v	56
ī	īīī	ice	v	58
y	yyyē	yard	v	60
er	urrr	brother	v	62
oo	oooooo	moon (not look)	v	65
j	j	judge	v	67
wh	www	why	w	69
ȳ	īīī	my	v	71
ū	ūūū	use	v	74
qu	kwww (or koo)	quick	v	74
x	ksss	ox	w	75
z	zzz	buzz	v	75
ea	ēēē	leave	v	79
ai	āāā	rain	v	88
ou	owww	loud	v	89

You should feel no vibration on your throat because all the sounds are whispered.

Now *say* the word **fuss** very slowly by holding each sound longer than you normally would. Do not try to whisper the word. Say the word in a normal speaking voice. You should feel no vibrations on your throat for the sounds **fff** and **sss.**

Now say the word **fun** slowly and feel your throat. Your throat should not buzz for the **fff** sound. But it should buzz for both **uuu** and **nnn.** The sound **nnn** is a voiced sound.

Now say the word **run** and feel your throat. Your throat should buzz for all sounds—**rrr, uuu,** and **nnn.** The **rrr** is a voiced sound.

Do not present a lesson that introduces a new sound until you can produce the sound accurately and consistently. (If you misteach a sound, your child will have a lot of trouble later in the program when trying to read words that include that sound.)

Pay particular attention to the pronunciation of the following sounds:

- **r.** Do not say "urrr" for this symbol or the child will have a lot of trouble reading words like **run.** The child will try to call the word "urun." Use the sound that is at the end of the word **bar.** It is a single sound that can be held.
- **th.** The sound for this symbol is *voiced.* There is a whispered **th** for words like **math** and **thing.** The voiced sound occurs in words like **them, then, that,** and **those.** This sound is the one that is taught in the program.
- **h.** The **h** sound is very tricky. It is produced quickly by letting out a little air *with no voice.*
- **y.** The sound we use for this symbol occurs only at the beginning of words **(yēard).** It is quite similar to the sound **ēēē** (as in **eat**), but it is slightly more restricted. If you have trouble with the sound, say **ēēē.** It will work pretty well.
- **oo.** This symbol refers to the sound in **boo, moon,** and **toot,** not to the sound in **look, soot,** or **book.**
- **wh.** This sound is pronounced differently in different parts of the country. In the East it is unvoiced. In the Midwest and West it is voiced. Use the pronunciation that is appropriate for your speech.

In addition to indicating whether a sound is voiced or whispered, the column of the sounds chart labeled "Pronounced" shows whether the sound can be held or must be said very rapidly. If a sound can be held, three symbols are shown for the sound (such as **mmm** and **sss**). These symbols tell you that you should be able to hold the sound for at least two seconds without distorting it. Note that you are not to say the sound repeatedly ("m—m—m"). You are to take a deep breath and say it one time, holding it for at least two seconds.

The sounds that cannot be held are shown in the "pronounced" column as single letters, **d, c, t.** These sounds must be said very quickly. Say the word **mad** slowly and loudly. The last sound you say is the appropriate pronunciation for the **d** sound. It is a voiced sound. (Feel your throat.) It does not have an "uh" sound following it (not "mmmaaad*uh*"), and it must be said very quickly.

To use the sounds chart, refer to the last column. That column tells you the lesson in which a new sound is introduced. In Lesson 1, the sounds for **m** and **s** are introduced. Practice these sounds before presenting the lesson. Both sounds are voiced. Check the column labeled "As in" to make sure that you are using the right pronunciation for the letter, particularly the vowels. The symbol **a** is introduced in Lesson 3. It has many different pronunciations when we deal with traditional orthography. For the beginning of the program that you will use, the symbol **a** refers to only one sound—the first sound in the word **and.** Note that you will *never* say "**aaa** as in **and**" to the child. The model word is to show *you* the sound you are to say for **a.**

Saying Words Slowly

Practice saying words without pausing between the sounds. As noted earlier, the child will have a much easier time identifying words that are sounded out if the child learns to blend the sounds by saying them without pausing between the sounds.

Beginning with Lesson 1, you will say words slowly, without pausing between the sounds. The words that you will say in Lesson 1 are **am, me, in,** and **she.**

Practice saying these words properly. Start with **am.** Put your hand on your throat. Take a deep breath. Say "aaammm," holding each sound for at least two seconds. Do not stop between the sounds. If you stop, you will feel your throat stop buzzing. Your throat should buzz from the first instant of "aaammm" to the last, with no interruption. Remember to hold both sounds for about an equal amount of time. Do not say a very fast **a** sound followed by a long **mmm** sound. Try to hold each sound for two seconds.

Practice the other words—**me, in,** and **she.** Note that when you practice **she,** your voice will not start until you say the sound **ēēē;** however, you should hold the **shshsh** sound for two seconds, and there should be no time during which there is silence. The **ēēē** sound should begin as soon as the **shshsh** sound stops, but there should not be the slightest pause (silence) between these two sounds.

Beginning with Lesson 1, your child will say words slowly after you say them. Make sure the child does not stop between the sounds. Correct mistakes immediately. Your child shouldn't have any serious problems with this task if you do a good job of saying the words slowly, one sound at a time.

The same rules that apply to pronouncing sounds in isolation apply to saying words slowly. Some sounds cannot be held for more than an instant. To say the word **mat** slowly, you would hold the first two sounds for two seconds each. Then you would quickly say the **t** sound: "mmmaaat." (Remember, this sound is whispered.) (Note that there is a silence immediately before the sounds **c, t,** and **p** when they occur at the end of words. This pause is acceptable because a pause occurs when we say the words at a normal speaking rate.)

Sounding Out Words

Beginning with Lesson 9, you will direct your child to sound out written words and then say them fast. The words to be read look like this:

For each word, you will first touch the big ball at the beginning of the arrow that runs under the word to be read. You tell the child to "sound it out." Then you move to each ball on the arrow and stop for at least *one second.* (One second is not one instant. It is a fairly long time.)

The illustration below shows what you are to do.

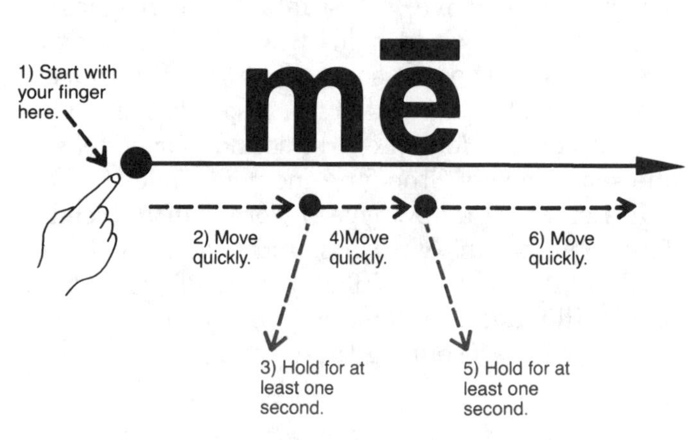

Practice moving quickly along the arrow and then stopping for at least one second at each ball. After you have stopped at the last ball for at least one second, move quickly to the end of the arrow.

The child is to say the sounds as soon as you touch the ball for each sound. The child is to keep holding the sound until you touch the ball for the next sound. The child is then to say the next sound without stopping. (The child is to say "mmmeee," not "mmm"—pause—"eee.") The child's task will be much easier if you remember to move fairly quickly from one sound to the next. (Note that if you move too quickly, the child will not know what sound to say next and will not be able to respond when you touch the next ball. If you move too slowly, the child will run out of air before saying the last sound.)

Some words end in sounds that cannot be held for a long period of time. You present these words almost the same way you present words with sounds that can be held. The only difference is that you don't stop at the last sound for a full second. You stop for an instant and then move quickly to the end of the arrow.

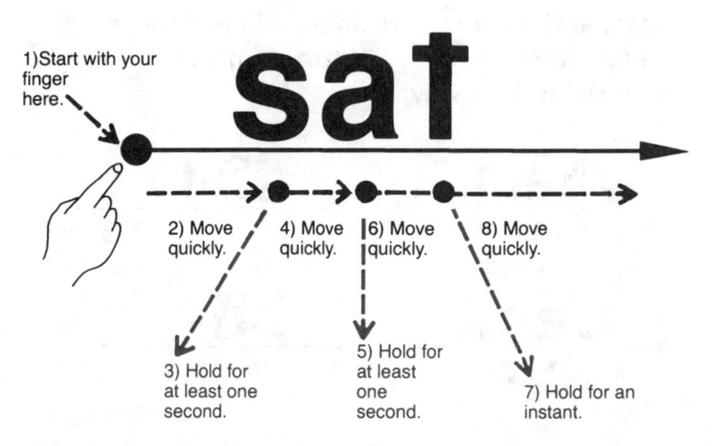

The program script for each task indicates the response the child is to produce. The response for the word above is "sssaaat." The response shows that the child holds the first sounds but does not hold the last sound. The way you touch the sounds should parallel the response the child is to produce. Hold the first sounds for at least one second each. Stop for a moment under the **t.**

In Lesson 21 a new type of word is introduced. This type begins with a sound that cannot be held. It is the most difficult type of word the child will read. The illustration below shows your behavior for presenting these words.

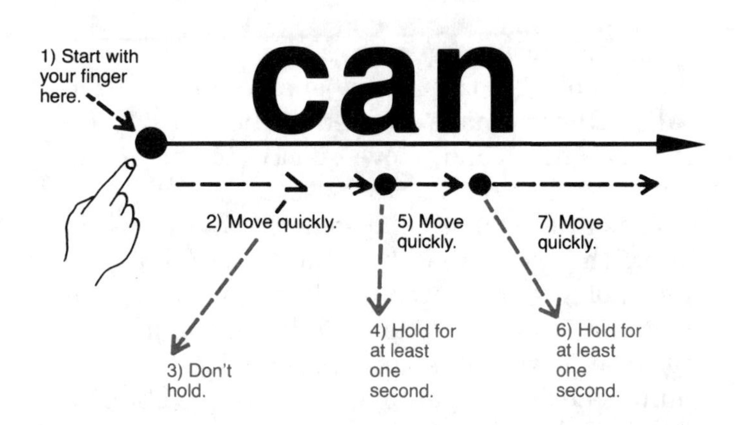

As you point, the child produces the response "caaannn." Note the symbol under the **c** in **can.** It is an arrow shape, not a ball. You do not stop under the **c.** The arrow symbol indicates that although you do not stop, the sound is to be pronounced. It is pronounced when you stop under the next sound **(a).** At that time the child says "caaa."

Remember, when an arrow shape appears under a letter, you do not stop or even pause under the sound. The child says the sound in combination with the next sound when you stop at the next ball.

Some words would be regular if they did not have "silent letters." Among these words are **meat, sail, came,** and **boat.** When these words are first introduced in **Distar** orthography, they are written this way:

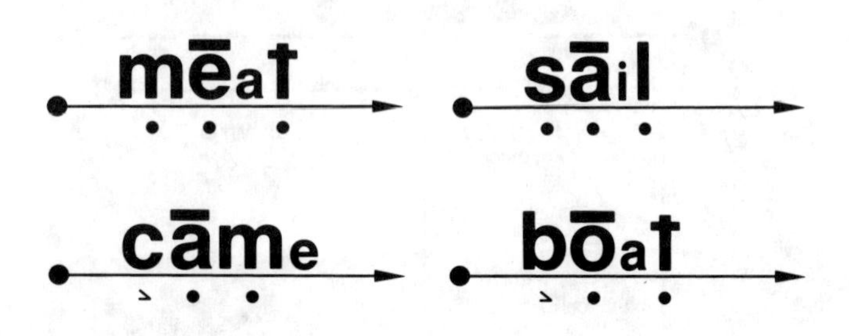

Note that there is neither a ball nor a small arrowhead under the silent letters. You do not pause for these letters or stop at them. When the child says the sounds for the letters that are marked with balls and arrowheads, the child says the sounds for the word. Later in the program, beginning with Lesson 74, the small letters become full-size. The child typically has no trouble reading them because the child has dealt with each word many times by Lesson 74. The transition is therefore not difficult.

No Skipping Allowed!

We have made this point several times, but it is extremely important. Do not push your child by skipping lessons or by introducing new procedures before the program presents them. It is possible that your child *may* be able to progress at a rate faster than that of the program sequence; however, before this possibility is a fact, you must consider the nature of the reading skill. The goal of decoding instruction is to make decoding an automatic practice, not something that requires a great deal of thinking time or a great deal of effort. Therefore, the program should progress at a rate somewhat slower than what would be possible if the only criterion for decoding were, Can the child do it? In other words, if your child is on Lesson 30 and you were to skip ahead to Lesson 50, you would find that indeed your child can read some of the words—maybe most of them. But simply being able to read the words is not enough. You must make sure that the child has enough practice to become relatively fluent. The task of decoding should not be a supreme effort. The goal of fluency and ease of reading is achieved if you stay well within the bounds of what the child is capable of doing. No harm will come of the child's reading the words **was** or **ram** ten or fifteen more times before reaching Lesson 50. The additional practice will simply make Lesson 50 easier and provide more reinforcement for the child. So do not skip.

Also, do not introduce such skills as "reading the fast way" (without sounding out words) before the program introduces them. Certainly the child can learn these skills earlier. But unless the child is very firm on sounding out, you may have no ready way to correct the mistakes made later when the child begins to "word guess." If the sounding out is very firm, you will easily be able to correct mistakes when the child later reads words the fast way. If the child has learned simply to say words, the child may have very little trouble early in the program but may encounter very serious problems when highly similar-looking words begin to appear. (After **that, this, those, them, then,** and **than** have been introduced, the child is not able to use a simple word-reading strategy that works when **the** and **that** are the only words that begin with **th.**)

Reinforcement and Corrections

To work effectively with your child, you must convey the information the child needs. You must also respond to your child's efforts. In responding to these efforts, you should reinforce appropriate behaviors and correct mistakes.

Although the lessons should be overwhelmingly reinforcing, do not confuse being reinforcing with being soft. You are soft if you "overlook" mistakes or if you let the child get by with a sloppy effort. This behavior is not reinforcing. Furthermore, it is not realistic. The skills that are taught early in the program will be used later—all of them. If they are weak when they are presented in their simplest form, early in the program, they will most certainly be weak later, when the child is expected to use them in complex tasks. If the child is weak in all the components of the complex task (which is what will happen if you use a very low standard on all skills), the child will fail hopelessly. The only remedy would be to take the child back to the beginning of the program and start over, this time with a firm criterion on performance.

Some statements of reinforcement are specified in the script for the daily lessons. However, the script does not tell you how to respond to all the good things that should be praised. To be reinforcing, follow these rules:

1. If the child is working hard, praise the child: "You are a really hard worker." (You can use this kind of praise even if the child's performance is not perfect.)
2. If the child performs well, praise the child: "That's amazing. You are really smart."
3. If the child performs well on a task that presented problems earlier, express surprise. "You got that right this time. I thought you'd have a lot more trouble than that. You're terrific."
4. Give the child a chance to show off skills that have been mastered. "Wait until your father sees you do that tonight. He'll never believe it."

Note that three of these four points express surprise. The most effective reinforcement that you can present is built around surprise, because the surprise shows that the child did not merely do what you expected, but more. Doing better than you expect is one of the most reinforcing experiences a child can have. Therefore, the most effective procedure you can use to assure that the child will find learning to read very reinforcing is to challenge the child. If you challenge the child to do something you think the child can do, and if the child succeeds, you can act amazed. Start by expressing a challenge. Ideally, the challenge should involve a group of tasks, not a single task. "Let's do the say-it-fast tasks for today. I'll bet that you can't do them all without making more than two mistakes. These are very hard words in the lesson today."

Present the tasks. If the child makes fewer than two mistakes (which will probably happen), respond by saying something like "You didn't make one mistake. I think you just got lucky. There is no way you could be that good at say-it-fast."

Even if the child does make more than two mistakes, you are in a good position to permit the child to save face without feeling defeated. "Those were hard words, weren't they? Let's go over them one more time and make sure that we can do them. I'll bet some of them will come up again tomorrow."

To make the challenge effective, pick a group of tasks that you are pretty sure the child can do. If the child is firm on sounds, say, "I don't think you'll be able to get all the sounds today without making a mistake."

Remember, the goal of the challenge is not to tease the child or to make fun of failure. The challenge is designed to let the child show you that she can do more than you expect. If you say, "I wouldn't be surprised if you missed two or three of the sounds today," the stage is set for the child to make *no* mistakes (or possibly one) and for you to say, "Wow, you did it. I don't believe it. Those were hard." Remember, if you cannot say, "Wow, you did it" at the end, the challenge was either a complete flop or less than a total success. The "Wow, you did it" is what the challenge is all about.

Two technical points about reinforcement:

1. If you reinforce the child after *every* task, you will actually be teaching the child to go off-task rather than to work through the lesson. The child learns that following each task will be a "reinforcement break."
2. The same thing will happen if you frequently use elaborate (lengthy) reinforcement.

Do not reinforce the child after every single task. The challenge should always be presented for a group of tasks. As you present each task within the group, make *very* brief comments such as "That's it" or "Good job." These interruptions should take no more than a second or two at most. Try to maintain very fast pacing from one task to the next. As soon as the child successfully completes a task, present the next task with the smallest interruption possible. This procedure is important not only from a "management" standpoint, but from a communication standpoint also. If the examples are presented quickly, one right after the other, the child will more readily see how the examples are the same and how they are different. If long pauses intervene, the child will not receive a message that is as clear.

If the child interrupts you while you are presenting, do not reinforce the behavior. If you listen to the child or permit the interruption, you reinforce interruptions, and they will occur with increasing frequency. Simply tell the child, "Whoa. Not now." Continue with the task. After you have completed a group of tasks (such as the say-it-fast tasks specified for the lesson), praise the child (if the child performed well). Then, "Now what was it you wanted to say earlier?"

In addition to discouraging the child from interrupting you, praise the child for not interrupting. Do not overdo this kind of reinforcement. But if the child has a tendency to interrupt and if the child does not interrupt during a group of tasks, say, "You are really a big person. You didn't interrupt one time. That's great. I didn't know you could work that hard."

A final reinforcement procedure: Occasionally a child becomes frustrated, has a bad day, and may produce a tear or two. A good way to respond to this behavior is to say, "Do you know how I know that everything is going to be all right tomorrow? You're crying. That means you care. That's good, because if you care, you'll keep working, and if you keep working, you'll get it. Do you know why? Because you're very smart."

Corrections

When the child makes a mistake, correct it immediately. If the child makes a mistake on the second letter of a word that is being sounded out, do not wait until the child finishes sounding out the word before correcting. Correct immediately. Correction procedures are specified for the most common mistakes the child will make. These corrections are based on the three things a good correction should do:

1. Alert the child to the mistake and where it occurred.
2. Provide practice with the skill the child needs to overcome the mistake.
3. Test the child within the context in which the mistake occurred.

If the child makes a mistake in identifying the third sound that is presented in a sound exercise:

1. Signal the mistake: "Stop."
2. Provide practice with the skill: "This sound is **aaa.** What sound?"
3. Test the child within the context in which the mistakes occurred. "Remember that sound. Let's go back and do those sounds again." Repeat the sounds in order, starting with sound 1. If the child is able to respond to the third sound correctly, the mistake has been corrected. (This assertion does not mean that the child will never misidentify the symbol again; it means that you know the child is able to handle the activity in which the mistake occurred.)

All three steps are important. If you simply tell the child the "answer" without testing the child, you have no way of knowing whether the correction was transmitted.

Step 2 of the correction does not always mean that you "tell the answer." The only way the child will know the sound that is called for by a given symbol is if you say it; however, some mistakes are different. If the child uses a particular skill, the child will be able to figure out the answer. For instance, if the child is sounding out the word **ram** but is unable to say the word after sounding it out, you would not tell the child the word. Instead, you would make it easier for the child to say the word fast.

Here is the correction:

1. You stop the child after a few seconds. You do not let the child flounder. "Stop."

2. "Listen: **rrraaammm.** Say that." (Child says:) "rrraaammm."
   "Now say it fast." (Child says:) "ram."
   "That's it."
3. Point to the written word **ram.** "Now do it here. Sound it out."
   (Child says:) "rrraaammm."
   "Say it fast." (Child says:) "ram."
   "You did it."

Learn this correction procedure. You will probably have many occasions to use it. Note that it follows the same three steps as the correction for sound identification. You first signal that a mistake has been made. You then provide practice in the skill needed to overcome the mistake. Finally, you test the child on the word in which the mistake occurred.

ADDITIONAL ACTIVITIES

The program includes sound writing as part of each lesson. It does not specify other activities that reinforce reading skills. Note that the purpose of sound writing is not to teach writing or penmanship. The rationale for sound writing is that if the child copies sounds, the child must attend to the shape details of the sounds. If the child attends to these details and associates them with the name of the sound, the child will learn the sounds faster and better. The sound-writing exercises, in other words, are included because of their reading-related value.

Note: It is not necessary to make **sh, th, wh, ch, er,** and **qu** so that they are actually joined. But identify each combination by the sound presented in the program.

To make it easier for the child to see how complex letters are formed (**a, w, t, h,** and other letters shown with two or more arrows), use two different-colored chalk (or pencil) lines. *Always* make the first part of complex letters with the same color and *always* make the second part with the same second color. (For instance, always make the first part with yellow and the second part with white.)

You may also teach writing and spelling. In fact, the reading program sets the stage for both additional activities. What follows is an outline for the more basic reinforcement activities that you might present.

Copying words. Beginning with Lesson 30, you can introduce copying words. Pick any words that have been presented in the reading lesson. Write three or four words on paper or the chalkboard (using **Distar** orthography). Leave a space below each word and a line on which the child is to copy the words. Direct the child to sound out the words that you have written, then to copy each word.

Writing words from "dictation." Beginning in Lesson 35, you can present a more sophisticated writing activity (one that is presented in addition to the copying activity, not as a substitute). Use this procedure:

"You're going to write a word that I say.

"Listen: **mat.** I'll say the word slowly: **mmmaaat.** Say that."

"Write the first sound in **mmmaaat.**

"Now listen again: **mmmaaat.** Write the next sound in *mat.*

"Listen again: **mmmaaat.** Write the last sound in *mat.*"

If the child has trouble isolating the sounds from the word, first say the word, then tell the child the first sound. Say the word again. Then say the next sound. After presenting the third sound in the same way, present the exercise above. Use any of the words that have been presented in the lessons.

Writing stories from pictures. Beginning in Lesson 50, present pictures to the child. For each picture tell the child, "Make up a story for this picture." Reinforce the child for spelling words phonetically. Do not expect the child to spell words conventionally (particularly irregular words). Typically, the child will have very few inhibitions about expressing very elaborate ideas and tackling any word composed of known sounds. The result will be horrible misspellings but very clever recordings of the way we say those words.

THE SCHEDULE

Typically, lessons do not take more than fifteen minutes. In fact, you may be able to present most lessons in twelve minutes. It is a good idea, however, to make a schedule that allows twenty minutes for each lesson. If you finish early, you

SOUND-WRITING CHART

m	Start with vertical line:	Add humps:
s	Start at top:	
a	Start with backward **s:**	Add ball:
e	Start with horizontal line: **Note:** Do not make long line over **e.**	Make **c** around it:
t	Start with vertical line:	Cross near top:
r	Start with vertical line:	Add curved line:
d	Start with **c:**	Add vertical line:
i	Start with vertical line:	Add dot:
c		
o	Start like **c:**	Close:
n	Make first part of **m:**	
f	Start with cane:	Add horizontal line:
u	Start with cane:	Add vertical line:
l	Make vertical line:	
g	Start with **c:**	Add:
h	Start with vertical line:	Add hump:

k	Start with vertical line:	Add **v** shape:
v	Make **v:**	
w	Start with **v:**	Add **v:**
th	Start with cane:	Add vertical line: Add hump and cross: th
sh	Start with **s:** S	Add **h:** sh
p	Start with vertical line:	Close with backward **c:**
ch	Start with **c:**	Add **h:** ch
b	Start with vertical line:	Close with backward **c:**
y	Start:	Add:
er	Start with **e:** e	Add **r:** er
j	Start with vertical line:	Add curve:
wh	Start with: w	Add **h:** wh
x	Start:	Cross: X
z	Start with horizontal line:	Add **v** shape:
qu	Start with **c:**	Add vertical line: q Add **u:** qu

can either quit at that time or permit the child to select a fun activity, such as the child playing teacher and presenting part of the lesson to you.

Schedule the lessons for a specific time each day. A good time is before dinner. Because the lessons do not take very long, you may decide to schedule the reading every day of the week (not just on Monday through Friday). The advantage of the every-day schedule is that the reading becomes a daily, nonnegotiable part of the day. When children understand that something is part of the daily schedule, they accept it far more readily than they do if it comes and goes or, even worse, if it is open to negotiation. Do not negotiate the schedule. Do not make deals over it. Discuss it after you have made it up. Change it if it is inconvenient or unworkable, but do not succumb to "I'm tired today" or "Do we have to? Huh?" Just smile and say, "Oh, come on, it only takes a few minutes and you're so smart you'll go through it like nothing," or "Well, let's work hard and see how quickly we can get it over with." Do not argue.

Some parents who have used **Distar** Fast Cycle have found that they can schedule two lessons a day—one early in the day, the other in the evening. These parents found that the early lessons go so quickly that presenting two lessons during one day is not a problem. Often they were right. Sometimes, however, this schedule overwhelms the child with information, even during the early lessons. If you feel that two lessons a day is possible for your child, try it. But remain extremely sensitive to the possibility that the new sounds and new skills introduced by the program may come so fast that the child does not have adequate time to digest them and become thoroughly facile with them. If you notice that your child does not have good retention of things that were presented in earlier lessons, abandon the schedule or modify it. A good modification is to present one entire lesson in the morning. In the evening, repeat the first part of that lesson. This part includes the work on sounds and blending (and, later in the program, word reading). Do not repeat the writing and comprehension activities for the lesson. If the child does well on the review of the lesson presented earlier (which should take no more than ten minutes), begin the next lesson. Stop when the twenty-minute period is over. Begin the next lesson where you left off.

Posting your schedule is a very good idea. In that way you can use the schedule as a symbol of the child's success. If you make up a schedule that looks like a calendar, you can end each lesson by writing the number of the lesson just completed on the schedule. You can indicate that the child has mastered the lesson by making a star or a smiling face next to the lesson number. From time to time refer to the number of lessons that have been mastered. "Wow. You've already got twenty stars. Look at that!" This technique makes your schedule a strong reinforcer.

Practicing the early lessons. Each lesson presents a script for all activities in the lesson, which indicates precisely what you are to say. It also indicates what the child is to do and what the child is to say when producing a correct response for each task that you present. Before you work with your child, make sure that you can present the tasks without fumbling or stopping while you figure out what to say or whether the child's response is correct. The only way to become facile with the scripts is to practice them. And practice means just that. Read the script out loud. Practice doing what the script tells you to do—for example, touching the ball at the beginning of the arrow for the sound exercises, and then moving along the arrow. After you present directions that call for a child's response, say that response to yourself.

These are the conventions for the script:

- What you *say* appears in red type.
- What you or the child does appears in parentheses.
- What the child says is presented within quotation marks.

Here is part of a task from Lesson 1:

5. Your turn to say the sound when I touch under it. (Touch first ball.) Get ready. (Move quickly to second ball. Hold.) "ssssss."

You first say, "Your turn to say the sound when I touch under it." You then touch the first ball. Then you say, "Get ready." You move quickly to the second ball and hold. As you do this, the child says, "Sssssss." For this task, the child produces the response, "sss." For other tasks, you will model or show the correct response. But remember, when the child is supposed to talk, you don't talk. And you don't move your lips to mouth the response or clue the child. You simply move under the ball and stop. The child produces the response.

PRACTICE PRESENTING LESSONS 1 AND 2

Assume that the child is sitting next to you.

Present each task of the lesson out loud. Remember, when the script indicates that the child is to respond, you are not to respond with the child or lead the child.

Go through the lesson a couple of times, until you can present it without looking at the book all the time. Remember, you are going to have to observe the child and respond to what the child says. Try to maintain fast pacing from task to task, but do not rush each task. Present each task in a conversational way, not in a stilted, schoolmarm manner.

Practice quick praises for quick response, and practice corrections.

After you take these steps you will be ready, and the preparation for the later lessons should not take more than a quick run-through before you present them to your child.

Lessons 1–100

INTRODUCING THE PROGRAM:

SAY TO YOUR CHILD:

I'm going to teach you how to read. We're going to work every day for about fifteen minutes. The work is hard, but I think you can do it. You're going to learn the sounds that you'll use when you read. And you're going to learn some good word games. Today we're going to do Lesson 1.

LESSON 1

TASK 1 SOUNDS INTRODUCTION

1. (Point to **m.**) I'm going to touch under this sound and say the sound. (Touch first ball of arrow. Move quickly to second ball. Hold two seconds.) **mmmmmm.** (Release point.)
2. Your turn to say the sound when I touch under it. (Touch first ball.) Get ready. (Move quickly to second ball. Hold.) "mmmmmm."

> (**To correct** child saying a wrong sound or not responding:) The sound is **mmmmmm.** (Repeat step 2.)

3. (Touch first ball.) Again. Get ready. (Move quickly to second ball. Hold.) "mmmmmm." (Repeat three more times.)

4. (Point to **s.**) I'm going to touch under this sound and say the sound. (Touch first ball of arrow. Move quickly to second ball. Hold.) **ssssss.** (Release point.)
5. Your turn to say the sound when I touch under it. (Touch first ball.) Get ready. (Move quickly to second ball. Hold.) "ssssss."

> (**To correct** child saying a wrong sound or not responding:) The sound is **ssssss.** (Repeat step 5.)

6. (Touch first ball.) Again. Get ready. (Move quickly to second ball. Hold.) "ssssss." (Repeat three more times.)

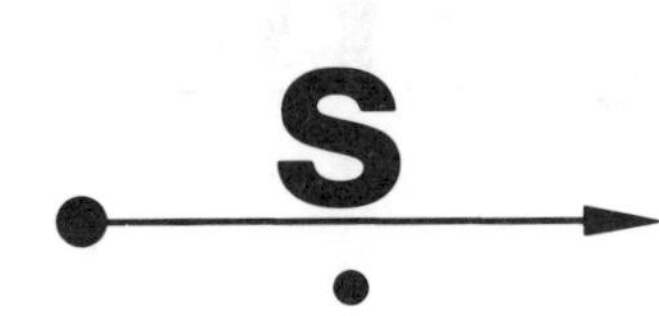

TASK 2 SAY IT FAST

1. Let's play say-it-fast. My turn: **motor** (pause) **boat.** (Pause.) Say it fast. **motorboat.**
2. Your turn. Wait until I tell you to say it fast. **motor** (pause) **boat.** (Pause.) Say it fast. "motorboat." (Repeat step 2 until firm.)

> (**To correct** child saying word slowly—for example, "motor [pause] boat":) You didn't say it fast. Here's saying it fast: **motorboat.** Say that. "motorboat." Now let's do that part again. (Repeat step 2.)

3. New word. Listen: **ice** (pause) **cream.** (Pause.) Say it fast. "icecream."
4. New word. Listen: **sis** (pause) **ter.** (Pause.) Say it fast. "sister."
5. New word. Listen: **ham** (pause) **burger.** (Pause.) Say it fast. "hamburger."
6. New word. Listen: **mmmēēē.** (Pause.) Say it fast. "me."
7. New word. Listen: **iiifff.** (Pause.) Say it fast. "if."
8. (Repeat any words child had trouble with.)

TASK 3 SAY THE SOUNDS

1. I'm going to say some words slowly, without stopping. Then you'll say them with me.
2. First I'll say **am** slowly. Listen: **aaammm.** Now I'll say **me** slowly. Listen: **mmmēēē.** Now I'll say **in** slowly. Listen: **iiinnn.** Now I'll say **she** slowly. Listen: **shshshēēē.**
3. Now it's your turn to say the words slowly with me. Take a deep breath and we'll say **aaammm.** Get ready. "aaammm."

> (**To correct** if child stops between sounds—for example, "aaa [pause] mmm":) Don't stop. Listen. (Don't pause between sounds **a** and **m** as you say **aaammm.**) Take a deep breath and we'll say **aaammm.** Get ready. "aaammm." (Repeat until child responds with you.)

4. Now we'll say **iiinnn.** Get ready. "iiinnn." Now we'll say **ooonnn.** Get ready. "ooonnn."
5. Your turn to say words slowly by yourself. Say **aaammm.** Get ready. "aaammm." Say **iiifff.** Get ready. "iiifff." Say **mmmēēē.** Get ready. "mmmēēē." Good saying the words slowly.

TASK 4 SOUNDS REVIEW

1. Let's do the sounds again. See if you remember them. (Touch first ball for **m.**) Get ready. (Quickly move to second ball. Hold.) "mmmmmm."

2. (Touch first ball for **s.**) Get ready. (Quickly move to second ball. Hold.) "ssssss."

TASK 5 SAY IT FAST

1. Let's play say-it-fast again. Listen: **motor** (pause) **cycle.** Say it fast. "motorcycle."
2. **mmmēēē.** (Pause.) Say it fast. "me." **iiifff.** (Pause.) Say it fast. "if." **shshshēēē.** (Pause.) Say it fast. "she."

TASK 6 SOUNDS WRITING

(Note: Refer to each symbol by its sound, not by its letter name. Make horizontal rules on paper or a chalkboard about two inches apart. Separate writing spaces by spaces about one inch apart. Optionally, divide writing spaces in half with a dotted line: - m - - - - .)

1. See chart on page 24 for steps in writing **m** and **s.**) You're going to write the sounds that I write. You're going to write a sound on each line. I'll show you how to make each sound. Then you'll write each sound. Here's the first sound you're going to write.
2. Here's how you make **mmm.** Watch. (Make **m** at the beginning of first line. Start with a vertical line: ↓

   Then add the humps: ↓↷↷

   (Point to **m.**) What sound? "mmm." First you're going to trace the **mmm** that I made. Then you're going to make more of them on the line.
3. (Help child trace sound two or three times. Child is then to make three to five **m**'s on top line. Help child if necessary. For each acceptable letter child makes, say:) Good writing **mmm.**
4. Here's how to make **sss.** Watch. (Make **s** at beginning of second line. Point to **s.**) What sound? "sss."
5. First you're going to trace the **sss** that I made. Then you're going to make more of them on the line. (Help child trace sound two or three times. Child is then to make three to five **s**'s on second line. Help child if necessary. For each acceptable letter child makes, say:) Good writing **sss.**

LESSON 2

TASK 1 SOUNDS REVIEW

1. (Point to **m.**) I'm going to touch under this sound and say the sound. (Touch first ball of arrow. Move quickly to second ball. Hold two seconds.) **mmmmmm.** (Release point.)
2. Your turn to say the sound when I touch under it. (Touch first ball.) Get ready. (Move quickly to second ball. Hold.) "mmmmmm."

> (**To correct** child saying a wrong sound or not responding:) The sound is **mmmmmm.** (Repeat step 2.)

3. (Touch first ball.) Again. Get ready. (Move quickly to second ball. Hold.) "mmmmmm." (Repeat three more times.)

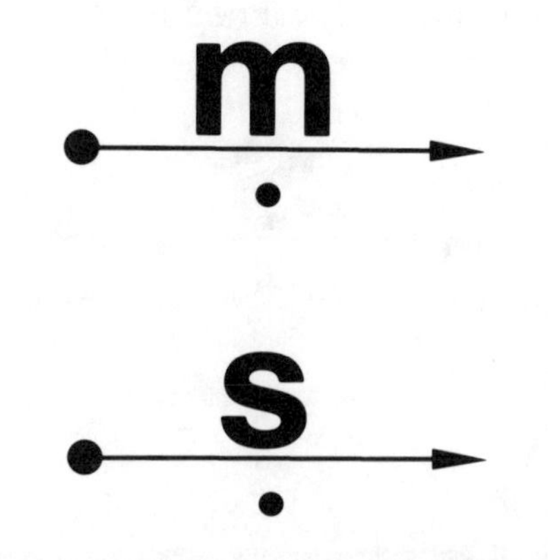

4. (Point to **s.**) I'm going to touch under this sound and say the sound. (Touch first ball of arrow. Move quickly to second ball. Hold.) **ssssss.** (Release point.)
5. Your turn to say the sound when I touch under it. (Touch first ball.) Get ready. (Move quickly to second ball. Hold.) "ssssss."

> (**To correct** child saying a wrong sound or not responding:) The sound is **ssssss.** (Repeat step 5.)

6. (Touch first ball.) Again. Get ready. (Move quickly to second ball. Hold.) "ssssss." (Repeat three more times.)

TASK 2 SAY IT FAST

1. Let's play say-it-fast. My turn: **lawn** (pause) **mower.** (Pause.) Say it fast. **lawnmower.**
2. Your turn. Wait until I tell you to say it fast. **lawn** (pause) **mower.** (Pause.) Say it fast. "lawnmower." (Repeat step 2 until firm.)

> (**To correct** child saying word slowly—for example, "lawn [pause] mower":) You didn't say it fast. Here's saying it fast: **lawnmower.** Say that. "lawnmower." Now let's do that part again. (Repeat step 2.)

3. New word. Listen: **side** (pause) **walk.** (Pause.) Say it fast. "sidewalk."
4. New word. Listen: **iiifff.** (Pause.) Say it fast. "if."
5. New word. Listen: **mmmēēē.** (Pause.) Say it fast. "me."
6. New word. Listen: **aaammm.** (Pause.) Say it fast. "am."
7. New word. Listen: **iiinnn.** (Pause.) Say it fast. "in."
8. New word. Listen: **shshshēēē.** (Pause.) Say it fast. "she."
9. (Repeat any words child had trouble with.)

TASK 3 SAY THE SOUNDS

1. I'm going to say some words slowly, without stopping. Then you'll say them with me.
2. First I'll say **she** slowly. Listen: **shshshēēē.** Now I'll say **me** slowly. Listen: **mmmēēē.** Now I'll say **ship** slowly. Listen: **shshshiiip.**
3. Now it's your turn to say the words slowly with me. Take a deep breath and we'll say **shshshēēē.** Get ready. "**shshshēēē.**"

> (**To correct** if child stops between sounds—for example, "shshsh [pause] ēēē":) Don't stop. Listen. (Don't pause between sounds **sh** and **ē** as you say **shshshēēē.**) Take a deep breath and we'll say **shshshēēē.** Get ready. "**shshshēēē.**" (Repeat until child responds with you.)

4. Now we'll say **mmmēēē.** Get ready. "**mmmēēē.**" Now we'll say **shshshiiip.** Get ready. "**shshshiiip.**" Now we'll say **aaammm.** Get ready. "**aaammm.**" Now we'll say **iiinnn.** Get ready. "**iiinnn.**" Now we'll say **iiifff.** Get ready. "**iiifff.**"
5. Your turn to say the words slowly by yourself. Say **shshshēēē.** Get ready. "shshshēēē." Say **mmmēēē.** Get ready. "mmmēēē." Say **shshshiiip.** Get ready. "shshshiiip." Say **aaammm.** Get ready. "aaammm." Say **iiinnn.** Get ready. "iiinnn." Say **iiifff.** Get ready. "iiifff." Good saying the words slowly.

TASK 4 SOUNDS REVIEW

1. Let's do the sounds again. See if you remember them. (Touch first ball for **m.**) Get ready. (Quickly move to second ball. Hold.) "mmmmmm."

2. (Touch first ball for **s.**) Get ready. (Quickly move to second ball. Hold.) "ssssss."

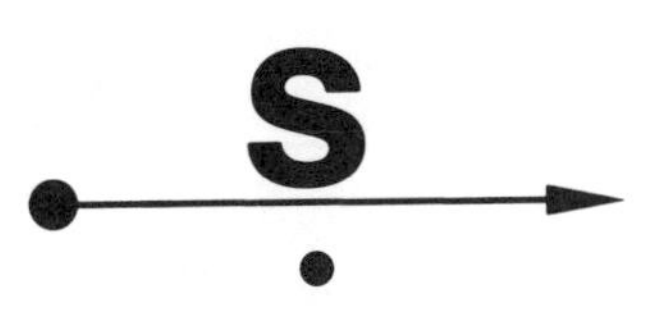

TASK 5 SAY IT FAST

1. Let's play say-it-fast again. Listen: **sis** (pause) **ter.** Say it fast. "sister."
2. **Mis** (pause) **ter.** (Pause.) Say it fast. "mister." **mo** (pause) **ther.** (Pause.) Say it fast. "mother." **iiifff.** (Pause.) Say it fast. "if." **sssēēē.** (Pause.) Say it fast. "see." **nnnōōō.** (Pause.) Say it fast. "no." **aaammm.** (Pause.) Say it fast. "am."

TASK 6 SAY THE SOUNDS

1. Your turn to say the words slowly. Say **mmmaaannn.** "mmmaaannn." Say **wwwiiilll.** "wwwiiilll." Say **shshshēēē.** "shshshēēē." Say **sssiiit.** "sssiiit."

(**To correct** child saying a wrong word or not responding:) Listen. (Don't pause between sounds **s, i,** and **t,** as you say **sssiiit.**) Take a deep breath and we'll say **sssiiit.** Get ready. "sssiiit." (Repeat until firm.)

TASK 7 SOUNDS WRITING

1. (See chart on page 24 for steps in writing **s** and **m.**)
2. You're going to write the sounds that I write. Here's the first sound you're going to write.
3. (Write **s** at beginning of first line. Point to **s.**) What sound? "sss."
4. First trace the **sss** that I made. Then make more of them on this line. (After tracing **s** several times, child is to make three to five **s**'s. Help child if necessary. For acceptable letters say:) Good writing **sss.**
5. Here's the next sound you're going to write. (Write **m** at beginning of second line. Point to **m.**) What sound? "mmm."
6. First trace the **mmm** that I made. Then make more of them on this line. (After tracing **m** several times, child is to make three to five **m**'s. Help child if necessary. For acceptable letters say:) Good writing **mmm.**

LESSON 3

TASK 1 SOUNDS INTRODUCTION

1. (Point to **a.**) Here's a new sound. I'm going to touch under this sound and say the sound. (Touch first ball of arrow. Move quickly to second ball. Hold.) **ăăăăăă.**
2. Your turn to say the sound when I touch under it. (Touch first ball.) Get ready. (Move quickly to second ball. Hold.) "ăăăăăă."

(**To correct** child saying a wrong sound or not responding:) The sound is **ăăăăăă.** (Repeat step 2.)

3. (Touch first ball.) Again. Get ready. (Move quickly to second ball. Hold.) "ăăăăăă."

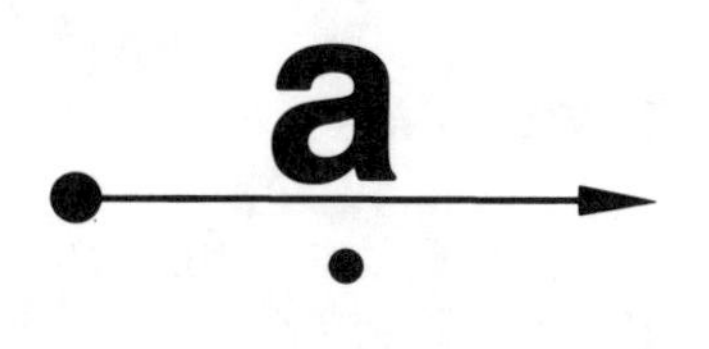

TASK 2 SOUNDS REVIEW

1. You're going to say all these sounds. (Touch first ball for **m.**) Get ready. (Quickly move to second ball. Hold.) "mmmmmm."

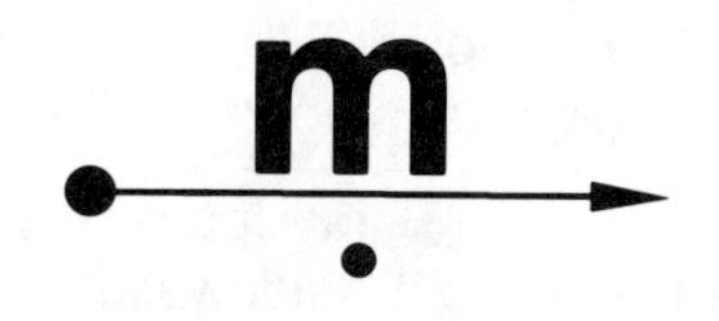

2. (Touch first ball for **a.**) Get ready. (Quickly move to second ball. Hold.) "aaaaaa."

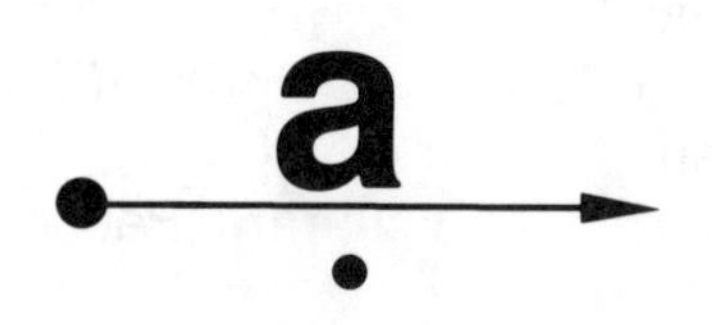

3. (Touch first ball for **s.**) Get ready. (Quickly move to second ball. Hold.) "ssssss."

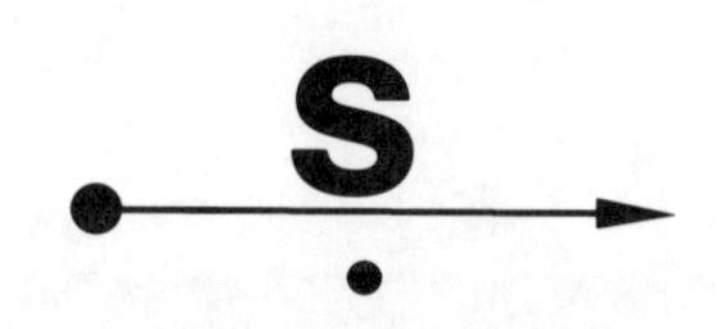

TASK 3 SAY THE SOUNDS

1. Your turn to say the words slowly. Say **rrruuunnn.** "rrruuunnn." Say **mmmaaannn.** "mmmaaannn." Say **thththiiisss.** "thththiiisss." Say **wwwēēē.** "wwwēēē." Say **shshshēēē.** "shshshēēē."

> (**To correct** child saying a wrong word or not responding:) Listen. (Don't stop between sounds **sh** and **ē** as you say **shshshēēē.**) Take a deep breath and we'll say **shshshēēē.** Get ready. "shshshēēē." (Repeat until firm.)

TASK 4 SOUNDS

1. Let's play say-it-fast with these sounds. My turn. (Touch first ball for **m.** Move quickly to second ball. Hold.) **mmmmmm.** (Release.) (Touch first ball.) Say it fast. (Move quickly to end of arrow.) **m.**
2. Your turn. First you'll say it slowly. Then you'll say it fast. (Touch first ball for **m.**) Say the sound slowly. (Move quickly to second ball. Hold.) "mmmmmm." (Release.) (Touch first ball.) Say it fast. (Move quickly to end of arrow.) "m."
3. (Touch first ball for **a.**) Say the sound slowly. (Move quickly to second ball. Hold.) "aaaaaa." (Release.) (Touch first ball for **a.**) Say it fast. (Move quickly to end of arrow.) "a."

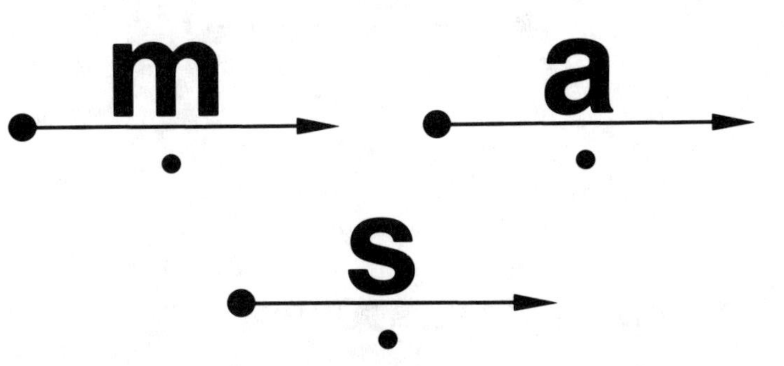

4. (Touch first ball for **m.**) Say the sound slowly. (Move quickly to second ball. Hold.) "mmmmmm." (Release.) (Touch first ball for **m.**) Say it fast. (Move quickly to end of arrow.) "m."
5. (Touch first ball for **s.**) Say the sound slowly. (Move quickly to second ball. Hold.) "ssssss." (Touch first ball for **s.** Hold.) Say it fast. (Move quickly to end of arrow.) "s."
6. (Touch first ball for **a.**) Say the sound slowly. (Move quickly to second ball. Hold.) "aaaaaa." (Touch first ball for **a.**) Say it fast. (Move quickly to end of arrow.) "a."

TASK 5 SAY THE SOUNDS

1. We're going to play a new say-it-fast game. First you'll say the word that I say slowly. Then you'll say it fast. Say (pause) **mmmēēē.** "mmmēēē." Now say it fast. "me."
2. Say (pause) **mmmaaannn.** "mmmaaannn." Now say it fast. "man." Say (pause) **iiifff.** "iiifff." Now say it fast. "if." Say **wwwēēē.** "wwwēēē." Now say it fast. "we."
3. Let's do those words again. (Repeat step 2 until firm.)

TASK 6 SAY THE SOUNDS

1. I'm going to say the sounds on the arrow. (Touch first ball. Quickly move to second ball. Hold for about three seconds. Quickly move to third ball and hold for about three seconds. Say **aaammm** without pausing between sounds as you touch under each sound. Repeat.)
2. This time I'm going to **say** the sounds. You **touch** under each sound as I say it. Put your finger on the first ball. Get ready. **aaammm.** (Hold each sound for about three seconds. Do not pause between sounds. Child touches under each sound as soon as you start to say it.)
3. Again, finger on the first ball. Get ready. **aaammm.** (Repeat until firm.)

> (**To correct:** Hold child's finger and move it to appropriate balls on arrow as you say **aaammm.** Then repeat.)

TASK 7 SAY THE SOUNDS

1. I'm going to say the sounds on the arrow. (Touch first ball. Quickly move to second ball. Hold for about three seconds. Quickly move to third ball and hold for about three seconds. Say **sssaaa** without pausing between sounds as you touch under each sound. Repeat.)
2. This time I'm going to **say** the sounds. You **touch** under each sound as I say it. Put your finger on the first ball. Get ready. **sssaaa.** (Hold each sound for about three seconds. Do not pause between sounds. Child touches under each sound as soon as you start to say it.)
3. Again, finger on the first ball. Get ready. **sssaaa.** (Repeat until firm.)

(**To correct:** Hold child's finger and move it to appropriate balls on arrow as you say **sssaaa.** Then repeat.)

sa

TASK 8 SOUNDS WRITING

1. (See chart on page 24 for steps in writing **a** and **m.**)
2. You're going to write the sounds that I write. Here's the first sound you're going to write.
3. (Write **a** at beginning of first line. Point to **a.**) What sound? "aaa."
4. First trace the **aaa** that I made. Then make more of them on this line. (After tracing **a** several times, child is to make three to five **a**'s. Help child if necessary. For each acceptable letter say:) Good writing **aaa.**
5. Here's the next sound you're going to write. (Write **m** at beginning of second line. Point to **m.**) What sound? "mmm."
6. First trace the **mmm** that I made. Then make more of them on this line. (After tracing **m** several times, child is to make three to five **m**'s. Help child if necessary. For acceptable letters say:) Good writing **mmm.**

LESSON 4

TASK 1 SOUNDS REVIEW

1. You're going to say all these sounds. (Touch first ball for **m.**) Get ready. (Quickly move to second ball. Hold.) "mmmmmm."

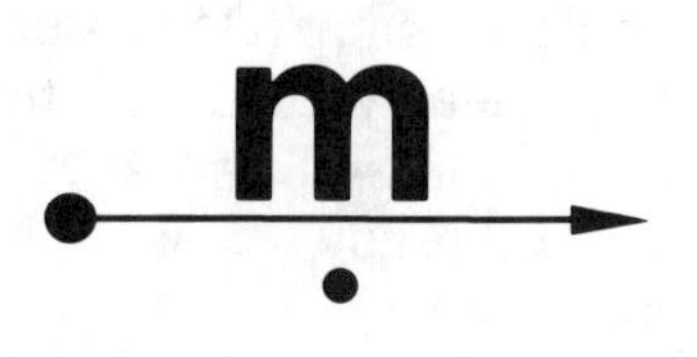

2. (Touch first ball for **a.**) Get ready. (Quickly move to second ball. Hold.) "aaaaaa."

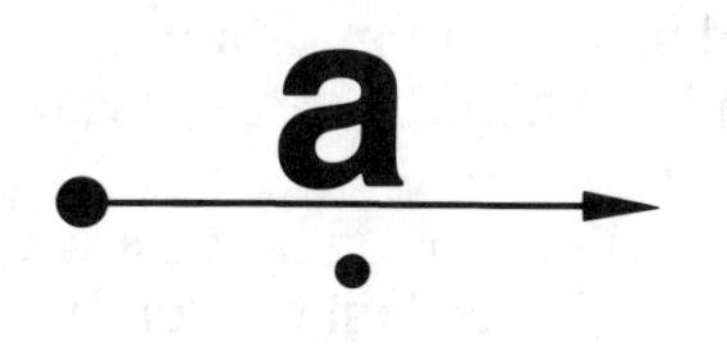

3. (Touch first ball for **s.**) Get ready. (Quickly move to second ball. Hold.) "ssssss."

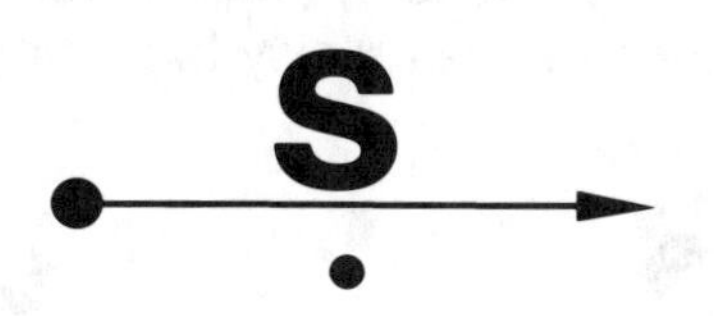

TASK 2 SAY THE SOUNDS

Your turn to say the words slowly.
Say **aaat.** "aaat."
Say **ēēēt.** "ēēēt."
Say **mmmaaat.** "mmmaaat."
Say **thththiiisss.** "thththiiisss."
Say **rrruuunnn.** "rrruuunnn."
Say **nnnooot.** "nnnooot."
Say **thththaaat.** "thththaaat."
Say **wwwēēē.** "wwwēēē."

TASK 3 SOUNDS

1. You're going to say sounds slowly, then you're going to say them fast. (Touch first ball for **s.**) Say the sound slowly. (Move quickly to second ball. Hold.) "ssssss." (Release.) (Return to first ball.) Say it fast. (Move quickly to end of arrow.) "s."
2. (Touch first ball for **m.**) Say the sound slowly. (Move quickly to second ball. Hold.) "mmmmmm." (Release.) (Return to first ball for **m.**) Say it fast. (Move quickly to end of arrow.) "m."
3. (Touch first ball for **a.**) Say the sound slowly. (Move quickly to second ball. Hold.) "aaaaaa." (Release.) (Return to first ball for **a.**) Say it fast. (Move quickly to end of arrow.) "a."

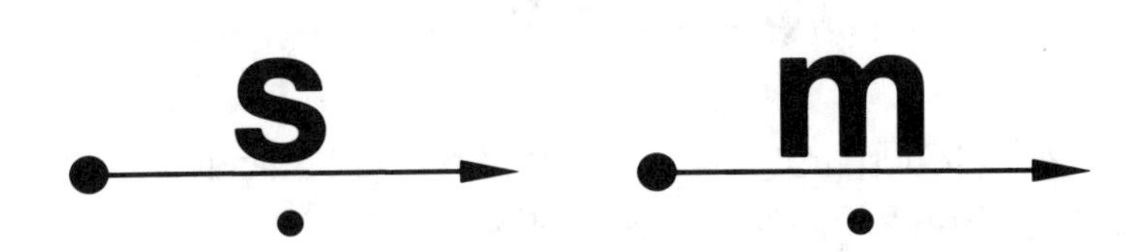

a

TASK 4 SAY THE SOUNDS

1. Say **rrruuunnn.** "rrruuunnn."
   Say it fast. "run."
   Say **aaat.** "aaat."
   Say it fast. "at."
   Say **nnnŏŏŏt.** "nnnŏŏŏt."
   Say it fast. "not."
   Say **thththiiisss.** "thththiiisss."
   Say it fast. "this."
   Say **mmmaaat.** "mmmaaat."
   Say it fast. "mat."
2. Let's do those words again. (Repeat step 1 until firm.)

TASK 5 SAY THE SOUNDS

1. I'm going to say the sounds on the arrow. (Touch first ball. Quickly move to second ball. Hold for about three seconds. Quickly move to third ball and hold for about three seconds. Say **mmmaaa** without pausing between sounds as you touch under each sound. Repeat.)
2. This time I'm going to say the sounds. You touch under each sound as I say it. Put your finger on the first ball. Get ready. **mmmaaa.** (Hold each sound for about three seconds. Do not pause between sounds. Child touches under each sound as soon as you start to say it.)
3. Again, finger on the first ball. Get ready. **mmmaaa.** (Repeat until firm.)

(**To correct:** Hold child's finger and move it to appropriate balls on arrow as you say **mmmaaa.** Then repeat.)

TASK 6 SAY THE SOUNDS

1. I'm going to say the sounds on the arrow. (Touch first ball. Quickly move to second ball. Hold for about three seconds. Quickly move to third ball and hold for about three seconds. Say **sssaaa** without pausing between sounds as you touch under each sound. Repeat.)
2. This time I'm going to say the sounds. You touch under each sound as I say it. Put your finger on the first ball. Get ready. **sssaaa.** (Hold each sound for about three seconds. Do not pause between sounds. Child touches under each sound as soon as you start to say it.)
3. Again, finger on the first ball. Get ready. **sssaaa.** (Repeat until firm.)

(**To correct:** Hold child's finger and move it to appropriate balls on arrow as you say **sssaaa.** Then repeat.)

TASK 7 SOUNDS WRITING

1. (See chart on page 24 for steps in writing **s** and **a.**)
2. You're going to write the sounds that I write. Here's the first sound you're going to write.
3. (Write **s** at beginning of first line. Point to **s.**) What sound? "sss."
4. First trace the **sss** that I made. Then make more of them on this line. (After tracing **s** several times, child is to make three to five **s**'s. Help child if necessary. For each acceptable letter say:) Good writing **sss.**
5. Here's the next sound you're going to write. (Write **a** at the beginning of second line. Point to **a.**) What sound? "aaa."
6. First trace the **a** that I made. Then make more of them on this line. (After tracing **a** several times, child is to make three to five **a**'s. Help child if necessary. For acceptable letters say:) Good writing **aaa.**

LESSON 5

TASK 1 SOUNDS INTRODUCTION

1. (Point to **ē.**) Here's a new sound. I'm going to touch under this sound and say the sound. (Touch first ball of arrow. Move quickly to second ball. Hold.) **ēēēēēē.**
2. Your turn to say the sound when I touch under it. (Touch first ball.) Get ready. (Move quickly to second ball. Hold.) "ēēēēēē."

(**To correct** child saying a wrong sound or not responding:) The sound is **ēēēēēē.** (Repeat step 2.)

3. (Touch first ball.) Again. Get ready. (Move quickly to second ball. Hold.) "ēēēēēē."

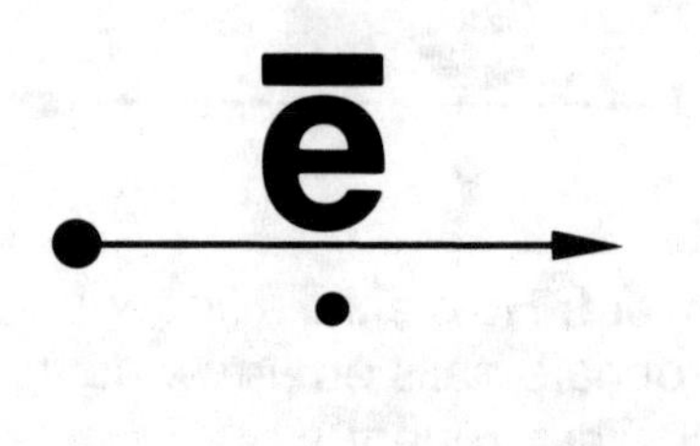

TASK 2 SOUNDS REVIEW

1. You're going to say all these sounds. (Touch first ball for **a.**) Get ready. (Quickly move to second ball. Hold.) "aaaaaa."

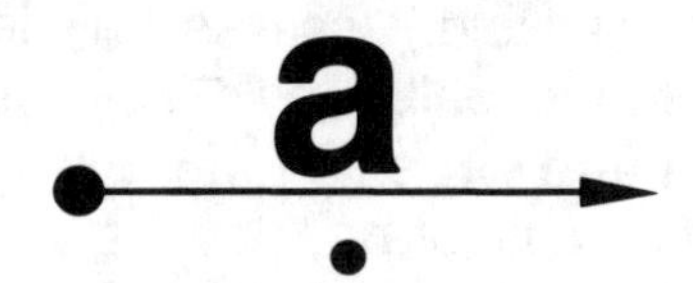

2. (Touch first ball for **s.**) Get ready. (Quickly move to second ball. Hold.) "ssssss."

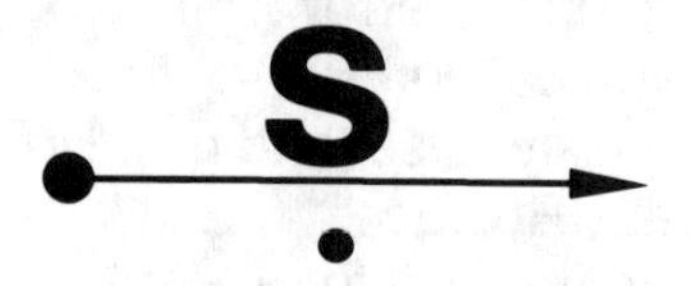

3. (Touch first ball for **m.**) Get ready. (Quickly move to second ball. Hold.) "mmmmmm."

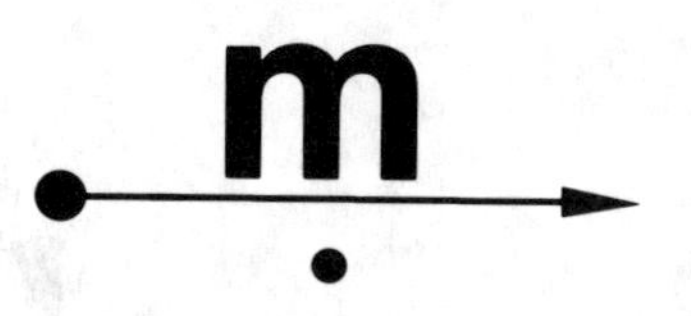

4. (Touch first ball for **ē.**) Get ready. (Quickly move to second ball. Hold.) "ēēēēēē."

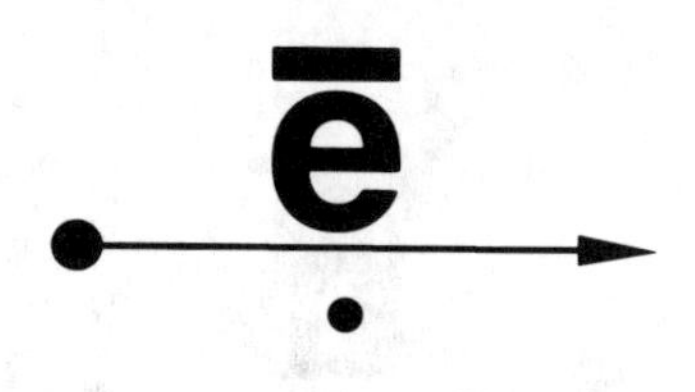

TASK 3 SAY THE SOUNDS

Your turn to say the words slowly.
Say **mmmēēē.** "mmmēēē."
Say **sssēēē.** "sssēēē."
Say **thththaaat.** "thththaaat."
Say **wwwēēē.** "wwwēēē."
Say **aaannnd.** "aaannnd."
Say **aaammm.** "aaammm."
Say **ēēēt.** "ēēēt."
Say **iiifff.** "iiifff."

TASK 4 SAY THE SOUNDS

1. Say **ssseee**. "sssēēē."
   Say it fast. "see."
   Say **thththaaat.** "thththaaat."
   Say it fast. "that."
   Say **iiifff.** "iiifff."

Say it fast. "if."
Say **aaat.** "aaat."
Say it fast. "at."
Say **aaammm.** "aaammm."
Say it fast. "am."

2. Let's do those words again. (Repeat step 1 until firm.)

TASK 5 SOUNDS

1. You're going to say sounds slowly, then you're going to say them fast. (Touch first ball for **ē.**) Say the sound slowly. (Move quickly to second ball. Hold.) "ēēēēēē." (Release.) (Return to first ball.) Say it fast. (Move quickly to end of arrow.) "ē."

2. (Touch first ball for **s.**) Say the sound slowly. (Move quickly to second ball. Hold.) "ssssss." (Release.)
(Return to first ball for **s.**) Say it fast. (Move quickly to end of arrow.) "s."

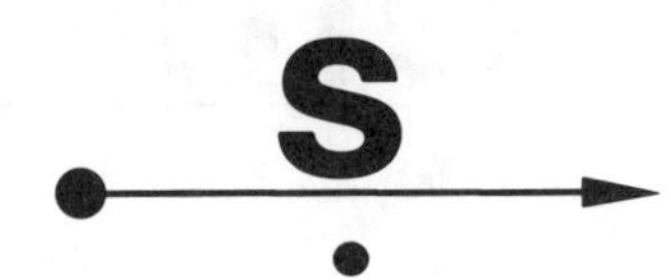

3. (Touch first ball for **m.**) Say the sound slowly. (Move quickly to second ball. Hold.) "mmmmmm." (Release.)
(Return to first ball for **m.**) Say it fast. (Move quickly to end of arrow.) "m."

4. (Touch first ball for **a.**) Say the sound slowly. (Move quickly to second ball. Hold.) "aaaaaa." (Release.)
(Return to first ball for **a.**) Say it fast. (Move quickly to end of arrow.) "a."

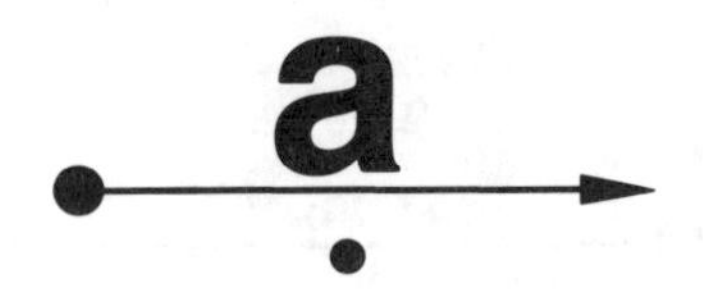

TASK 6 CHILD TOUCHES SOUNDS

1. (Point to **ē**.) Your turn to touch the sounds and say them. First you're going to say this sound slowly and then say it fast. Touch the first ball of the arrow. You're going to move to the next ball on the arrow and stop. When you stop, say the sound slowly. Do it. "ēēēēēē." Now say it fast. (Child slides finger quickly under ē.) "ē."

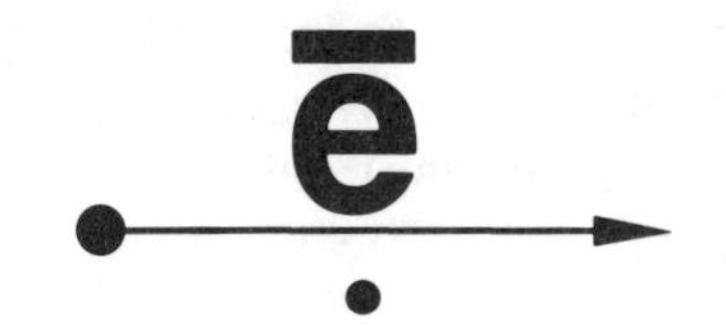

> **(To correct:** Hold child's finger and move it appropriately as you say:) Do it with me. Say the sound slowly. **"ēēē."** Now say it fast. **"ē."** (Repeat until child responds correctly. Then repeat step 1.)

2. Touch the first ball for the next sound. Move to the next ball and say the sound slowly. "ssssss." Now say it fast. "s."

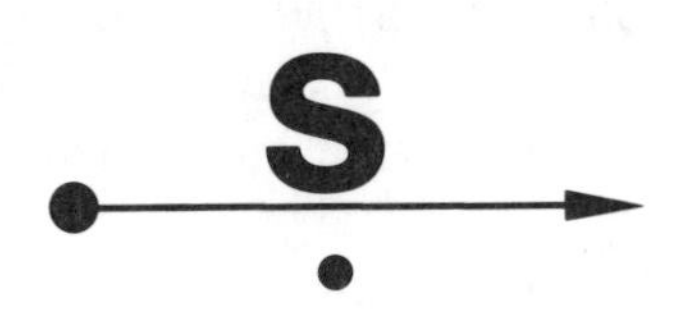

3. Touch the first ball for the next sound. Move to the next ball and say the sound slowly. "mmmmmm." Now say it fast. "m."

4. Touch the first ball for the next sound. Move to the next ball and say the sound slowly. "aaaaaa." Now say it fast. "a."

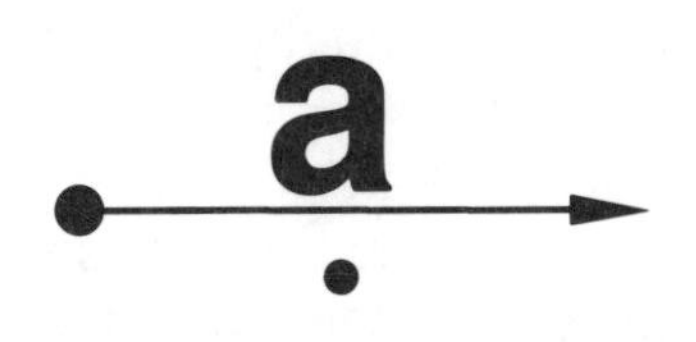

TASK 7 RHYMING

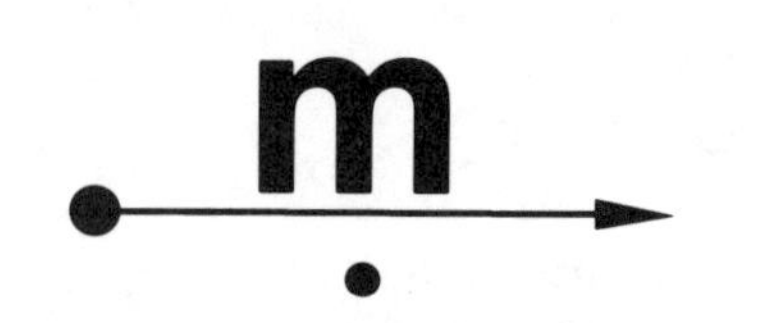

1. I'm going to rhyme. (Touch first ball for **m.**) This is the sound I'm going to start with. Get ready to say the sound. (Quickly slide to second ball and hold.) "mmm."
2. (Return to first ball.) I'm going to rhyme with (pause) **eat.** What am I going to rhyme with? "eat." (Slide quickly to second ball under **m.** Hold for about three seconds, then slide quickly to end of arrow as you say:) **mmmeat.** (Return to first ball.) Say it fast. (Slide to end of arrow as you say:) **meat.** I rhymed with (pause) **eat.**
3. (Touch first ball.) Now I'm going to rhyme with (pause) **at.** What am I going to rhyme with? "at." (Slide quickly to second ball under **m.** Hold for about three seconds, then slide quickly to end of arrow as you say:) **mmmat.** (Return to first ball.) Say it fast. (Slide to end of arrow as you say:) **mat.** I rhymed with (pause) **at.**
4. (Touch first ball.) Now I'm going to rhyme with (pause) **ē.** What am I going to rhyme with? "ē." (Slide quickly to second ball under **m.** Hold for about three seconds, then slide quickly to end of arrow as you say:) **mmme.** (Return to first ball.) Say it fast. (Slide to end of arrow as you say:) **me.** I rhymed with (pause) **ē.**
5. (Touch first ball.) Now it's your turn to rhyme with (pause) **ē.** (Slide quickly to second ball. Hold for about three seconds, then slide quickly to end of arrow.) "mmme."

> (**To correct** if child does not respond or says "mmm" only:) Do it with me. (Touch first ball.) Rhymes with (pause) **ē.** (Slide to second ball. Touch for three seconds and then slide quickly to end of arrow as you say **mmme** without pausing between sounds. Repeat correction until child responds with you, then repeat step 5.)

(Return to first ball.) Say it fast. (Slide to end of arrow.) "mē." You rhymed with (pause) **ē.**

6. (Touch first ball.) Your turn to rhyme with (pause) **at.** What are you going to rhyme with? "at." Rhyming with (pause) **at.** (Slide quickly to second ball. Hold for about three seconds, then slide quickly to end of arrow.) "mmmat." (Return to first ball.) Say it fast. (Slide to end of arrow.) "mat." You rhymed with (pause) **at.**
7. (Touch first ball.) Your turn to rhyme with (pause) **eat.** What are you going to rhyme with? "eat." Rhyming with (pause) **eat.** (Slide quickly to second ball. Hold for about three seconds, then slide quickly to end of arrow.) "mmmeat." (Return to first ball.) Say it fast. (Slide to end of arrow.) "meat." You rhymed with (pause) **eat.**

TASK 8 SAY THE SOUNDS

1. (Point to **ēm.**) You're going to touch under these sounds and say them. Here's what you're going to say. (Pause.) **ēēēmmm.** Say that. "ēēēmmm." Again. "ēēēmmm."
2. Touch the first ball of the arrow. Get ready to touch under the sounds and say them. (Child touches under **ē** and **m** and says "ēēēmmm" without pausing between sounds.) Good sounding out.

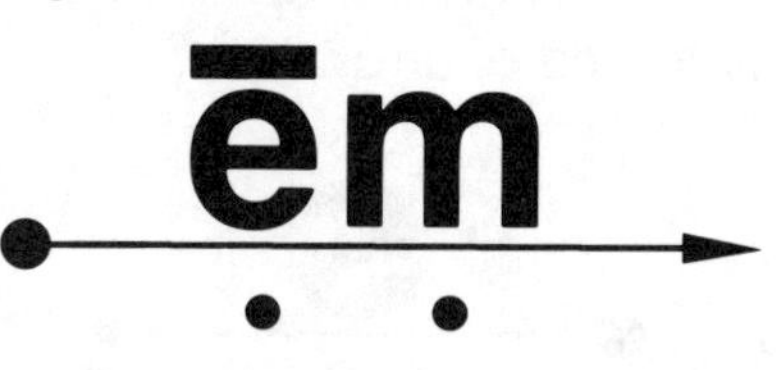

> (**To correct** if child pauses between sounds or does not touch and say sounds at the same time:) Let's say the sounds. (Hold child's finger and move it to appropriate balls as you say **ēēēmmm** without pausing between sounds. Repeat until child responds with you. Repeat step 2.)

3. (Point to **ēs.**) You're going to touch under these sounds and say them. Here's what you're going to say (Pause.) **ēēēsss.** Say that. "ēēēsss." Again "ēēēsss."
4. Touch the first ball of the arrow. Get ready to touch under the sounds and say them. Go. (Child touches under **ē** and **s** and says "ēēēsss" without pausing between sounds.) Good sounding out.

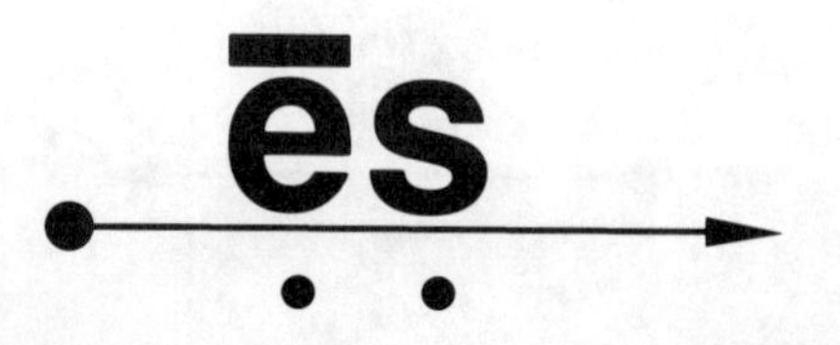

TASK 9 SOUNDS WRITING

1. (See chart on page 24 for steps in writing **e** and **a**.)
2. You're going to write the sounds that I write. Here's the first sound you're going to write.
3. (Point to **e**.) What sound? "ēēē." Yes, we're going to write **ēēē** without a line.
4. First trace the **ēēē** that I made. Then make more of them on this line. (After tracing **e** several times, child is to make three to five **e**'s. Help child if necessary. For each acceptable letter say:) Good writing **ēēē.**
5. Here's the next sound you're going to write. (Write **a** at beginning of second line. Point to **a**.) What sound? "aaa."
6. First trace the **aaa** that I made. Then make more of them on this line (After tracing **a** several times, child is to make three to five **a**'s. Help child if necessary. For acceptable letters say:) Good writing **aaa.**

LESSON 6

TASK 1 SOUNDS

1. (Touch first ball for **ē.**) You're going to say the sound slowly. Then you'll say it fast. (Move quickly to second ball. Hold.) "ēēē."
(Release.)
(Return to first ball.) Say it fast. (Move quickly to end of arrow.) "ē."

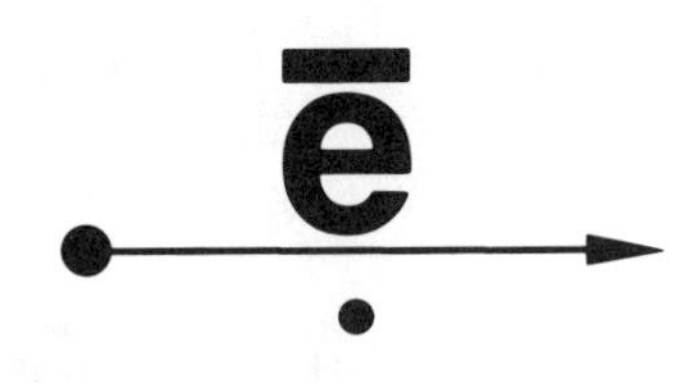

2. (Touch first ball for **s.**) Say the sound slowly. (Move quickly to second ball. Hold.) "sss."
(Release.)
(Return to first ball for **s.**) Say it fast. (Move quickly to end of arrow.) "s."

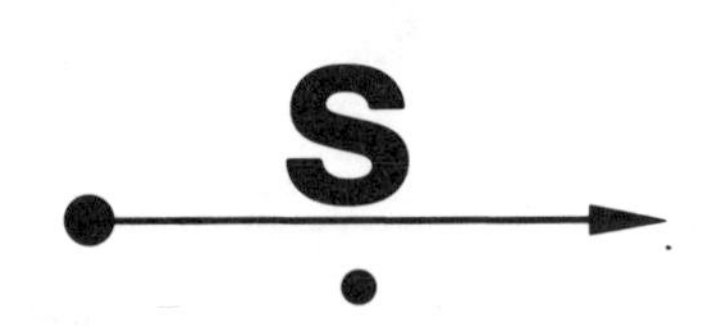

3. (Touch first ball for **a.**) Say the sound slowly. (Move quickly to second ball. Hold.) "aaa."
(Release.)
(Return to first ball for **a.**) Say it fast. (Move quickly to end of arrow.) "a."

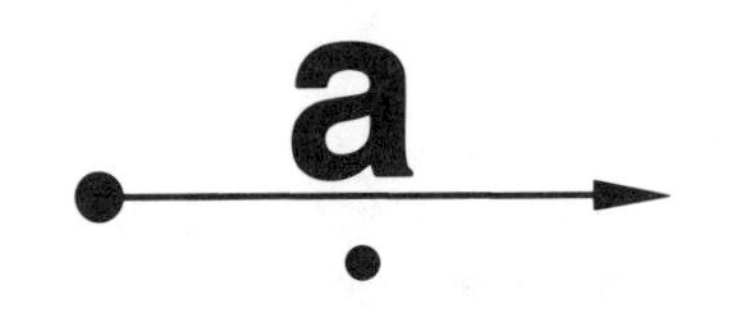

4. (Touch first ball for **m.**) Say the sound slowly. (Move quickly to second ball. Hold.) "mmm."
(Release.)
(Return to first ball for **m.**) Say it fast. (Move quickly to end of arrow.) "m."

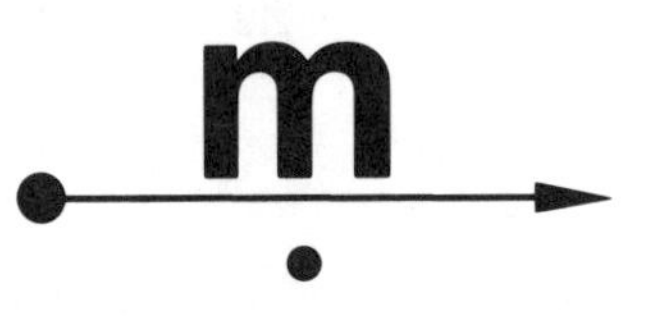

TASK 2 SAY THE SOUNDS

Your turn to say the words slowly.
Say **wwwēēē.** "wwwēēē."
Say **iiinnn.** "iiinnn."
Say **rrruuunnn.** "rrruuunnn."
Say **nnnooot.** "nnnooot."
Say **fffiiinnn.** "fffiiinnn."
Say **ēēēt.** "ēēēt."
Say **thththaaat.** "thththaaat."
Say **fffēeet.** "fffēēēt."
Say **sssēēē.** "sssēēē."
Say **sssaaat.** "sssaaat."
Say **sssēēēnnn.** "sssēēēnnn."
Say **sssiiinnn.** "sssiiinnn."

TASK 3 RHYMING

1. I'm going to rhyme. (Touch first ball for **m.**) This is the sound I'm going to start with. Get ready to say the sound. (Quickly slide to second ball and hold.) "mmm."
2. (Return to first ball.) I'm going to rhyme with (pause) **ē.** What am I going to rhyme with? "ē." (Slide quickly to second ball under **m.** Hold for about three seconds, then slide quickly to end of arrow as you say:) **mmme.** (Return to first ball.) Say it fast. (Slide to end of arrow as you say:) **me.** I rhymed with (pause) **ē.**
3. (Touch first ball.) Now I'm going to rhyme with (pause) **eat.** What am I going to rhyme with? "eat." (Slide quickly to second ball under **m.** Hold for about three seconds, then slide quickly to end of arrow as you say:) **mmmeat.** (Return to first ball.) Say it fast. (Slide to end of arrow as you say:) **meat.** I rhymed with (pause) **eat.**
4. (Touch first ball.) Now I'm going to rhyme with (pause) **ēn.** What am I going to rhyme with?" "ēn." (Slide quickly to second ball under **m.** Hold for about three seconds, then slide quickly to end of arrow as you say:) **mmmean.** (Return to first ball.) Say it fast. (Slide to end of arrow as you say:) **mean.** I rhymed with (pause) **ēn.**
5. (Touch first ball.) Now I'm going to rhyme with (pause) **at.** What am I going to rhyme with? "at." (Slide quickly to second ball under **m.** Hold for about three seconds, then slide quickly to end of arrow as you say:) **mmmat.** (Return to first ball.) Say it fast. (Slide to end of arrow as you say:) **mat.** I rhymed with (pause) **at.**
6. (Touch first ball.) Now it's your turn to rhyme with (pause) **at.** (Slide quickly to second ball. Hold for about three seconds, then slide quickly to end of arrow.) "mmmat." (Return to first ball.) Say it fast. (Slide to end of arrow.) "mat." You rhymed with (pause) **at.**
7. (Touch first ball.) Your turn to rhyme with (pause) **ēn.** What are you going to rhyme with? "ēn." Rhyming with (pause) **ēn.** (Slide quickly to second ball. Hold for about three seconds, then slide quickly to end of arrow.) "mmmean." (Return to first ball.) Say it fast. (Slide to end of arrow.) "mean." You rhymed with (pause) **ēn.**
8. (Touch first ball.) Your turn to rhyme with (pause) **eat.** What are you going to rhyme with? "eat." Rhyming with (pause) **eat.** (Slide quickly to second ball. Hold for about three seconds, then slide quickly to end of arrow.) "mmmeat." (Return to first ball.) Say it fast. (Slide to end of arrow.) "meat." You rhymed with (pause) **eat.**
9. (Touch first ball.) Your turn to rhyme with (pause) **ē.** What are you going to rhyme with? "ē." Rhyming with (pause) **ē.** (Slide quickly to second ball. Hold for about three seconds, then slide quickly to end of arrow.) "mmme." (Return to first ball.) Say it fast. (Slide to end of arrow.) "me." You rhymed with (pause) **ē.**

(**To correct** if child does not respond or says "mmm" only:) Do it with me. (Touch first ball.) Rhymes with (pause) **at.** (Slide to second ball. Touch for three seconds and then slide quickly to end of arrow as you say **mmmat** without pausing between sounds. Repeat correction until child responds with you, then repeat step 6.)

m

TASK 4 CHILD TOUCHES SOUNDS

1. Your turn to touch the sounds and say them. Touch the first ball for the first sound. Move to the next ball and say the sound slowly. "ēēē." Now say it fast. "ē."
2. Touch the first ball for the next sound. Move to the next ball and say the sound slowly. "aaa." Now say it fast. "a."

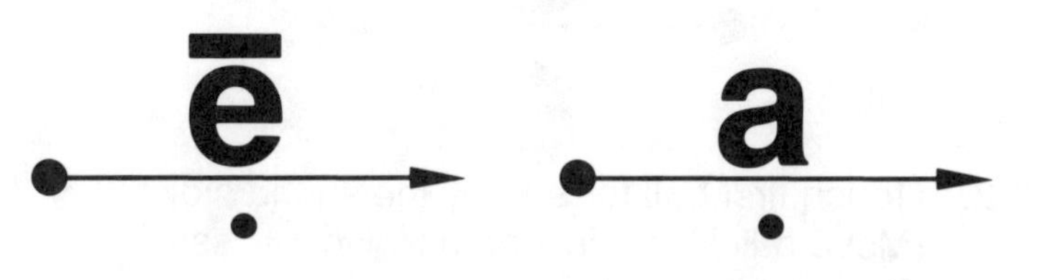

3. Touch the first ball for the next sound. Move to the next ball and say the sound slowly. "mmm." Now say it fast. "m."
4. Touch the first ball for the next sound. Move to the next ball and say the sound slowly. "sss." Now say it fast. "s."

m **s**

TASK 5 SAY THE SOUNDS

1. Say **aaat.** "aaat."
   Say it fast. "at."
   Say **sssaaat.** "sssaaat."
   Say it fast. "sat."
   Say **fffēēēt.** "fffēēēt."
   Say it fast. "feet."
   Say **sssiiinnn.** "sssiiinnn."
   Say it fast. "sin."
   Say **sssēēē.** "sssēēē."
   Say it fast. "see."
   Say **sssēēēnnn.** "sssēēēnnn."
   Say it fast. "seen."
   Say **wwwēēē.** "wwwēēē."
   Say it fast. "we."
2. Let's do those words again. (Repeat step 1 until firm.)

TASK 6 RHYMING

1. I'm going to rhyme. (Touch first ball for **s.**) This is the sound I'm going to start with. Get ready to say the sound. (Quickly slide to second ball and hold.) **"sss."**
2. (Return to first ball.) I'm going to rhyme with (pause) **at.** What am I going to rhyme with? "at." (Slide quickly to second ball under **s.** Hold for about three seconds, then slide quickly to end of arrow as you say:) **sssat.** (Return to first ball.) Say it fast. (Slide to end of arrow as you say:) **sat.** I rhymed with (pause) **at.**
3. (Touch first ball.) Now I'm going to rhyme with (pause) **eat.** What am I going to rhyme with? "eat." (Slide quickly to second ball under **s.** Hold for about three seconds, then slide quickly to end of arrow as you say:) **ssseat.** (Return to first ball.) Say it fast. (Slide to end of arrow as you say:) **seat.** I rhymed with (pause) **eat.**
4. (Touch first ball.) Now I'm going to rhyme with (pause) **ē.** What am I going to rhyme with? "ē." (Slide quickly to second ball under **s.** Hold for about three seconds, then slide quickly to end of arrow as you say:) **sssee.** (Return to first ball.) Say it fast. (Slide to end of arrow as you say:) **see.** I rhymed with (pause) **ē.**

s

5. (Touch first ball.) Now it's your turn to rhyme with (pause) **ē.** (Slide quickly to second ball. Hold for about three seconds, then slide quickly to end of arrow.) "sssee." (Return to first ball.) Say it fast. (Slide to end of arrow.) "see." You rhymed with (pause) **ē.**
6. (Touch first ball.) Your turn to rhyme with (pause) **eat.** What are you going to rhyme with? "eat." Rhyming with (pause) **eat.** (Slide quickly to second ball. Hold for about three seconds, then slide quickly to end of arrow.) "ssseat." (Return to first ball.) Say it fast. (Slide to end of arrow.) "seat." You rhymed with (pause) **eat.**
7. (Touch first ball.) Your turn to rhyme with (pause) **at.** What are you going to rhyme with? "at." Rhyming with (pause) **at.** (Slide quickly to second ball. Hold for about three seconds, then slide quickly to end of arrow.) "sssat." (Return to first ball.) Say it fast. (Slide to end of arrow.) "sat." You rhymed with (pause) **at.**

TASK 7 SAY THE SOUNDS

1. (Point to **mē.**) You're going to touch under these sounds and say them. Here's what you're going to say. (Pause.) **mmmēēē.** Say that. "mmmēēē." Again. "mmmēēē."
2. Touch the first ball of the arrow. Get ready to touch under the sounds and say them. (Child touches under **m** and **ē** and says "mmmēēē" without pausing between sounds.) Good sounding out.

(**To correct** if child pauses between sounds or does not touch and say sounds at the same time:) Let's say the sounds. (Hold child's finger and move it to appropriate balls as you say **mmmēēē** without pausing between sounds. Repeat until child responds with you. Repeat step 2.)

mē

3. (Point to **sē.**) You're going to touch under these sounds and say them. Here's what you're going to say. (Pause.) **sssēēē.** Say that. "sssēēē." Again. "sssēēē."
4. Touch the first ball of the arrow. Get ready to touch under the sounds and say them. Go. (Child touches under **s** and **ē** and says "sssēēē" without pausing between sounds.) Good sounding out.

TASK 8 SOUNDS WRITING

1. (See chart on page 24 for steps in writing **ē** and **s.**)
2. You're going to write the sounds that I write. Here's the first sound you're going to write.
3. (Write **ē** at beginning of first line. Point to **e.**) What sound? "ēēē."
4. First trace the **ēēē** that I made. Then make more of them on this line. (After tracing **ē** several times, child is to make three to five **ē**'s. Help child if necessary. For each acceptable letter say:) Good writing **ēēē.**
5. Here's the next sound you're going to write. (Write **s** at beginning of second line. Point to **s.**) What sound? "sss."
6. First trace the **sss** that I made. Then make more of them on this line. (After tracing **s** several times, child is to make three to five **s**'s. Help child if necessary. For acceptable letters say:) Good writing **sss.**

LESSON 7

TASK 1 SOUNDS INTRODUCTION

1. (Touch ball for **t.**) We always have to say this sound fast. My turn to say it fast. (Quickly move to end of arrow as you say sound.) **t.**
2. My turn to say it fast again. (Touch ball for **t.**) Say it fast. (Quickly move to end of arrow.) **t.**
3. (Touch ball.) Your turn. (Pause.) Say it fast. (Quickly move to end of arrow.) "t."

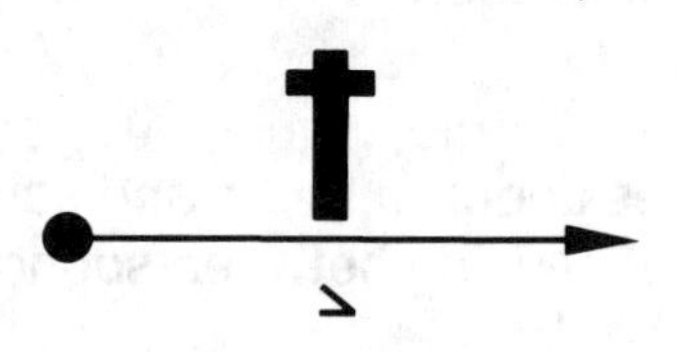

(**To correct** if child says "tuh," "tah," or "tih":) Listen: **t.** Say it fast. (Repeat steps 1–3.)

TASK 2 SOUNDS

1. You're going to say sounds slowly, then you're going to say them fast. (Touch first ball for **ē.**) Say the sound slowly. (Move quickly to second ball. Hold.) "ēēē." (Release.) (Return to first ball.) Say it fast. (Move quickly to end of arrow.) "ē."
2. (Touch first ball for **s.**) Say the sound slowly. (Move quickly to second ball. Hold.) "sss." (Release.)
(Return to first ball for **s.**) Say it fast. (Move quickly to end of arrow.) "s."

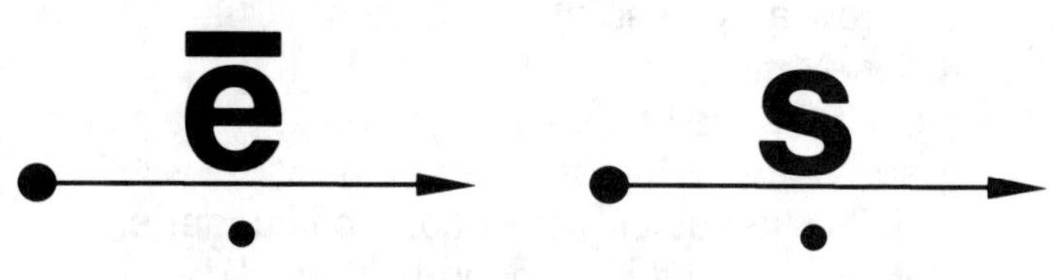

3. (Touch first ball for **m.**) Say the sound slowly. (Move quickly to second ball. Hold.) "mmm." (Release.)
(Return to first ball for **m.**) Say it fast. (Move quickly to end of arrow.) "m."
4. (Touch first ball for **a.**) Say the sound slowly. (Move quickly to second ball. Hold.) "aaa." (Release.)
(Return to first ball for **a.**) Say it fast. (Move quickly to end of arrow.) "a."

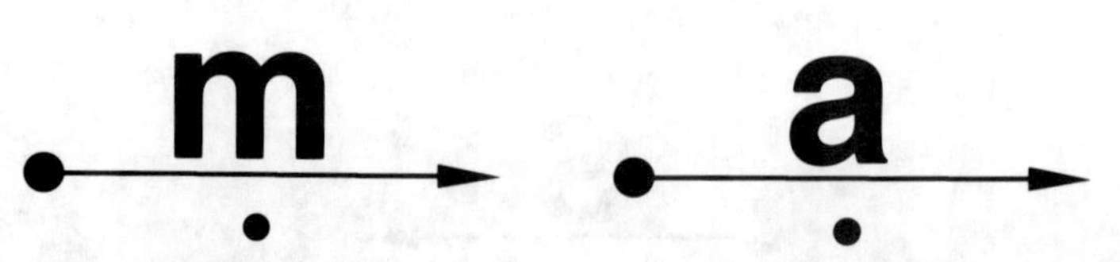

TASK 3 RHYMING

1. I'm going to rhyme. (Touch first ball for **s.**) This is the sound I'm going to start with. Get ready to say the sound. (Quickly slide to second ball and hold.) "sss."
2. (Return to first ball.) I'm going to rhyme with (pause) **ē.** What am I going to rhyme with? "ē." (Slide quickly to second ball under **s.** Hold for about three seconds, then slide quickly to end of arrow as you say:) **sssee.** (Return to first ball.) Say it fast. (Slide to end of arrow as you say:) **see.** I rhymed with (pause) **ē.**
3. (Touch first ball.) Now I'm going to rhyme with (pause) **at.** What am I going to rhyme with? "at." (Slide quickly to second ball under **s.** Hold for about three seconds, then slide quickly to end of arrow as you say:) **sssat.** (Return to first ball.) Say it fast. (Slide to end of arrow as you say:) **sat.** I rhymed with (pause) **at.**
4. (Touch first ball.) Now I'm going to rhyme with (pause) **eat.** What am I going to rhyme with? "eat." (Slide quickly to second ball under **s.** Hold for about three seconds, then slide quickly to end of arrow as you say:) **ssseat.** (Return to first ball.) Say it fast. (Slide to end of arrow as you say:) **seat.** I rhymed with (pause) **eat.**
5. (Touch first ball.) Now I'm going to rhyme with (pause) **ēn.** What am I going to rhyme with? "ēn." (Slide quickly to second ball under **s.** Hold for about three seconds, then slide quickly to end of arrow as you say:) **ssseēn.** (Return to first ball.) Say it fast. (Slide to end of arrow as you say:) **seen.** I rhymed with (pause) **ēn.**
6. (Touch first ball.) Now it's your turn to rhyme with (pause) **ēn.** (Slide quickly to second ball. Hold for about three seconds, then slide quickly to end of arrow.) "ssseen."

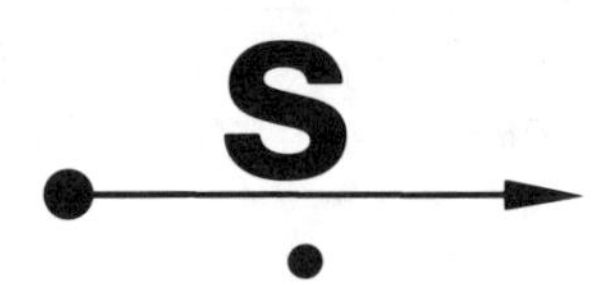

(**To correct** if child does not respond or says "sss" only:) Do it with me. (Touch first ball.) Rhymes with (pause) **ēn.** (Slide to second ball. Touch for three seconds and then slide quickly to end of arrow as you say **ssseen** without pausing between sounds. Repeat correction until child responds with you, then repeat step 6.)

(Return to first ball.) Say it fast. (Slide to end of arrow.) "sēēn." You rhymed with (pause) **ēn.**

7. (Touch first ball.) Your turn to rhyme with (pause) **eat.** What are you going to rhyme with? "eat." Rhyming with (pause) **eat.** (Slide quickly to second ball. Hold for about three seconds, then slide quickly to end of arrow.) "ssseat." (Return to first ball.) Say it fast. (Slide to end of arrow.) "seat." You rhymed with (pause) **eat.**
8. (Touch first ball.) Your turn to rhyme with (pause) **at.** What are you going to rhyme with? "at." Rhyming with (pause) **at.** (Slide quickly to second ball. Hold for about three seconds, then slide quickly to end of arrow.) "sssat." (Return to first ball.) Say it fast. (Slide to end of arrow.) "sat." You rhymed with (pause) **at.**
9. (Touch first ball.) Your turn to rhyme with (pause) **ē.** What are you going to rhyme with? "ē." Rhyming with (pause) **ē.** (Slide quickly to second ball. Hold for about three seconds, then slide quickly to end of arrow.) "sssee." (Return to first ball.) Say it fast. (Slide to end of arrow.) "see." You rhymed with (pause) **ē.**

TASK 4 SAY THE SOUNDS

Your turn to say the words slowly.
Say **sssēēē.** "sssēēē."
Say **fffēēēt.** "fffēēēt."
Say **sssēēēt.** "sssēēēt."
Say **mmmēēēt.** "mmmēēēt."
Say **sssaaat.** "sssaaat."
Say **aaat.** "aaat."
Say **sssēēēnnn.** "sssēēēnnn."

TASK 5 SOUNDS REVIEW

1. Let's do sounds again. See if you remember all of them. (Touch first ball for **m.**) Get ready. (Quickly move to second ball. Hold.) "mmm."
2. (Touch first ball for **a.**) Get ready. (Quickly move to second ball. Hold.) "aaa."
3. (Touch ball for **t.**) Take a good look and get ready. (Pause.) Say it fast. (Move quickly to end of arrow.) "t." (Repeat until firm.)
4. (Touch first ball for **s.**) Get ready. (Quickly move to second ball. Hold.) "sss."
5. (Touch first ball for **ē.**) Get ready. (Quickly move to second ball. Hold.) "ēēē."

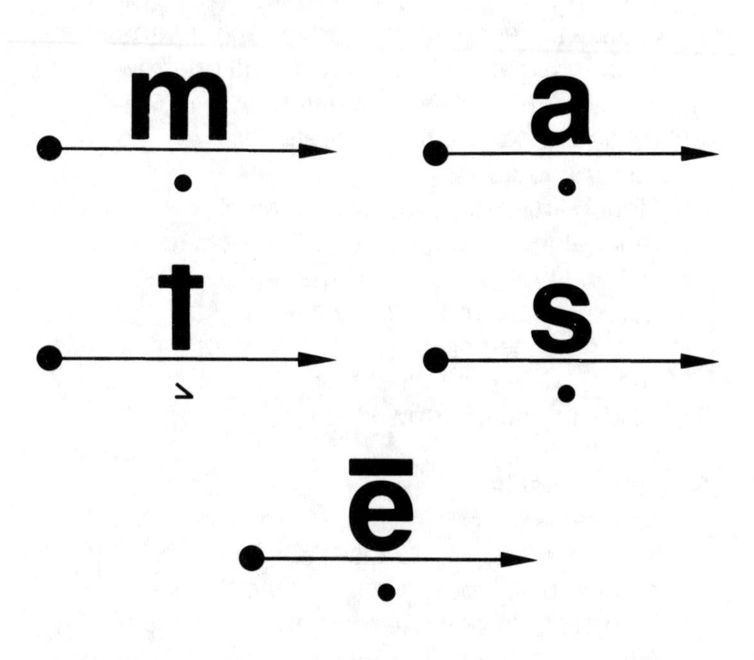

TASK 6 SAY THE SOUNDS

1. Say **aaammm.** "aaammm."
   Say it fast. "am."
   Say **rrruuunnn.** "rrruuunnn."
   Say it fast. "run."
   Say **nnnooot.** "nnnooot."
   Say it fast. "not."
   Say **ēēēt.** "ēēēt."
   Say it fast. "eat."
   Say **sssēēē.** "sssēēē."
   Say it fast. "see."
   Say **sssēēēnnn.** "sssēēēnnn."
   Say it fast. "seen."
   Say **sssēēēt.** "sssēēēt."
   Say it fast. "seat."
2. Let's do those words again. (Repeat step 1 until firm.)

TASK 7 RHYMING

1. I'm going to rhyme. (Touch first ball for **m.**) This is the sound I'm going to start with. Get ready to say the sound. (Quickly slide to second ball and hold.) "mmm."
2. (Return to first ball.) I'm going to rhyme with (pause) **ē.** What am I going to rhyme with? "ē." (Slide quickly to second ball under **m.** Hold for about three seconds, then slide quickly to end of arrow as you say:) **mmme.** (Return to first ball.) Say it fast. (Slide to end of arrow as you say:) **me.** I rhymed with (pause) **ē.**
3. (Touch first ball.) Now I'm going to rhyme with (pause) **at.** What am I going to rhyme with? "at." (Slide quickly to second ball under **m.** Hold for about three seconds, then slide quickly to end of arrow as you say:) **mmmat.** (Return to first ball.) Say it fast. (Slide to end of arrow as you say:) **mat.** I rhymed with (pause) **at.**
4. (Touch first ball.) Now I'm going to rhyme with (pause) **ēn.** What am I going to rhyme with? "ēn." (Slide quickly to second ball under **m.** Hold for about three seconds, then slide quickly to end of arrow as you say:) **mmmean.** (Return to first ball.) Say it fast. (Slide to end of arrow as you say:) **mean.** I rhymed with (pause) **ēn.**
5. (Touch first ball.) Now it's your turn to rhyme with (pause) **ēn.** (Slide quickly to second ball. Hold for about three seconds, then slide quickly to end of arrow.) "mmmean."

> (**To correct** if child does not respond or says "mmm" only:) Do it with me. (Touch first ball.) Rhymes with (pause) **ēn.** (Slide to second ball. Touch for three seconds, then slide quickly to end of arrow as you say **mmmean** without pausing between sounds. Repeat correction until child responds with you, then repeat step 5.)

(Return to first ball.) Say it fast. (Slide to end of arrow.) "mean." You rhymed with (pause) **ēn.**

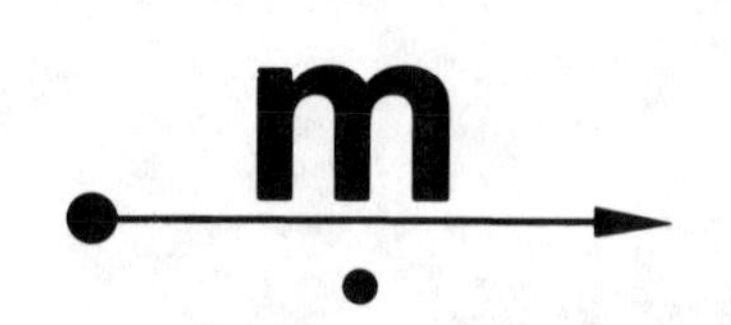

6. (Touch first ball.) Your turn to rhyme with (pause) **at.** What are you going to rhyme with? "at." Rhyming with (pause) **at.** (Slide quickly to second ball. Hold for about three seconds, then slide quickly to end of arrow.) "mmmat." (Return to first ball.) Say it fast. (Slide to end of arrow.) "mat." You rhymed with (pause) **at.**
7. (Touch first ball.) Your turn to rhyme with (pause) **ē.** What are you going to rhyme with? "ē." Rhyming with (pause) **ē.** (Slide quickly to second ball. Hold for about three seconds, then slide quickly to end of arrow.) "mmme." (Return to first ball.) Say it fast. (Slide to end of arrow.) "me." You rhymed with (pause) **ē.**

TASK 8 SAY THE SOUNDS

1. (Point to **at.**) You're going to touch under these sounds and say them. Here's what you're going to say. (Pause.) **aaat.** Say that. "aaat." Again. "aaat."
2. Touch the first ball of the arrow. Get ready to touch under the sounds and say them. Go. (Child touches under **a** and **t** and says "aaat" without pausing between sounds.) Good sounding out.

3. (Point to **ēt.**) You're going to touch under these sounds and say them. Here's what you're going to say. (Pause.) **ēēēt.** Say that. "ēēēt." Again. "ēēēt."
4. Touch the first ball of the arrow. Get ready to touch under the sounds and say them. Go. (Child touches under **ē** and **t** and says "ēēēt" without pausing between sounds.) Good sounding out.

5. (Point to **mēt.**) You're going to touch under these sounds and say them. Here's what you're going to say. (Pause.) **mmmēēēt.** Say that. "mmmēēēt." Again. "mmmēēēt."
6. Touch the first ball of the arrow. Get ready to touch under the sounds and say them. Go. (Child touches under **m, e,** and **t** and says "mmmēēēt" without pausing between sounds.) Good sounding out.

TASK 9 SOUNDS WRITING

1. (See chart on page 24 for steps in writing **t** and **m.**)
2. You're going to write the sounds that I write. Here's the first sound you're going to write.
3. (Write **t** at beginning of first line. Point to **t.**) What sound? "t."
4. First trace the **t** that I made. Then make more of them on this line. (After tracing **t** several times, child is to make three to five **t**'s. Help child if necessary. For each acceptable letter say:) Good writing **t.**
5. Here's the next sound you're going to write. (Write **m** at beginning of second line. Point to **m.**) What sound? "mmm."
6. First trace the **mmm** that I made. Then make more of them on this line. (After tracing **m** several times, child is to make three to five **m**'s. Help child if necessary. For acceptable letters say:) Good writing **mmm.**

LESSON 8

TASK 1 SOUNDS REVIEW

1. You're going to say all these sounds. (Touch first ball for **m.**) Get ready. (Quickly move to second ball. Hold.) "mmm."
2. (Touch first ball for **ē.**) Get ready. (Quickly move to second ball. Hold.) "ēēē."

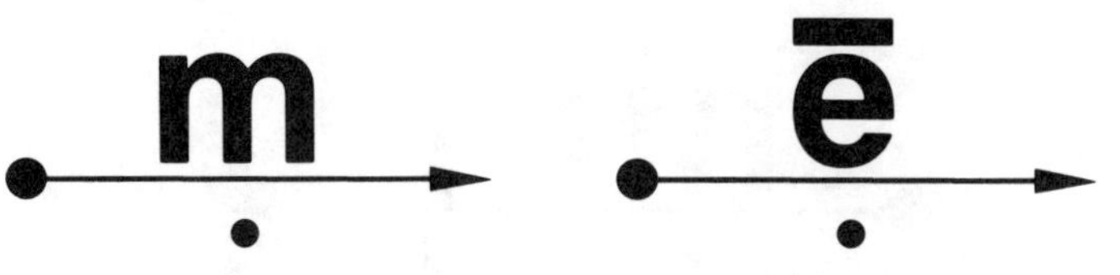

3. (Touch ball for **t.**) Take a good look and get ready. (Pause.) Say it fast. (Move quickly to end of arrow.) "t." (Repeat until firm.)
4. (Touch first ball for **s.**) Get ready. (Quickly move to second ball. Hold.) "sss."

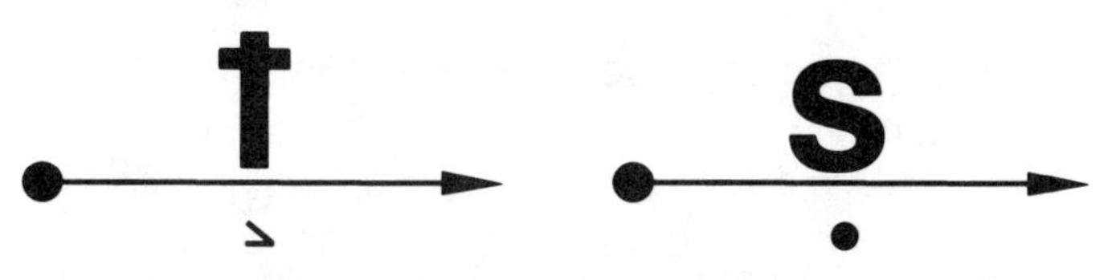

5. (Touch first ball for **a.**) Get ready. (Quickly move to second ball. Hold.) "aaa."

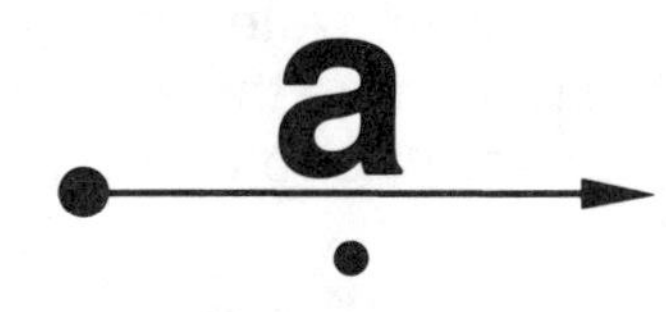

TASK 2 RHYMING

1. You're going to rhyme. (Touch first ball for **s.**) This is the sound you're going to start with. Get ready to say the sound. (Quickly slide to second ball and hold.) **"sss."**
2. (Return to first ball.) Yes, you're going to start with **sss.** And you're going to rhyme with (pause) **ēn.** What are you going to rhyme with? "ēn."
3. Rhyming with (pause) **ēn.** (Slide quickly to second ball. Hold for about three seconds, then slide quickly to end of arrow.) "ssseen."

s

4. (Return to first ball.) Say it fast. (Slide to end of arrow.) "seen." You rhymed with (pause) **ēn.**
5. (Touch first ball.) Now you're going to rhyme with (pause) **eat.** What are you going to rhyme with? "eat." Rhyming with (pause) **eat.** (Slide quickly to second ball. Hold for about three seconds, then slide quickly to end of arrow.) "ssseat." (Return to first ball.) Say it fast. (Slide to end of arrow.) "seat." You rhymed with (pause) **eat.**

TASK 3 RHYMING

1. You're going to rhyme again. (Touch first ball for **m.**) This is the sound you're going to start with. Get ready to say the sound. (Quickly slide to second ball and hold.) "mmm."
2. (Return to first ball.) Yes, you're going to start with **mmm.** And you're going to rhyme with (pause) **ē.** What are you going to rhyme with? "ē."
3. Rhyming with (pause) **ē.** (Slide quickly to second ball. Hold for about three seconds, then slide quickly to end of arrow.) "mmme."
4. (Return to first ball.) Say it fast. (Slide to end of arrow.) "me." You rhymed with (pause) **ē.**
5. (Touch first ball.) Now you're going to rhyme with (pause) **at.** What are you going to rhyme with? "at." Rhyming with (pause) **at.** (Slide quickly to second ball. Hold for about three seconds, then slide quickly to end of arrow.) "mmmat." (Return to first ball.) Say it fast. (Slide to end of arrow.) "mat." You rhymed with (pause) **at.**
6. (Touch first ball.) Now you're going to rhyme with (pause) **ēn.** What are you going to rhyme with? "ēn." Rhyming with (pause) **ēn.** (Slide quickly to second ball. Hold for about three seconds, then slide quickly to end of arrow.) "mmmean." (Return to first ball.) Say it fast. (Slide to end of arrow.) "mean." You rhymed with (pause) **ēn.**

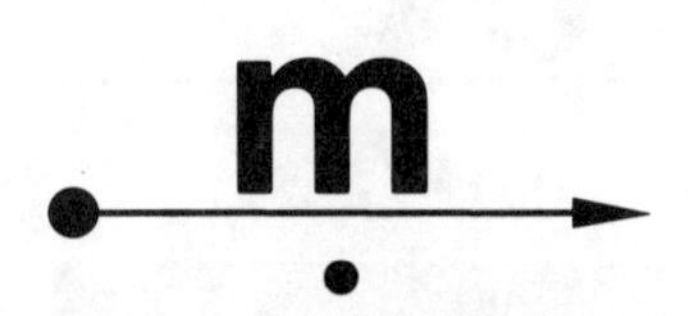

TASK 4 SAY THE SOUNDS

Your turn to say the words slowly.
Say **sssaaammm.** "sssaaammm."
Say **iiifff.** "iiifff."
Say **iiinnn.** "iiinnn."
Say **sssuuunnn.** "sssuuunnn."
Say **rrruuunnn.** "rrruuunnn."
Say **rrrōōōd.** "rrrōōōd."
Say **mmmēēēt.** "mmmēēēt."
Say **sssiiit.** "sssiiit."
Say **sssaaat.** "sssaaat."
Say **rrraaat.** "rrraaat."
Say **aaammm.** "aaammm."
Say **rrraaammm.** "rrraaammm."

TASK 5 CHILD TOUCHES SOUNDS

1. Your turn. Touch the ball for the first sound. You have to say this sound fast. So say it fast when you touch under it. Say it fast. "t."

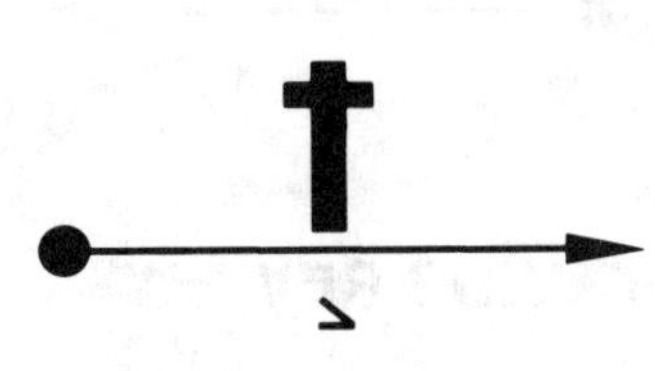

2. Touch the first ball for the next sound. Move to the next ball and say the sound slowly. "ēēē." Now say it fast. "ē."

3. Touch the first ball for the next sound. Move to the next ball and say the sound slowly. "mmm." Now say it fast. "m."

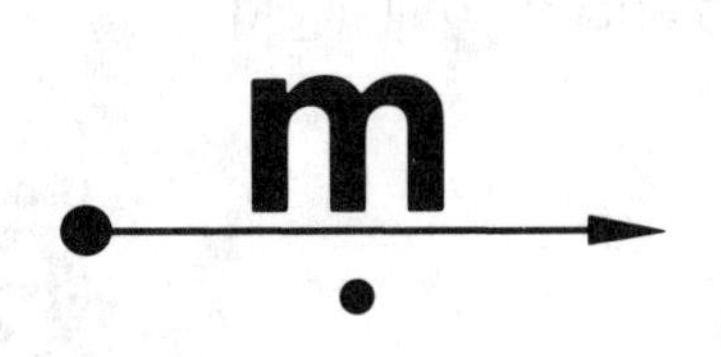

4. Touch the first ball for the next sound. Move to the next ball and say the sound slowly. "sss." Now say it fast. "s."

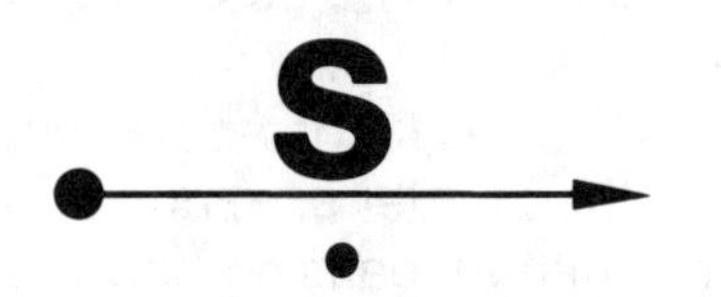

5. Touch the first ball for the next sound. Move to the next ball and say the sound slowly. "aaa." Now say it fast. "a."

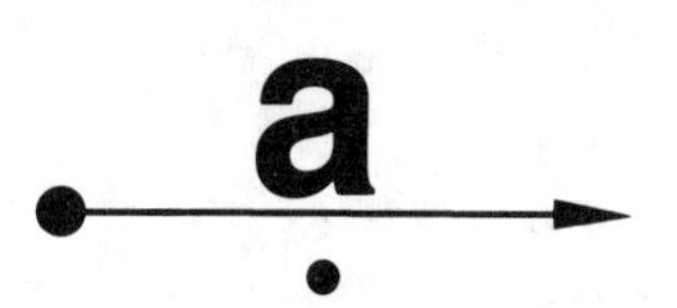

TASK 6 SAY THE SOUNDS

1. Say **rrruuunnn.** "rrruuunnn."
   Say it fast. "run."
   Say **rrraaat.** "rrraaat."
   Say it fast. "rat."
   Say **rrrōōōd.** "rrrōōōd."
   Say it fast. "road."
   Say **thththaaat.** "thththaaat."
   Say it fast. "that."
   Say **sssiiit.** "sssiiit."
   Say it fast. "sit."
   Say **sssaaat.** "sssaaat."
   Say it fast. "sat."
   Say **mmmaaat.** "mmmaaat."
   Say it fast. "mat."
2. Let's do those words again. (Repeat step 1 until firm.)

TASK 7 SAY THE SOUNDS

1. (Point to **mat.**) You're going to touch under these sounds and say them. Here's what you're going to say. (Pause.) **mmmaaat.** Say that. "mmmaaat." Again. "mmmaaat."
2. Touch the first ball of the arrow. Get ready to touch under the sounds and say them. Go. (Child touches under **m, a,** and **t** and says "mmmaaat" without pausing between sounds.) Good sounding out.

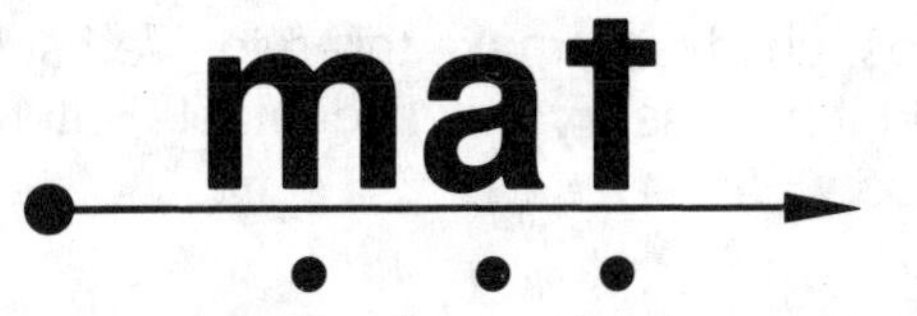

3. (Point to **sēt.**) You're going to touch under these sounds and say them. Here's what you're going to say. (Pause.) **sssēēēt.** Say that. "sssēēēt." Again. "sssēēēt."
4. Touch the first ball of the arrow. Get ready to touch under the sounds and say them. Go. (Child touches under **s, ē,** and **t** and says "sssēēēt" without pausing between sounds.) Good sounding out.

5. (Point to **am.**) You're going to touch under these sounds and say them. Here's what you're going to say. (Pause.) **aaammm.** Say that. "aaammm." Again. "aaammm."
6. Touch the first ball of the arrow. Get ready to touch under the sounds and say them. Go. (Child touches under **a** and **m** and says "aaammm" without pausing between sounds.) Good sounding out.

TASK 8 SOUNDS WRITING

1. (See chart on page 24 for steps in writing **s** and **t.**)
2. You're going to write the sounds that I write.
3. Here's the first sound you're going to write. (Write **s** at beginning of first line. Point to **s.**) What sound? "sss."
4. First trace the **sss** that I made. Then make more of them on this line. (After tracing **s** several times, child is to make three to five **s**'s. Help child if necessary. For acceptable letters say:) Good writing **sss.**
5. Here's the next sound you're going to write. (Write **t** at beginning of second line. Point to **t.**) What sound? "t."
6. First trace the **t** that I made. Then make more of them on this line. (After tracing **t** several times, child is to make three to five **t**'s. Help child if necessary. For acceptable letters say:) Good writing **t.**

LESSON 9

TASK 1 SOUNDS INTRODUCTION

1. (Point to **r.**) Here's a new sound. I'm going to touch under this sound and say the sound. (Touch first ball of arrow. Move quickly to second ball. Hold.) **rrr.**
2. Your turn to say the sound when I touch under it. (Touch first ball.) Get ready. (Move quickly to second ball. Hold.) "rrr."

(**To correct** child saying a wrong sound or not responding:) The sound is **rrr.** (Repeat step 2.)

3. (Touch first ball.) Again. Get ready. (Move quickly to second ball. Hold.) "rrr."

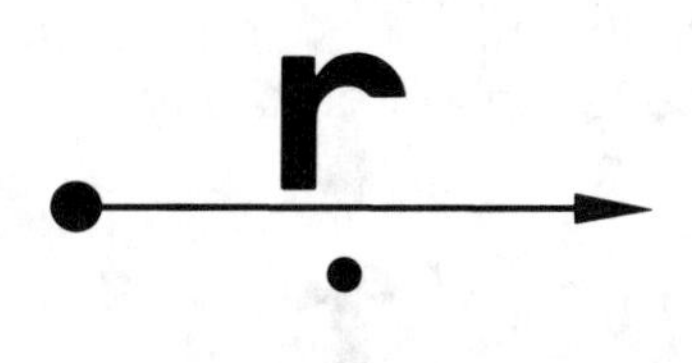

TASK 2 SOUNDS REVIEW

1. You're going to say all these sounds. (Touch first ball for **m.**) Get ready. (Quickly move to second ball. Hold.) "mmm."
2. (Touch first ball for **a.**) Get ready. (Quickly move to second ball. Hold.) "aaa."

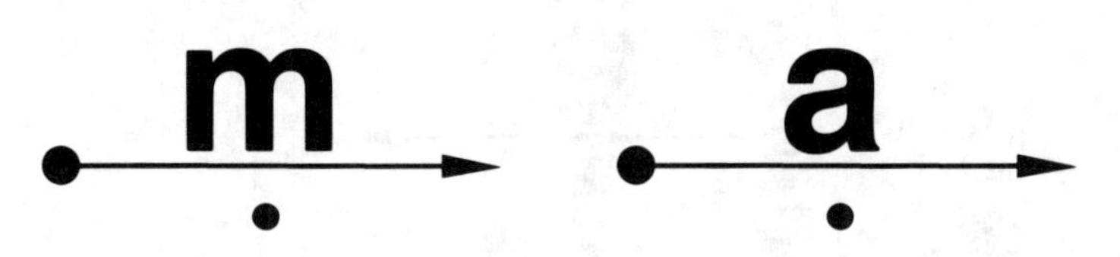

3. (Touch first ball for **s.**) Get ready. (Quickly move to second ball. Hold.) "sss."
4. (Touch first ball for **ē.**) Get ready. (Quickly move to second ball. Hold.) "ēēē."

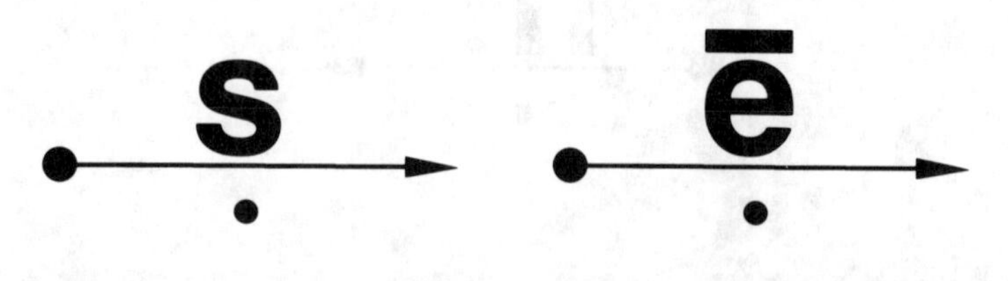

5. (Touch ball for **t.**) Take a good look and get ready. (Pause.) Say it fast. (Move quickly to end of arrow.) "t." (Repeat until firm.)
6. (Touch first ball for **r.**) Get ready. (Quickly move to second ball. Hold.) "rrr."

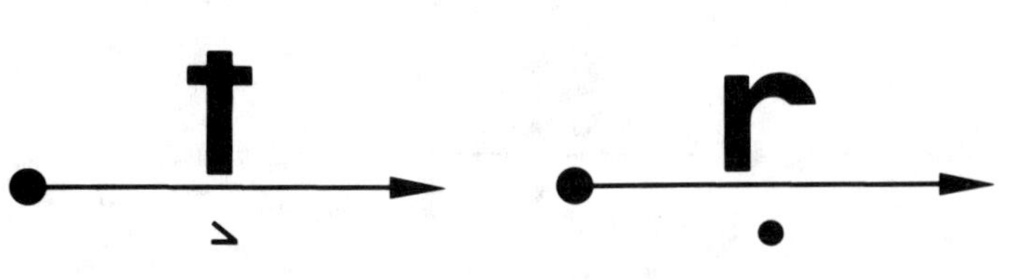

TASK 3 SAY THE SOUNDS

1. Say **rrraaat.** "rrraaat."
   Say it fast. "rat."
   Say **rrrōōōd.** "rrrōōōd.
   Say it fast. "road."
   Say **rrruuunnn.** "rrruuunnn."
   Say it fast. "run."
   Say **rrraaammm.** "rrraaammm."
   Say it fast. "ram."
   Say **aaammm.** "aaammm."
   Say it fast. "am."
   Say **mmmēēēnnn.** "mmmēēēnnn."
   Say it fast. "mean."
   Say **ēēēt.** "ēēēt."
   Say it fast. "eat."
   Say **sssēēēt.** "sssēēēt."
   Say it fast. "seat."
2. Let's do those words again. (Repeat step 1 until firm.)

TASK 4 WORD READING

1. (Touch first ball for **mat.**) I'm going to sound out this word. Then you'll say it fast. (Point to ball under **m.**)
2. What's the first sound I'm going to say? (Touch for two seconds.) "mmm." (Release.) (Point to ball under **a.**) What's the next sound I'm going to say? (Touch for two seconds.) "aaa." (Point to ball under **t.**) What's the next sound I'm going to say? "t." (Return to first ball. Repeat until firm.)

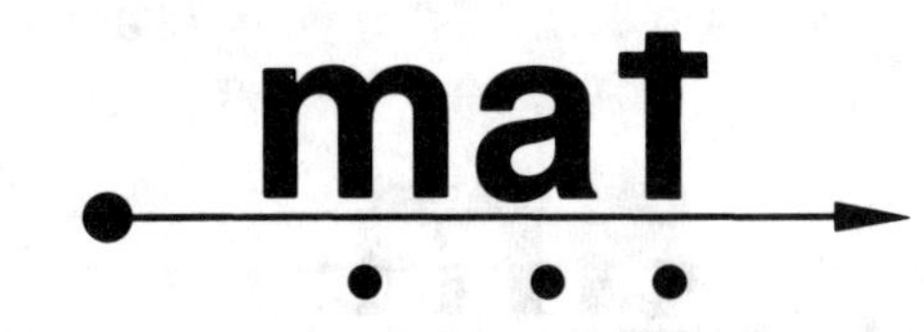

3. (Return to first ball.) My turn to sound it out. (Touch under **m, a,** and **t** as you say:) **mmmaaat.** (Return to first ball.) Say it fast. (Slide quickly to end of arrow.) "mat."
4. (Touch first ball.) You're going to sound out this word, then say it fast. Sound it out. Get ready. (Touch under **m, a,** and **t** as child says "mmmaaat" without pausing between sounds. Repeat until firm.)
   (Return to first ball.) Say it fast. (Slide to end of arrow.) "mat." Yes, what word? "mat." You read the word **mat.** Good reading.

TASK 5 WORD READING

1. (Touch first ball for **sat.**) I'm going to sound out this word. Then you'll say it fast. (Point to ball under **s.**)
2. What's the first sound I'm going to say? (Touch for two seconds.) "sss." (Release.) (Point to ball under **a.**) What's the next sound I'm going to say? (Touch for two seconds.) "aaa." (Point to ball under **t.**) What's the next sound I'm going to say? "t." (Return to first ball. Repeat until firm.)
3. (Return to first ball.) My turn to sound it out. (Touch under **s, a,** and **t** as you say:) **sssaaat.** (Return to first ball.) Say it fast. (Slide quickly to end of arrow.) "sat."
4. (Touch first ball.) You're going to sound out this word, then say it fast. Sound it out. Get ready. (Touch under **s, a,** and **t** as child says "sssaaat" without pausing between sounds. Repeat until firm.)
   (Return to first ball.) Say it fast. (Slide to end of arrow.) "sat." Yes, what word? "sat." You read the word **sat.** Good reading.

TASK 6 WORD READING

1. (Touch first ball for **am.**) I'm going to sound out this word. Then you'll say it fast. (Point to ball under **a.**)
2. What's the first sound I'm going to say? (Touch for two seconds.) "aaa." (Release.) (Point to ball under **m.**) What's the next sound I'm going to say? (Touch for two seconds.) "mmm." (Return to first ball. Repeat until firm.)
3. (Return to first ball.) My turn to sound it out. (Touch under **a** and **m** as you say:) **aaammm.** (Return to first ball.) Say it fast. (Slide quickly to end of arrow.) "am."
4. (Touch first ball.) You're going to sound out this word, then say it fast. Sound it out. Get ready. (Touch under **a** and **m** as child says "aaammm" without pausing between sounds. Repeat until firm.)
   (Return to first ball.) Say it fast. (Slide to end of arrow.) "am." Yes, what word? "am." You read the word **am.** Good reading.

TASK 7 SOUNDS

1. (Touch first ball for **e.**) Your turn to say the sound slowly. Then you'll say it fast. (Move quickly to second ball. Hold.) "ēēē." (Release.) (Return to first ball.) Say it fast. (Move quickly to end of arrow.) "ē."

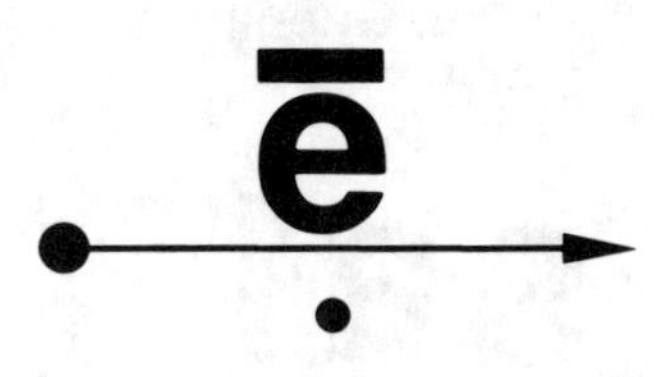

2. (Touch first ball for **a.**) Say the sound slowly. (Move quickly to second ball. Hold.) "aaa." (Release.)
   (Return to first ball for **a.**) Say it fast. (Move quickly to end of arrow.) "a."

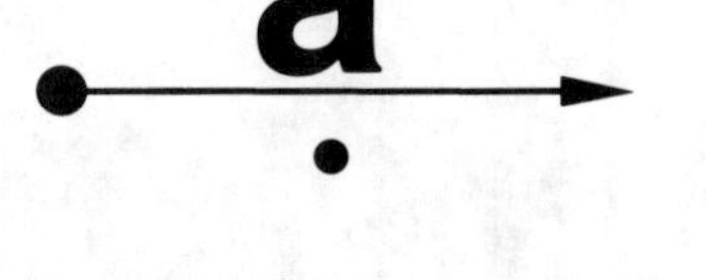

3. (Touch first ball for **s.**) Say the sound slowly. (Move quickly to second ball. Hold.) "sss." (Release.)
   (Return to first ball for **s.**) Say it fast. (Move quickly to end of arrow.) "s."

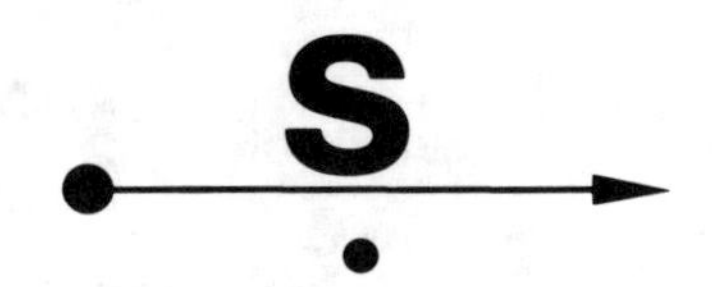

4. (Touch first ball for **m.**) Say the sound slowly. (Move quickly to second ball. Hold.) "mmm." (Release.)
   (Return to first ball for **m.**) Say it fast. (Move quickly to end of arrow.) "m."

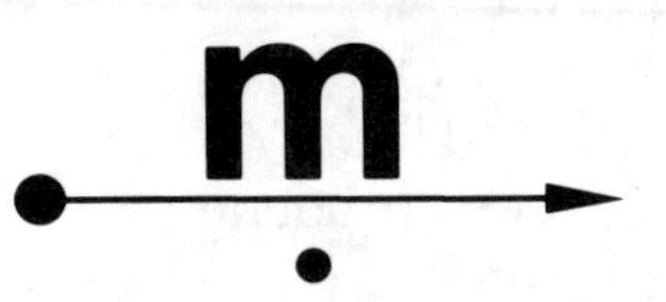

5. (Touch first ball for **r.**) Say the sound slowly. (Move quickly to second ball. Hold.) "rrr." (Release.)
   (Return to first ball for **r.**) Say it fast. (Move quickly to end of arrow.) "r."

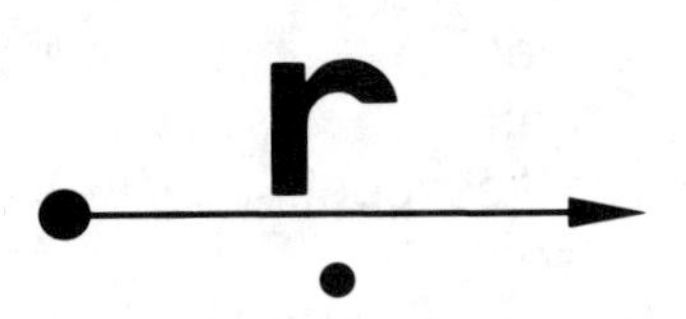

TASK 8 WORD READING

1. (Point to **am.**) You're going to **touch** under the sounds as **you** sound out this word and say it fast. (Touch under **a.**) What's the first sound you're going to say? "aaa." (Touch under **m.**) What's the next sound you're going to say? "mmm."
2. Touch the first ball of the arrow. Take a deep breath and say the sounds as you touch under them. Get ready. Go. (Child touches under **a** and **m** and says "aaammm" without pausing between sounds.) Touch the first ball and sound it out again. "aaammm." (Repeat until firm.)
3. Say it fast. "am." Yes, what word? "am." You read the word **am.** Good reading.

TASK 9 WORD READING

1. (Point to **sat.**) You're going to touch under the sounds as you sound out this word and say it fast. (Touch under **s.**) What's the first sound you're going to say? "sss." (Touch under **a.**) What's the next sound you're going to say? "aaa." (Touch under **t.**) What's the next sound you're going to say? "t."
2. Touch the first ball of the arrow. Take a deep breath and say the sounds as you touch under them. Get ready. Go. (Child touches under **s, a,** and **t** and says "sssaaat" without pausing between sounds.) Touch the first ball and sound it out again. "sssaaat." (Repeat until firm.)
3. Say it fast. "sat." Yes, what word? "sat." You read the word **sat.** Good reading.

TASK 10 RHYMING

1. You're going to rhyme. (Touch first ball for **s.**) This is the sound you're going to start with. Get ready to say the sound. (Quickly slide to second ball and hold.) "sss."
2. (Return to first ball.) Yes, you're going to start with **sss.** And you're going to rhyme with (pause) **at.** What are you going to rhyme with? "at."
3. Rhyming with (pause) **at.** (Slide quickly to second ball. Hold for about three seconds, then slide quickly to end of arrow.) "sssat."
4. (Return to first ball.) Say it fast. (Slide to end of arrow.) "sat." You rhymed with (pause) **at.**
5. (Touch first ball.) Now you're going to rhyme with (pause) **un.** What are you going to rhyme with? "un." Rhyming with (pause) **un.** (Slide quickly to second ball. Hold for about three seconds, then slide quickly to end of arrow.) "rrrun." (Return to first ball.) Say it fast. (Slide to end of arrow.) "run." You rhymed with (pause) **un.**

s

6. (Touch first ball.) Now you're going to rhyme with (pause) **am.** What are you going to rhyme with? "am." Rhyming with (pause) **am.** (Slide quickly to second ball. Hold for about three seconds, then slide quickly to end of arrow.) "rrram." (Return to first ball.) Say it fast. (Slide to end of arrow.) "ram." You rhymed with (pause) **am.**

TASK 11 RHYMING

1. You're going to rhyme again. (Touch first ball for **r.**) This is the sound you're going to start with. Get ready to say the sound. (Quickly slide to second ball and hold.) "rrr."
2. (Return to first ball.) Yes, you're going to start with **rrr.** And you're going to rhyme with (pause) **at.** What are you going to rhyme with? "at."
3. Rhyming with (pause) **at.** (Slide quickly to second ball. Hold for about three seconds, then slide quickly to end of arrow.) "rrrat."
4. (Return to first ball.) Say it fast. (Slide to end of arrow.) "rat." You rhymed with (pause) **at.**
5. (Touch first ball.) Now you're going to rhyme with (pause) **un.** What are you going to rhyme with? "un." Rhyming with (pause) **un.** (Slide quickly to second ball. Hold for about three seconds, then slide quickly to end of arrow.) "rrrun." (Return to first ball.) Say it fast. (Slide to end of arrow.) "run." You rhymed with (pause) **un.**
6. (Touch first ball.) Now you're going to rhyme with (pause) **am.** What are you going to rhyme with? "am." Rhyming with (pause) **am.** (Slide quickly to second ball. Hold for about three seconds, then slide quickly to end of arrow.) "rrram." (Return to first ball.) Say it fast. (Slide to end of arrow.) "ram." You rhymed with (pause) **am.**

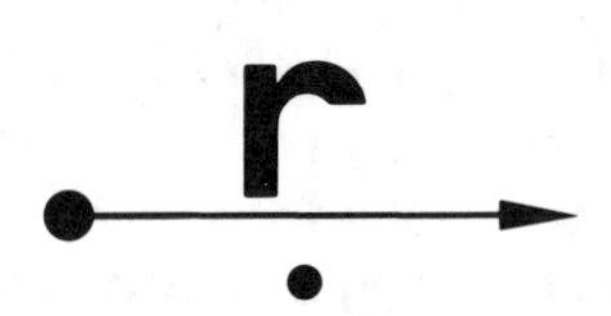

TASK 12 RHYMING

1. You're going to rhyme again. (Touch first ball for **m.**) This is the sound you're going to start with. Get ready to say the sound. (Quickly slide to second ball and hold.) "mmm."
2. (Return to first ball.) Yes, you're going to start with **mmm.** And you're going to rhyme with (pause) **ē.** What are you going to rhyme with? "ē."
3. Rhyming with (pause) **ē.** (Slide quickly to second ball. Hold for about three seconds, then slide quickly to end of arrow.) "mmme."
4. (Return to first ball.) Say it fast. (Slide to end of arrow.) "me." You rhymed with (pause) **ē.**
5. (Touch first ball.) Now you're going to rhyme with (pause) **at.** What are you going to rhyme with? "at." Rhyming with (pause) **at.** (Slide quickly to second ball. Hold for about three seconds, then slide quickly to end of arrow.) "mmmat." (Return to first ball.) Say it fast. (Slide to end of arrow.) "mat." You rhymed with (pause) **at.**

TASK 13 SOUNDS WRITING

1. (See chart on page 24 for steps in writing **r** and **a.**)
2. You're going to write the sounds that I write. Here's the first sound you're going to write.
3. (Write **r** at beginning of first line. Point to **r.**) What sound? "rrr."
4. First trace the **rrr** that I made. Then make more of them on this line. (After tracing **r** several times, child is to make three to five **r**'s. Help child if necessary. For each acceptable letter say:) Good writing **rrr.**
5. Here's the next sound you're going to write. (Write **a** at beginning of second line. Point to **a.**) What sound? "'aaa."
6. First trace the **aaa** that I made. Then make more of them on this line. (After tracing **a** several times, child is to make three to five **a**'s. Help child if necessary. For acceptable letters say:) Good writing **aaa.**

TASK 14 SAY THE SOUNDS

Your turn to say the words slowly.
Say **thththiiisss.** "thththiiisss."
Say **fffēēēt.** "fffēēēt."
Say **wwwēēē.** "wwwēēē."
Say **mmmēēēt.** "mmmēēēt."
Say **sssēēē.** "sssēēē."
Say **sssuuummm.** "sssuuummm."
Say **rrraaat.** "rrraaat."
Say **rrrōōōd.** "rrrōōōd."
Say **rrruuunnn.** "rrruuunnn."
Say **iiifff.** "iiifff."
Say **mmmēēēnnn.** "mmmēēēnnn."

LESSON 10

TASK 1 SOUNDS REVIEW

1. You're going to say all these sounds. (Touch first ball for **r.**) Get ready. (Quickly move to second ball. Hold.) "rrr."
2. (Touch first ball for **m.**) Get ready. (Quickly

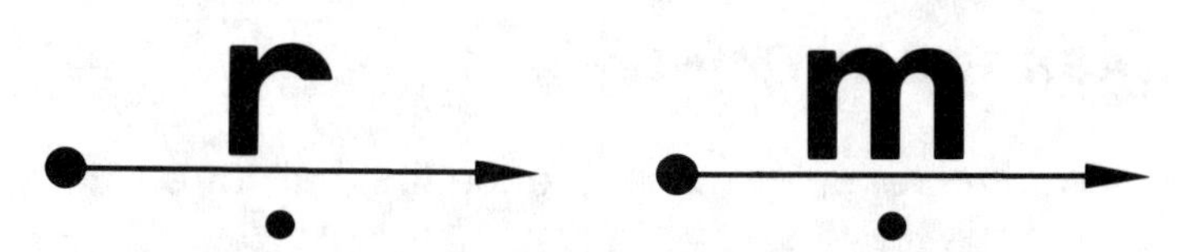

move to second ball. Hold.) "mmm."
3. (Touch ball for **t.**) Take a good look and get ready. (Pause.) Say it fast. (Move quickly to end of arrow.) "t." (Repeat until firm.)
4. (Touch first ball for **a.**) Get ready. (Quickly move to second ball. Hold.) "aaa."

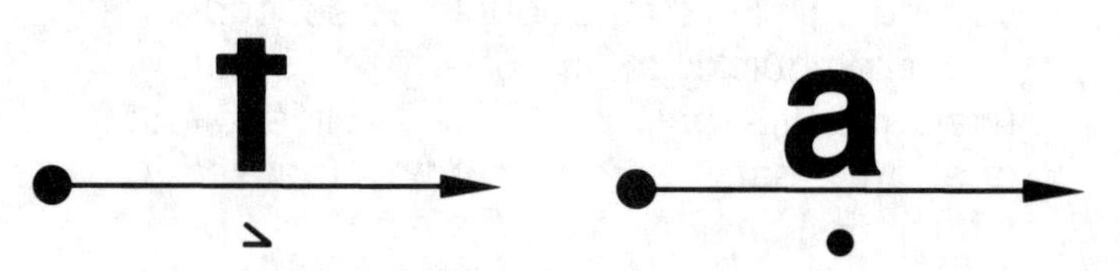

5. (Touch first ball for **s.**) Get ready. (Quickly move to second ball. Hold.) "sss."
6. (Touch first ball for **ē.**) Get ready. (Quickly move to second ball. Hold.) "ēēē."

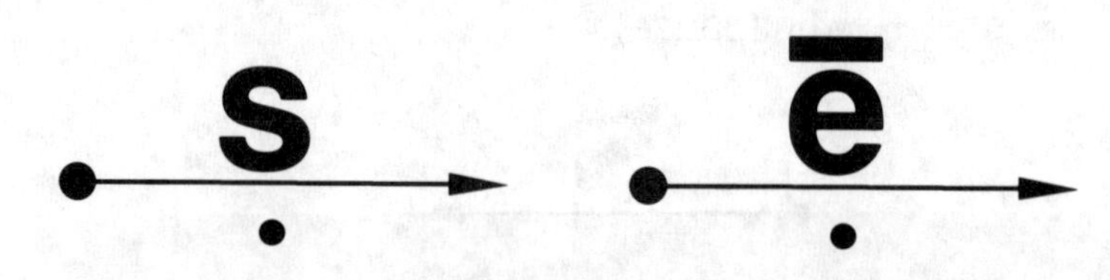

TASK 2 SAY THE SOUNDS

1. Say **rrruuunnn.** "rrruuunnn."
   Say it fast. "run."
   Say **iiifff.** "iiifff."
   Say it fast. "if."
   Say **rrrēēēd.** "rrrēēēd."
   Say it fast. "read."
   Say **rrrōōōp.** "rrrōōōp."
   Say it fast. "rope."
   Say **sssōōōp.** "sssōōōp."
   Say it fast. "soap."
   Say **sssēēē.** "sssēēē."
   Say it fast. "see."
   Say **mmmaaat.** "mmmaaat."
   Say it fast. "mat."
   Say **mmmēēē.** "mmmēēē."
   Say it fast. "me."
   Say **aaammm.** "aaammm."
   Say it fast. "am."
2. Let's do those words again. (Repeat step 1 until firm.)

TASK 3 SOUNDS

1. You're going to do these sounds a new way. We're going to say all of them fast.
2. (Touch ball for **m.**) Say it fast. (Move quickly to end of arrow.) "m."
3. (Touch ball for **a.**) Say it fast. (Move quickly to end of arrow.) "a."

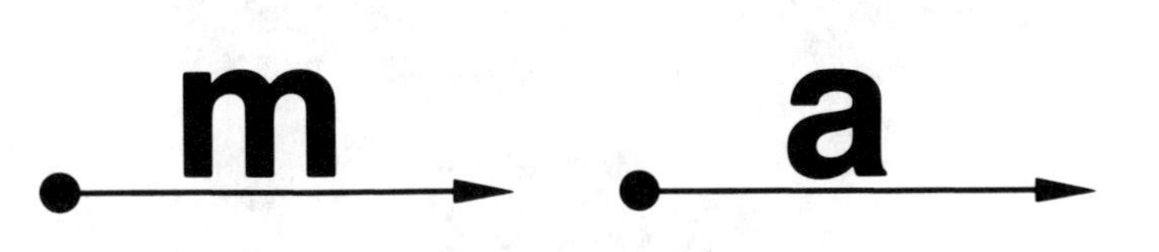

4. (Touch ball for **t.**) Say it fast. (Move quickly to end of arrow.) "t."
5. (Touch ball for **s.**) Say it fast. (Move quickly to end of arrow.) "s."

t s

6. (Touch ball for **ē.**) Say it fast. (Move quickly to end of arrow.) "ē."
7. (Touch ball for **r.**) Say it fast. (Move quickly to end of arrow.) "r."

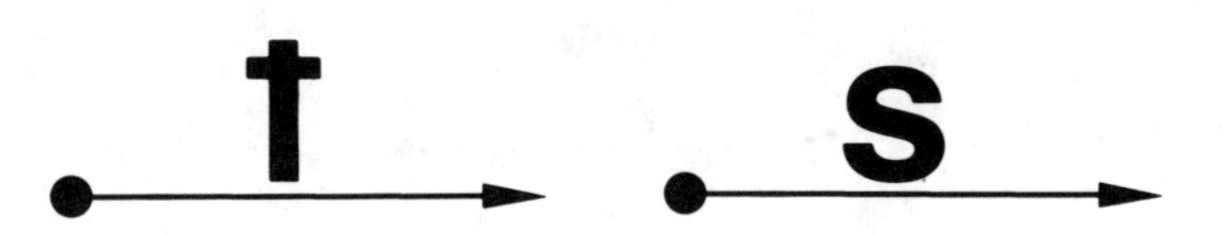

TASK 4 WORD READING

1. (Touch first ball for **am.**) I'm going to sound out this word. Then you'll say it fast. (Point to ball under **a.**)
2. What's the first sound I'm going to say? (Touch for two seconds.) "aaa." (Release.) (Point to ball under **m.**) What's the next sound I'm going to say? (Touch for two seconds.) "mmm." (Return to first ball. Repeat until firm.)
3. (Return to first ball.) My turn to sound it out. (Touch under **a** and **m** as you say:) **aaammm.** (Return to first ball.) Say it fast. (Slide quickly to end of arrow.) "am."
4. (Touch first ball.) You're going to sound out this word, then say it fast. Sound it out. Get ready. (Touch under **a** and **m** as child says "aaammm" without pausing between sounds. Repeat until firm.)
   (Return to first ball.) Say it fast. (Slide to end of arrow.) "am." Yes, what word? "am." You read the word **am.** Good reading.

TASK 5 WORD READING

1. (Touch first ball for **mē.**) I'm going to sound out this word. Then you'll say it fast. (Point to ball under **m.**)
2. What's the first sound I'm going to say? (Touch for two seconds.) "mmm." (Release.) (Point to ball under **ē.**) What's the next sound I'm going to say? (Touch for two seconds.) "ēēē." (Return to first ball. Repeat until firm.)
3. (Return to first ball.) My turn to sound it out. (Touch under **m** and **ē** as you say:) **mmmēēē.** (Return to first ball.) Say it fast. (Slide quickly to end of arrow.) "mē."
4. (Touch first ball.) You're going to sound out this word, then say it fast. Sound it out. Get ready. (Touch under **m** and **ē** as child says "mmmēēē" without pausing between sounds. Repeat until firm.)
(Return to first ball.) Say it fast. (Slide to end of arrow.) "mē." Yes, what word? "me." You read the word **me.** Good reading.

TASK 6 WORD READING

1. (Touch first ball for **sēē.**) I'm going to sound out this word. Then you'll say it fast. (Point to ball under **s.**)
2. What's the first sound I'm going to say? (Touch for two seconds.) "sss." (Release.) (Point to ball under **ē.**) What's the next sound I'm going to say? (Touch for two seconds.) "ēēē." (Return to first ball. Repeat until firm.)
3. (Return to first ball.) My turn to sound it out. (Touch under **s** and **ē** as you say:) **sssēēē.** (Return to first ball.) Say it fast. (Slide quickly to end of arrow.) "sēē."
4. (Touch first ball.) You're going to sound out this word, then say it fast. Sound it out. Get ready. (Touch under **s** and **ē** as child says "sssēēē" without pausing between sounds. Repeat until firm.)
(Return to first ball.) Say it fast. (Slide to end of arrow.) "sēē." Yes, what word? "see." You read the word **see.** Good reading.

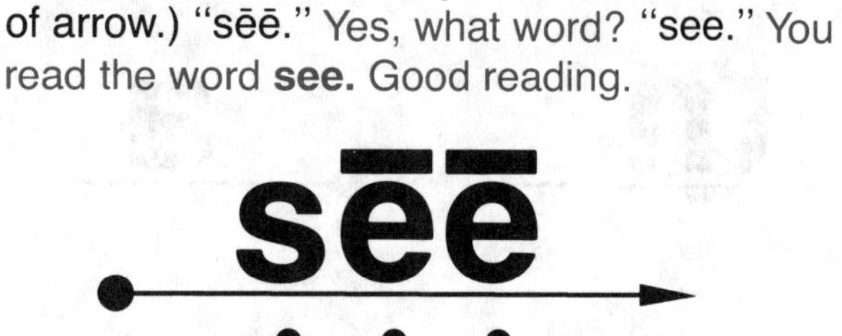

TASK 7 RHYMING

1. I'm going to rhyme. (Point to **r, m,** and **s.**) These are the sounds I'm going to start with. (Touch first ball for **r.**) Say the sound. (Quickly slide to second ball and hold.) "rrr." (Touch first ball for **m.**) Say the sound. (Quickly slide to second ball and hold.) "mmm." (Touch first ball for s.) Say the sound. (Quickly slide to second ball and hold.) "sss."
2. (Touch first ball for **r.**) I'm going to rhyme with (pause) **at.** What am I going to rhyme with? "at." (Quickly slide to second ball and hold for about three seconds, then slide to end of arrow as you say:) **rrrat.** (Touch first ball for **m.** Quickly slide to second ball and hold for about three seconds. Then slide to end of arrow as you say:) **mmmat.** (Touch first ball for **s.** Quickly slide to second ball and hold for about three seconds. Then slide to end of arrow as you say:) **sssat.**

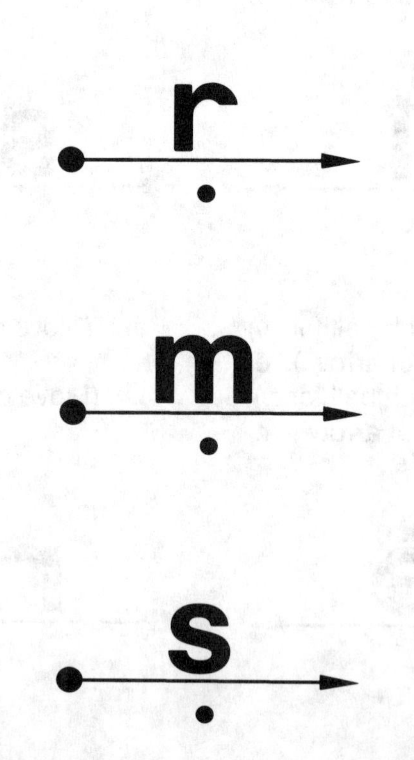

3. (Touch first ball for **r.**) Your turn. Rhyming with (pause) **at.** (Quickly slide to second ball and hold. Then slide to end of arrow as child says:) "rrrat." (Return to first ball.) Say it fast. (Slide.) "rat."
4. (Touch first ball for **m.**) Rhyming with (pause) **at**. (Quickly slide to second ball and hold. Then slide to end of arrow as child says:) "mmmat." (Return to first ball.) Say it fast. (Slide.) "mat."
5. (Touch first ball for **s.**) Rhyming with (pause) **at.** (Quickly slide to second ball and hold. Then slide to end of arrow as child says:) "sssat." (Return to first ball.) Say it fast. (Slide.) "sat."
6. (Repeat steps 3–5 until firm.) You rhymed with (pause) **at.** Good rhyming.

TASK 8 RHYMING

1. You're going to rhyme. (Touch first ball for **r.**) This is the sound you're going to start with. Get ready to say the sound. (Quickly slide to second ball and hold.) "rrr."
2. (Return to first ball.) Yes, you're going to start with **rrr.** And you're going to rhyme with (pause) **un.** What are you going to rhyme with? "un."
3. Rhyming with (pause) **un.** (Slide quickly to second ball. Hold for about three seconds, then slide quickly to end of arrow.) "rrrun."
4. (Return to first ball.) Say it fast. (Slide to end of arrow.) "run." You rhymed with (pause) **un.**
5. (Touch first ball.) Now you're going to rhyme with (pause) **ōd.** What are you going to rhyme with? "ōd." Rhyming with (pause) **ōd.** (Slide quickly to second ball. Hold for about three seconds, then slide quickly to end of arrow.) "rrrōd." (Return to first ball.) Say it fast. (Slide to end of arrow.) "rōde." You rhymed with (pause) **ōd.**
6. (Touch first ball.) Now you're going to rhyme with (pause) **at.** What are you going to rhyme with? "at." Rhyming with (pause) **at.** (Slide quickly to second ball. Hold for about three seconds, then slide quickly to end of arrow.) "rrrat." (Return to first ball.) Say it fast. (Slide to end of arrow.) "rat." You rhymed with (pause) **at.**

r

TASK 9 WORD READING

1. (Point to **sēē.**) You're going to touch under the sounds as you sound out this word and say it fast. (Touch under **s.**) What's the first sound you're going to say? "sss." (Touch under first ē.) What's the next sound you're going to say? "ēēē." (Touch under second **ē.**) What's the next sound you're going to say? "ēēē."
2. Touch the first ball of the arrow. Take a deep breath and say the sounds as you touch under them. Get ready. Go (Child touches under **s** and **ēē** and says "sssēēē" without pausing between sounds.) Touch the first ball and sound it out again. "sssēēē." (Repeat until firm.)
3. Say it fast. "sēē." Yes, what word? "see." You read the word **see.** Good reading.

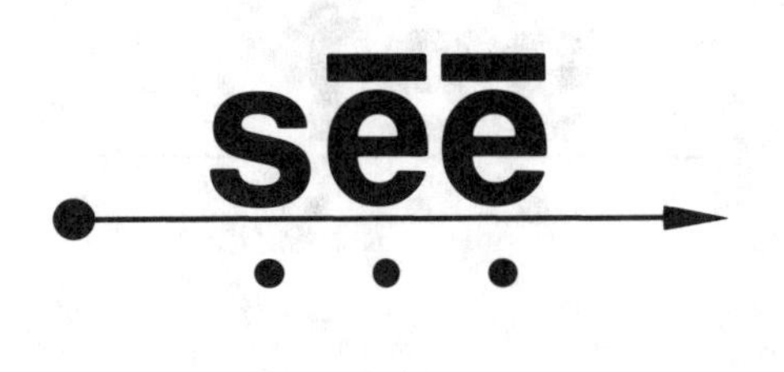

TASK 10 WORD READING

1. (Point to **mē.**) You're going to touch under the sounds as you sound out this word and say it fast. (Touch under **m.**) What's the first sound you're going to say? "mmm." (Touch under **ē.**) What's the next sound you're going to say? "ēēē."
2. Touch the first ball of the arrow. Take a deep breath and say the sounds as you touch under them. Get ready. Go. (Child touches under **m** and **ē** and says "mmmēēē" without pausing between sounds.) Touch the first ball and sound it out again. "mmmēēē." (Repeat until firm.)
3. Say it fast. "mē." Yes, what word? "me." You read the word **me.** Good reading.

TASK 11 WORD READING

1. (Point to **sat.**) You're going to touch under the sounds as you sound out this word and say it fast. (Touch under **s.**) What's the first sound you're going to say? "sss." (Touch under **a.**) What's the next sound you're going to say? "aaa." (Touch under **t.**) What's the next sound you're going to say? "t."
2. Touch the first ball of the arrow. Take a deep breath and say the sounds as you touch under them. Get ready. Go. (Child touches under **s, a,** and **t** and says "sssaaat" without pausing between sounds.) Touch the first ball and sound it out again. "sssaaat." (Repeat until firm.)
3. Say it fast. "sat." Yes, what word? "sat." You read the word **sat.** Good reading.

sat

TASK 12 SOUNDS WRITING

1. (See chart on page 24 for steps in writing **r** and **a.**)
2. You're going to write the sounds that I write.
3. Here's the first sound you're going to write. (Write **r** at beginning of first line. Point to **r.**) What sound? "rrr."
4. First trace the **rrr** that I made. Then make more of them on this line. (After tracing **r** several times, child is to make three to five **r**'s. Help child if necessary. For acceptable letters say:) Good writing **rrr.**
5. Here's the next sound you're going to write. (Write **a** at beginning of second line. Point to **a.**) What sound? "aaa."
6. First trace the **aaa** that I made. Then make more of them on this line. (After tracing **a** several times, child is to make three to five **a**'s. Help child if necessary. For acceptable letters say:) Good writing **aaa.**

LESSON 11

TASK 1 SOUNDS REVIEW

1. You're going to say all these sounds. (Touch first ball for **r.**) Get ready. (Quickly move to second ball. Hold.) "rrr."

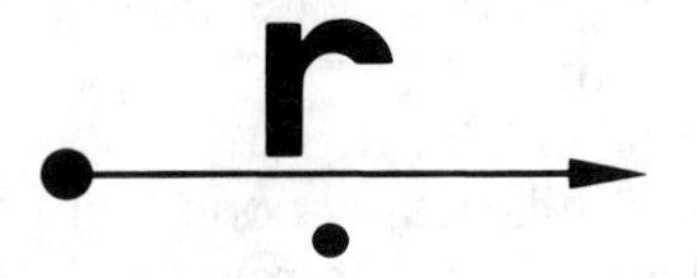

2. (Touch first ball for **a.**) Get ready. (Quickly move to second ball. Hold.) "aaa."

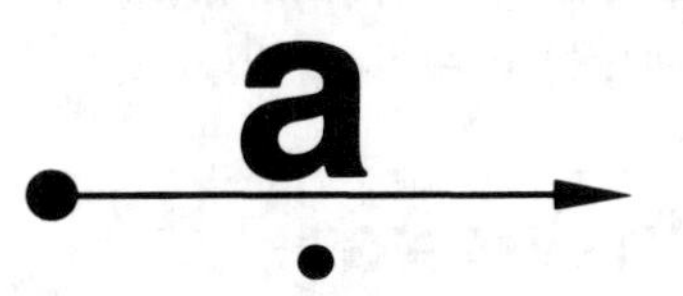

3. (Touch first ball for **ē.**) Get ready. (Quickly move to second ball. Hold.) "ēēē."

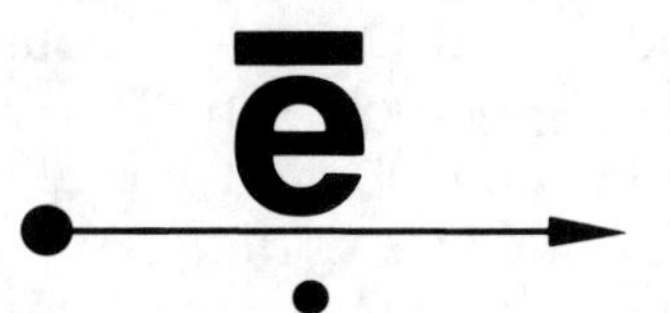

4. (Touch first ball for **s.**) Get ready. (Quickly move to second ball. Hold.) "sss."

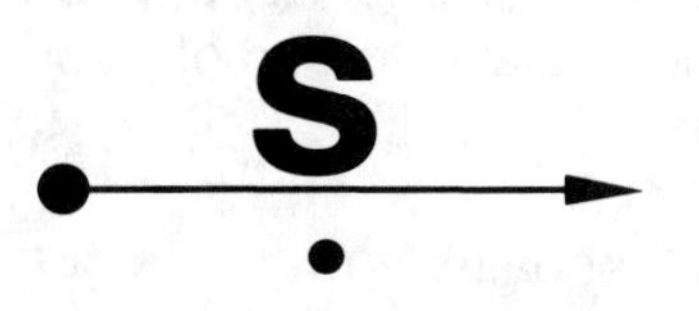

5. (Touch ball for **t.**) Take a good look and get ready. (Pause.) Say it fast. (Move quickly to end of arrow.) "t." (Repeat until firm.)

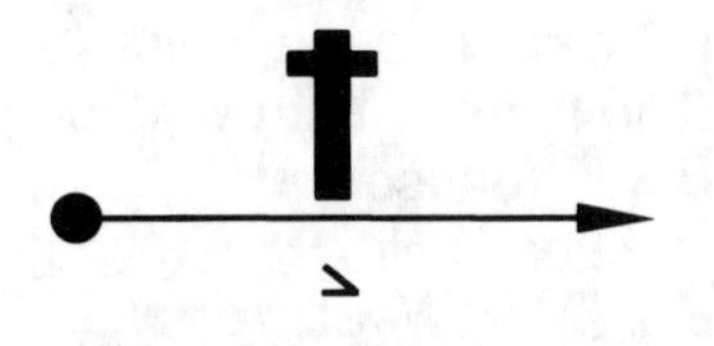

6. (Touch first ball for **m.**) Get ready. (Quickly move to second ball. Hold.) "mmm."

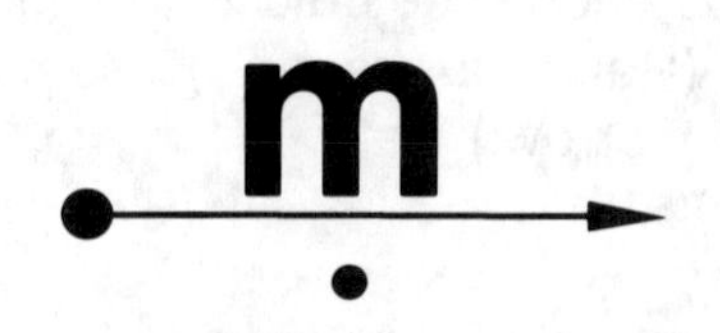

TASK 2 RHYMING

1. I'm going to rhyme. (Point to **r** and **s.**) These are the sounds I'm going to start with. (Touch first ball for **r.**) Say the sound. (Quickly slide to second ball and hold.) "rrr." (Touch first ball for **s.**) Say the sound. (Quickly slide to second ball and hold.) "sss."
2. (Touch first ball for **r.**) I'm going to rhyme with (pause) **am.** What am I going to rhyme with? "am." (Quickly slide to second ball and hold for about three seconds, then slide to end of arrow as you say:) **rrram.** (Touch first ball for **s.** Quickly slide to second ball and hold for about three seconds. Then slide to end of arrow as you say:) **sssam.**
3. (Touch first ball for **r.**) Your turn. Rhyming with (pause) **am.** (Quickly slide to second ball and hold. Then slide to end of arrow as child says:) "rrram." (Return to first ball.) Say it fast. (Slide.) "ram."
4. (Touch first ball for **s.**) Rhyming with (pause) **am.** (Quickly slide to second ball and hold. Then slide to end of arrow as child says:) "sssam." (Return to first ball.) Say it fast. (Slide.) "sam."
5. (Repeat steps 3–4 until firm.) You rhymed with (pause) **am.** Good rhyming.

r

s

TASK 3 RHYMING

1. I'm going to rhyme again. (Point to **s** and **m.**) These are the sounds I'm going to start with. (Touch first ball for **s.**) Say the sound. (Quickly slide to second ball and hold.) "sss." (Touch first ball for **m.**) Say the sound. (Quickly slide to second ball and hold.) "mmm."
2. (Touch first ball for **s.**) I'm going to rhyme with (pause) **ēn.** What am I going to rhyme with? "ēn." (Quickly slide to second ball and hold for about three seconds, then slide to end of arrow as you say:) **ssseen.** (Touch first ball for **m.** Quickly slide to second ball and hold for about three seconds. Then slide to end of arrow as you say:) **mmmean.**
3. (Touch first ball for **s.**) Your turn. Rhyming with (pause) **ēn.** (Quickly slide to second ball and hold. Then slide to end of arrow as child says:) "ssseen." (Return to first ball.) Say it fast. (Slide.) "seen."
4. (Touch first ball for **m.**) Rhyming with (pause) **ēn.** (Quickly slide to second ball and hold. Then slide to end of arrow as child says:) "mmmean." (Return to first ball.) Say it fast. (Slide.) "mean."
5. (Repeat steps 3–4 until firm.) You rhymed with (pause) **ēn.** Good rhyming.

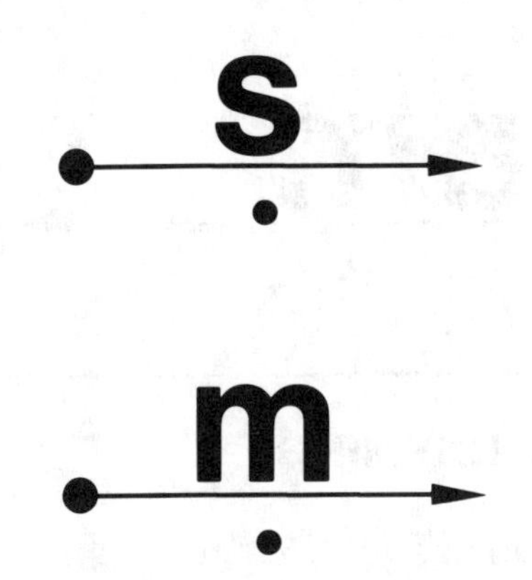

TASK 4 SAY THE SOUNDS

1. Say **rrrēēēd.** "rrrēēēd."
   Say it fast. "read."
   Say **sssēēēd.** "sssēēēd."
   Say it fast. "seed."
   Say **iiifff.** "iiifff."
   Say it fast. "if."
   Say **iiit.** "iiit."
   Say it fast. "it."
   Say **rrrōōōp.** "rrrōōōp."
   Say it fast. "rope."
   Say **sssōōōp.** "sssōōōp."
   Say it fast. "soap."
   Say **mmmēēēnnn.** "mmmēēēnnn."
   Say it fast. "mean."
2. Let's do those words again. (Repeat step 1 until firm.)

TASK 5 WORD READING

1. (Touch under first ball for **am.**) You're going to read this word. You're going to sound it out. Then you're going to say it fast.
2. Sound it out. (Touch under **a** and **m** as child says "aaammm" without pausing between sounds.)
   (Return to first ball.) Say it fast. (Slide quickly to end of arrow.) "am." What word? "am."

> (**To correct** if child misidentifies a sound—for example, says "ēēē" instead of "aaa"—immediately say sound:) **aaa.** (Point to sound.) This sound is **aaa.** What sound? (Touch **a.**) "aaa." Yes, **aaa.** Let's start again. (Repeat step 2.)

3. (Touch **a** in **ēat.**) This word has a little sound in it. We don't say that sound. Just say the big sounds. (Return to first ball.) Sound it out. (Touch under **ē** and **t** as child says "ēēēt" without pausing between sounds.)
   (Return to first ball.) Say it fast. (Slide quickly to end of arrow.) "eat." What word? "eat."
4. (Touch first ball for **ram.**) You're going to read this word. You're going to sound it out. Then you're going to say it fast. Sound it out. (Touch under **r, a,** and **m** as child says "rrraaammm" without pausing between sounds.)
   (Return to first ball.) Say it fast. (Slide quickly to end of arrow.) "ram." What word? "ram."
5. (Touch first ball for **sēē.**) You're going to read this word. You're going to sound it out. Then you're going to say it fast. Sound it out. (Touch under **s, ē,** and **ē** as child says "sssēēē" without pausing between sounds.) (Return to first ball.) Say it fast. (Slide quickly to end of arrow.) "see." What word? "see."
6. (Touch first ball for **rat.**) You're going to read this word. You're going to sound it out. Then you're going to say it fast. Sound it out. (Touch under **r, a,** and **t,** as child says "rrraaat" without pausing between sounds.) (Return to first ball.) Say it fast. (Slide quickly to end of arrow.) "rat." What word? "rat."

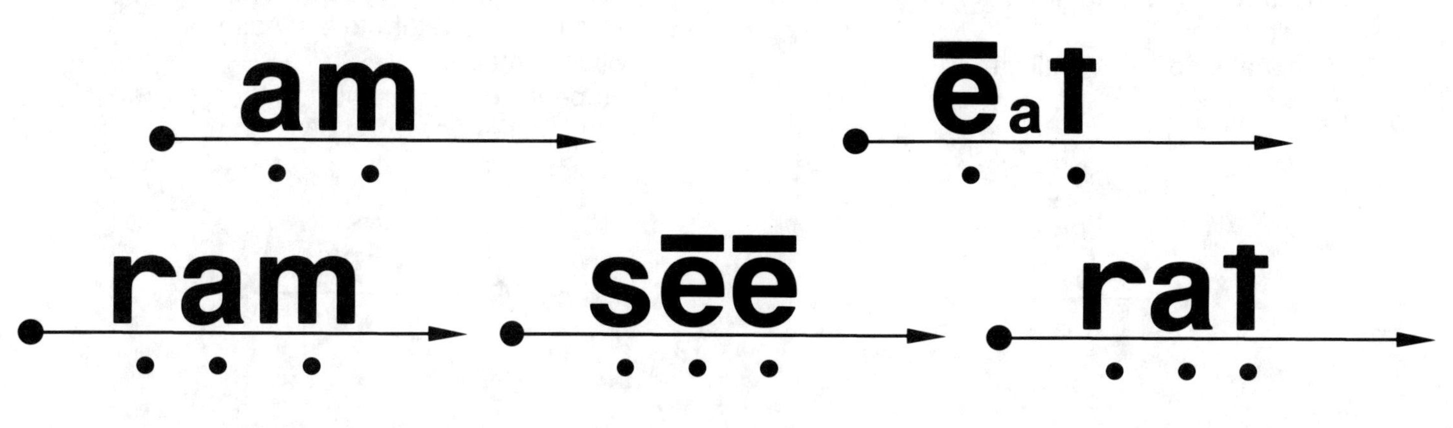

TASK 6 RHYMING

1. (Point to **m** and **r.**) You're going to rhyme. These are the sounds you're going to start with. (Touch first ball for **m.**) Say the sound. (Quickly slide to second ball and hold.) "mmm." (Touch first ball for **r.**) Say the sound. (Quickly slide to second ball and hold.) "rrr."
2. (Touch first ball for **m.**) You're going to rhyme with (pause) **at.** What are you going to rhyme with? "at." Rhyming with (pause) **at.** (Quickly slide to second ball and hold. Then slide to end of arrow as child says:) "mmmat." (Return to first ball.) Say it fast. (Slide.) "mat."
3. (Touch first ball for **r.**) You're going to rhyme with (pause) **at.** What are you going to rhyme with? "at." Rhyming with (pause) **at.** (Quickly slide to second ball and hold. Then slide to end of arrow as child says:) "rrrat." (Return to first ball.) Say it fast. (Slide.) "rat."

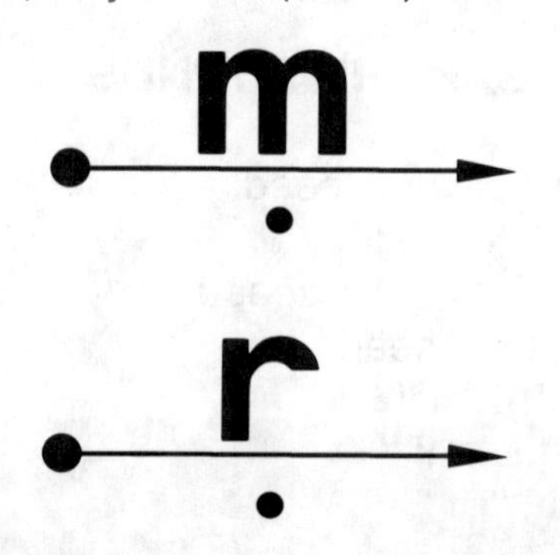

TASK 7 SOUNDS

1. You're going to say all these sounds fast.
2. (Touch ball for **s.**) Say it fast. (Move to end of arrow.) "s."
3. (Repeat step 2 for each sound.)

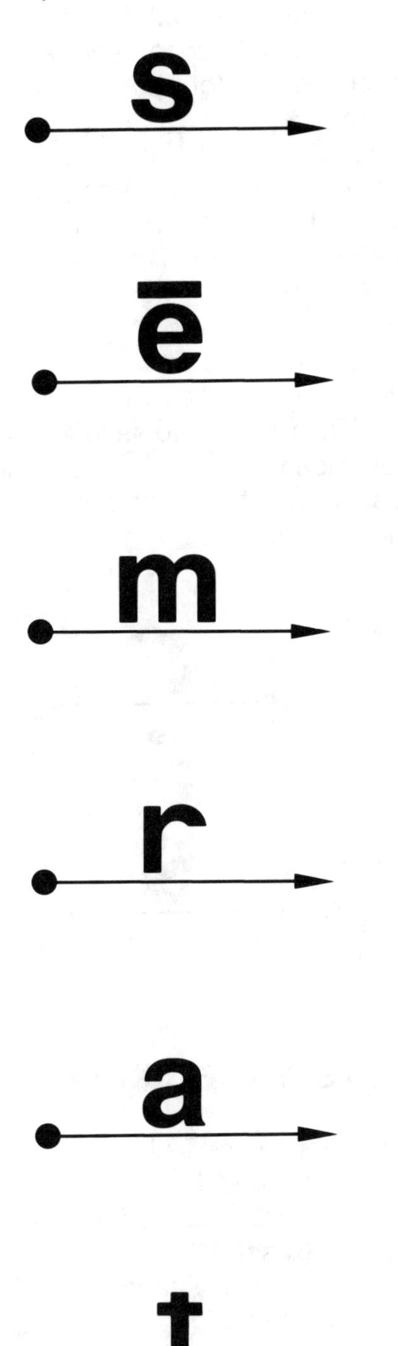

TASK 8 WORD READING

1. (Point to **at** and **sat.**) You're going to read these words.
2. (Point to **at.**) Touch the first ball of the arrow for this word. Sound it out. (Child touches under sounds and says "aaat" without pausing between sounds.) Touch the first ball and sound it out again. "aaat." Say it fast. "at." What word? "at." Yes, **at.**

> (**To correct** if child misidentifies a sound—for example, says "ēēē" instead of "aaa"—immediately say sound:) **aaa.** (Point to sound.) This sound is **aaa.** What sound? (Touch **a.**) "aaa." Yes, **aaa.** Let's start again. (Repeat step 2.)

3. (Point to **sat.**) Touch the first ball of the arrow for this word. Sound it out. (Child touches under sounds and says "sssaaat" without pausing between sounds.) Touch the first ball and sound it out again. "sssaaat." Say it fast. "sat." What word? "sat." Yes, **sat.**

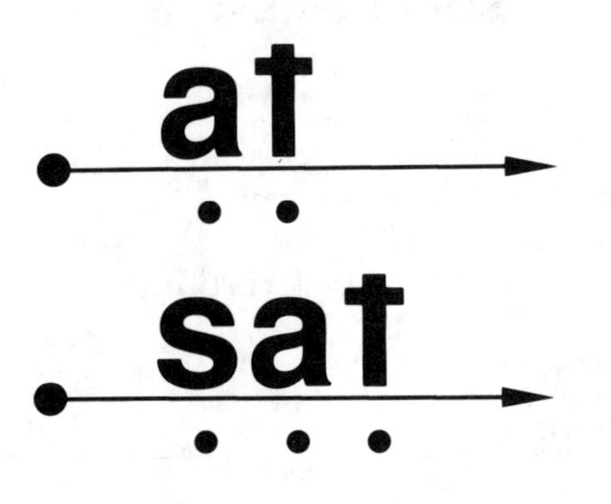

TASK 9 SOUNDS WRITING

1. Here's the first sound you're going to write. (Write **t** at beginning of first line. Point to **t.**) What sound? "t."
2. First trace the **t** that I made. Then make more of them on this line. (After tracing **t** several times, child is to make three to five **t**'s. Help child if necessary. For acceptable letters say:) Good writing **t.**
3. Here's the next sound you're going to write. (Write **ē** at beginning of second line. Point to **ē.**) What sound? "ēēē."
4. First trace the **ēēē** that I made. Then make more of them on this line. (After tracing **ē** several times, child is to make three to five **ē**'s. Help child if necessary. For acceptable letters say:) Good writing **ēēē.**

LESSON 12

TASK 1 SOUNDS INTRODUCTION

1. (Touch ball for **d.**) We always have to say this sound fast. My turn to say it fast. (Quickly move to end of arrow as you say sound.) **d.**
2. My turn to say it fast again. (Touch ball for **d.**) Say it fast. (Quickly move to end of arrow.) **d.**
3. (Touch ball.) Your turn. (Pause.) Say it fast. (Quickly move to end of arrow.) "d."

> (**To correct** if child says "duh," "dah," or "dih":) Listen: **d.** Say it fast. (Repeat steps 1–3.)

d

TASK 2 SOUNDS REVIEW

1. You're going to say all these sounds. (Touch first ball for **a.**) Get ready. (Quickly move to second ball. Hold.) "aaa."
2. (Touch first ball for **ē.**) Get ready. (Quickly move to second ball. Hold.) "ēēē."

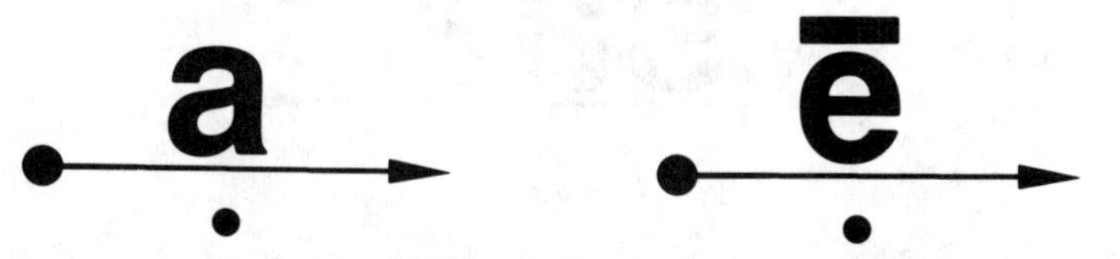

3. (Touch ball for **t.**) Take a good look and get ready. (Pause.) Say it fast. (Move quickly to end of arrow.) "t." (Repeat until firm.)
4. (Touch first ball for **r.**) Get ready. (Quickly move to second ball. Hold.) "rrr."

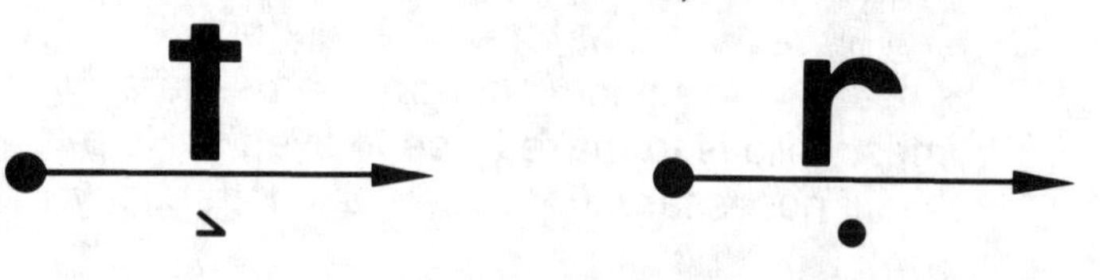

5. (Touch ball for **d.**) Take a good look and get ready. (Pause.) Say it fast. (Move quickly to end of arrow.) "d." (Repeat until firm.)

d

TASK 3 RHYMING

1. (Point to **r** and **s.**) You're going to rhyme. These are the sounds you're going to start with. (Touch first ball for **r.**) Say the sound. (Quickly slide to second ball and hold.) "rrr." (Touch first ball for **s.**) Say the sound. (Quickly slide to second ball and hold.) "sss."
2. (Touch first ball for **r.**) You're going to rhyme with (pause) **ēēd.** What are you going to rhyme with? "ēēd." Rhyming with (pause) **ēēd.** (Quickly slide to second ball and hold. Then slide to end of arrow as child says:) "rrrēēd." (Return to first ball.) Say it fast. (Slide.) "reed."
3. (Touch first ball for **s.**) You're going to rhyme with (pause) **ēēd.** What are you going to rhyme with? "ēēd." Rhyming with (pause) **ēēd.** (Quickly slide to second ball and hold. Then slide to end of arrow as child says:) "sssēēd." (Return to first ball.) Say it fast. (Slide.) "seed."

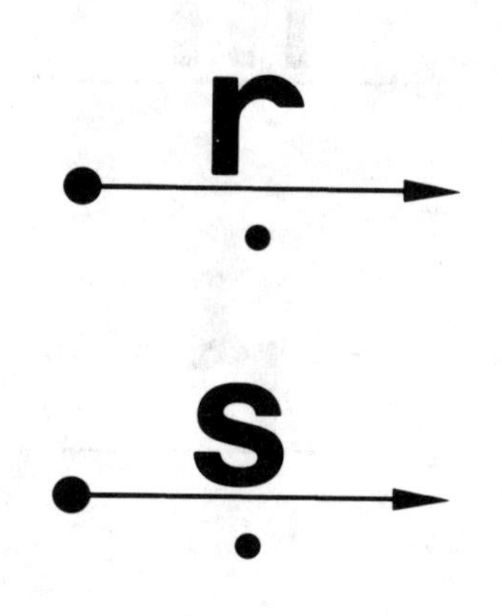

TASK 4 SAY THE SOUNDS

1. Say **rrrēēēd.** "rrrēēēd."
   Say it fast. "read."
   Say **sssēēēd.** "sssēēēd."
   Say it fast. "seed."
   Say **sssaaad.** "sssaaad."
   Say it fast. "sad."
   Say **sssēēēt.** "sssēēēt."
   Say it fast. "seat."
   Say **mmmaaad.** "mmmaaad."
   Say it fast. "mad."
2. Let's do those words again. (Repeat step 1 until firm.)

TASK 5 WORD READING

1. (Touch under first ball for **seed.**) You're going to read this word. You're going to sound it out. Then you're going to say it fast. Sound it out. (Touch under **s, ē, ē,** and **d,** as child says "sssēēēd" without pausing between sounds.) (Return to first ball.) Say it fast. (Slide quickly to end of arrow.) "seed." What word? "seed."
2. (Touch under first ball for **sam.**) You're going to read this word. You're going to sound it out. Then you're going to say it fast. Sound it out. (Touch under **s, a,** and **m,** as child says "sssaaammm" without pausing between sounds.)
(Return to first ball.) Say it fast. (Slide quickly to end of arrow.) "sam." What word? "sam."
3. (Touch under first ball for **rat.**) You're going to read this word. You're going to sound it out. Then you're going to say it fast. Sound it out. (Touch under **r, a,** and **t** as child says "rrraaat" without pausing between sounds.) (Return to first ball.) Say it fast. (Slide quickly to end of arrow.) "rat." What word? "rat."
4. (Touch under first ball for **mē.**) You're going to read this word. You're going to sound it out. Then you're going to say it fast. Sound it out. (Touch under **m** and **ē** as child says "mmmēēē" without pausing between sounds.)
(Return to first ball.) Say it fast. (Slide quickly to end of arrow.) "me." What word? "me."

sēēd

sam

rat

mē

TASK 6 RHYMING

1. (Point to **m, r,** and **s.**) You're going to rhyme. These are the sounds you're going to start with. (Touch first ball for **m.**) Say the sound. (Quickly slide to second ball and hold.) "mmm." (Touch first ball for **r.**) Say the sound.

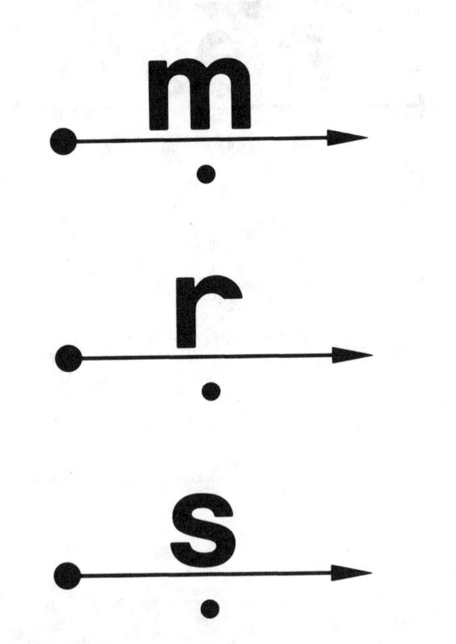

(Quickly slide to second ball and hold.) "rrr." (Touch first ball for **s.**) Say the sound. (Quickly slide to second ball and hold.) "sss."
2. (Touch first ball for **m.**) You're going to rhyme with (pause) **at.** What are you going to rhyme with? "at." Rhyming with (pause) **at.** (Quickly slide to second ball and hold. Then slide to end of arrow as child says:) "mmmat." (Return to first ball.) Say it fast. (Slide.) "mat."
3. (Touch first ball for **r.**) You're going to rhyme with (pause) **at.** What are you going to rhyme with? "at." Rhyming with (pause) **at.** (Quickly slide to second ball and hold. Then slide to end of arrow as child says:) "rrrat." (Return to first ball.) Say it fast. (Slide.) "rat."
4. (Touch first ball for **s.**) You're going to rhyme with (pause) **at.** What are you going to rhyme with? "at." Rhyming with (pause) **at.** (Quickly slide to second ball and hold. Then slide to end of arrow as child says:) "sssat." (Return to first ball.) Say it fast. (Slide.) "sat."

TASK 7 SOUNDS REVIEW

1. Let's do sounds again. See if you remember all of them. (Touch ball for **d.**) Take a good look and get ready. (Pause.) Say it fast. (Move quickly to end of arrow.) "d." (Repeat until firm.)

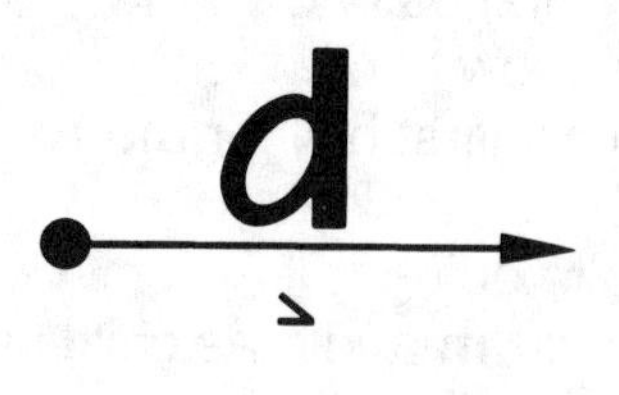

2. (Touch first ball for **ē.**) Get ready. (Move to second ball. Hold.) "ēēē."

3. (Touch ball for **t.**) Take a good look and get ready. (Pause.) Say it fast. (Move quickly to end of arrow.) "t." (Repeat until firm.)

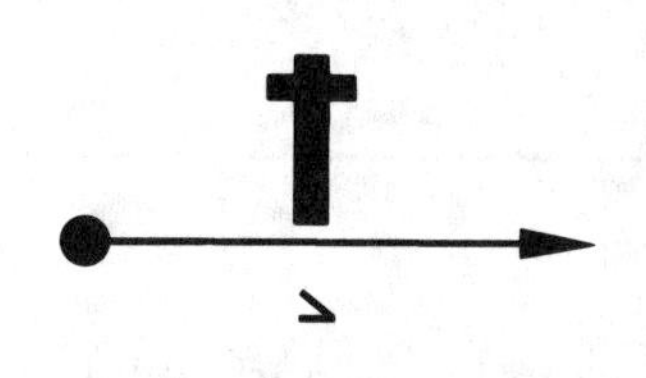

4. (Touch first ball for **s.**) Get ready. (Move to second ball. Hold.) "sss."

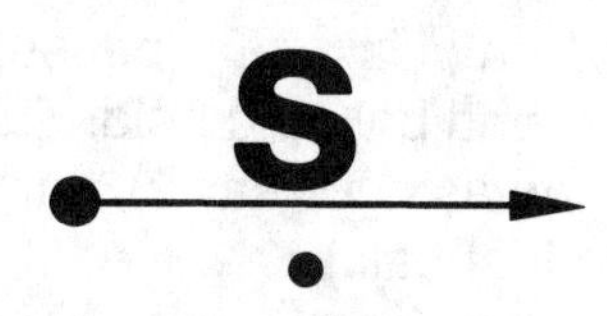

5. (Touch first ball for **r.**) Get ready. (Move to second ball. Hold.) "rrr."

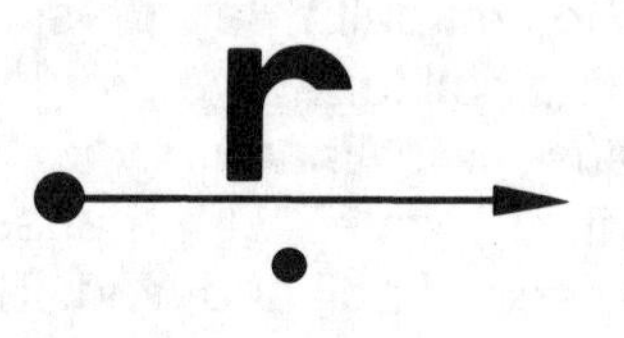

TASK 8 WORD READING

1. (Point to **ēat** and **sēat.**) You're going to read these words.
2. (Point to **ēat.**) Touch the first ball of the arrow for this word. Remember, don't say anything for the little sound. Just touch under and say the big sounds. Sound it out. (Child touches under sounds and says "ēēēt" without pausing between sounds.) Touch the first ball and sound it out again. "ēēēt." Say it fast. "eat." What word? "eat." Yes, **eat.**

> (**To correct** if child misidentifies a sound—for example, says "d" instead of "t"—immediately say sound:) **t.** (Point to sound.) This sound is **t.** What sound? (Touch **t.**) "t." Yes, **t.** Let's start again. (Repeat step 2.)

3. (Point to **sēat.**) Touch the first ball of the arrow for this word. Remember, don't say anything for the little sound. Just touch under and say the big sounds. Sound it out. (Child touches under sounds and says "sssēēēt" without pausing between sounds.) Touch the first ball and sound it out again. "sssēēēt." Say it fast. "seat." What word? "seat." Yes, **seat.**

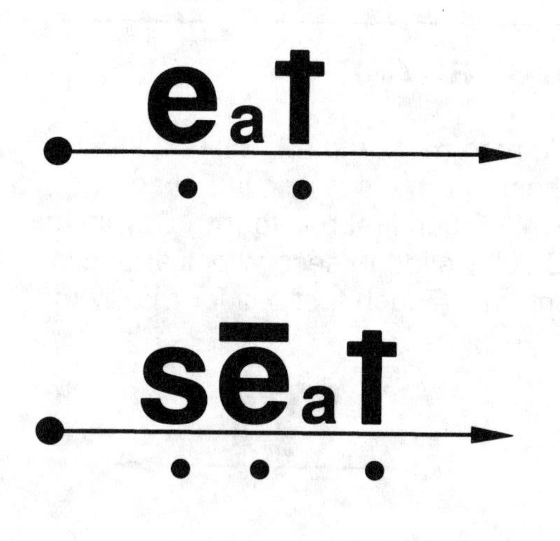

TASK 9 SOUNDS WRITING

1. (Write **d** at beginning of first line. Point to **d.**) What sound? "d."
2. First trace the **d** that I made. Then make more of them on this line. (After tracing **d** several times, child is to make three to five **d**'s. Help child if necessary. For each acceptable letter say:) Good writing **d.**
3. Here's the next sound you're going to write. (Write **a** at beginning of second line. Point to **a.**) What sound? "aaa."
4. First trace the **aaa** that I made. Then make more of them on this line. (After tracing **a** several times, child is to make three to five **a**'s. Help child if necessary. For acceptable letters say:) Good writing **aaa.**

(**Important:** Practice correction procedures for word-reading errors (page 22) before presenting this lesson.)

LESSON 13

TASK 1 SOUNDS REVIEW

1. You're going to say all these sounds. (Touch first ball for **s.**) Get ready. (Quickly move to second ball. Hold.) "sss."
2. (Touch first ball for **a.**) Get ready. (Quickly move to second ball. Hold.) "aaa."

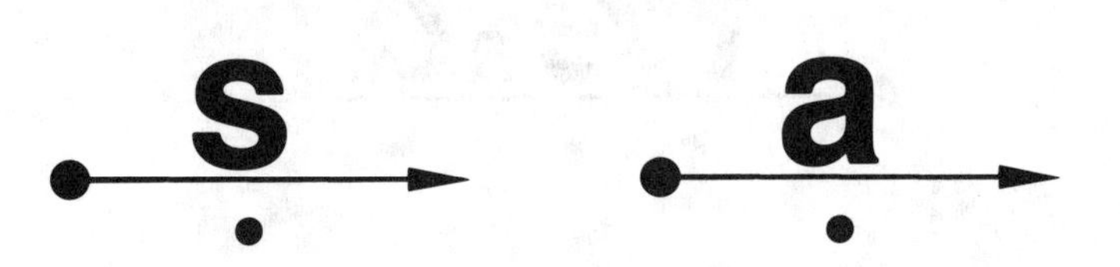

3. (Touch ball for **t.**) Take a good look and get ready. (Pause.) Say it fast. (Move quickly to end of arrow.) "t." (Repeat until firm.)
4. (Touch ball for **d.**) Take a good look and get ready. (Pause.) Say it fast. (Move quickly to end of arrow.) "d." (Repeat until firm.)

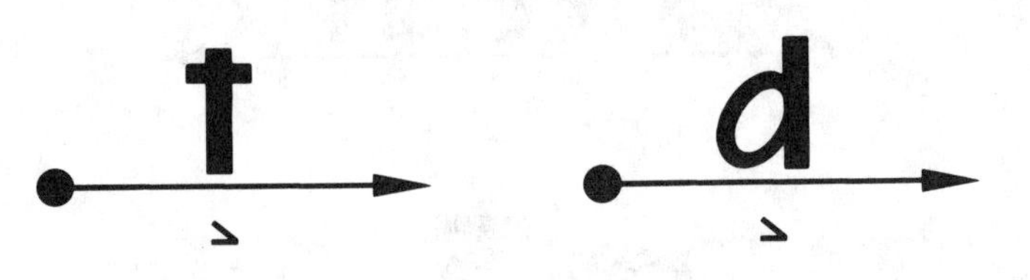

5. (Touch first ball for **ē.**) Get ready. (Quickly move to second ball. Hold.) "ēēē."
6. (Touch first ball for **r.**) Get ready. (Quickly move to second ball. Hold.) "rrr."

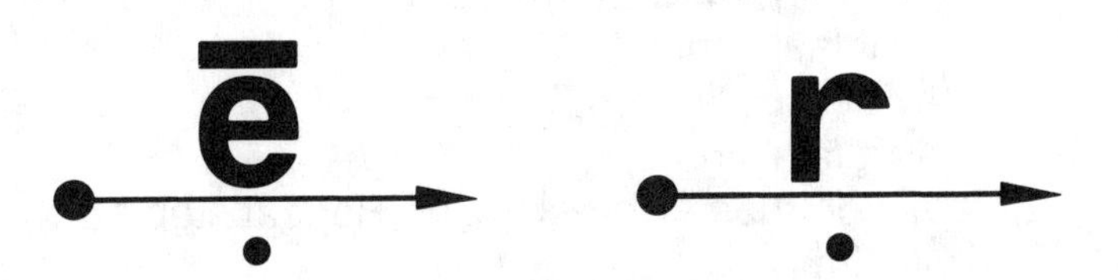

TASK 2 RHYMING

1. (Point to **r** and **s.**) You're going to rhyme. These are the sounds you're going to start with. (Touch first ball for **r.**) Say the sound. (Quickly slide to second ball and hold.) "rrr." (Touch first ball for **s.**) Say the sound. (Quickly slide to second ball and hold.) "sss."
2. (Touch first ball for **r.**) You're going to rhyme with (pause) **ōp.** What are you going to rhyme with? "ōp." Rhyming with (pause) **ōp.** (Quickly slide to second ball and hold. Then slide to end of arrow as child says:) "rrrōp." (Return to first ball.) Say it fast. (Slide.) "rōp."
3. (Touch first ball for **s.**) You're going to rhyme with (pause) **ōp.** What are you going to rhyme with? "ōp." Rhyming with (pause) **ōp.** (Quickly slide to second ball and hold. Then slide to end of arrow as child says:) "sssōp." (Return to first ball.) Say it fast. (Slide.) "sōp."

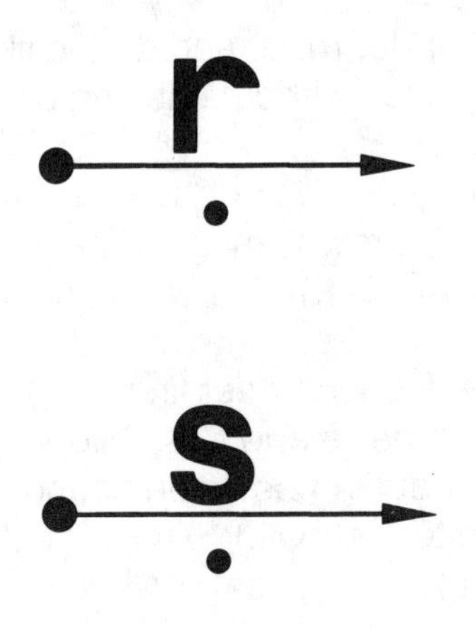

TASK 3 SAY THE SOUNDS

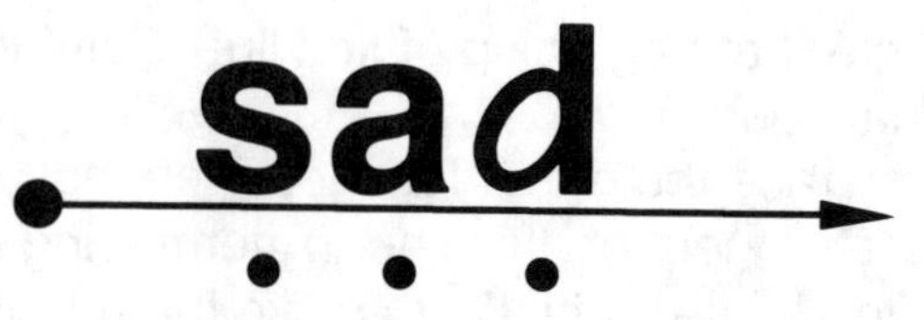

1. Say **sssaaad.** "sssaaad."
   Say it fast. "sad."
   Say **mmmaaad.** "mmmaaad."
   Say it fast. "mad."
   Say **ēēērrr.** "ēēērrr."
   Say it fast. "ear."
2. Let's do those words again. (Repeat step 1 until firm.)

TASK 4 WORD READING

1. (Touch under first ball for **sad.**) You're going to read this word. You're going to sound it out. Then you're going to say it fast. Sound it out. (Touch under **s, a,** and **d** as child says "sssaaad" without pausing between sounds.) (Return to first ball.) Say it fast. (Slide quickly to end of arrow.) "sad." What word? "sad."

> (**To correct** if child breaks between sounds, is unable to say word after sounding it out, or says "ad":) Stop. Listen. **sssaaad.** Say that. "sssaaad." Now say it fast. "sad." That's it. (Point to first ball of arrow for **sad.**) Now do it here. Sound it out. "sssaaad." Say it fast. "sad." You did it.

2. (Touch under first ball for **mad.**) You're going to read this word. You're going to sound it out. Then you're going to say it fast. Sound it out. (Touch under **m, a,** and **d** as child says "mmmaaad" without pausing between sounds.)
   (Return to first ball.) Say it fast. (Slide quickly to end of arrow.) "mad." What word? "mad."
3. (Touch **a** in **ēat.**) This word has a little sound in it. We don't say that sound. Just say the big sounds. (Touch under first ball.) Sound it out. (Touch under **ē** and **t** as child says "ēēēt" without pausing between sounds.)
   (Return to first ball.) Say it fast. (Slide quickly to end of arrow.) "eat." What word? "eat."

mad

ēat

mēat

rēad

am

ram

mē

4. (Touch **a** in **mēat.**) This word has a little sound in it. We don't say that sound. Just say the big sounds. (Touch under first ball.) Sound it out. (Touch under **m, ē,** and **t** as child says "mmmēēēt" without pausing between sounds.)
(Return to first ball.) Say it fast. (Slide quickly to end of arrow.) "meat." What word? "meat."
5. (Touch **a** in **rēad.**) This word has a little sound in it. We don't say that sound. Just say the big sounds. (Touch under first ball.) Sound it out. (Touch under **r, ē,** and **d** as child says "rrrēēēd" without pausing between sounds.)
(Return to first ball.) Say it fast. (Slide quickly to end of arrow.) "read." What word? "read."
6. (Touch under first ball for **am.**) You're going to read this word. You're going to sound it out. Then you're going to say it fast. Sound it out. (Touch under **a** and **m** as child says "aaammm" without pausing between sounds.)
(Return to first ball.) Say it fast. (Slide quickly to end of arrow.) "am." What word? "am."
7. (Touch under first ball for **ram.**) You're going to read this word. You're going to sound it out. Then you're going to say it fast. Sound it out. (Touch under **r, a,** and **m** as child says "rrraaammm" without pausing between sounds.)
(Return to first ball.) Say it fast. (Slide quickly to end of arrow.) "ram." What word? "ram."
8. (Touch under first ball for **me.**) You're going to read this word. You're going to sound it out. Then you're going to say it fast. Sound it out. (Touch under **m** and **ē** as child says "mmmēēē" without pausing between sounds.)
(Return to first ball.) Say it fast. (Slide quickly to end of arrow.) "me." What word? "me."

TASK 5 CHILD TOUCHES SOUNDS

1. Your turn. Touch the first ball for the first sound. You have to say this sound fast. So say it fast when you touch under it. Say it fast. "d."

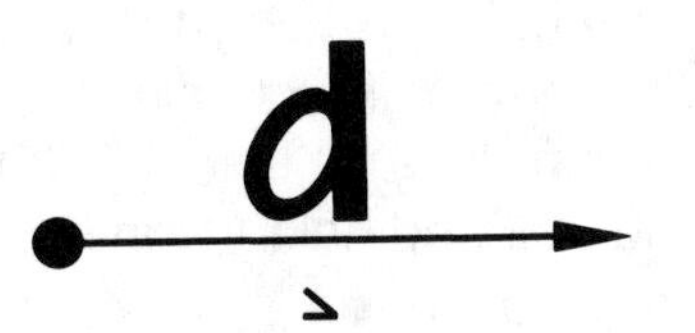

2. Touch the first ball for the next sound. Move to the next ball and say the sound slowly. "rrr." Now say it fast. "r."

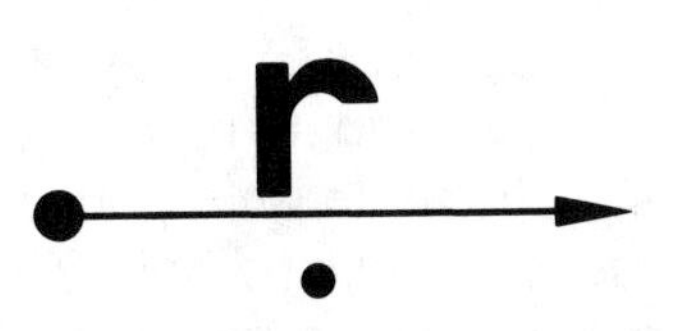

3. Touch the first ball for the next sound. You have to say this sound fast. So say it fast when you touch under it. Say it fast. "t."

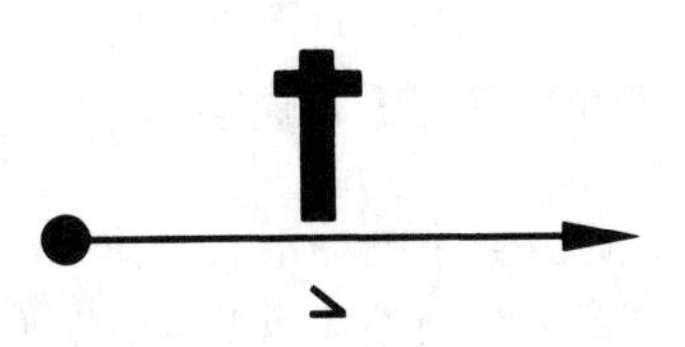

4. Touch the first ball for the next sound. Move to the next ball and say the sound slowly. "ēēē." Now say it fast. "ē."

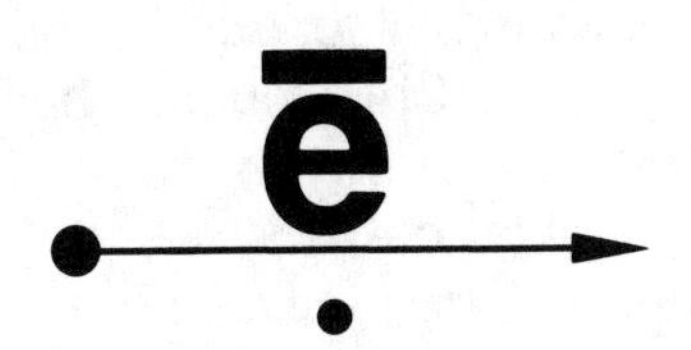

5. Touch the first ball for the next sound. Move to the next ball and say the sound slowly. "mmm." Now say it fast. "m."

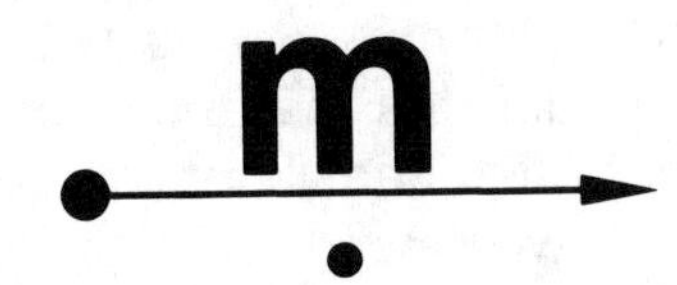

TASK 6 RHYMING

1. (Point to **s**, **r**, and **m.**) You're going to rhyme. These are the sounds you're going to start with. (Touch first ball for **s.**) Say the sound. (Quickly slide to second ball and hold.) "sss." (Touch first ball for **r.**) Say the sound. (Quickly slide to second ball and hold.) "rrr." (Touch first ball for **m.**) Say the sound. (Quickly slide to second ball and hold.) "mmm."
2. (Touch first ball for **s.**) You're going to rhyme with (pause) **at**. What are you going to rhyme with? "at." Rhyming with (pause) **at.** (Quickly slide to second ball and hold. Then slide to end of arrow as child says:) "sssat." (Return to first ball.) Say it fast. (Slide.) "sat."
3. (Touch first ball for **r.**) You're going to rhyme with (pause) **at**. What are you going to rhyme with? "at." Rhyming with (pause) **at.** (Quickly slide to second ball and hold. Then slide to end of arrow as child says:) "rrrat." (Return to first ball.) Say it fast. (Slide.) "rat."
4. (Touch first ball for **m.**) You're going to rhyme with (pause) **at**. What are you going to rhyme with? "at." Rhyming with (pause) **at** (Quickly slide to second ball and hold. Then slide to end of arrow as child says:) "mmmat." (Return to first ball.) Say it fast (Slide.) "mat."

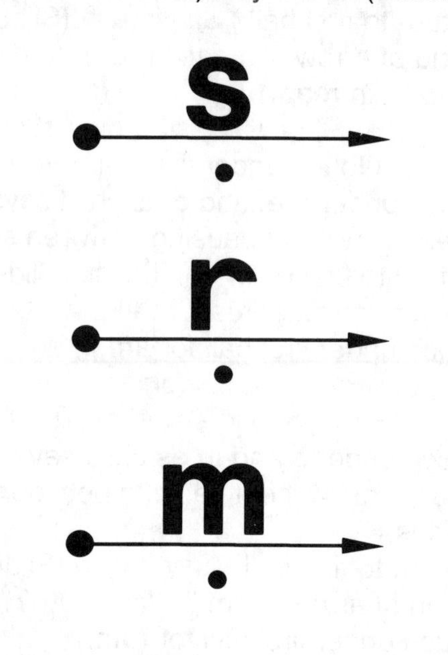

TASK 7 FIRST READING

1. (Point to words in sentence.) This is a story. I'll touch the words in this story (Touch first ball for **sēē.**) This is the first word. (Touch the first ball for **mē.**) This is the next word (Touch the first ball for **ēat.**) This is the next word.
2. Your turn to touch the ball for the first word. (Child touches ball for **sēē.**) Touch the ball for the next word. (Child touches ball for **mē.**) Touch the ball for the next word (Child touches ball for **ēat.**)
3. Touch the ball for the first word again. Sound out the first word. (Child touches under **s, ē,** and **ē** and says:) "sssēēē." (Repeat if not firm.) Say it fast. "see " Yes, what word? "see " You just read the first word.
4. Touch the ball for the next word. (Child touches ball for **mē.**) Sound it out. (Child touches under **m** and **ē** and says:) "mmmēēē." (Repeat if not firm.) Say it fast. "me." Yes, what word? "me."
5. Touch the ball for the next word. (Child touches ball for **ēat.**) Sound it out. (Child touches under **ē** and **t** and says:) "ēēēt." (Repeat if not firm.) Say it fast. "eat." Yes, what word? "eat."

TASK 8 SECOND READING

1. Get ready to read the story again. Touch the ball for the first word. Sound it out. "sssēēē." (Repeat if not firm.) Say it fast "see." Yes, what word? "see."
2. Touch the ball for the next word. Sound it out. "mmmēēē." (Repeat if not firm.) Say it fast. "me." Yes, what word? "me."
3. Touch the ball for the next word. Sound it out. "ēēēt." (Repeat if not firm.) Say it fast. "eat." Yes, what word? "eat."

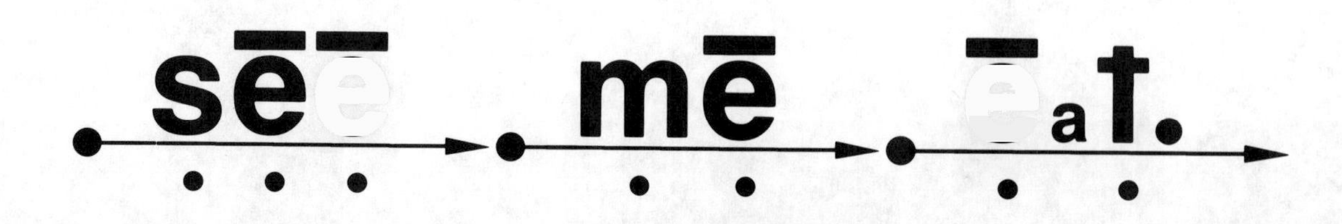

TASK 9 PARENT READS THE FAST WAY

1. I'm going to read the words in the story the fast way. You don't know how to do this yet, so watch.
2. (Touch ball for **sēē.** Slide quickly under **sēē.**) **sēē.** (Pause. Touch ball for **mē.** Slide quickly under **mē.**) **mē.** (Pause. Touch ball for **ēat.** Slide quickly under **ēat.**) **ēat.** I'll do it again. (Repeat step 2.)

TASK 10 PICTURE COMPREHENSION

1. You just read (pause) **see me eat.** (Point to picture.) This picture shows what you read. The story says (pause) **see me eat.** So what do you think the boy in this picture is saying?
2. What is the boy doing?
3. Do you think he likes to eat?
4. What do you see in the picture that shows he likes to eat?
5. What is he eating?
6. What do you like to eat?

For all lessons, cover the picture until you are ready to begin picture comprehension task.

TASK 11 SOUNDS WRITING

1. Here's the first sound you're going to write. (Write **s** at beginning of first line. Point to **s.**) What sound? "sss."
2. First trace the **sss** that I made. Then make more of them on this line. (After tracing **s** several times, child is to make three to five **s**'s. Help child if necessary. For acceptable letters say:) Good writing **sss.**
3. Here's the next sound you're going to write. (Write **d** at beginning of second line. Point to **d.**) What sound? "d."
4. First trace the **d** that I made. Then make more of them on this line. (After tracing **d** several times, child is to make three to five **d**'s. Help child if necessary. For acceptable letters say:) Good writing **d.**

LESSON 14

TASK 1 SOUNDS INTRODUCTION

1. (Point to **i.**) Here's a new sound. I'm going to touch under this sound and say the sound. (Touch first ball of arrow. Move quickly to second ball. Hold.) **ĭĭĭ.**
2. Your turn to say the sound when I touch under it. (Touch first ball.) Get ready. (Move quickly to second ball. Hold.) "ĭĭĭ."

> (**To correct** child saying a wrong sound or not responding:) The sound is **ĭĭĭ.** (Repeat step 2.)

3. (Touch first ball.) Again. Get ready. (Move quickly to second ball. Hold.) "ĭĭĭ."

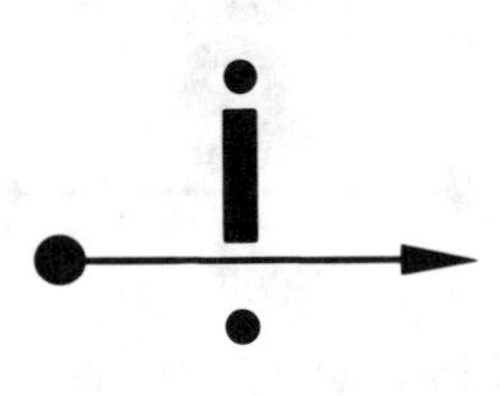

TASK 2 SOUNDS

1. You can say some of these sounds slowly. Other sounds you have to say fast.
2. Take a good look at each sound. Say it slowly if you can. Don't get fooled.
3. (Touch first ball for **r.**) Get ready. (Quickly move to second ball. Hold.) "rrr."

> (**To correct** saying **r** fast:) You can say that sound slowly. Listen: **rrr.** (Repeat step 3.)

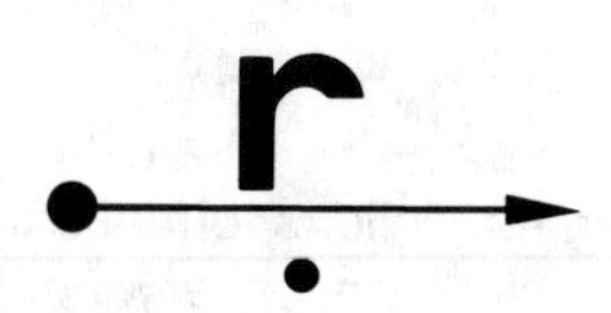

4. (Touch ball for **d.**) Get ready. (Quickly move to end of arrow.) "d."

> (**To correct** holding **d:**) You say that sound fast. Listen: **d.** (Repeat step 4.)

5. (Touch ball for **t.**) Get ready. (Quickly move to end of arrow.) "t."

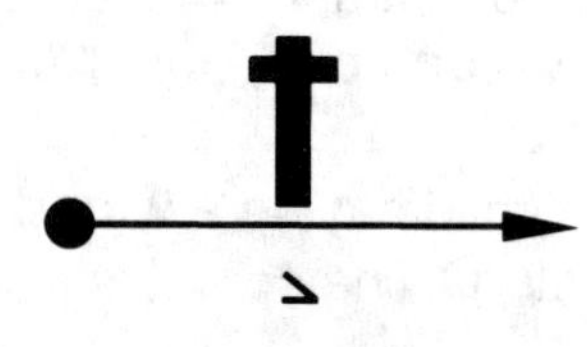

6. (Touch first ball for **ē.**) Get ready. (Quickly move to second ball.) "ēēē."

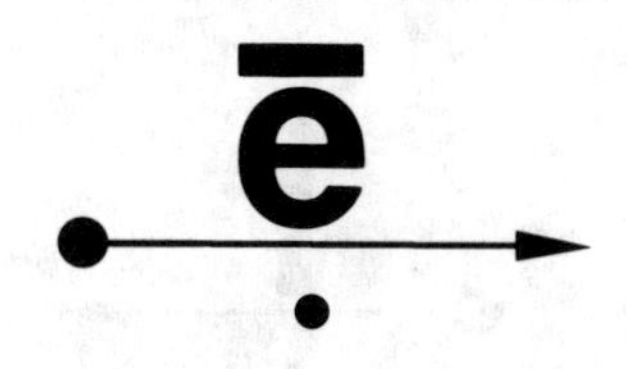

7. (Touch first ball for **i.**) Get ready. (Quickly move to second ball.) "iii."

TASK 3 RHYMING

1. (Point to **s** and **r.**) You're going to rhyme. These are the sounds you're going to start with. (Touch first ball for **s.**) Say the sound. (Quickly slide to second ball and hold.) "sss." (Touch first ball for **r.**) Say the sound. (Quickly slide to second ball and hold.) "rrr."
2. (Touch first ball for **s.**) You're going to rhyme with (pause) **ēēd.** What are you going to rhyme with? "ēēd." Rhyming with (pause) **ēēd.** (Quickly slide to second ball and hold. Then slide to end of arrow as child says:) "sssēēd."
   (Return to first ball.) Say it fast. (Slide.) "seed."
3. (Touch first ball for **r.**) You're going to rhyme with (pause) **ēēd.** What are you going to rhyme with? "ēēd." Rhyming with (pause) **ēēd.** (Quickly slide to second ball and hold. Then slide to end of arrow as child says:) "rrrēēd."
   (Return to first ball.) Say it fast. (Slide.) "reed."

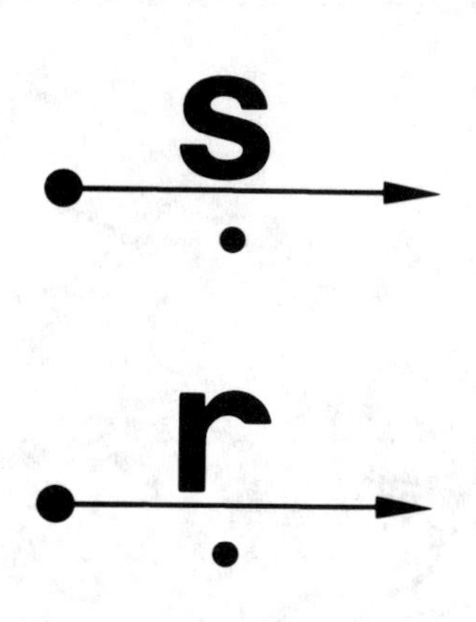

TASK 4 SAY THE SOUNDS

1. Say **sssēēēd.** "sssēēēd."
   Say it fast. "seed."
   Say **rrrēēēd.** "rrrēēēd."
   Say it fast. "read."
   Say **sssaaad** "sssaaad."
   Say it fast. "sad."
   Say **ēēērrr.** "ēēērrr."
   Say it fast. "ear."
2. Let's do those words again. (Repeat step 1 until firm.)

TASK 5 WORD READING

1. (Point to words.) Now you get to read these words.
   (Touch first ball for **sēē.**) Sound it out. (Touch balls for sounds as child says "sssēēē." Repeat until firm.)
   (Return to first ball.) Say it fast (Slide to end of arrow.) "see." What word? "see."
2. (Touch first ball for **sēēd.**) Sound it out. (Touch balls for sounds as child says "sssēēēd." Repeat until firm.)
   (Return to first ball.) Say it fast. (Slide to end of arrow.) "seed." What word? "seed."
3. (Touch first ball for **rat.**) Sound it out. (Touch balls for sounds as child says "rrraaat." Repeat until firm.)
   (Return to first ball.) Say it fast. (Slide to end of arrow.) "rat." What word? "rat."

(**To correct** if child breaks between sounds, is unable to say word after sounding it out, or says "at":) Stop. Listen. **rrraaat.** Say that. "rrraaat." Now say it fast. "rat." That's it. (Point to first ball of arrow for **rat.**) Now do it here. Sound it out. "rrraaat." Say it fast. "rat." You did it.

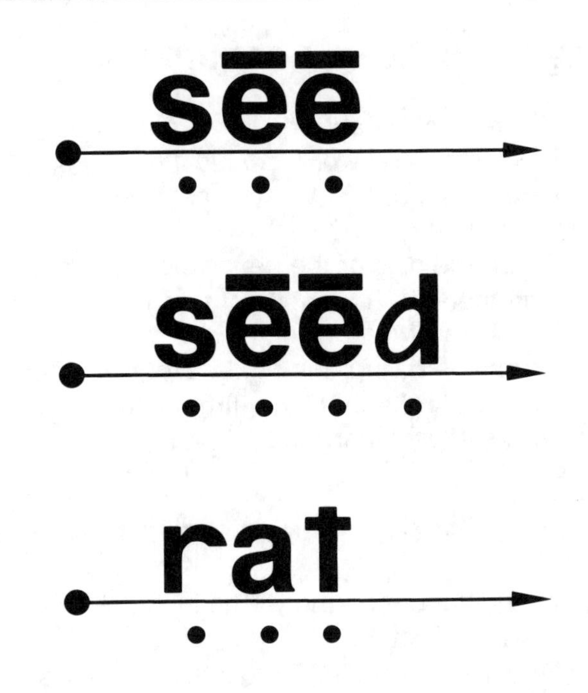

4. (Touch first ball for **rēad.**) Sound it out (Touch balls for sounds as child says "rrrēēēd." Repeat until firm.) (Return to first ball.) Say it fast (Slide to end of arrow.) "read." What word? "read."
5. (Repeat step 4 for **mad, sad, am, ēar,** and **at.**)

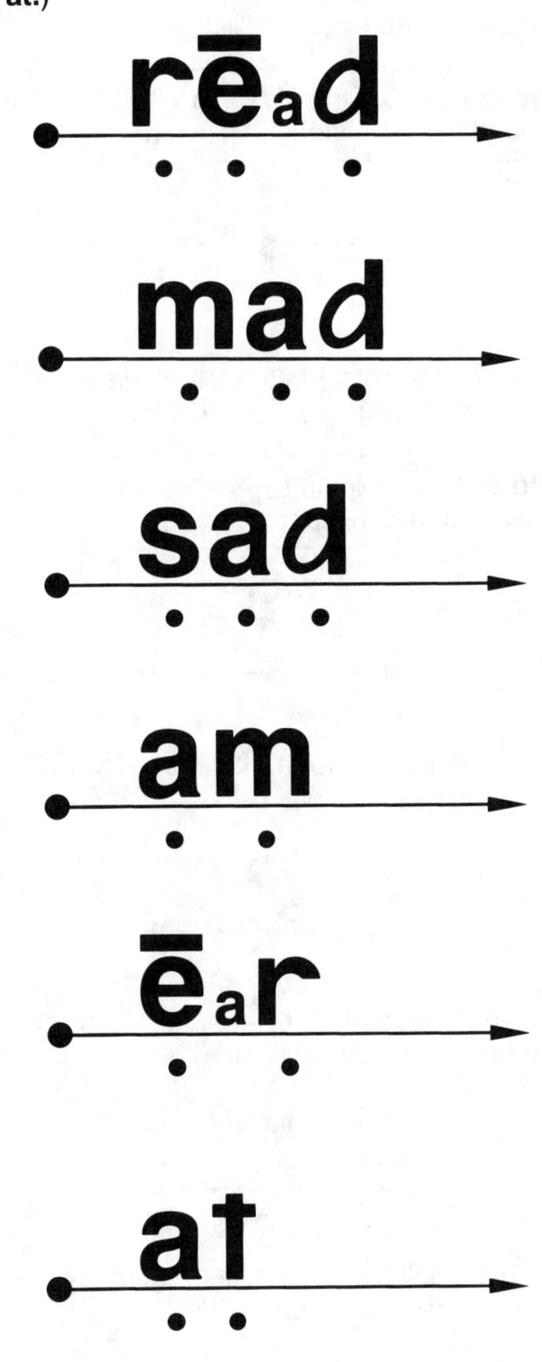

TASK 6 SOUNDS

1. You can say some of these sounds slowly. Other sounds you have to say fast.
2. Take a good look at each sound. Say it slowly if you can. Don't get fooled.
3. (Touch first ball for **i.**) Get ready. (Quickly move to second ball.) "iii."

(**To correct** saying **i** fast:) You can say that sound slowly. Listen: **iii.** (Repeat step 3.)

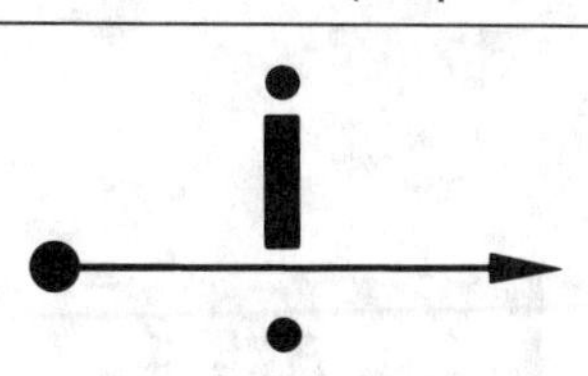

4. (Touch ball for **t.**) Get ready. (Quickly move to end of arrow.) "t."

(**To correct** holding **t:**) You say that sound fast. Listen: **t.** (Repeat step 4.)

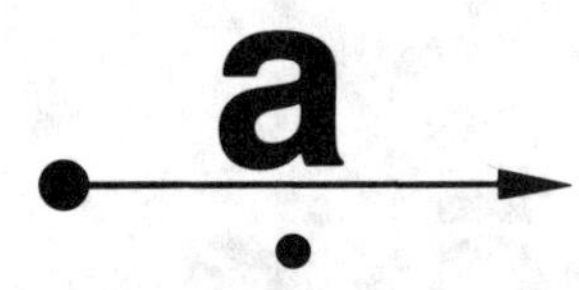

5. (Touch first ball for **a.**) Get ready. (Quickly move to second ball.) "aaa."

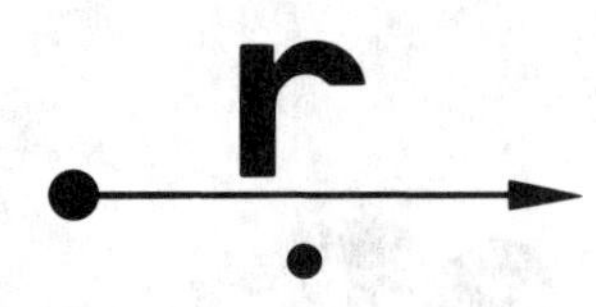

6. (Touch first ball for **r.**) Get ready. (Quickly move to second ball.) "rrr."

7. (Touch ball for **d.**) Get ready. (Quickly move to end of arrow.) "d."

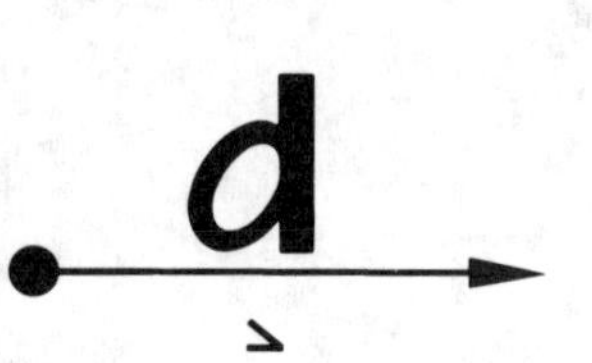

TASK 7 FIRST READING

1. (Point to words in sentence.) This is a story. I'll touch the words in this story. (Touch first ball for **sēē.**) This is the first word. (Touch first ball for **mē.**) This is the next word. (Touch first ball for **rēad.**) This is the next word.
2. Your turn to touch the ball for the first word. (Child touches ball for **sēē.**) Touch the ball for the next word. (Child touches ball for **mē.**) Touch the ball for the next word. (Child touches ball for **rēad.**)
3. Touch the ball for the first word again. Sound out the first word. (Child touches under **s, ē,** and **ē** and says:) "sssēēē." (Repeat if not firm.) Say it fast. "see." Yes, what word? "see." You just read the first word.
4. Touch the ball for the next word. (Child touches ball for **mē.**) Sound it out. (Child touches under **m** and **ē** and says:) "mmmēēē." (Repeat if not firm.) Say it fast. "me." Yes, what word? "me."
5. Touch the ball for the next word. (Child touches ball for **rēad.**) Sound it out. (Child touches under **r, ē,** and **d** and says:) "rrrēēēd." (Repeat if not firm.) Say it fast. "read." Yes, what word? "read."

TASK 8 SECOND READING

1. Get ready to read the story again. Touch the ball for the first word. Sound it out. "sssēēē." (Repeat if not firm.) Say it fast. "see." Yes, what word? "see."
2. Touch the ball for the next word. Sound it out. "mmmēēē." (Repeat if not firm.) Say it fast. "me." Yes, what word? "me."
3. Touch the ball for the next word. Sound it out. "rrrēēēd." (Repeat if not firm.) Say it fast. "read." Yes, what word? "read."

TASK 9 PARENT READS THE FAST WAY

1. I'm going to read the words in the story the fast way. Watch.
2. (Touch ball for **sēē.** Slide quickly under **sēē.**) **see.** (Pause. Touch ball for **mē.** Slide quickly under **mē.**) **me.** (Pause. Touch ball for **rēad.** Slide quickly under **rēad.**) **read.** I'll do it again. (Repeat step 2.)

sēē mē rēad.

TASK 10 PICTURE COMPREHENSION

1. You just read (pause) **see me read.** Now you're going to see a picture. Somebody in the picture is saying (pause) **see me read.** What will somebody be doing in the picture?
2. Look at the picture.
3. Who is saying (pause) **see me read?**
4. What is he reading?
5. Can dogs really read? No, of course not. But *you* can read.
6. Why do you think the dog is wearing those glasses?

TASK 11 SOUNDS WRITING

1. (Write **i** at beginning of first line. Point to **i.**) What sound? "iii."
2. First trace the **iii** that I made. Then make more of them on this line. (After tracing **i** several times, child is to make three to five **i**'s. Help child if necessary. For each acceptable letter say:) Good writing **iii.**
3. Here's the next sound you're going to write. (Write **e** at beginning of second line. Point to **e.**) What sound? "ēēē."
4. First trace the **ēēē** that I made. Then make more of them on this line. (After tracing **e** several times, child is to make three to five **e**'s. Help child if necessary. For acceptable letters say:) Good writing **ēēē.**

LESSON 15

TASK 1 SOUNDS

1. You can say some of these sounds slowly. Other sounds you have to say fast.
2. Take a good look at each sound. Say it slowly if you can. Don't get fooled.
3. (Touch first ball for **r.**) Get ready. (Quickly move to second ball. Hold.) "rrr."

> (**To correct** saying **r** fast:) You can say that sound slowly. Listen: **rrr.** (Repeat step 3.)

4. (Touch ball for **t.**) Get ready (Quickly move to end of arrow.) "t."

> (**To correct** holding **t:**) Say that sound fast. Listen: **t.** (Repeat step 4.)

5. (Touch first ball for **ē.**) Get ready. (Quickly move to second ball.) "ēēē."
6. (Touch first ball for **a.**) Get ready. (Quickly move to second ball.) "aaa."
7. (Touch first ball for **i.**) Get ready. (Quickly move to second ball.) "iii."
8. (Touch ball for **d.**) Get ready. (Quickly move to end of arrow.) "d."

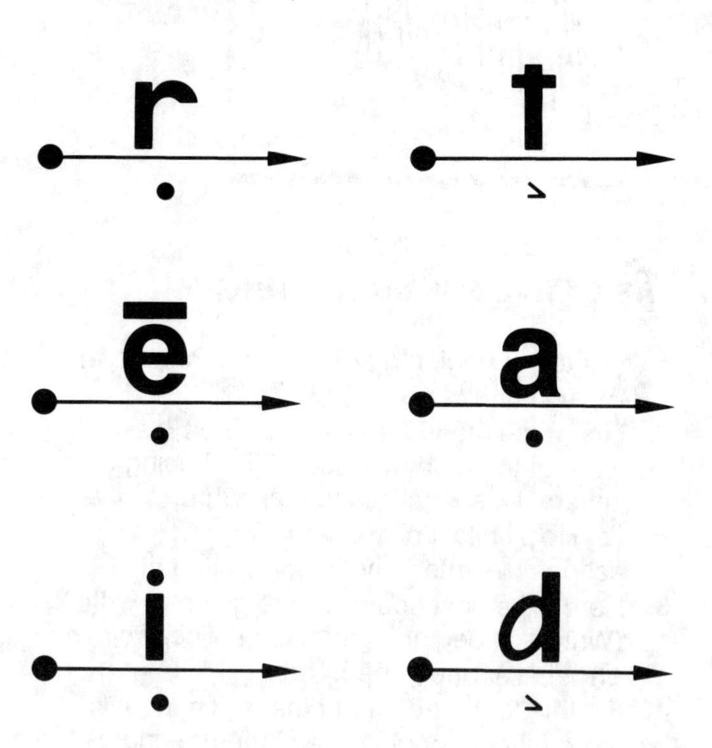

TASK 2 RHYMING

1. (Point to **m** and **s.**) You're going to rhyme. These are the sounds you're going to start with. (Touch first ball for **m.**) Say the sound. (Quickly slide to second ball and hold.) "mmm." (Touch first ball for **s.**) Say the sound. (Quickly slide to second ball and hold.) "sss."
2. (Touch first ball for **m.**) You're going to rhyme with (pause) **eat.** What are you going to rhyme with? "eat." Rhyming with (pause) **eat.** (Quickly slide to second ball and hold. Then slide to end of arrow as child says:) "mmmeat."
   (Return to first ball.) Say it fast. (Slide.) "meat."
3. (Touch first ball for **s.**) You're going to rhyme with (pause) **eat.** What are you going to rhyme with? "eat." Rhyming with (pause) **eat.** (Quickly slide to second ball and hold. Then slide to end of arrow as child says:) "ssseat." (Return to first ball.) Say it fast. (Slide.) "seat."

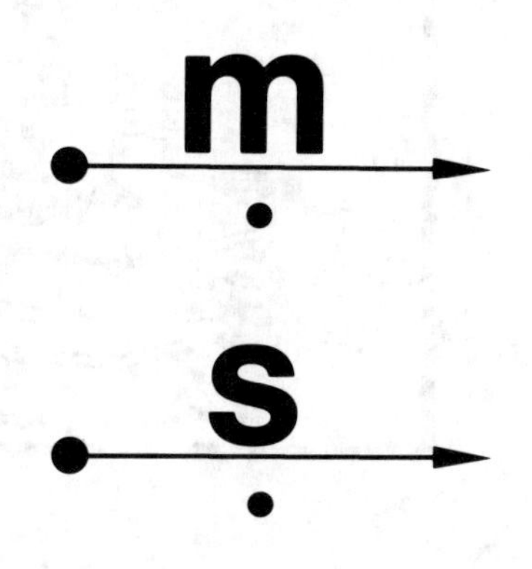

TASK 3 SAY THE SOUNDS

1. Say **sssēēēd.** "sssēēēd."
   Say it fast. "seed."
   Say **rrrēēēd.** "rrrēēēd."
   Say it fast. "read."
   Say **ēēērrr.** "ēēērrr."
   Say it fast. "ear."
   Say **mmmēēēt.** "mmmēēēt."
   Say it fast. "meet."
2. Let's do those words again. (Repeat step 1 until firm.)

TASK 4 WORD READING

1. (Point to words.) Now you're going to read these words.
   (Touch first ball for **it.**) Sound it out. (Touch balls for sounds as child says:) "iiit." (Repeat until firm.)
   (Return to first ball.) Say it fast. (Slide to end of arrow.) "it." What word? "it."
2. (Touch first ball for **sit.**) Sound it out. (Touch balls for sounds as child says:) "sssiiit." (Repeat until firm.)
   (Return to first ball.) Say it fast. (Slide to end of arrow.) "sit." What word? "sit."
3. (Touch first ball for **ēar.**) Sound it out. (Touch balls for sounds as child says:) "ēēērrr." (Repeat until firm.)
   (Return to first ball.) Say it fast. (Slide to end of arrow.) "ear." What word? "ear."
4. (Touch first ball for **sēēd.**) Sound it out. (Touch balls for sounds as child says:) "sssēēēd." (Repeat until firm.)
   (Return to first ball.) Say it fast. (Slide to end of arrow.) "seed." What word? "seed."
5. (Touch first ball for **rat.**) Sound it out. (Touch balls for sounds as child says:) "rrraaat." (Repeat until firm.)
   (Return to first ball.) Say it fast. (Slide to end of arrow.) "rat." What word? "rat."
6. (Touch first ball for **mēēt.**) Sound it out. (Touch balls for sounds as child says:) "mmmēēēt." (Repeat until firm.) (Return to first ball.) Say it fast. (Slide to end of arrow.) "meet." What word? "meet."

(**To correct** if child breaks between sounds, is unable to say word after sounding it out, or says "ēt":) Stop. Listen. **mmmēēēt.** Say that. "mmmēēēt." Now say it fast. "meet." That's it. (Point to first ball of arrow for **mēēt.**) Now do it here. Sound it out. "mmmēēēt." Say it fast. "meet." You did it.

7. (Touch first ball for **mad.**) Sound it out. (Touch balls for sounds as child says:) "mmmaaad." (Repeat until firm.)
   (Return to first ball.) Say it fast. (Slide to end of arrow.) "mad." What word? "mad."

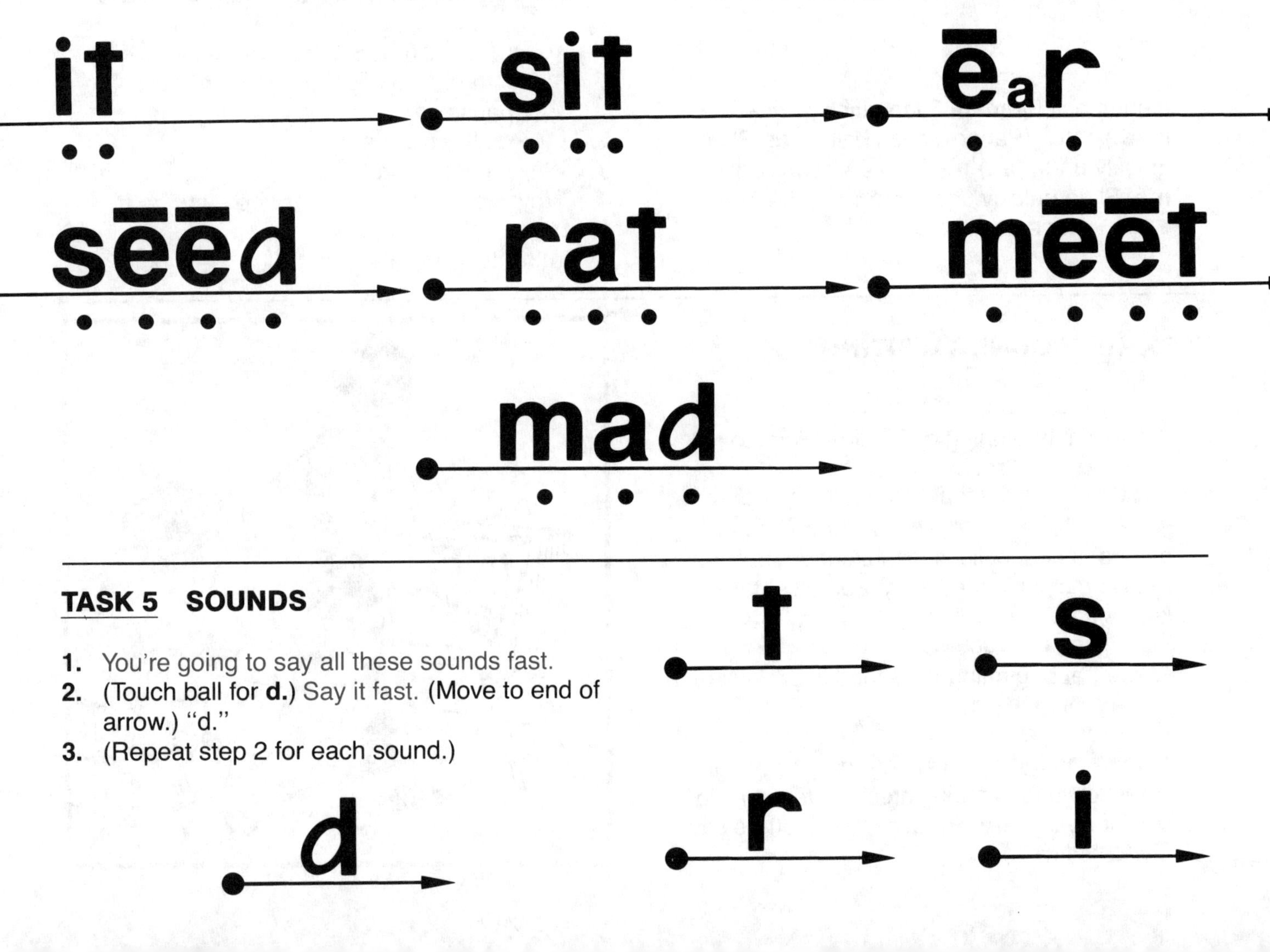

TASK 5 SOUNDS

1. You're going to say all these sounds fast.
2. (Touch ball for **d.**) Say it fast. (Move to end of arrow.) "d."
3. (Repeat step 2 for each sound.)

mad at mē.

TASK 6 FIRST READING

1. (Point to story.) Now you're going to read this story. Finger on the ball of the first word. (Child touches ball for **mad.**) Sound it out. (Child touches under **m, a,** and **d** and says:) "mmmaaad." (Repeat if not firm.) Say it fast. "mad." Yes, what word? "mad."
2. Touch the ball for the next word. Sound it out. (Child touches under **a** and **t** and says:) "aat." (Repeat if not firm.) Say it fast. "at." Yes, what word? "at."
3. Touch the ball for the next word. Sound it out. (Child touches under **m** and **ē** and says:) "mmmēēē." (Repeat if not firm.) Say it fast. "me." Yes, what word? "me."

TASK 7 SECOND READING

1. Get ready to read the story again. Touch the ball for the first word. Sound it out. "mmmaaad." (Repeat if not firm.) Say it fast. "mad." Yes, what word? "mad."
2. Touch the ball for the next word. Sound it out. "aaat." (Repeat if not firm.) Say it fast. "at." Yes, what word? "at."
3. Touch the ball for the next word. Sound it out. "mmmēēē." (Repeat if not firm.) Say it fast. "me." Yes, what word? "me."

TASK 8 PARENT READS THE FAST WAY

1. I'm going to read the words in the story the fast way. Watch.
2. (Touch ball for **mad.** Slide quickly under **mad.**) **mad.** (Pause. Touch ball for **at.** Slide quickly under **at.**) **at.** (Pause. Touch ball for **me.** Slide quickly under **me.**) **me.** I'll do it again. (Repeat step 2.)

TASK 9 PICTURE COMPREHENSION

1. You just read (pause) **mad at me.** One girl in the picture is asking the other girl, "Why are you (pause) mad at me?"
2. Look at the picture.
3. Which girl is mad?
4. Why is she mad at the other girl?
5. Did anybody ever get mad at you for standing in front of the TV?

TASK 10 SOUNDS WRITING

1. Here's the first sound you're going to write. (Write **r** at beginning of first line. Point to **r.**) What sound? "rrr."
2. First trace the **rrr** that I made. Then make more of them on this line. (After tracing **r** several times, child is to make three to five **r**'s. Help child if necessary. For acceptable letters say:) Good writing **rrr.**
3. Here's the next sound you're going to write. (Write **t** at beginning of second line. Point to **t.**) What sound? "t."
4. First trace the **t** that I made. Then make more of them on this line. (After tracing **t** several times, child is to make three to five **t**'s. Help child if necessary. For acceptable letters say: Good writing **t.**)

LESSON 16

TASK 1 SOUNDS INTRODUCTION

1. (Point to **th.**) Here's a new sound. I'm going to touch under this sound and say the sound. (Touch first ball of arrow. Move quickly to second ball. Hold.) **ththth.**
2. Your turn to say the sound when I touch under it. (Touch first ball.) Get ready. (Move quickly to second ball. Hold.) "ththth."

> (**To correct** child saying a wrong sound or not responding:) The sound is **ththth.** (Repeat step 2.)

3. (Touch first ball.) Again. Get ready. (Move quickly to second ball. Hold.) "ththth."

4. (Touch first ball for **i.**) Get ready. (Quickly move to second ball.) "iii."

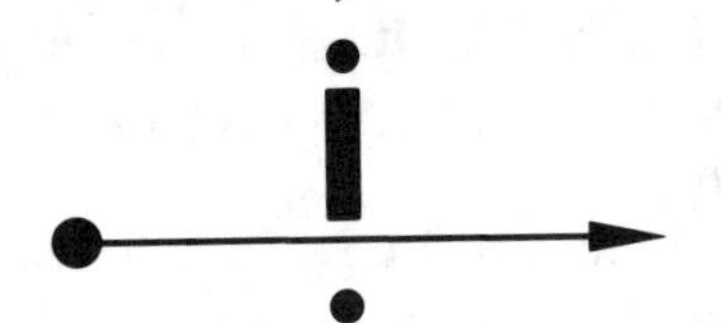

5. (Touch first ball for **th.**) Get ready. (Quickly move to second ball.) "ththth."

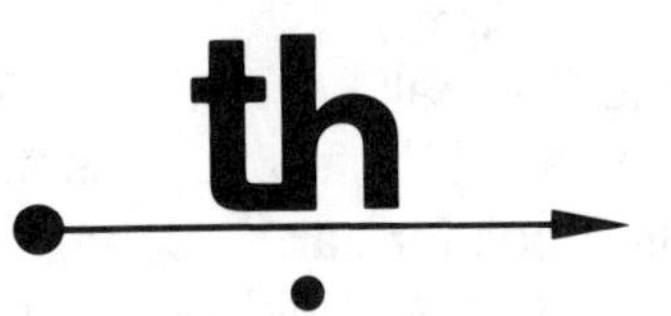

6. (Touch first ball for **r.**) Get ready. (Quickly move to second ball.) "rrr."

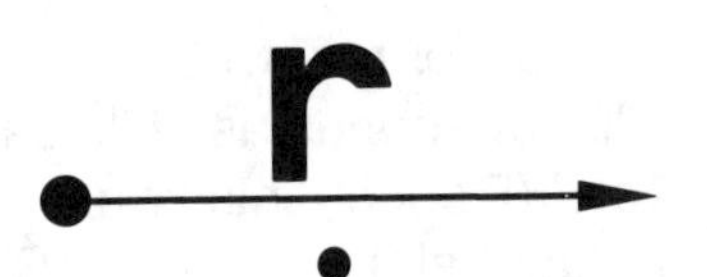

7. (Touch ball for **t.**) Get ready. (Quickly move to end of arrow.) "t."

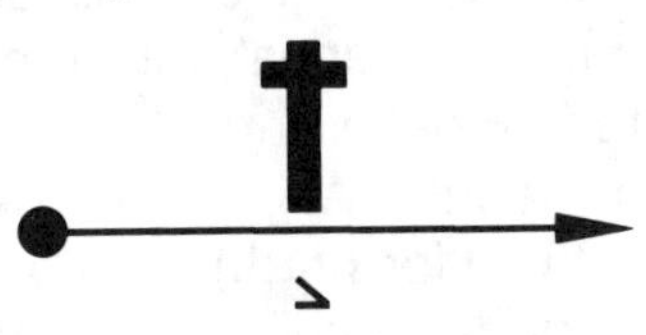

TASK 2 SOUNDS

1. Take a good look at each sound. Say it slowly if you can. Don't get fooled.
2. (Touch ball for **d.**) Get ready. (Quickly move to end of arrow.) "d."

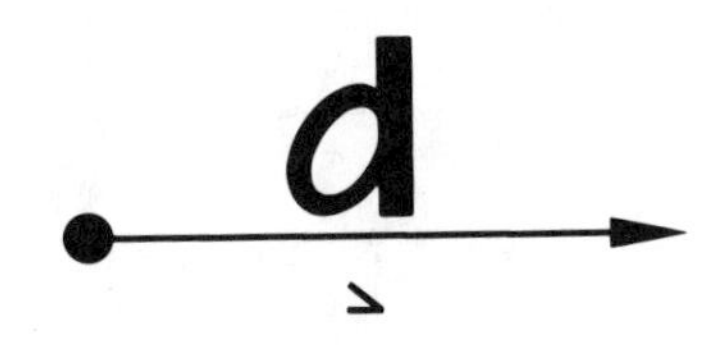

3. (Touch first ball for **ē.**) Get ready. (Quickly move to second ball.) "ēēē."

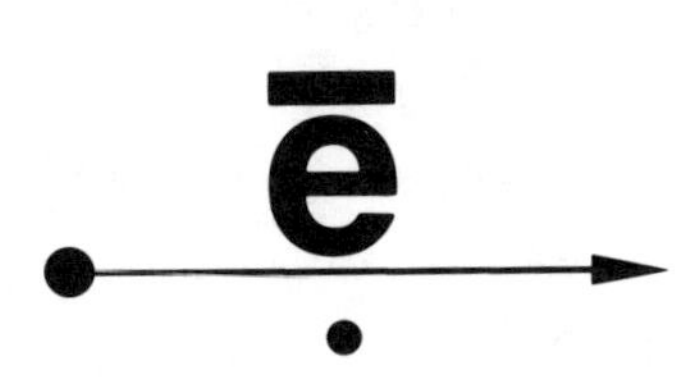

TASK 3 WORD READING

1. Now you're going to read some words. (Touch first ball for **is.**) Sound it out. (Touch balls for sounds as child says:) "iiisss."

> (**To correct** if child says "iiizzz," touch under **s.**) This sound is **sss.** You've got to say the sounds I touch. (Repeat sounding out.)

2. That's how we sound out the word. Here's how we say the word. (pause.) is **(iz).** How do we say the word? **"is."**
3. (Return to first ball.) Sound it out again. (Touch balls for sounds as child says:) "iiisss." Now say the word. "is." Yes, **is.** Reading **is** fun.

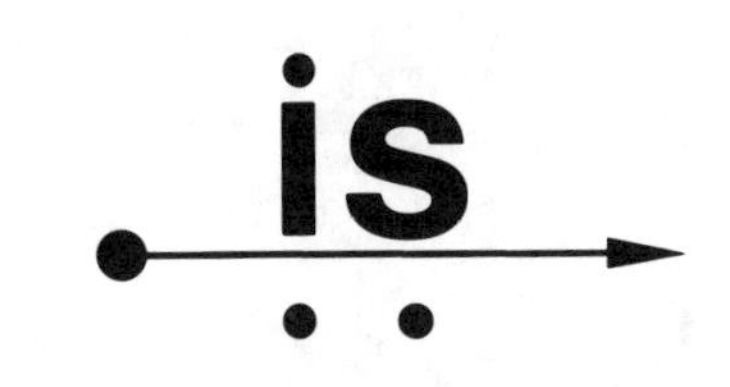

TASK 4 WORD READING

1. (Touch first ball for **it.**) Sound it out. (Touch balls for sounds as child says:) "iiit." (Repeat until firm.)
   (Return to first ball.) Say it fast. (Slide to end of arrow.) "it." What word? "it."
2. (Touch first ball for **sat.**) Sound it out. (Touch balls for sounds as child says:) "sssaaat." (Repeat until firm.)
   (Return to first ball.) Say it fast. (Slide to end of arrow.) "sat." What word? "sat."
3. (Touch first ball for **ēar.**) Sound it out. (Touch balls for sounds as child says:) "ēēērrr." (Repeat until firm.)
   (Return to first ball.) Say it fast. (Slide to end of arrow.) "ear." What word? "ear."
4. (Touch first ball for **mēēt.**) Sound it out. (Touch balls for sounds as child says:) "mmmēēēt." (Repeat until firm.)
   (Return to first ball.) Say it fast. (Slide to end of arrow.) "meet." What word? "meet."
5. (Touch first ball for **sēēm.**) Sound it out. (Touch balls for sounds as child says:) "sssēēēmmm." (Repeat until firm.)
   (Return to first ball.) Say it fast. (Slide to end of arrow.) "seem." What word? "seem."
6. (Touch first ball for **rēad.**) Sound it out. (Touch balls for sounds as child says:) "rrrēēēd." (Repeat until firm.)
   (Return to first ball.) Say it fast. (Slide to end of arrow.) "read." What word? "read."

it

sat

ēar

mēēt

sēēm

rēad

TASK 5 RHYMING

1. (Point to **r, s,** and **m.**) You're going to rhyme. These are the sounds you're going to start with. (Touch first ball for **r.**) Say the sound. (Quickly slide to second ball and hold.) "rrr." (Touch first ball for **s.**) Say the sound. (Quickly slide to second ball and hold.) "sss." (Touch first ball for **m.**) Say the sound. (Quickly slide to second ball and hold.) "mmm."
2. (Touch first ball for **r.**) You're going to rhyme with (pause) **am.** What are you going to rhyme with? "am." Rhyming with (pause) **am.** (Quickly slide to second ball and hold. Then slide to end of arrow as child says:) "rrram." (Return to first ball.) Say it fast. (Slide.) "ram."
3. (Touch first ball for **s.**) You're going to rhyme with (pause) **am.** What are you going to rhyme with? "am." Rhyming with (pause) **am.** (Quickly slide to second ball and hold. Then slide to end of arrow as child says:) "sssam." (Return to first ball.) Say it fast. (Slide.) "sam."
4. (Touch first ball for **m.**) You're going to rhyme with (pause) **am.** What are you going to rhyme with? "am." Rhyming with (pause) **am.** (Quickly slide to second ball and hold. Then slide to end of arrow as child says:) "mmmam." (Return to first ball.) Say it fast. (Slide.) "mam."

r

s

m

TASK 6 CHILD TOUCHES SOUNDS

1. Your turn to touch the sounds and say them. Touch the first ball for the first sound. Move to the next ball and say the sound slowly. "ththth." Now say it fast. "th."
2. Touch the ball for the next sound. You have to say this sound fast. So say it fast when you touch under it. Say it fast. "d."
3. Touch the first ball for the next sound. Move to the next ball and say the sound slowly. "mmm." Now say it fast. "m."
4. Touch the first ball for the next sound. Move to the next ball and say the sound slowly. "rrr." Now say it fast. "r."
5. Touch the first ball for the next sound. Move to the next ball and say the sound slowly. "iii." Now say it fast. "i."
6. Touch the ball for the next sound. You have to say this sound fast. So say it fast when you touch under it. Say it fast. "t."

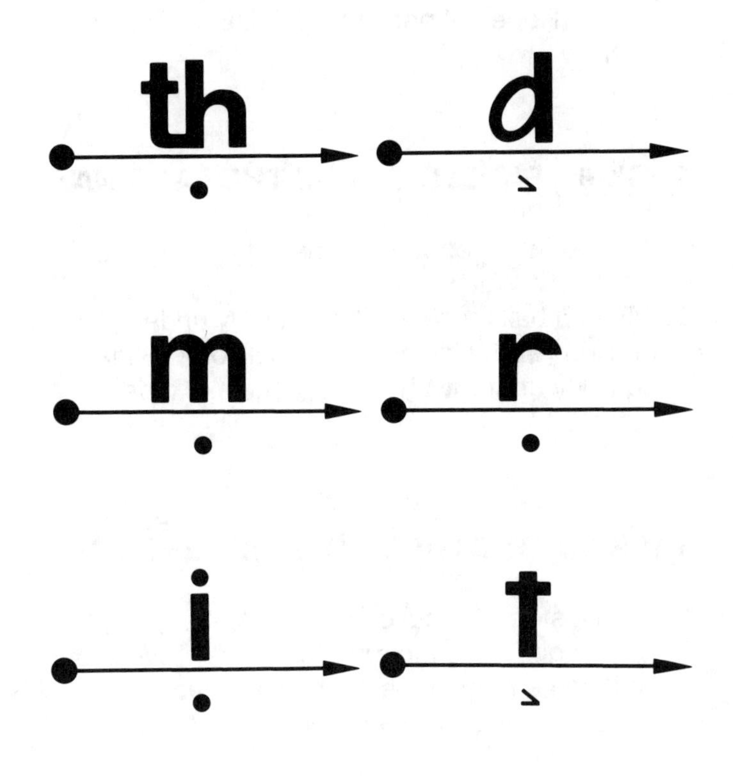

TASK 7 FIRST READING

1. (Point to story.) Now you're going to read this story. Finger on the ball of the first word. (Child touches ball for **read.**) Sound it out. (Child touches under **r, ē,** and **d,** and says:) "rrrēēēd." (Repeat if not firm.) Say it fast. "read." Yes, what word? "read."
2. Touch the ball for the next word. Sound it out. (Child touches under **i** and **t** and says:) "iiit." (Repeat if not firm.) Say it fast. "it." Yes, what word? "it."

TASK 8 SECOND READING

1. Get ready to read the story again. Touch the ball for the first word. Sound it out. "rrrēēēd." (Repeat if not firm.) Say it fast. "read." Yes, what word? "read."
2. Touch the ball for the next word. Sound it out. "iiit." (Repeat if not firm.) Say it fast. "it." Yes, what word? "it."

TASK 9 PARENT READS THE FAST WAY

1. I'm going to read the words in the story the fast way. Watch.
2. (Touch ball for **rēad.** Slide quickly under **rēad.**) **read.** (Pause. Touch ball for **it.** Slide quickly under **it.**) **it.** I'll do it again. (Repeat step 2.)

TASK 10 PICTURE COMPREHENSION

1. You just read (pause) **read it.** You're going to see a girl in the picture. Somebody gave this girl something and said (pause) **read it.**
2. Look at the picture and see what somebody gave the girl.
3. What did somebody give the girl?
4. Do you think she can read that great big book?
5. Do you think you're going to get smart enough to read such a big book? Sure, you'll be smart enough to read any book there is.

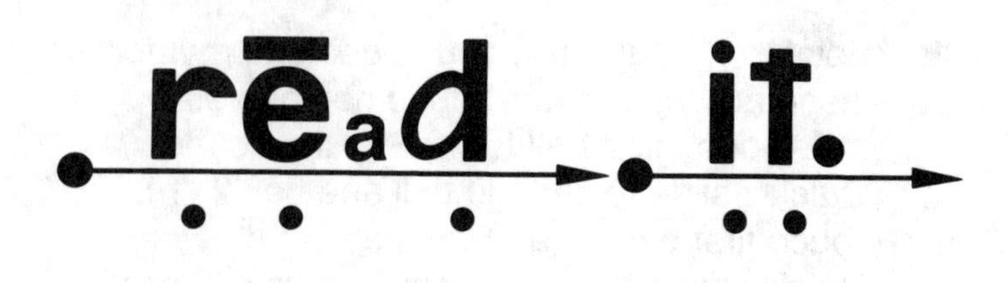

TASK 11 SOUNDS WRITING

1. Here's the first sound you're going to write. (Write **d** at beginning of first line. Point to **d.**) What sound? "d."
2. First trace the **d** that I made. Then make more of them on this line. (After tracing **d** several times, child is to make three to five **d**'s. Help child if necessary. For acceptable letters say:) Good writing **d.**
3. Here's the next sound you're going to write. (Write **i** at beginning of second line. Point to **i.**) What sound? "iii."
4. First trace the **iii** that I made. Then make more of them on this line. (After tracing **i** several times, child is to make three to five **i**'s. Help child if necessary. For acceptable letters say:) Good writing **iii.**

LESSON 17

TASK 1 SOUNDS

1. Take a good look at each sound. Say it slowly if you can. Don't get fooled.
2. (Touch first ball for **th.**) Get ready. (Quickly move to second ball.) "ththth."

3. (Touch first ball for **s.**) Get ready. (Quickly move to second ball.) "sss."

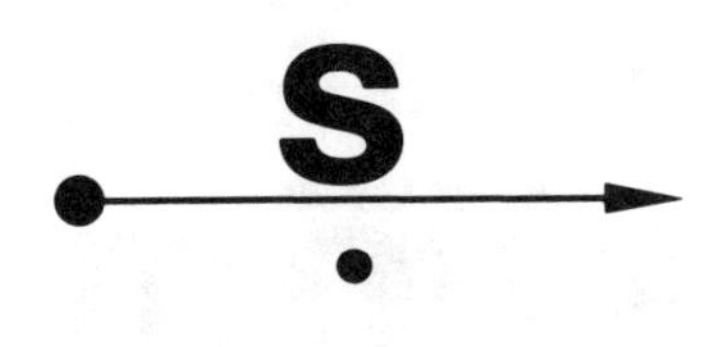

4. (Touch first ball for **r.**) Get ready. (Quickly move to second ball.) "rrr."

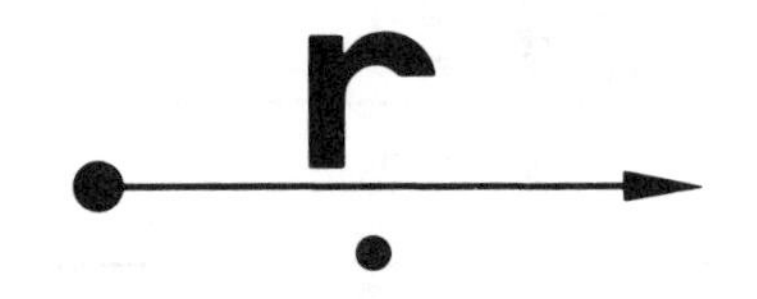

5. (Touch first ball for **m.**) Get ready. (Quickly move to second ball.) "mmm."

6. (Touch ball for **t.**) Get ready. (Quickly move to end of arrow.) "t."

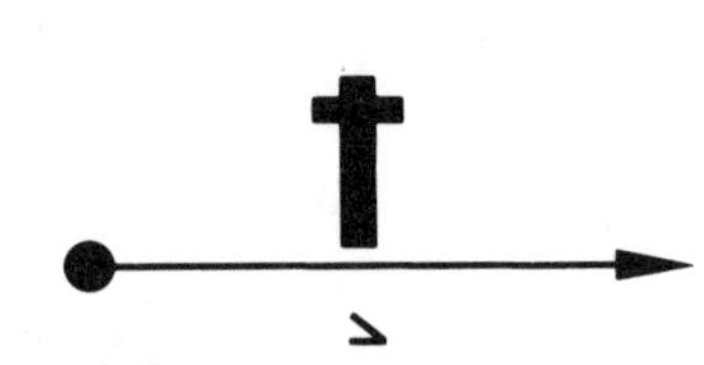

7. Touch first ball for **i.**) Get ready. (Quickly move to second ball.) "iii."

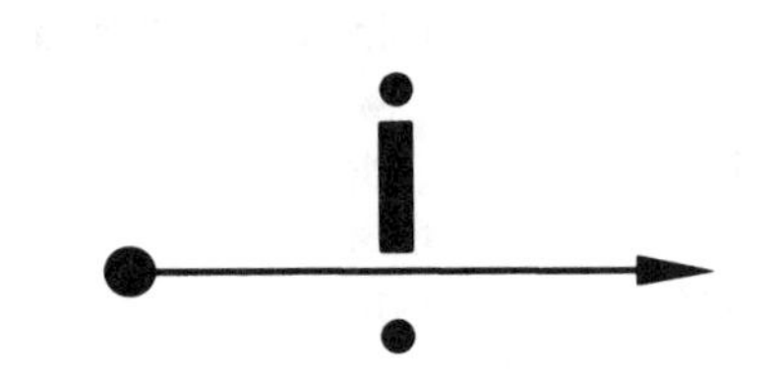

8. (Touch ball for **d.**) Get ready. (Quickly move to end of arrow.) "d."

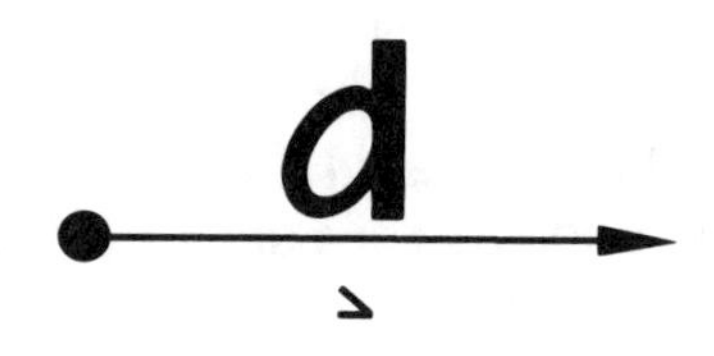

TASK 2 WORD READING

1. Now you're going to read these words. (Touch first ball for **is.**) Sound it out. (Touch balls for sounds as child says:) "iiisss."

(**To correct** if child says "iiizzz" touch under **s.**) This sound is **sss.** You've got to say the sounds I touch. (Repeat sounding out.)

2. That's how we **sound out** the word. Here's how we **say** the word. (pause.) **is.** How do we say the word? "is."
3. (Return to first ball.) **Sound it out** again. (Touch balls for sounds as child says:) "iiisss." Now **say** the word. "is." Yes, **is.** (Repeat until firm.)

a ▪ rat ▪ is ▪ in
a ▪ sack. ▪ that ▪ rat
is ▪ not ▪ sad.

TASK 6 SECOND READING

1. This time you read the story again and I'll ask questions. Touch the ball on the top line and get ready to read the words. (Repeat steps from first reading for each word. Ask following comprehension questions after child has read indicated sentences.)
2. (After child has read:) (You say:)

(After child has read:)	(You say:)
"A rat is in a sack."	Who is in a sack?
"That rat is not sad."	Is the rat sad?
	We'll have to find out why he's happy.

TASK 7 PICTURE COMPREHENSION

1. What animal will you see in the picture?
2. Where will the rat be?
3. Will the rat be sad?
4. Look at the picture and get ready to answer some questions.
5. Where is the rat?
6. Why do you think he's happy? Right, he's got packages and a toy airplane.
7. What would you do with that toy airplane?

TASK 8 READING THE FAST WAY

1. Let's read this story the fast way. (Touch under **not.**) This word is (pause) **not.** (Touch under **sad.**) This word is (pause) **sad.**
2. (Point to **not.**) What are you going to say when I touch this word? "not." (Point to **sad.**) What are you going to say when I touch this word? "sad." (Repeat until firm.)
3. My turn. (Point to **that.** Pause two seconds.) **that.** (Point to **rat.** Pause two seconds.) **rat.** (Point to **is.** Pause two seconds.) **is.**
4. Your turn. (Touch under words as child says:) "not . . . sad."
5. (Repeat steps 1–4 until firm.)

TASK 9 WORD FINDING

1. Now get ready to find the words I say.
2. Find the word (pause) **sad. sad.**
3. (Repeat step 2 for **sad, sack, that, sack, that, sad, that, sack, sad.**)
4. Good finding those words.

TASK 10 SOUNDS WRITING

1. (Write **n** at beginning of first line. Point to **n.**) What sound? "nnn."
2. First trace the **nnn** that I made. Then make more of them on this line. (After tracing **n** several times, child is to make three to five **n**'s. Help child if necessary. For each acceptable letter say:) Good writing **nnn.**
3. Here's the next sound you're going to write. (Write **d** at beginning of second line. Point to **d.**) What sound? "d."
4. First trace the **d** that I made. Then make more of them on this line. (After tracing **d** several times, child is to make three to five **d**'s. Help child if necessary. For acceptable letters say:) Good writing **d.**

LESSON 25

TASK 1 SOUNDS INTRODUCTION

1. (Point to **f.**) Here's a new sound. I'm going to touch under this sound and say the sound. (Touch first ball of arrow. Move quickly to second ball. Hold.) **fff.**
2. Your turn to say the sound when I touch under it. (Touch first ball.) Get ready. (Move quickly to second ball. Hold.) "fff."

(**To correct** child saying a wrong sound or not responding:) The sound is **fff.** (Repeat step 2.)

3. (Touch first ball.) Again. Get ready. (Move quickly to second ball. Hold.) "fff."

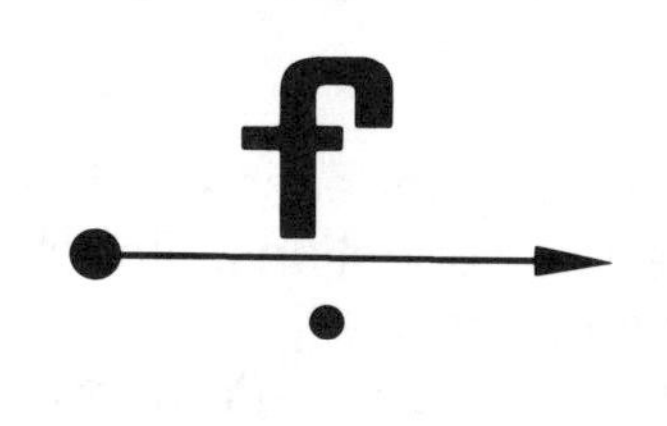

TASK 2 SOUNDS

1. Take a good look at each sound. Say it slowly if you can. Don't get fooled.
2. (Touch first ball for **i.**) Get ready. (Quickly move to second ball. Hold.) "iii."
3. (Repeat step 2 for **r, o, n,** and **c.** Remember to move quickly to end of arrow if there is no ball on arrow for sound.)

i

r

o

n

c

TASK 3 WORD READING

1. You're going to read these words. (Touch first ball for **an.**) Sound it out. (Touch balls for sounds.) "aaannn." (Repeat until firm.) What word? "an."
2. (Touch first ball for **man.**) Sound it out. (Touch balls for sounds.) "mmmaaannn." (Repeat until firm.) What word? "man."
3. (Touch arrow under **c.**) Remember, I can't stop under this sound, but you have to say the sound with the next sound I stop at. (Touch first ball for **can.**) Sound it out. Get ready. (Slide past **c,** touch **a** for two seconds, move quickly to **n,** hold for two seconds.) "caaannn." (Repeat until firm.) What word? "can." Yes, **can.**
4. (Touch first ball for **on.**) Sound it out. (Touch balls for sounds.) "ooonnn." (Repeat until firm.) What word? "on."
5. (Touch first ball for **not.**) Sound it out. (Touch balls for sounds.) "nnnooot." (Repeat until firm.) What word? "not."
6. (Touch first ball for **mē.**) Sound it out. (Touch balls for sounds.) "mmmēēē." (Repeat until firm) What word? "me."
7. (Touch first ball for **in.**) Sound it out. (Touch balls for sounds.) "iiinnn." (Repeat until firm.) What word? "in."
8. (Touch first ball for **sit.**) Sound it out. (Touch balls for sounds.) "sssiiit." (Repeat until firm.) What word? "sit."
9. (Touch first ball for **ant.**) Sound it out. (Touch balls for sounds.) "aaannnt." (Repeat until firm.) What word? "ant."

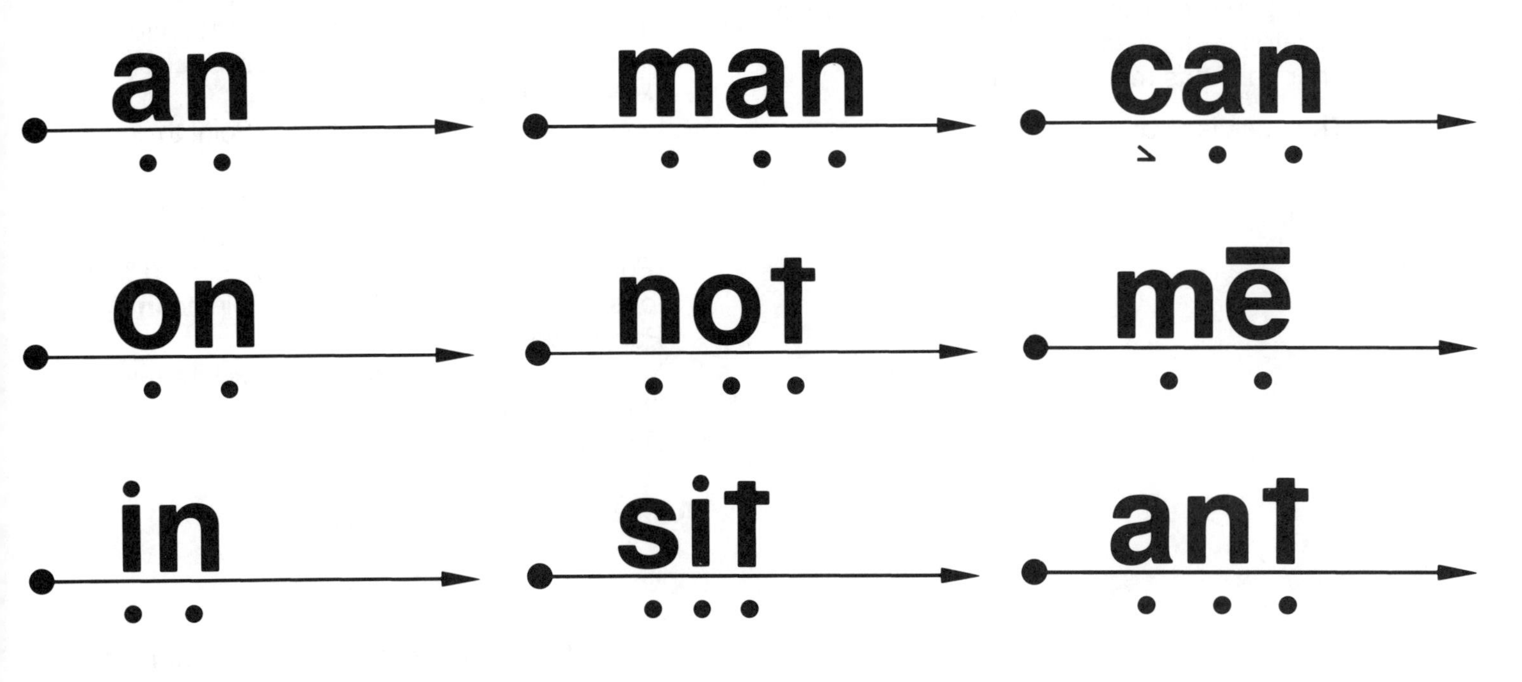

TASK 4 SOUNDS

1. Take a good look at each sound. Say it slowly if you can. Don't get fooled.
2. (Touch first ball for **f.**) Get ready. (Quickly move to second ball. Hold.) "fff."
3. (Repeat step 2 for **n, o, i, ē,** and **c.** Remember to move quickly to end of arrow if there is no ball on arrow for sound.)

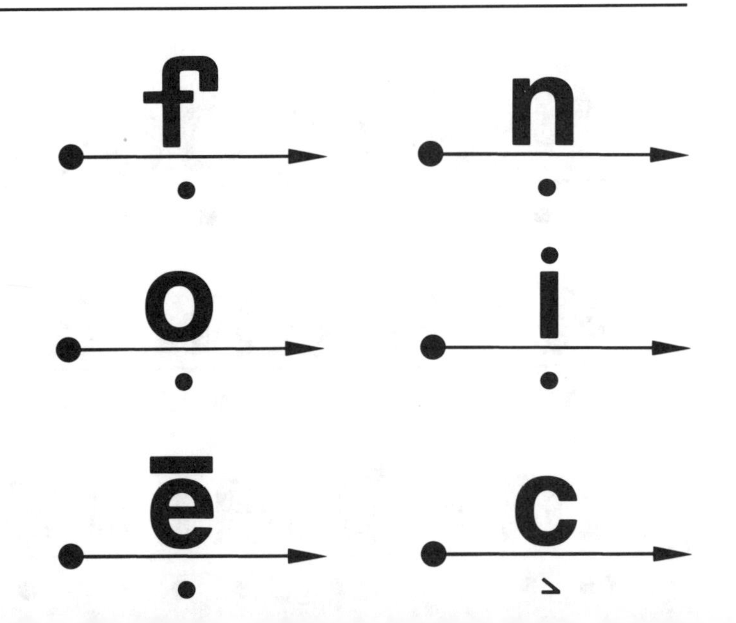

TASK 5 FIRST READING

1. Now you're going to read the story. Finger on the ball of the top line. Sound out the first word. (Child touches under and says:) "thththēēē." What word? "the."
2. Sound out the next word. (Child touches under and says:) "sssoook." What word? "sock."
3. (Repeat step 2 for remaining words in story.)

TASK 6 SECOND READING

1. This time you read the story and I'll ask questions. Touch the ball on the top line and get ready to read the words. (Repeat steps from first reading for each word. Ask following comprehension questions after child has read indicated sentences.)
2. (After child has read:) (You say:)

(After child has read:)	(You say:)
"The sock is near a man."	Where is the sock?
"A cat is in that sock."	And what is in that sock?
	I wonder why the cat is in a sock.

TASK 7 PICTURE COMPREHENSION

1. What will you see in the picture?
2. Where will the sock be?
3. Where will the cat be?
4. Look at the picture and get ready to answer some questions.
5. What kind of tree is that? Yes, a Christmas tree.
6. And where is the sock hanging?
7. What kind of present is in the sock?
8. Does the man look happy with that present?
9. What would you do if you got a cat as a Christmas present?

TASK 8 READING THE FAST WAY

1. Let's read this story the fast way. (Touch under **that.**) This word is (pause) **that.** (Touch under **sock.**) This word is (pause) **sock.**
2. (Point to **that.**) What are you going to say when I touch this word? "that." (Point to **sock.**) What are you going to say when I touch this word? "sock." (Repeat until firm.)
3. My turn. (Point to **a.** Pause two seconds.) **a.** (Point to **cat.** Pause two seconds.) **cat.** (Point to **is.** Pause two seconds.) **is.** (Point to **in.** Pause two seconds.) **in.**
4. Your turn. (Touch under words as child says:) "that . . . sock."
5. (Repeat steps 1–4 until firm.)

TASK 9 WORD FINDING

1. Now get ready to find the words I say.
2. Find the word (pause) **cat. cat.**
3. (Repeat step 2 for **man, cat, sock, cat, man, sock, man, cat, sock.**)
4. Good finding those words.

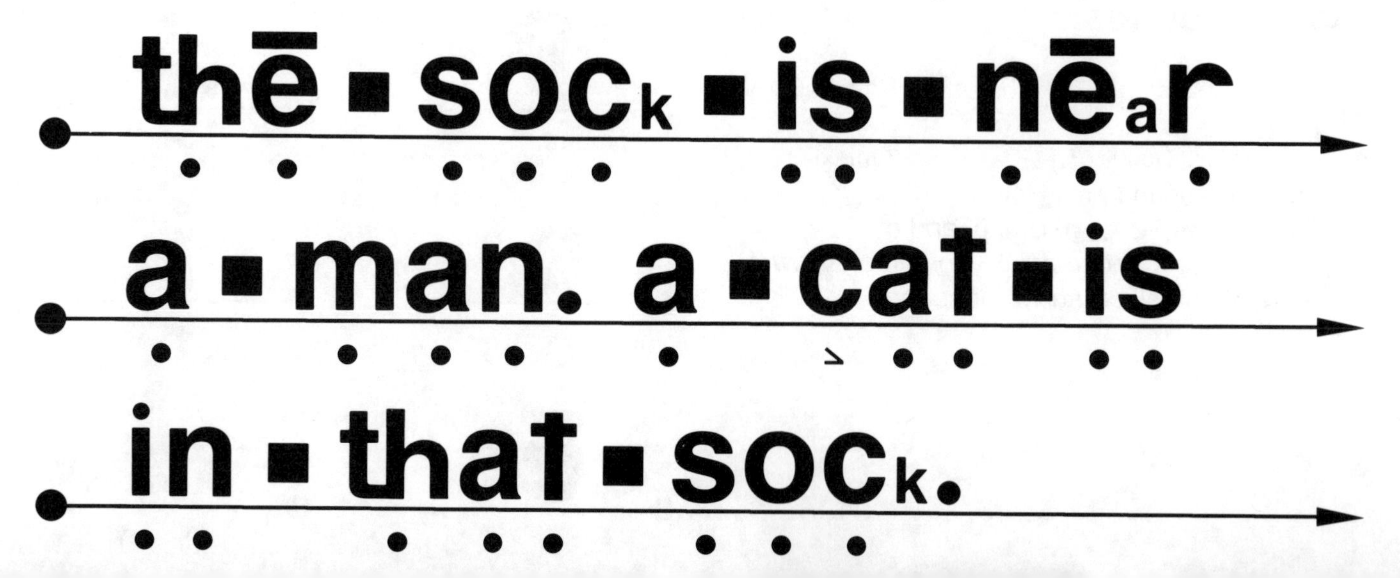

TASK 10 SOUNDS WRITING

1. Here's the first sound you're going to write. (Write **n** at beginning of first line. Point to **n.**) What sound? "nnn."
2. First trace the **nnn** that I made. Then make more of them on this line. (After tracing **n** several times, child is to make three to five **n**'s. Help child if necessary. For acceptable letters say:) Good writing **nnn.**
3. Here's the next sound you're going to write. (Write **o** at beginning of second line. Point to **o.**) What sound? "ooo."
4. First trace the **ooo** that I made. Then make more of them on this line. (After tracing **o** several times, child is to make three to five **o**'s. Help child if necessary. For acceptable letters say:) Good writing **ooo.**

LESSON 26

TASK 1 SOUNDS

1. Take a good look at each sound. Say it slowly if you can. Don't get fooled.
2. (Touch first ball for **o.**) Get ready. (Quickly move to second ball. Hold.) "ooo."
3. (Repeat step 2 for **f, r, i, d,** and **th.** Remember to move quickly to end of arrow if there is no ball on arrow for sound.)

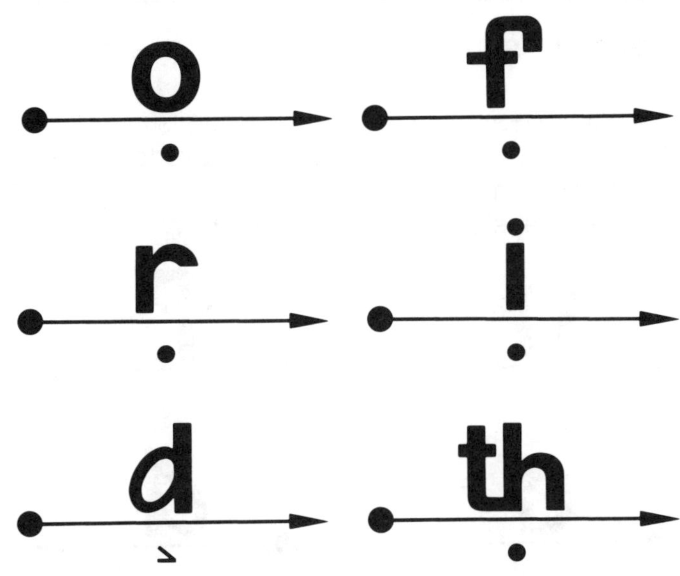

TASK 2 WORD READING

1. Now here are the words you get to read. (Touch first ball for **fat.**) Sound it out. (Touch balls for sounds.) "fffaaat." (Repeat until firm.) What word? "fat."
2. (Touch first ball for **fan.**) Sound it out. (Touch balls for sounds.) "fffaaannn." (Repeat until firm.) What word? "fan."
3. (Touch first ball for **feet.**) Sound it out. (Touch balls for sounds.) "fffēēēt." (Repeat until firm.) What word? "feet."

4. (Touch first ball for **if.**) Sound it out. (Touch balls for sounds.) "iiifff." (Repeat until firm.) What word? "if."
5. (Touch first ball for **on.**) Sound it out. (Touch balls for sounds.) "ooonnn." (Repeat until firm.) What word? "on."
6. (Touch arrow under **c.**) Remember, I can't stop under this sound, but you have to say the sound with the next sound I stop at. (Touch first ball for **can.**) Sound it out. Get ready. (Slide past **c,** touch **a** for two seconds, move quickly to **n,** hold for two seconds.) "caaannn." (Repeat until firm.) What word? "can." Yes, **can.**
7. (Touch first ball for **and.**) Sound it out. (Touch balls for sounds.) "aaannnd." (Repeat until firm.) What word? "and."
8. (Touch first ball for **not.**) Sound it out. (Touch balls for sounds.) "nnnooot." (Repeat until firm.) What word? "not."
9. (Touch first ball for **in.**) Sound it out. (Touch balls for sounds.) "iiinnn." (Repeat until firm.) What word? "in."

if **on** **can**

and **not** **in**

TASK 3 SOUNDS

1. You're going to say all these sounds fast.
2. (Touch ball for **n.**) Say it fast. (Move to end of arrow.) "n."
3. (Repeat step 2 for each sound.)

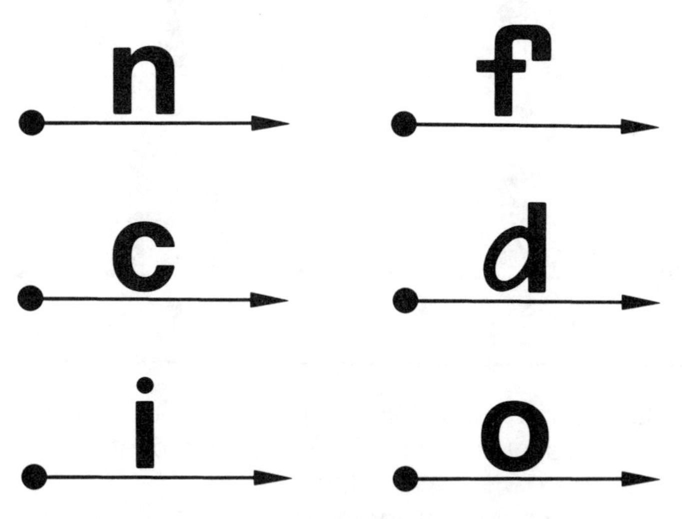

TASK 4 FIRST READING

1. Now you're going to read the story. Finger on the ball of the top line. Touch under the first word. What word? "uh."
2. Sound out the next word. (Child touches under and says:) "mmmaaannn." What word? "man."
3. (Repeat step 2 for remaining words in story.)

TASK 5 SECOND READING

1. This time you read the story again and I'll ask questions. Touch the ball on the top line and get ready to read the words. (Repeat steps from first reading for each word. Ask following comprehension questions after child has read indicated sentences.)
2. (After child has read:) (You say:)

(After child has read:)	(You say:)
"A man sat on a ram."	Where did the man sit?
"That ram can not see."	What's the matter with the ram?

TASK 6 PICTURE COMPREHENSION

1. What will you see in the picture?
2. Where will the man be sitting?
3. And what's the matter with the ram?
4. Look at the picture and get ready to answer some questions.
5. Why can't the ram see?
6. Can the man see?
7. Why are they wearing those big hats? Yes, it's raining.
8. What do you wear when it's raining outside?

a ▪ man ▪ sat on ▪ a ▪ ram. that ▪ ram ▪ can not ▪ sēē.

TASK 7 READING THE FAST WAY

1. Let's read this story the fast way. (Touch under **not.**) This word is (pause) **not.** (Touch under **sēē.**) This word is (pause) **see.**
2. (Point to **not.**) What are you going to say when I touch this word? "not." (Point to **see.**) What are you going to say when I touch this word? "see." (Repeat until firm.)
3. My turn. (Point to **that.** Pause two seconds.) **that.** (Point to **ram.** Pause two seconds.) **ram.** (Point to **can.** Pause two seconds.) **can.**
4. Your turn. (Touch under words as child says:) "not . . . see."
5. (Repeat steps 1–4 until firm.)

TASK 8 WORD FINDING

1. Now get ready to find the words I say.
2. Find the word (pause) **ram. ram.**
3. (Repeat step 2 for **man, see, ram, see, ram, man, see, man, ram.**)
4. Good finding those words.

TASK 9 SOUNDS WRITING

1. (Write **f** at beginning of first line. Point to **f.**) What sound? "fff."
2. First trace the **fff** that I made. Then make more of them on this line. (After tracing **f** several times, child is to make three to five **f**'s. Help child if necessary. For each acceptable letter say:) Good writing **fff.**
3. Here's the next sound you're going to write. (Write **s** at the beginning of the second line. Point to **s.**) What sound? "sss."
4. First trace the **sss** that I made. Then make more of them on this line. (After tracing **s** several times, child is to make three to five **s**'s. Help child if necessary. For acceptable letters say:) Good writing **sss.**

LESSON 27

TASK 1 SOUNDS INTRODUCTION

1. (Point to **u.**) Here's a new sound. I'm going to touch under this sound and say the sound. (Touch first ball of arrow. Move quickly to second ball. Hold.) **ŭŭŭ.**
2. Your turn to say the sound when I touch under it. (Touch first ball.) Get ready. (Move quickly to second ball. Hold.) "ŭŭŭ."

(**To correct** child saying a wrong sound or not responding:) The sound is **ŭŭŭ.** (Repeat step 2.)

3. (Touch first ball.) Again. Get ready. (Move quickly to second ball. Hold.) "ŭŭŭ."

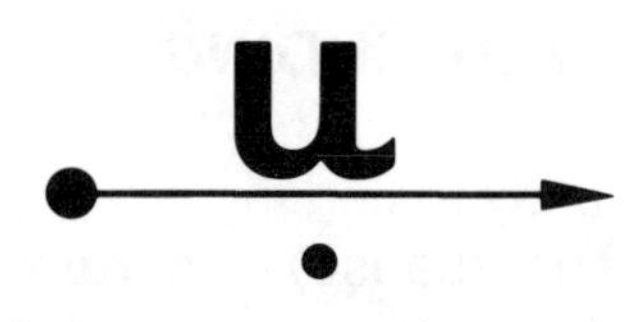

TASK 2 SOUNDS

1. Take a good look at each sound. Say it slowly if you can. Don't get fooled.
2. (Touch first ball for **f.**) Get ready. (Quickly move to second ball. Hold.) "fff."
3. (Repeat step 2 for **n, o, c,** and **th.** Remember to move quickly to end of arrow if there is no ball on arrow for sound.)

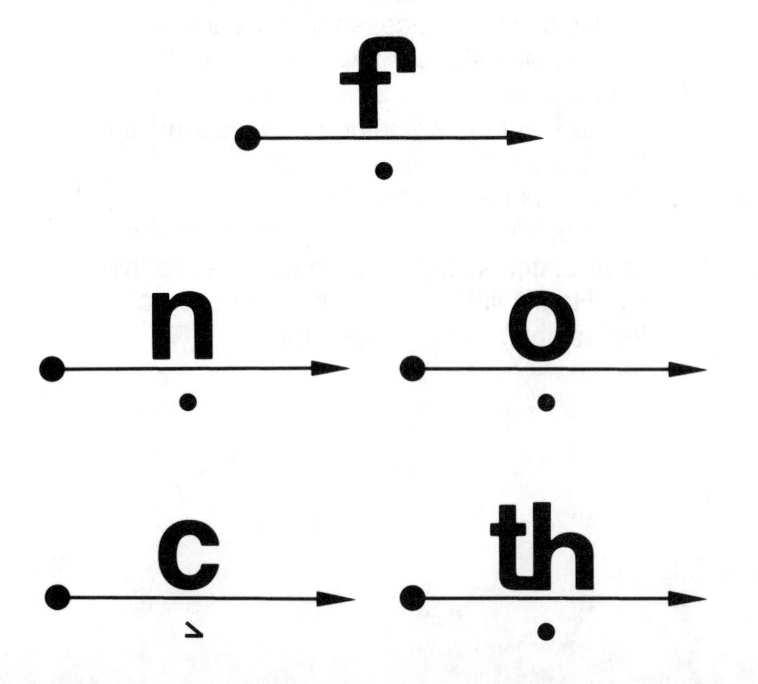

TASK 3 WORD READING

1. (Point to **fan, fin,** and **fun.**) We're going to do something new today. (Touch first ball for **fan.**) First sound it out. (Touch balls for sounds.) "fffaaannn." What word? "fan." Yes, **fan.**
2. (Return to first ball.) You're going to read this word the fast way. But first I'm going to move my finger down the arrow three times. Take a good look at the sounds and see if you can remember this word. But don't say the sounds out loud until you read it the fast way. (Move down arrow three times, stopping at each ball. Return to first ball.) Read it the fast way. (Slide.) "fan." Yes, **fan.** Good reading. (Repeat step 1, then step 2 if not firm.)
3. (Touch first ball for **fin.**) Sound it out. (Touch balls for sounds.) "fffiiinnn." What word? "fin." Yes, **fin.**
4. (Return to first ball.) I'm going to move my finger down the arrow three times. Then you're going to read the word the fast way. (Move down arrow three times, stopping at each ball. Return to first ball.) Read it the fast way. (Slide.) "fin." Yes, **fin.** Good reading.
5. (Touch first ball for **fun.**) Sound it out. (Touch balls for sounds.) "fffuuunnn." What word? "fun." Yes, **fun.**
6. (Return to first ball.) I'm going to move my finger down the arrow three times. Then you're going to read the word the fast way. (Move down arrow three times, stopping at each ball. Return to first ball.) Read it the fast way. (Slide.) "fun." Yes, **fun.** Good reading.

fan

fin

fun

TASK 4 WORD READING

1. Here are some more words. (Touch first ball for **run.**) Sound it out. (Touch balls for sounds.) "rrruuunnn." (Repeat until firm.) What word? "run."
2. (Touch first ball for **ēat.**) Sound it out. (Touch balls for sounds.) "ēēēt." (Repeat until firm.) What word? "eat."
3. (Touch first ball for **that.**) Sound it out. (Touch balls for sounds.) "thththaaat." (Repeat until firm.) What word? "that."
4. (Touch first ball for **rod.**) Sound it out. (Touch balls for sounds.) "rrroood." (Repeat until firm.) What word? "rod."
5. (Touch first ball for **if.**) Sound it out. (Touch balls for sounds.) "iiifff." (Repeat until firm.) What word? "if."
6. (Touch first ball for **and.**) Sound it out. (Touch balls for sounds.) "aaannnd." (Repeat until firm.) What word? "and."

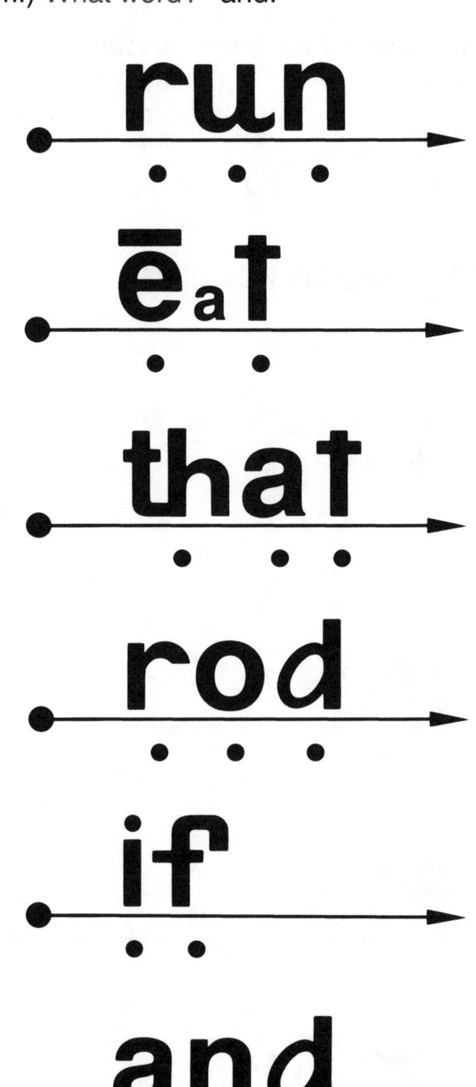

TASK 5 SOUNDS

1. Take a good look at each sound. Say it slowly if you can. Don't get fooled.
2. (Touch first ball for **n.**) Get ready. (Quickly move to second ball. Hold.) "nnn."
3. (Repeat step 2 for **u, i, a, s,** and **m.**)

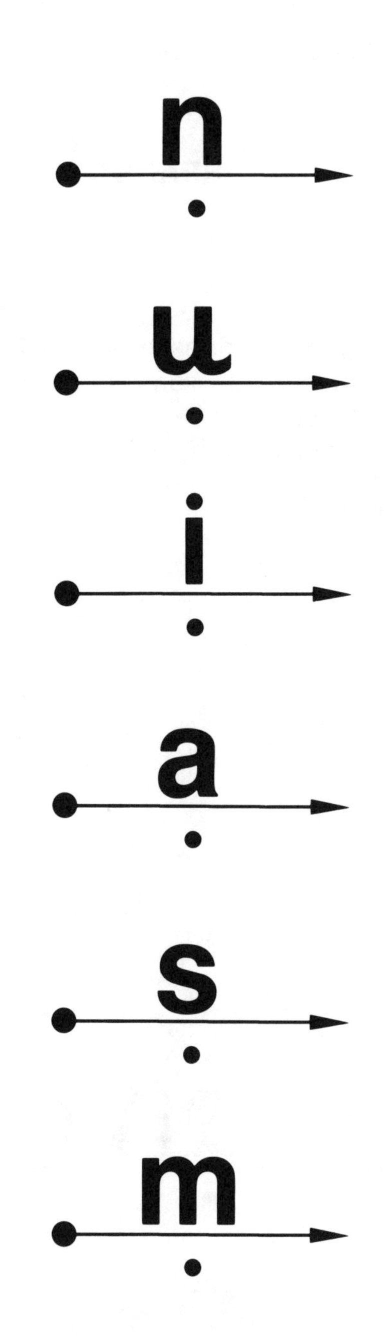

TASK 6 FIRST READING

1. Now you're going to read the story. Finger on the ball of the top line. Sound out the first word. (Child touches under and says:) "aaannn." What word? "an."
2. Sound out the next word. (Child touches under and says:) "aaannnt." What word? "ant."
3. (Repeat step 2 for remaining words in story.)

TASK 7 SECOND READING

1. This time you read the story again and I'll ask questions. Touch the ball on the top line and get ready to read the words. (Repeat steps from first reading for each word. Ask following comprehension questions after child has read indicated sentences.)
2.

(After child has read:)	(You say:)
"An ant is fat."	Tell me about the ant.
"It can sit and eat."	Yes, it's fat.
	What can this ant do?
	It must be a funny ant.

TASK 8 PICTURE COMPREHENSION

1. What will you see in the picture?
2. Look at the picture and get ready to answer some questions.
3. Is the ant fat?
4. What is it sitting on?
5. And what is it eating? Maybe that's why it's so fat.
6. What would you eat if you were an ant?

TASK 9 READING THE FAST WAY

1. Let's read this story the fast way. (Touch under **and.**) This word is (pause) **and.** (Touch under **ēat.**) This word is (pause) **eat.**
2. (Point to **and.**) What are you going to say when I touch this word? "and." (Point to **ēat.**) What are you going to say when I touch this word? "eat." (Repeat until firm.)
3. My turn. (Point to **it.** Pause two seconds.) **it.** (Point to **can.** Pause two seconds.) **can.** (Point to **sit.** Pause two seconds.) **sit.**
4. Your turn. (Touch under words as child says "and . . . eat.")
5. (Repeat steps 1–4 until firm.)

TASK 10 WORD FINDING

1. Now get ready to find the words I say.
2. Find the word (pause) **an. an.**
3. (Repeat step 2 for **fat, an, ant, an, fat, ant, fat, ant, an.**)
4. Good finding those words.

an ▪ ant ▪ is

fat. it ▪ can

sit ▪ and ▪ ēat.

TASK 11 SOUNDS WRITING

1. Here's the first sound you're going to write. (Write **o** at beginning of first line. Point to **o.**) What sound? "ooo."
2. First trace the **ooo** that I made. Then make more of them on this line. (After tracing **o** several times, child is to make three to five **o**'s. Help child if necessary. For acceptable letters say:) Good writing **ooo.**
3. Here's the next sound you're going to write. (Write **c** at beginning of second line. Point to **c.**) What sound? "c."
4. First trace the **c** that I made Then make more of them on this line. (After tracing **c** several times, child is to make three to five **c**'s. Help child if necessary. For acceptable letters say:) Good writing **c.**

LESSON 28

TASK 1 SOUNDS

1. Take a good look at each sound. Say it slowly if you can. Don't get fooled.
2. (Touch ball for **d.**) Get ready. (Quickly move to end of arrow.) "d."
3. (Repeat step 2 for **u, n, f, c,** and **th.** Remember to move quickly to end of arrow if there is no ball on arrow for sound.)

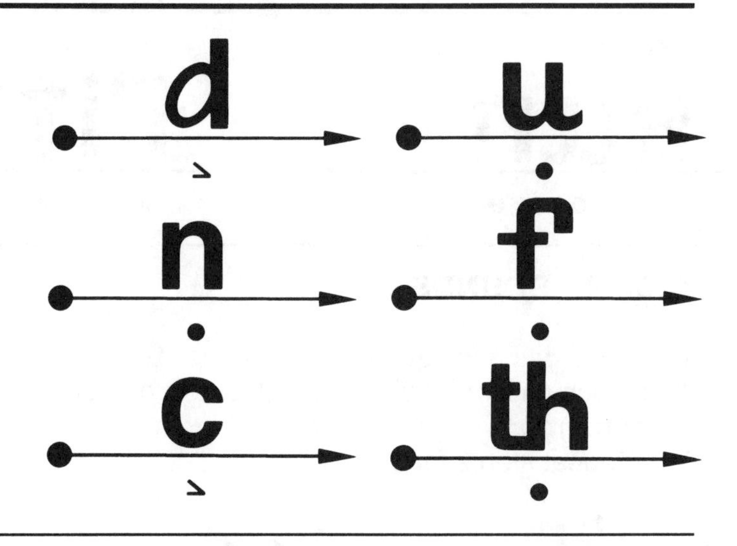

TASK 2 WORD READING

1. Now you're going to read these words. (Touch first ball for **ant.**) Sound it out. (Touch balls for sounds.) "aaannnt." What word? "ant." Yes, **ant.**
2. (Return to first ball.) You're going to read this word the fast way. But first I'm going to move my finger down the arrow three times. Take a good look at the sounds and see if you can remember this word. But don't say the sounds out loud until you read it the fast way. (Move down arrow three times, stopping at each ball. Return to first ball.) Read it the fast way. (Slide.) "ant." Yes, **ant.** Good reading. (Repeat step 1, then step 2 if not firm.)
3. (Touch first ball for **fun.**) Sound it out. (Touch balls for sounds.) "fffuuunnn." What word? "fun." Yes, **fun.**
4. (Return to first ball.) I'm going to move my finger down the arrow three times. Then you're going to read the word the fast way. (Move down arrow three times, stopping at each ball. Return to first ball.) Read it the fast way. (Slide.) "fun." Yes, **fun.** Good reading.
5. (Touch first ball for **fat.**) Sound it out (Touch balls for sounds.) "fffaaat." What word? "fat." Yes, **fat.**
6. (Return to first ball.) I'm going to move my finger down the arrow three times. Then you're going to read the word the fast way. (Move down arrow three times, stopping at each ball. Return to first ball.) Read it the fast way. (Slide.) "fat." Yes, **fat.** Good reading.

ant **fun** **fat**

TASK 3 WORD READING

1. (Touch first ball for **in.**) Sound it out. (Touch balls for sounds.) "iiinnn." (Repeat until firm.) What word? "in."
2. (Touch first ball for **at.**) Sound it out. (Touch balls for sounds.) "aaat." (Repeat until firm.) What word? "at."
3. (Touch first ball for **on.**) Sound it out. (Touch balls for sounds.) "ooonnn." (Repeat until firm.) What word? "on."
4. (Touch first ball for **mud.**) Sound it out. (Touch balls for sounds.) "mmmuuud." (Repeat until firm.) What word? "mud."
5. (Touch first ball for **sun.**) Sound it out. (Touch balls for sounds.) "sssuuunnn." (Repeat until firm.) What word? "sun."
6. (Touch first ball for **fit.**) Sound it out. (Touch balls for sounds.) "fffiiit." (Repeat until firm.) What word? "fit."
7. (Touch first ball for **fēēd.**) Sound it out. (Touch balls for sounds.) "fffēēēd." (Repeat until firm.) What word? "feed."

TASK 4 SOUNDS

1. You're going to say all these sounds fast.
2. (Touch ball for **ē.**) Say it fast. (Move to end of arrow.) "ē."
3. (Repeat step 2 for each sound.)

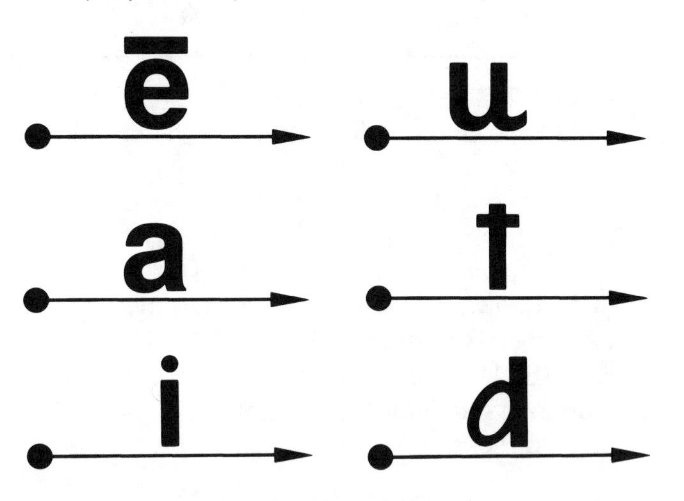

TASK 5 FIRST READING

1. Now you're going to read the story. Finger on the ball of the top line. Sound out the first word. What word? "uh."
2. Sound out the next word. (Child touches under and says:) "sssoook." What word? "sock."
3. (Repeat step 2 for remaining words in story.)

TASK 6 SECOND READING

1. This time you read the story again and I'll ask questions. Touch the ball on the top line and get ready to read the words. (Repeat steps from first reading for each word. Ask following comprehension questions after child has read indicated sentences.)
2. (After child has read:) (You say:)

(After child has read:)	(You say:)
"A sock is in the sun."	Where is the sock?
"The sock is on me."	The person in the picture will be saying

TASK 7 PICTURE COMPREHENSION

1. What will you see in the picture?
2. What will the person be wearing?
3. Look at the picture and get ready to answer some questions.
4. Where is the woman in this picture?
5. Show me the sun. Show me the sock.
6. Why do you suppose she's wearing only one sock?

a ▪ sock ▪ is
in ▪ thē ▪ sun.
thē ▪ sock ▪ is
on ▪ mē.

TASK 8 READING THE FAST WAY

1. Let's read this story the fast way. (Touch under **on.**) This word is (pause) **on.** (Touch under **me.**) This word is (pause) **me.**
2. (Point to **on.**) What are you going to say when I touch this word? "on." (Point to **me.**) What are you going to say when I touch this word? "me." (Repeat until firm.)

3. My turn. (Point to **the.** Pause two seconds.) **the.** (Point to **sock.** Pause two seconds.) **sock.** (Point to **is.** Pause two seconds.) **is.**
4. Your turn. (Touch under words as child says:) "on . . . me."
5. (Repeat steps 1–4 until firm.)

TASK 9 WORD FINDING

1. Now get ready to find the words I say.
2. Find the word (pause) **on. on.**
3. (Repeat step 2 for **on, in, sun, in, on, sun, on, in, on.**)
4. Good finding those words.

TASK 10 SOUNDS WRITING

1. Here's the first sound you're going to write. (Write **n** at beginning of first line. Point to **n.**) What sound? "nnn."
2. First trace the **nnn** that I made. Then make more of them on this line. (After tracing **n** several times, child is to make three to five **n**'s. Help child if necessary. For acceptable letters say:) Good writing **n.**
3. Here's the next sound you're going to write. (Write **ē** at beginning of second line. Point to **ē.**) What sound? "ēēē."
4. First trace the **ēēē** that I made. Then make more of them on this line. (After tracing **ē** several times, child is to make three to five **ē**'s. Help child if necessary. For acceptable letters say:) Good writing **ēēē.**

LESSON 29

TASK 1 SOUNDS INTRODUCTION

1. (Point to **l.**) Here's a new sound. I'm going to touch under this sound and say the sound. (Touch first ball of arrow. Move quickly to second ball. Hold.) **lll.**
2. Your turn to say the sound when I touch under it. (Touch first ball.) Get ready. (Move quickly to second ball. Hold.) "lll."

(**To correct** child saying a wrong sound or not responding:) The sound is **lll.** (Repeat step 2.)

3. (Touch first ball.) Again. Get ready. (Move quickly to second ball. Hold.) "lll."

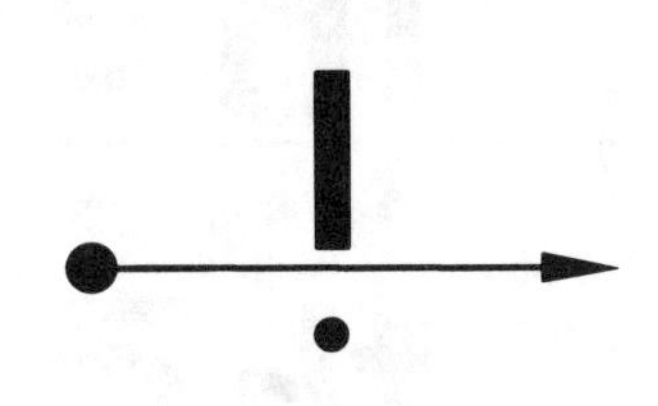

TASK 2 SOUNDS

1. Take a good look at each sound. Say it slowly if you can. Don't get fooled.
2. (Touch first ball for **f.**) Get ready. (Quickly move to second ball. Hold.) "fff."
3. (Repeat step 2 for **u, n, i, o,** and **c.** Remember to move quickly to end of arrow if there is no ball on arrow for sound.)

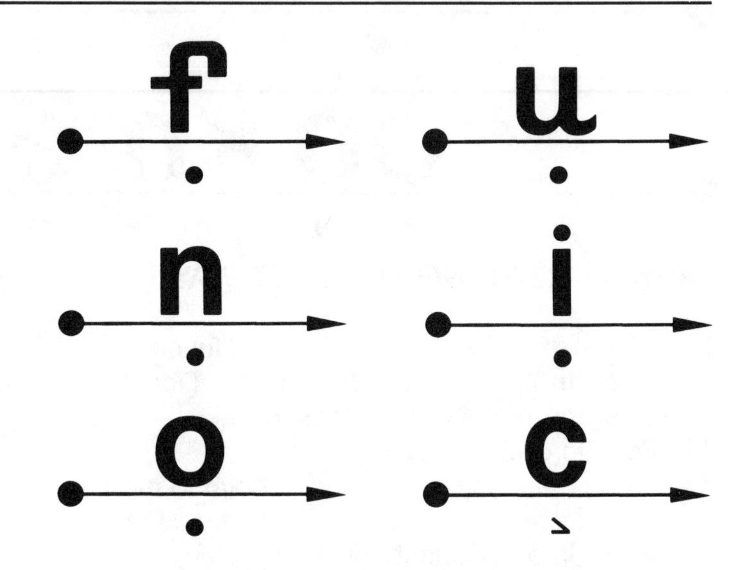

TASK 3 WORD READING

1. Here are the words you're going to read. (Touch first ball for **nut.**) Sound it out. (Touch balls for sounds.) "nnnuuut." What word? "nut." Yes, **nut.**
2. (Return to first ball.) You're going to read this word the fast way. But first I'm going to move my finger down the arrow three times. Take a good look at the sounds and see if you can remember this word. But don't say the sounds out loud until you read it the fast way. (Move down arrow three times, stopping at each ball. Return to first ball.) Read it the fast way. (Slide.) "nut." Yes, **nut.** Good reading. (Repeat step 1, then step 2 if not firm.)
3. (Touch first ball for **not.**) Sound it out. (Touch balls for sounds.) "nnnooot." What word? "not." Yes, **not.**
4. (Return to first ball.) I'm going to move my finger down the arrow three times. Then you're going to read the word the fast way. (Move down arrow three times, stopping at each ball. Return to first ball.) Read it the fast way. (Slide.) "not." Yes, **not.** Good reading.
5. (Touch first ball for **fēēt.**) Sound it out. (Touch balls for sounds.) "fffēēēt." What word? "feet." Yes, **feet.**
6. (Return to first ball.) I'm going to move my finger down the arrow three times. Then you're going to read the word the fast way. (Move down arrow three times, stopping at each ball. Return to first ball.) Read it the fast way. (Slide.) "feet." Yes, **feet.** Good reading.

nut not fēēt

TASK 4 WORD READING

1. (Touch first ball for **sēēd.**) Sound it out. (Touch balls for sounds.) "sssēēēd." (Repeat until firm.) What word? "seed."
2. (Touch first ball for **run.**) Sound it out. (Touch balls for sounds.) "rrruuunnn." (Repeat until firm.) What word? "run."
3. (Touch first ball for **fin.**) Sound it out. (Touch balls for sounds.) "fffiiinnn." (Repeat until firm.) What word? "fin."
4. (Touch first ball for **sun.**) Sound it out. (Touch balls for sounds.) "sssuuunnn." (Repeat until firm.) What word? "sun."
5. (Touch first ball for **mud.**) Sound it out. (Touch balls for sounds.) "mmmuuud." (Repeat until firm.) What word? "mud."
6. (Touch first ball for **it.**) Sound it out. (Touch balls for sounds.) "iiit." (Repeat until firm.) What word? "it."

run

fin

mud

it

TASK 5 SOUNDS

1. Take a good look at each sound. Say it slowly if you can. Don't get fooled.
2. (Touch first ball for **u.**) Get ready. (Quickly move to second ball. Hold.) "uuu."
3. (Repeat step 2 for **l, f, th, c,** and **o.** Remember to move quickly to end of arrow if there is no ball on arrow for sound.)

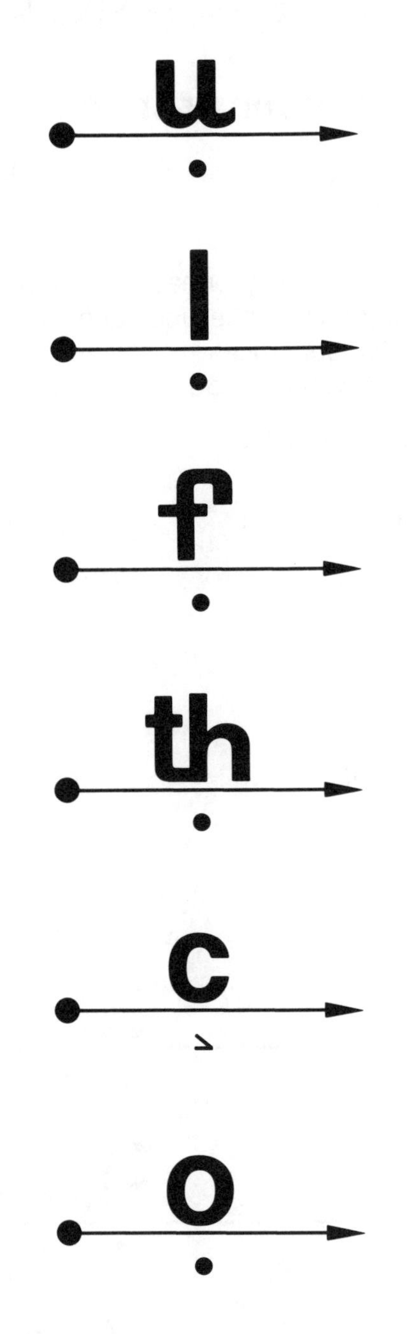

TASK 6 FIRST READING

1. Now you're going to read the story. Finger on the ball of the top line. Sound out the first word. (Child touches under and says:) "aaannn." What word? "an."
2. Sound out the next word. (Child touches under and says:) "aaannnt." What word? "ant."
3. (Repeat step 2 for remaining words in story.)

TASK 7 SECOND READING

1. This time you read the story again and I'll ask questions. Touch the ball on the top line and get ready to read the words. (Repeat steps from first reading for each word. Ask following comprehension questions after child has read indicated sentences.)
2. (After child has read:) (You say:)

(After child has read:)	(You say:)
"An ant can eat a seed."	Tell me what an ant can do.
"That seed is in the mud."	Where is that seed?

TASK 8 PICTURE COMPREHENSION

1. What will you see in the picture?
2. Where will the seed be?
3. Look at the picture and get ready to answer some questions.
4. Where is the seed?
5. Where is the ant sitting?
6. What is that ant doing? Yes, eating the seed.
7. Would you eat something that was covered with mud?

TASK 9 READING THE FAST WAY

1. Let's read this story the fast way. (Touch under **the.**) This word is (pause) **the.** (Touch under **mud.**) This word is (pause) **mud.**
2. (Point to **the.**) What are you going to say when I touch this word? "the." (Point to **mud.**) What are you going to say when I touch this word? "mud." (Repeat until firm.)
3. My turn. (Point to **that.** Pause two seconds.) **that.**
   (Point to **seed.** Pause two seconds.) **seed.**
   (Point to **is.** Pause two seconds.) **is.**
   (Point to **in.** Pause two seconds.) **in.**
4. Your turn. (Touch under words as child says:) "the . . . mud."
5. (Repeat steps 1–4 until firm.)

TASK 10 WORD FINDING

1. Now get ready to find the words I say.
2. Find the word (pause) **an. an.**
3. (Repeat step 2 for **can, an, seed, an, can, seed, can, an, seed.**)
4. Good finding those words.

an · ant · can

ēat · a · sēēd.

that · sēēd · is

in · thē · mud.

TASK 11 SOUNDS WRITING

1. (Write **u** at beginning of first line. Point to **u.**) What sound? "uuu."
2. First trace the **uuu** that I made. Then make more of them on this line. (After tracing **u** several times, child is to make three to five **u**'s. Help child if necessary. For each acceptable letter say:) Good writing **uuu.**
3. Here's the next sound you're going to write. (Write **n** at beginning of second line. Point to **n.**) What sound? "nnn."
4. First trace the **nnn** that I made. Then make more of them on this line. (After tracing **n** several times, child is to make three to five **n**'s. Help child if necessary. For acceptable letters say:) Good writing **nnn.**

LESSON 30

TASK 1 SOUNDS

1. Take a good look at each sound. Say it slowly if you can. Don't get fooled.
2. (Touch first ball for **u.**) Get ready. (Quickly move to second ball. Hold.) "uuu."
3. (Repeat step 2 for **l, i, n, f,** and **o.**)

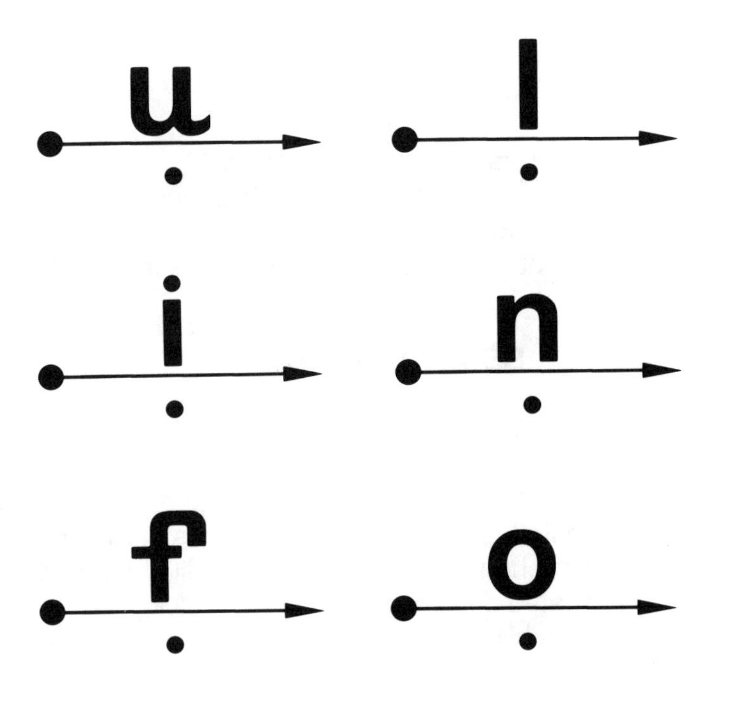

TASK 2 WORD READING

1. Now you get to read these words. (Touch first ball for **and.**) Sound it out. (Touch balls for sounds.) "aaannnd." What word? "and." Yes, **and.**
2. (Return to first ball.) You're going to read this word the fast way. But first I'm going to move my finger down the arrow three times. Take a good look at the sounds and see if you can remember this word. But don't say the sounds out loud until you read it the fast way. (Move down arrow three times, stopping at each ball. Return to first ball.) Read it the fast way. (Slide.) "and."Yes, **and.** Good reading. (Repeat step 1, then step 2 if not firm.)
3. (Touch first ball for **sand.**) Sound it out. (Touch balls for sounds.) "sssaaannnd." What word? "sand." Yes, **sand.**
4. (Return to first ball.) I'm going to move my finger down the arrow three times. Then you're going to read the word the fast way. (Move down arrow three times, stopping at each ball. Return to first ball.) Read it the fast way. (Slide.) "sand." Yes, **sand.** Good reading.

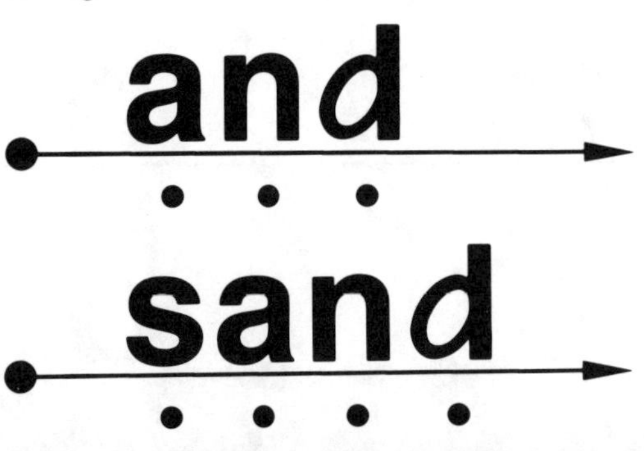

5. (Touch first ball for **land.**) Sound it out. (Touch balls for sounds.) "lllaaannnd." What word? "land." Yes, **land.**
6. (Return to first ball.) I'm going to move my finger down the arrow three times. Then you're going to read the word the fast way. (Move down arrow three times, stopping at each ball. Return to first ball.) Read it the fast way. (Slide.) "land." Yes. **land.** Good reading.

TASK 3 WORD READING

1. (Touch first ball for **little.**) Sound it out. (Touch balls for sounds.) "llliiitlll." (Repeat until firm.) What word? "little."
2. (Touch first ball for **fill.**) Sound it out. (Touch balls for sounds.) "fffiiilll." (Repeat until firm.) What word? "fill."
3. (Touch first ball for **lot.**) Sound it out. (Touch balls for sounds.) "lllooot." (Repeat until firm.) What word? "lot."
4. (Touch first ball for **lid.**) Sound it out. (Touch balls for sounds.) "llliiid." (Repeat until firm.) What word? "lid."
5. (Touch first ball for **sick.**) Sound it out. (Touch balls for sounds.) "sssiiik." (Repeat until firm.) What word? "sick."
6. (Touch first ball for **lick.**) Sound it out. (Touch balls for sounds.) "llliiik." (Repeat until firm.) What word? "lick."

TASK 4 SOUNDS

1. You're going to say all these sounds fast.
2. (Touch ball for **i.**) Say it fast. (Move to end of arrow.) "i."
3. (Repeat step 2 for each sound.)

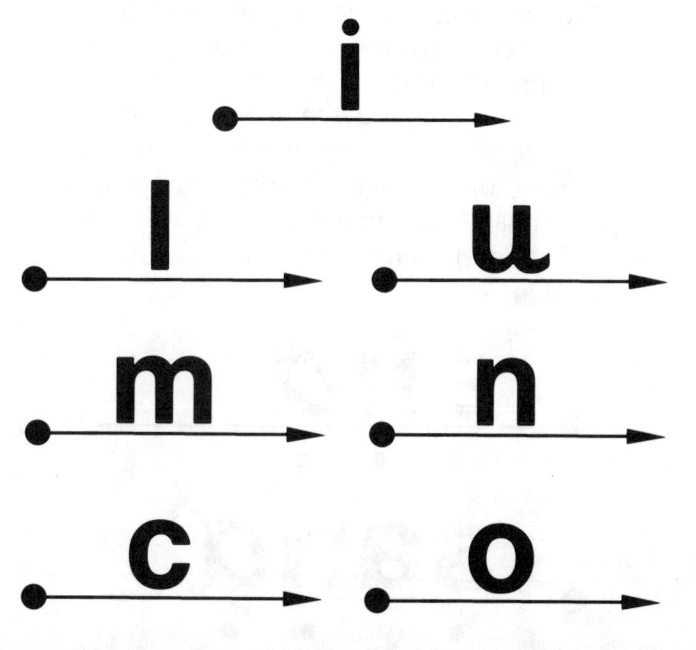

TASK 5 FIRST READING

1. Now you're going to read the story. Finger on the ball of the top line. Sound out the first word. (Child touches under and says:) "thththiiisss." What word? "this."
2. Sound out the next word. (Child touches under and says:) "iiisss." What word? "is."
3. (Repeat step 2 for remaining words in story.)

TASK 6 SECOND READING

1. This time you read the story again and I'll ask questions. Touch the ball on the top line and get ready to read the words. (Repeat steps from first reading for each word. Ask following comprehension questions after child has read indicated sentences.)
2. (After child has read:) (You say:)

(After child has read:)	(You say:)
"This is a cat."	What is this?
"The cat can run."	What can the cat do?
"Mud is on the cat."	What is on the cat?

this · is · a · cat.

thē · cat · can

run. mud · is

on · thē · cat.

TASK 7 PICTURE COMPREHENSION

1. What will you see in the picture?
2. What is this cat going to look like? Right, we know he can run and we know he has mud on him.
3. Look at the picture and get ready to answer some questions.
4. What is that cat doing?
5. What's that stuff all over the cat?
6. Where could that cat be going?
7. Do you think the man will let him into the house?
8. What would you do if you were that man?

TASK 8 READING THE FAST WAY

1. Let's read this story the fast way. (Touch under **the.**) This word is (pause) **the.** (Touch under **cat.**) This word is (pause) **cat.**
2. (Point to **the.**) What are you going to say when I touch this word? "the." (Point to **cat.**) What are you going to say when I touch this word? "cat." (Repeat until firm.)
3. My turn. (Point to **mud.** Pause two seconds.) **mud.** (Point to **is.** Pause two seconds.) **is.** (Point to **on.** Pause two seconds.) **on.**
4. Your turn. (Touch under words as child says:) "the . . . cat."
5. (Repeat steps 1–4 until firm.)

TASK 9 WORD FINDING

1. Now get ready to find the words I say.
2. Find the word (pause) **the. the.**
3. (Repeat step 2 for **this, run, the, run, this, the, this, the, run.**)
4. Good finding those words.

TASK 10 SOUNDS WRITING

1. Here's the first sound you're going to write. (Write **u** at beginning of first line. Point to **u.**) What sound? "uuu."
2. First trace the **uuu** that I made. Then make more of them on this line. (After tracing **u** several times, child is to make three to five **u**'s. Help child if necessary. For acceptable letters say:) Good writing **uuu.**
3. Here's the next sound you're going to write. (Write **f** at beginning of second line. Point to **f.**) What sound? "fff."
4. First trace the **fff** that I made. Then make more of them on this line. (After tracing **f** several times, child is to make three to five **f**'s. Help child if necessary. For acceptable letters say:) Good writing **fff.**

LESSON 31

TASK 1 SOUNDS INTRODUCTION

1. (Point to **w.**) Here's a new sound. I'm going to touch under this sound and say the sound. (Touch first ball of arrow. Move quickly to second ball. Hold.) **www.**
2. Your turn to say the sound when I touch under it. (Touch first ball.) Get ready. (Move quickly to second ball. Hold.) "www."

> **To correct** child saying a wrong sound or not responding:) The sound is **www.** (Repeat step 2.)

3. (Touch first ball.) Again. Get ready. (Move quickly to second ball. Hold.) "www."

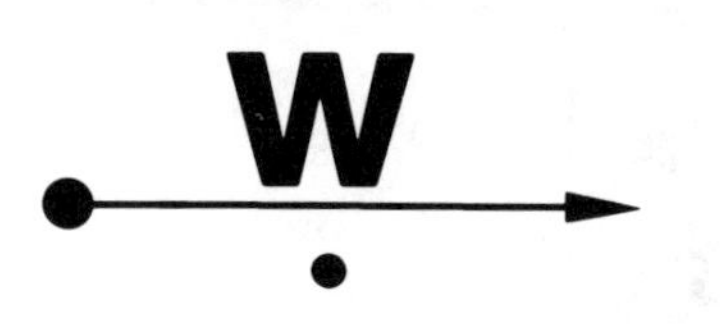

TASK 2 SOUNDS

1. Take a good look at each sound. Say it slowly if you can. Don't get fooled.
2. (Touch first ball for **l.**) Get ready (Quickly move to second ball. Hold.) "lll."
3. (Repeat step 2 for **n, i, m,** and **f.** Remember to move quickly to end of arrow if there is no ball on arrow for sound.)

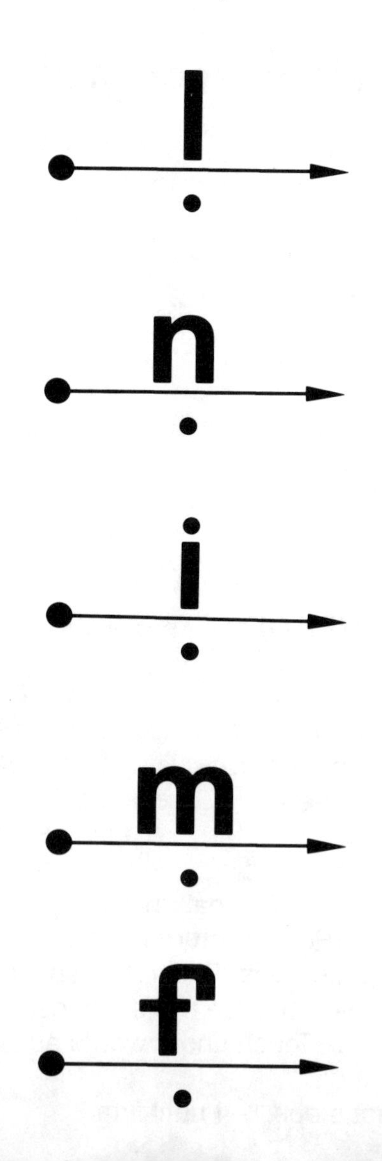

TASK 3 WORD READING

1. Now you're going to read these words. (Touch first ball for **lock.**) Sound it out. (Touch balls for sounds.) "Illoook." (Repeat until firm.) What word? "lock."
2. (Repeat step 1 for **and, sand, fun, luck, sun, little,** and **lick.**)

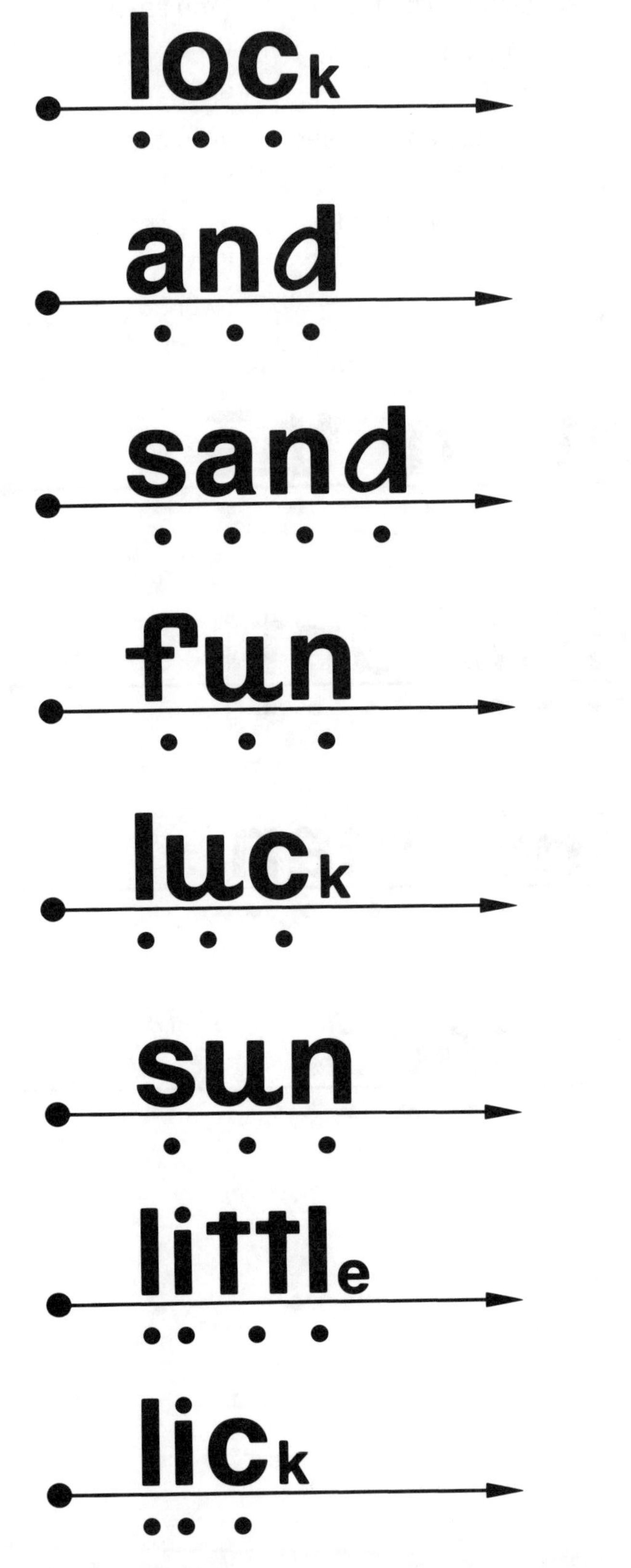

TASK 4 WORD READING

1. Now you get to read all the words on this page the fast way.
2. (Touch the first ball for **lock.**) I'll go down the arrow one time and touch the sounds. Figure out the word. But don't say anything out loud until I tell you to read the fast way.
3. (Go down arrow, stopping at each ball. Return to first ball.) Read it the fast way. (Slide.) "lock." Yes, **lock.**
4. (Repeat step 3 for each remaining word on page.)

> (**To correct** if child misidentifies a word—for example, **lock:**) (Touch first ball for **lock.**) Sound it out. (Touch balls for sounds.) "Illoook." What word? "lock." Yes, **lock.** Remember that word, because I'm going to come back to it after you do the rest of the words on this page. (Return to any words that were missed.)

TASK 5 SOUNDS

1. Take a good look at each sound. Say it slowly if you can. Don't get fooled.
2. (Touch first ball for **l.**) Get ready. (Quickly move to second ball. Hold.) "lll."
3. (Repeat step 2 for **w, u, a, i,** and **ē.** Remember to move quickly to end of arrow if there is no ball on arrow for sound.)

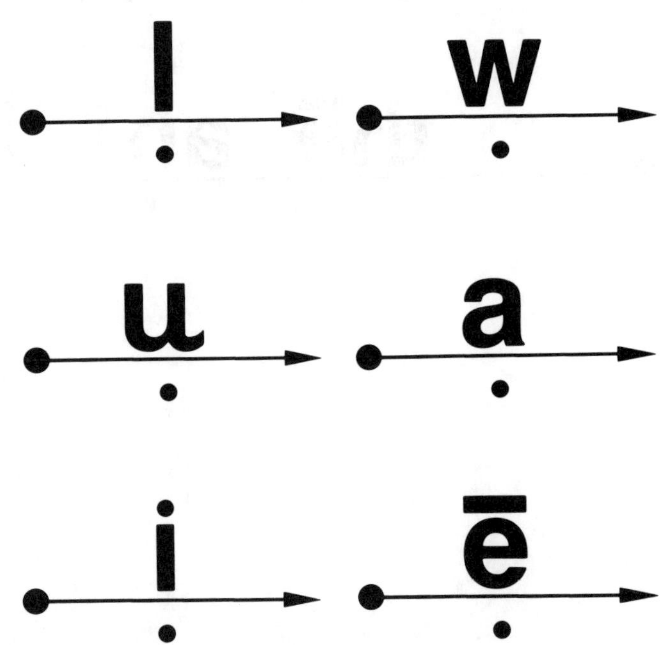

TASK 6 WORD FINDING

1. Look at the story. There are no boxes between the words. But you can see the words. Touch the first word.
2. Touch the next word.
3. (Repeat step 2 for remaining words in story.)
4. Good touching the words.

TASK 7 FIRST READING

1. Now you're going to read the story. Finger on the ball of the top line. Touch under the first word. What word? "uh."
2. Sound out the next word. (Child touches under and says:) "mmmaaannn." What word? "man."
3. (Repeat step 2 for remaining words in story.)

TASK 8 SECOND READING

1. This time you read the story again and I'll ask questions. Touch the ball on the top line and get ready to read the words. (Repeat steps from first reading for each word. Ask following comprehension questions after child has read indicated sentences.)
2. (After child has read:) (You say:)

(After child has read:)	(You say:)
"A man sat in the sand."	Where did the man sit?
"A little ant can see the man."	Who can see the man?
"The ant is mad."	How does that ant feel?
	I wonder why the ant is mad.

a man sat in thē

sand. a little ant

can sēē thē man.

thē ant is mad.

TASK 9 PICTURE COMPREHENSION

1. What will you see in the picture?
2. We know the ant is little. What else do we know about him?
3. Look at the picture and get ready to answer some questions.
4. What do we call that thing the man is sitting in? Yes, a sandbox where children play.
5. Why do you suppose the little ant is mad?
6. What do you think the ant will do?

TASK 10 READING THE FAST WAY

1. I'm going to read the first part of this story the fast way. Later, you'll get to read that part the fast way.
2. (Point to **a.** Pause.) **a.**
3. (Repeat step 2 for remaining words in first sentence: **man, sat, in, the,** and **sand.**)

TASK 11 WORD FINDING

1. Now get ready to find the words I say.
2. Find the word (pause) **man. man.**
3. (Repeat step 2 for **sat, a, man, a, sat, man, sat, man, a, man.**)
4. Good finding those words.

TASK 12 CHILD READS THE FAST WAY

1. Now it's your turn to read the first part of the story the fast way. Touch the first word and read it the fast way. Don't sound it out loud. Just figure it out to yourself and read it the fast way. (Allow child time to sound out each word silently.) "uh." Yes, **uh.**
2. Read the next word the fast way. (Allow child time to sound out silently.) "man." Yes, **man.**
3. (Repeat step 2 for **sat, in, the,** and **sand.**) Good reading the fast way.

(**To correct** if child misidentifies a word:) Sound it out. What word? . . . Good. Now start over. (Point to first word in sentence.) Take your time. See if you can read with no mistakes.

TASK 13 SOUNDS WRITING

1. (Write **l** at beginning of first line. Point to **l.**) What sound? "lll."
2. First trace the **lll** that I made. Then make more of them on this line. (After tracing **l** several times, child is to make three to five **l**'s. Help child if necessary. For each acceptable letter say:) Good writing **lll.**
3. Here's the next sound you're going to write. (Write **m** at beginning of second line. Point to **m.**) What sound? "mmm."
4. First trace the **mmm** that I made. Then make more of them on this line. (After tracing **m** several times, child is to make three to five **m**'s. Help child if necessary. For acceptable letters say:) Good writing **mmm.**

LESSON 32

TASK 1 SOUNDS

1. Take a good look at each sound. Say it slowly if you can. Don't get fooled.
2. (Touch first ball for **o.**) Get ready. (Quickly move to second ball. Hold.) "ooo."
3. (Repeat step 2 for **w, ē, a, i,** and **u.** Remember to move quickly to end of arrow if there is no ball on arrow for sound.)

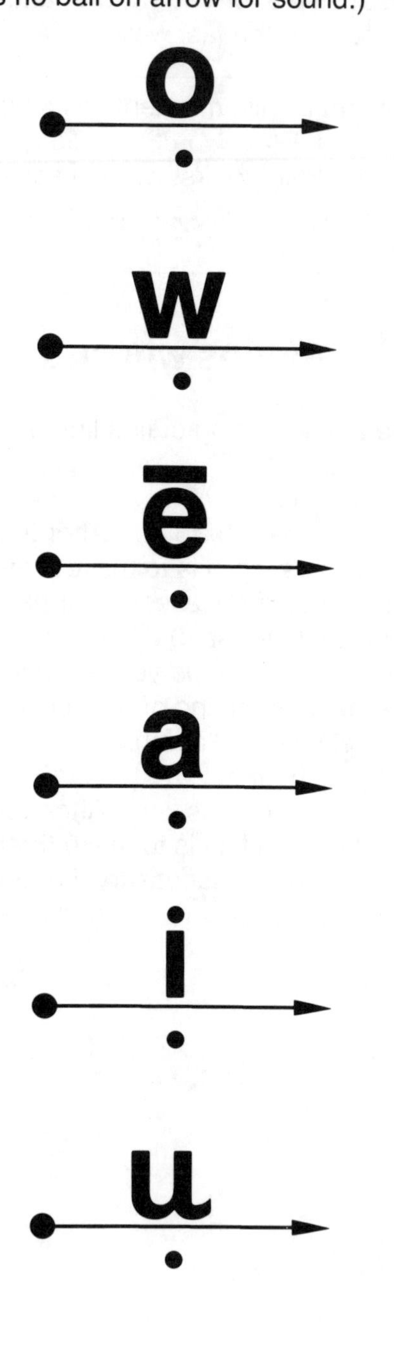

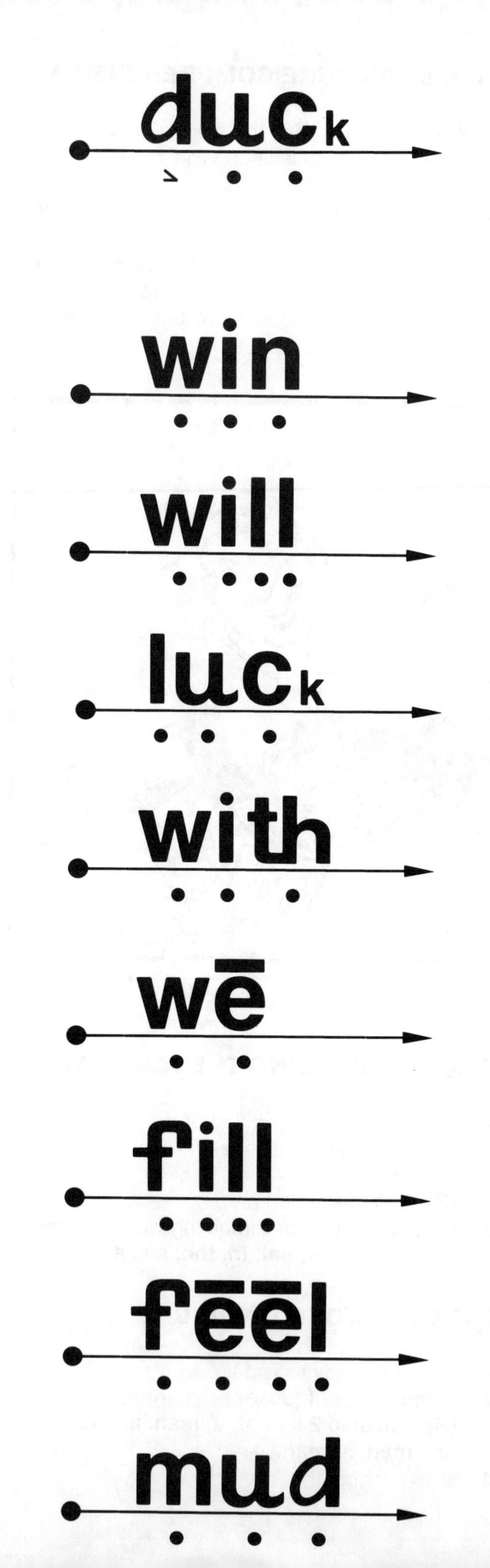

TASK 2 WORD READING

1. Here's a new word. You're going to sound out (slide under **u, c,** and **k**) this part. (Point to ball for **u.**) Get ready. (Touch balls for **u** and **c** as child says:) "uuuk." (Return to ball for **u.**) Say it fast. "uk." (Touch first ball for **duck.**) This word rhymes with (pause) **uk.** (Slide quickly to end of arrow.) "duck." (Return to first ball.) What word? (Slide quickly to end of arrow.) "duck."
2. (Point to arrow under **d.**) This arrow tells me that I can't stop under this sound. But you must say the sound with the next sound when I stop.
3. (Point to first ball for **duck.**) Sound out (pause) **duck.** Get ready. (Slide past **d.** Stop at balls for other sounds.) "duuuk."
4. (Demonstrate sounding out if response is not firm. Child should not stop between **d** and **uuu.** Then repeat step 3.) What word? "duck." Good reading.

TASK 3 WORD READING

1. (Touch first ball for **win.**) Sound it out. (Touch balls for sounds.) "wwwiiinnn." (Repeat until firm.) What word? "win."
2. (Repeat step 1 for **will, luck, with, we, fill, feel,** and **mud.**)

TASK 4 WORD READING

1. Now you get to read all the words on this page the fast way.
2. (Touch first ball for **duck.**) I'll go down the arrow one time and touch the sounds. Figure out the word. But don't say anything out loud until I tell you to read the fast way.
3. (Go down arrow, stopping at each ball. Return to first ball.) Read it the fast way. (Slide.) "duck." Yes, **duck.**
4. (Repeat step 3 for each remaining word on page.)

(**To correct** if child misidentifies a word—for example, **duck:**) (Touch first ball for **duck.**) Sound it out. (Touch balls for sounds.) "duuuk." What word? "duck." Yes, **duck.** Remember that word, because I'm going to come back to it after you do the rest of the words on this page. (Return to any words that were missed.)

TASK 5 SOUNDS

1. Take a good look at each sound. Say it slowly if you can. Don't get fooled.
2. (Touch first ball for **w.**) Get ready. (Quickly move to second ball. Hold.) "www."
3. (Repeat step 2 for **u, f, n, l,** and **th.** Remember to move quickly to end of arrow if there is no ball on arrow for sound.)

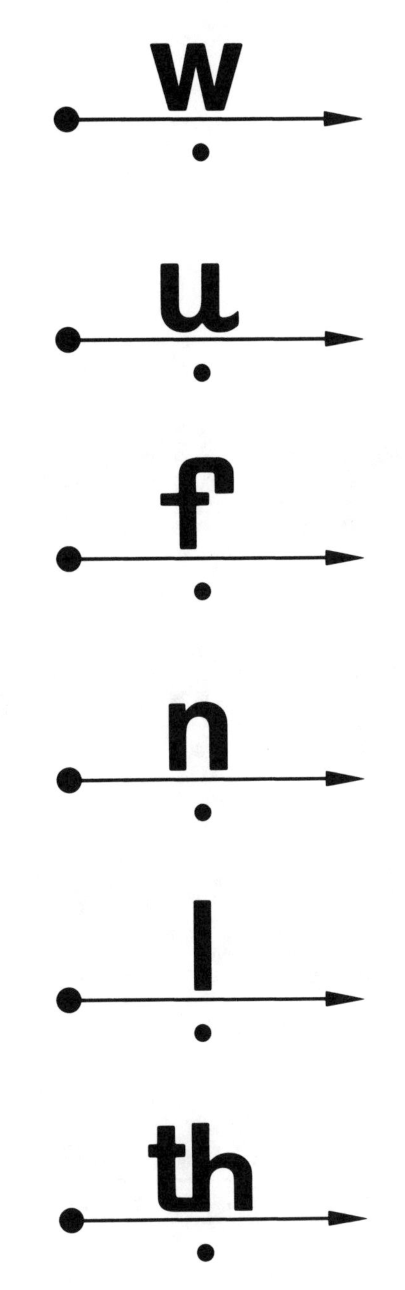

TASK 6 FIRST READING

1. Now you're going to read the story. Finger on the ball of the top line. Sound out the first word. (Child touches under and says:) "thththiiisss." What word? "this."
2. Sound out the next word. (Child touches under and says:) "llliiitlll." What word? "little."
3. (Repeat step 2 for remaining words in story.)

TASK 7 SECOND READING

1. This time you read the story again and I'll ask questions. Touch the ball on the top line and get ready to read the words. (Repeat steps from first reading for each word. Ask following comprehension questions below after child has read indicated sentences.)
2. (After child has read:) (You say:)

(After child has read:)	(You say:)
"This little cat can run in sand."	What can this little cat do?
"That little cat can sit on sand."	What else can that little cat do?
"See the feet."	What are you going to see?

this little cat can

run in sand. that

little cat can sit

on sand. see the feet.

TASK 8 PICTURE COMPREHENSION

1. What will you see in the picture?
2. What will that cat be doing?
3. Look at the picture and get ready to answer some questions.
4. What's that cat running in?
5. How many feet do you see?
6. What does the cat have on his feet?
7. Did you ever get sand on your feet?

TASK 9 READING THE FAST WAY

1. I'm going to read the first part of this story the fast way. Later, you'll get to read that part the fast way.
2. (Point to **this.** Pause.) **this.**
3. (Repeat step 2 for remaining words in first sentence: **little, cat, can, run, in,** and **sand.**)

TASK 10 WORD FINDING

1. You're going to find words that are in the top line of the story.
2. Find the word (pause) **little.**
3. (Repeat step 2 for **can, little, can, cat, little, can, cat.**)
4. Good finding those words.

TASK 11 CHILD READS THE FAST WAY

1. Now it's your turn to read the first part of the story the fast way. Touch the first word and read it the fast way. Don't sound it out aloud. Just figure it out to yourself and read it the fast way. "this."
2. Read the next word the fast way. "little."
3. (Repeat step 2 for **cat, can, run, in,** and **sand.**) Good reading the fast way.

TASK 12 SOUNDS WRITING

1. Here's the first sound you're going to write. (Write **o** at beginning of first line. Point to **o.**) What sound? "ooo."
2. First trace the **ooo** that I made. Then make more of them on this line. (After tracing **o** several times, child is to make three to five **o**'s. Help child if necessary. For acceptable letters say:) Good writing **ooo.**
3. Here's the next sound you're going to write. (Write **t** at beginning of second line. Point to **t.**) What sound? "t."
4. First trace the **t** that I made. Then make more of them on this line. (After tracing **t** several times, child is to make three to five **t**'s. Help child if necessary. For acceptable letters say:) Good writing **t.**

LESSON 33

TASK 1 SOUNDS INTRODUCTION

1. (Touch ball for **g.**) We always have to say this sound fast. My turn to say it fast. (Quickly move to end ot arrow as you say sound.) **g.**
2. My turn to say it fast again. (Touch ball for **g.**) Say it fast. (Quickly move to end of arrow.) **g.**
3. (Touch ball.) Your turn. (Pause.) Say it fast. (Quickly move to end of arrow.) "g."

(**To correct** if child says "guh," "gah," or "gih":) Listen: **g.** Say it fast. "g." Yes, **g.**

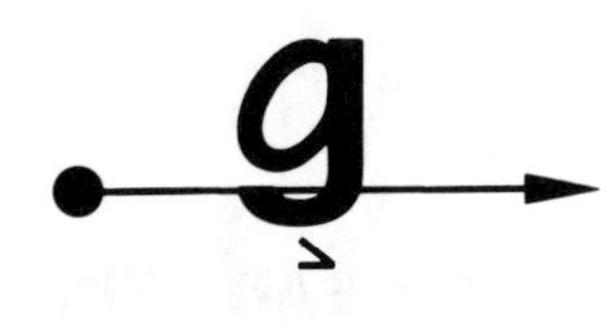

TASK 2 SOUNDS

1. Take a good look at each sound. Say it slowly if you can. Don't get fooled.
2. (Touch first ball for **w.**) Get ready. (Quickly move to second ball. Hold.) "www."
3. (Repeat step 2 for **g, i, a, o,** and **c.** Remember to move quickly to end of arrow if there is no ball on arrow for sound.)

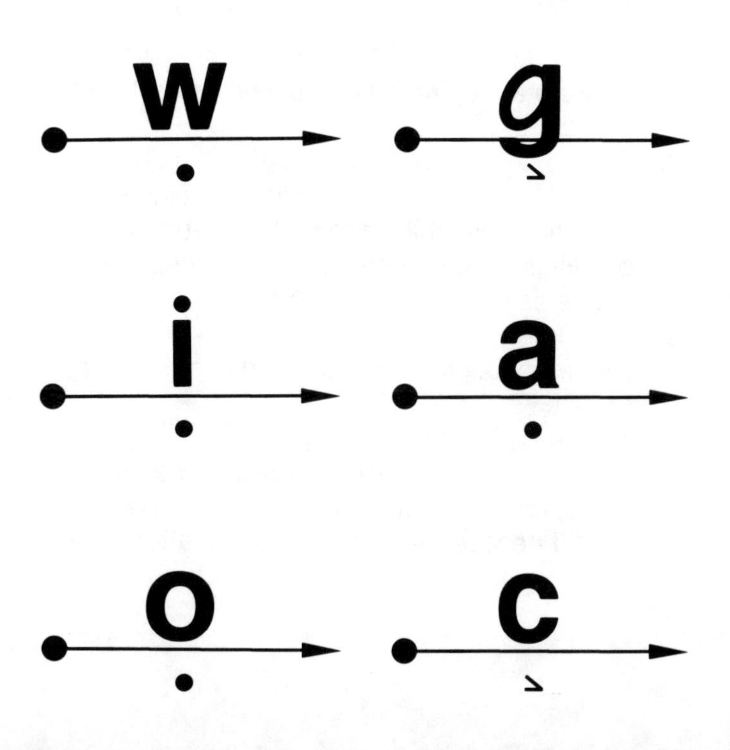

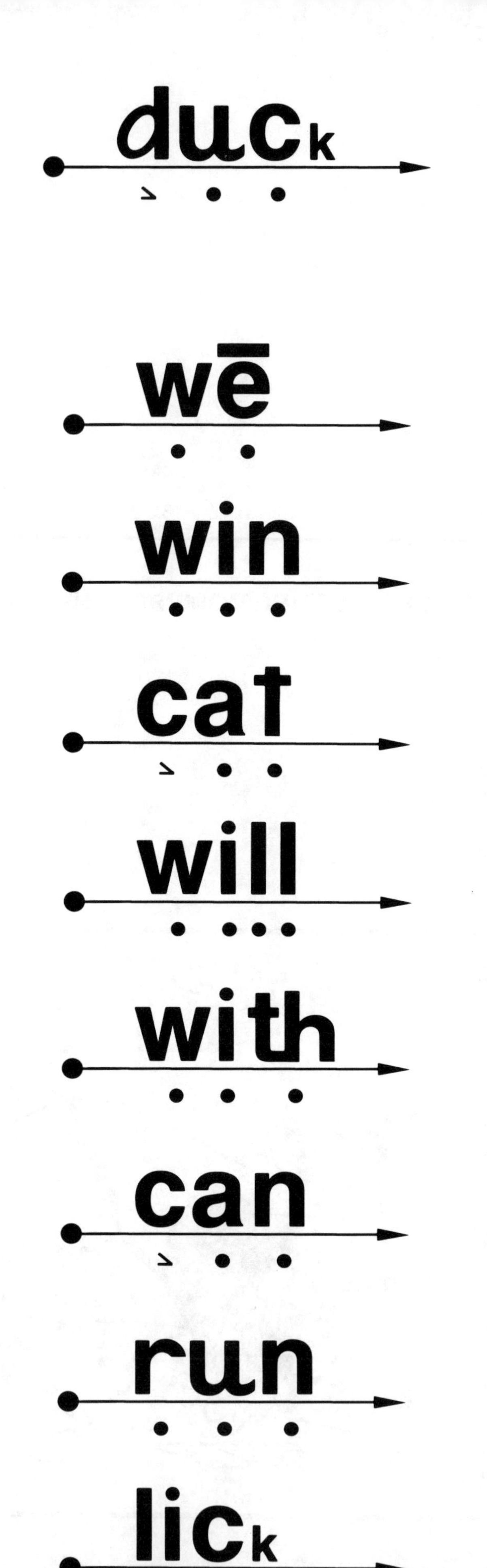

TASK 3 WORD READING

1. Look at this word. You're going to sound out (slide under **u, c,** and **k**) this part. (Point to ball for **u.**) Get ready. (Touch balls for **u, c,** and **k** as child says:) "uuuk." (Return to ball for **u.**) Say it fast. "uk." (Touch first ball for **duck.**) This word rhymes with (pause) **uk.** (Slide quickly to end of arrow.) "duck." What word? (Slide quickly to end of arrow.) "duck."
2. (Point to arrow under **d.**) This arrow tells me that I can't stop under this sound. But you must say the sound with the next sound when I stop.
3. (Point to first ball.) Sound out (pause) **duck.** Get ready. (Slide past **d.** Stop at balls for other sounds.) "duuuk."
4. (Demonstrate sounding out if response is not firm. Child should not stop between **d** and **uuu.** Then repeat step 3.) What word? "duck." Good reading.

TASK 4 WORD READING

1. (Touch first ball for **we.**) Sound it out. (Touch balls for sounds.) "wwwēēē." (Repeat until firm.) What word? "we."
2. (Repeat step 1 for **win, cat, will, with, can, run,** and **lick.**)

TASK 5 WORD READING

1. Now you get to read all the words on this page the fast way.
2. (Touch first ball for **duck.**) I'll go down the arrow one time and touch the sounds. Figure out the word. But don't say anything out loud until I tell you to read the fast way. (Go down arrow, stopping at each ball. Return to first ball.) Read it the fast way. (Slide.) "duck." Yes, **duck.**
3. (Repeat step 2 for each remaining word on page.)

TASK 6 SOUNDS

1. You're going to say all these sounds fast.
2. (Touch ball for **g.**) Say it fast. (Move to end of arrow.) "g."
3. (Repeat step 2 for each sound.)

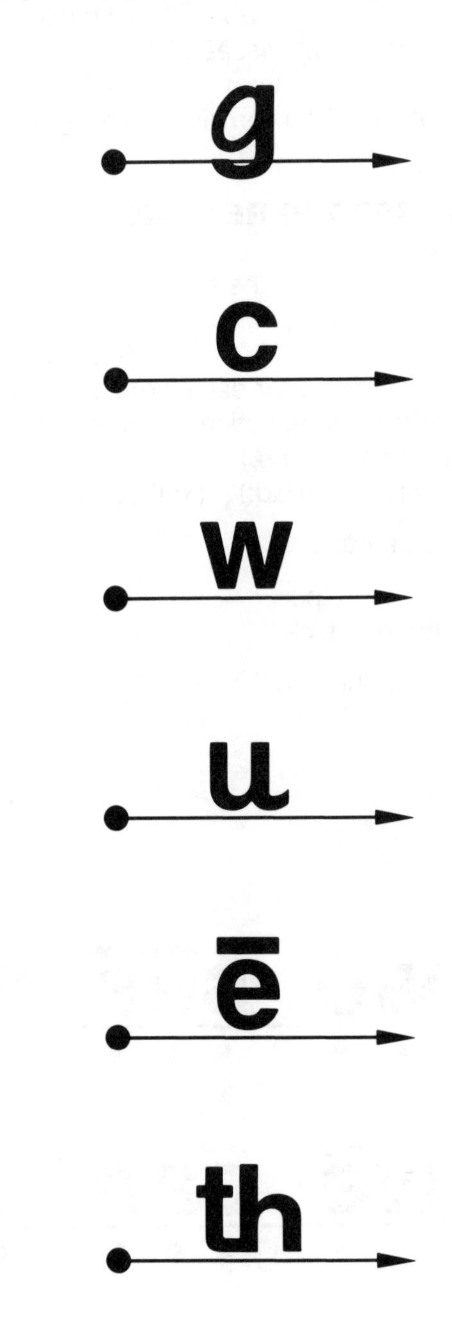

TASK 7 FIRST READING

1. Now you're going to read the story. Finger on the ball of the top line. Sound out the first word. **(Child touches under and says:)** "wwwēēē." What word? "we."
2. Sound out the next word. **(Child touches under and says:)** "sssēēē." What word? "see."
3. **(Repeat step 2 for remaining words in story.)**

TASK 8 SECOND READING

1. This time you read the story again and I'll ask questions. Touch the ball on the top line and get ready to read the words. **(Repeat steps from first reading for each word. Ask following comprehension questions after child has read indicated sentences.)**
2. **(After child has read:)** **(You say:)**

(After child has read:)	(You say:)
"We see a duck."	What do we see?
"We can sit in the sun with that duck."	What can we do with that duck?
"It is fun in the sun."	Where are we having fun?

TASK 9 PICTURE COMPREHENSION

1. What will you see in the picture? Yes, people and a duck.
2. What will the people be doing?
3. Look at the picture and get ready to answer some questions.
4. What are we doing in this picture? Yes, having a picnic.
5. Is a picnic fun?
6. Where is the duck?
7. What is that duck doing?
8. Did you ever have a picnic with a duck?

TASK 10 READING THE FAST WAY

1. I'm going to read the first part of this story the fast way. Later, you'll get to read that part the fast way.
2. **(Point to we. Pause.)** we.
3. **(Repeat step 2 for remaining words in first sentence: see, a, and duck.)**

TASK 11 WORD FINDING

1. You're going to find words that are in the top line of the story.
2. Find the word **(pause)** **we.**
3. **(Repeat step 2 for see, we, duck, see, duck, we, we.)**
4. Good finding those words.

wē sēē a duck.

wē can sit in thē

sun with that duck.

it is fun in thē sun.

LESSON 34

TASK 1 SOUNDS

1. Take a good look at each sound. Say it slowly if you can. Don't get fooled.
2. (Touch ball for **g.**) Get ready. (Quickly move to end of arrow.) "g."
3. (Repeat step 2 for **l, c, u, f,** and **n.** Remember to move quickly to end of arrow if there is no ball on arrow for sound.)

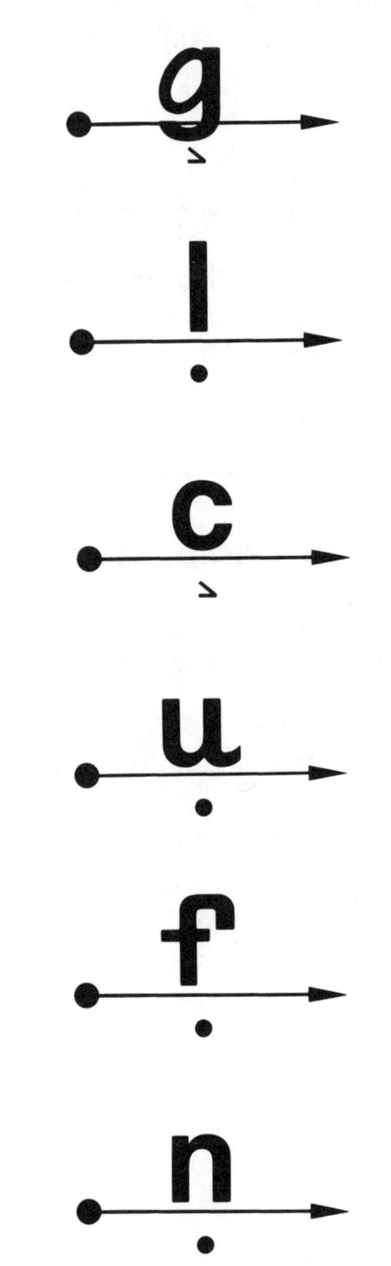

TASK 12 CHILD READS THE FAST WAY

1. Now it's your turn to read the first part of the story the fast way. Touch the first word and read it the fast way. Don't sound it out aloud. Just figure it out to yourself and read it the fast way. "we."
2. Read the next word the fast way. "see."
3. (Repeat step 2 for **a,** and **duck.**) Good reading the fast way.

TASK 13 SOUNDS WRITING

1. Here's the first sound you're going to write. (Write **a** at beginning of first line. Point to **a.**) What sound? "aaa."
2. First trace the **aaa** that I made. Then make more of them on this line. (After tracing **a** several times, child is to make three to five **a**'s. Help child if necessary. For acceptable letters say:) Good writing **aaa.**
3. Here's the next sound you're going to write. (Write **f** at beginning of second line. Point to **f.**) What sound? "fff."
4. First trace the **fff** that I made. Then make more of them on this line. (After tracing **f** several times, child is to make three to five **f**'s. Help child if necessary. For acceptable letters say:) Good writing **fff.**

TASK 2 WORD READING

(Point to **I.**) I'll tell you this word: **I.** What word? "I." Remember this word. You'll see it in the story.

I

TASK 3 WORD READING

1. (Point to **got.**) You're going to sound out (slide under **o** and **t**) this part. (Point to ball for **o.**) Get ready. (Touch balls for **o** and **t** as child says:) "ooot." (Return to ball for **o.**) Say it fast. "ot." (Touch first ball for **got.**) This word rhymes with (pause) **ot.** (Slide quickly to end of arrow.) "got." What word? (Slide quickly to end of arrow.) "got."
2. (Point to arrow under **g.**) This arrow tells me that I can't stop under this sound. But you must say the sound with the next sound when I stop.
3. (Point to first ball.) Sound out (pause) **got.** Get ready. (Slide past **g.** Stop at balls for other sounds.) "gooot."
4. (Demonstrate sounding out if response is not firm. Child should not stop between **g** and **ooo.** Then repeat step 3.) What word? "got." Good reading.

TASK 4 WORD READING

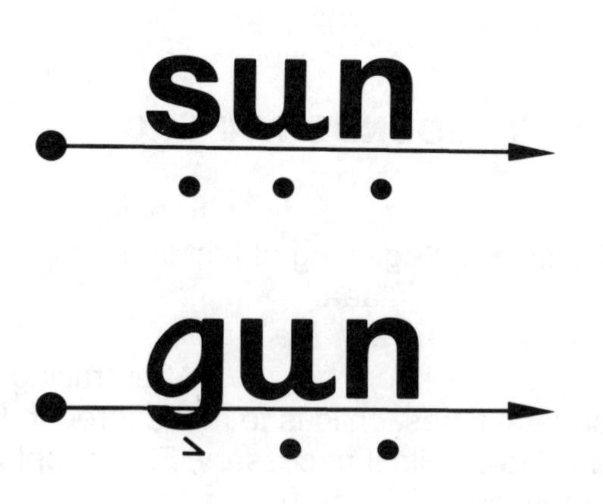

1. (Touch first ball for **sun.**) Sound it out. (Touch ball for sounds.) "sssuuunnn." What word? "sun." Yes, **sun.**
2. (Return to first ball. Pause.) This word rhymes with (pause) **un.** Read it the fast way. (Slide.) "sun."
3. (Touch first ball for **gun.**) This word also rhymes with (pause) **un.** Read it the fast way. (Slide.) "gun." Yes, **gun.** Good rhyming.

TASK 5 WORD READING

1. (Touch first ball for **win.**) Sound it out. (Touch balls for sounds.) "wwwiiinnn." (Repeat until firm.) What word? "win."
2. (Repeat step 1 for **rug, rag, duck, luck,** and **with.**)

TASK 6 WORD READING

1. Now you get to read all the words on this page the fast way.
2. (Touch first ball for **I.**) I'll go down the arrow one time and touch the sound. Figure out the word. But don't say anything out loud until I tell you to read the fast way. (Go down arrow, stopping at second ball. Return to first ball.) Read it the fast way. (Slide.) "I." Yes, **I.**
3. (Repeat step 2 for each remaining word on page.)

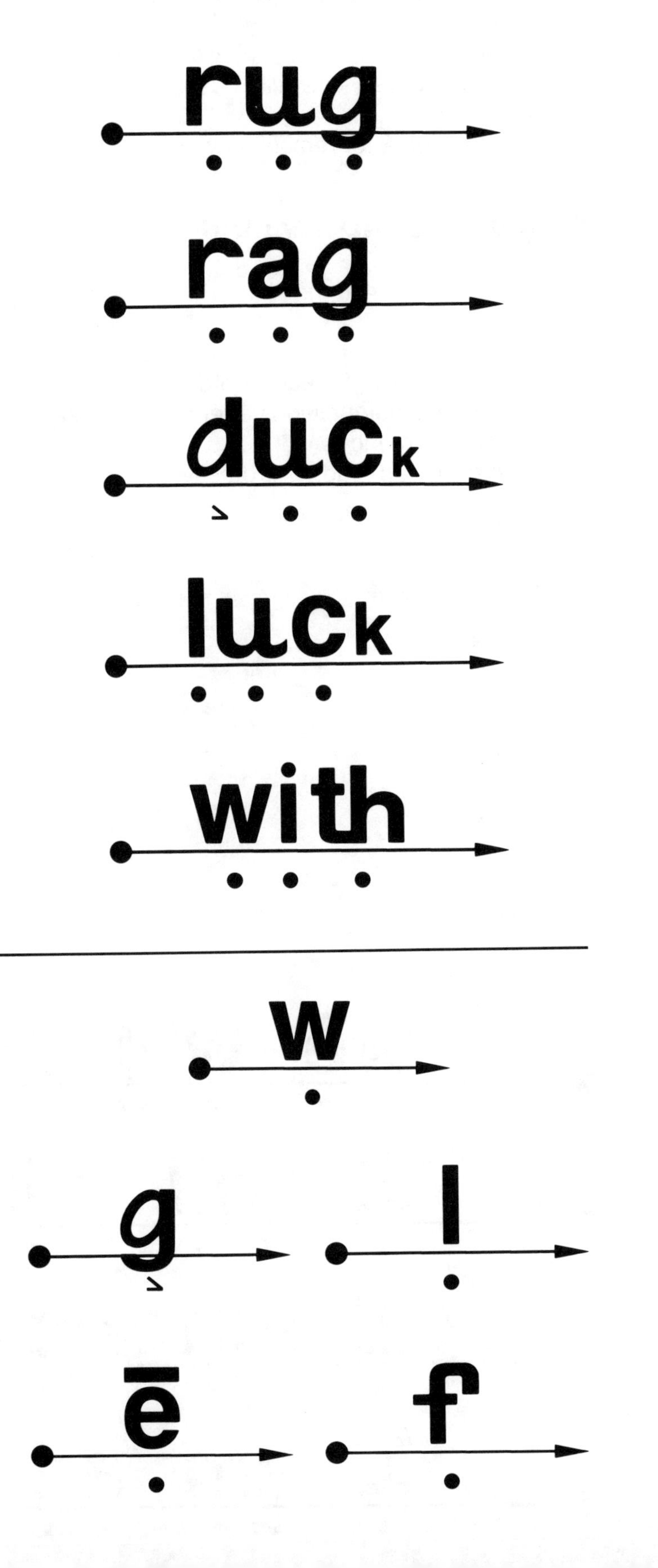

TASK 7 SOUNDS

1. Take a good look at each sound. Say it slowly if you can. Don't get fooled.
2. (Touch first ball for **w.**) Get ready. (Quickly move to second ball. Hold.) "www."
3. Repeat step 2 for **g, l, e,** and **f.** Remember to move quickly to end of arrow if there is no ball on arrow for sound.)

TASK 8 FIRST READING

1. Now you're going to read the story. Finger on the ball of the top line. Sound out the first word. (Child touches under and says:) "wwweee." What word? "we."
2. Sound out the next word. (Child touches under and says:) "wwwiiilll." What word? "will."
3. (Repeat step 2 for remaining words in story.)

TASK 9 SECOND READING

1. This time you read the story again and I'll ask questions. Touch the ball on the top line and get ready to read the words. (Repeat steps from first reading for each word. Ask following comprehension questions after child has read indicated sentences.)
2. (After child has read:) (You say:)

(After child has read:)	(You say:)
"We will run."	What will we do?
"I will win."	Who will win?
"I am not a duck."	Yes, I will win. Am I a duck?
"I am an ant."	Let's read some more and see who is telling this story. What am I? Yes, who's telling this story?

TASK 10 PICTURE COMPREHENSION

1. What will you see in the picture?
2. And what does the ant say he'll do?
3. Look at the picture and get ready to answer some questions.
4. What are those ants getting ready to do? Yes, it looks to me as if they'll have a running race.
5. Which ant do you think will win?
6. Have you ever won a race?

TASK 11 READING THE FAST WAY

1. I'm going to read the first part of this story the fast way. Later, you'll get to read that part the fast way.
2. (Point to **we.** Pause.) **we.**
3. (Repeat step 2 for remaining words in first sentence: **will** and **run.**)

TASK 12 WORD FINDING

1. You're going to find words that are in the top line of the story.
2. Find the word (pause) **we.**
3. (Repeat step 2 for **will, we, run, we, run, will, we.**)
4. Good finding those words.

TASK 13 CHILD READS THE FAST WAY

1. Your turn to read the first part of the story the fast way. First word. "we."
2. Next word. "will."
3. Next word. "run." Good reading the fast way.

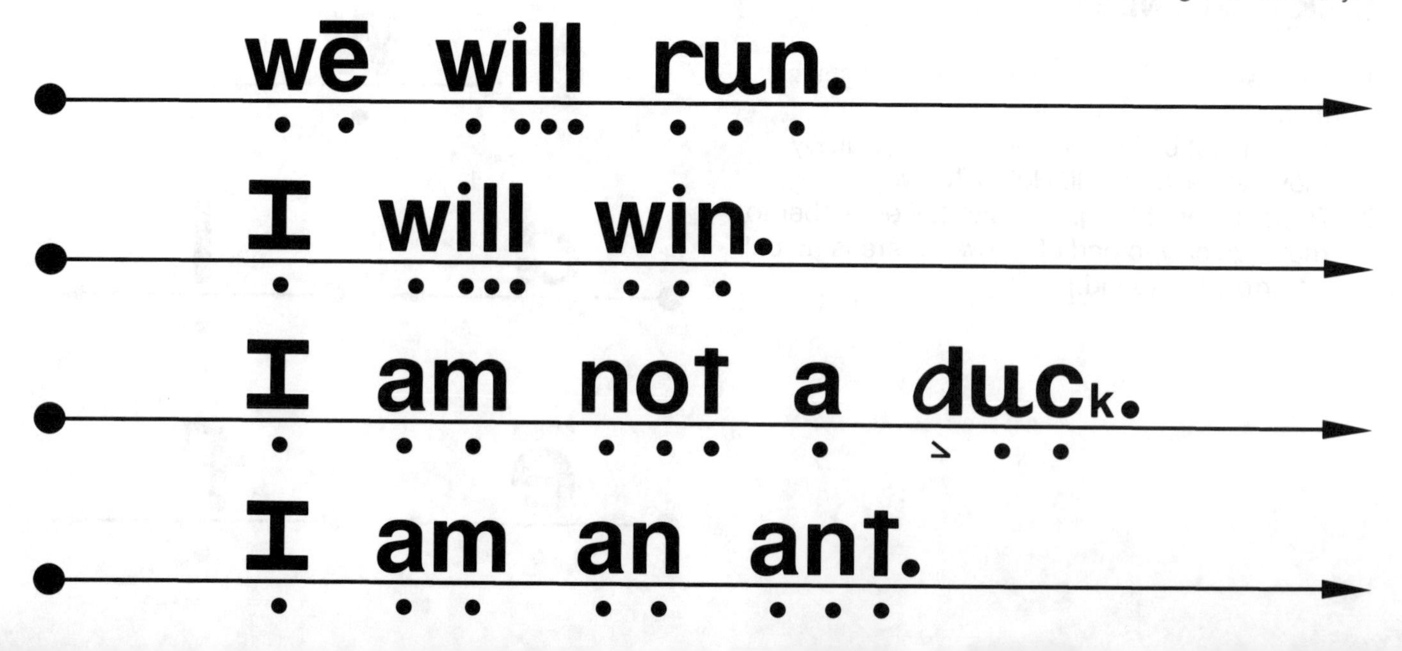

TASK 14 SOUNDS WRITING

1. Here's the first sound you're going to write. (Write **c** at beginning of first line. Point to **c.**) What sound? "c."
2. First trace the **c** that I made. Then make more of them on this line. (After tracing **c** several times, child is to make three to five **c**'s. Help child if necessary. For acceptable letters say:) Good writing **c.**
3. Here's the next sound you're going to write. (Write **g** at beginning of second line. Point to **g.**) What sound? "g."
4. First trace the **g** that I made. Then make more of them on this line. (After tracing **g** several times, child is to make three to five **g**'s. Help child if necessary. For acceptable letters say:) Good writing **g.**

LESSON 35

TASK 1 SOUNDS INTRODUCTION

1. (Point to **sh.**) Here's a new sound. I'm going to touch under this sound and say the sound. (Touch first ball of arrow. Move quickly to second ball. Hold.) **shshsh.**
2. Your turn to say the sound when I touch under it. (Touch first ball.) Get ready. (Move quickly to second ball. Hold.) "shshsh."

(**To correct** child saying a wrong sound or not responding:) The sound is **shshsh.** (Repeat step 2.)

3. (Touch first ball.) Again. Get ready. (Move quickly to second ball. Hold.) "shshsh."

sh

TASK 2 SOUNDS

1. Take a good look at each sound. Say it slowly if you can. Don't get fooled.
2. (Touch ball for **g.**) Get ready. (Quickly move to end of arrow.) "g."
3. (Repeat step 2 for **w, l, sh, d,** and **o.** Remember to move quickly to end of arrow if there is no ball on arrow for sound.)

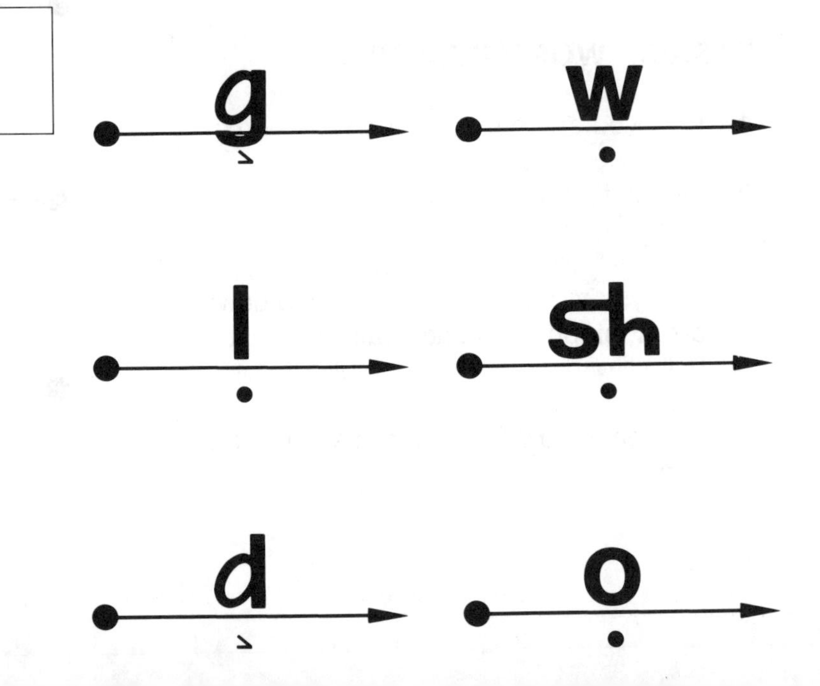

TASK 3 WORD READING

1. You're going to read these words. (Touch first ball for **lot.**) Sound it out. (Touch balls for sounds.) "lllooot." (Repeat until firm.) What word? "lot."
2. (Repeat step 1 for **rug, got, log, little, lick, win, we,** and **duck.**)

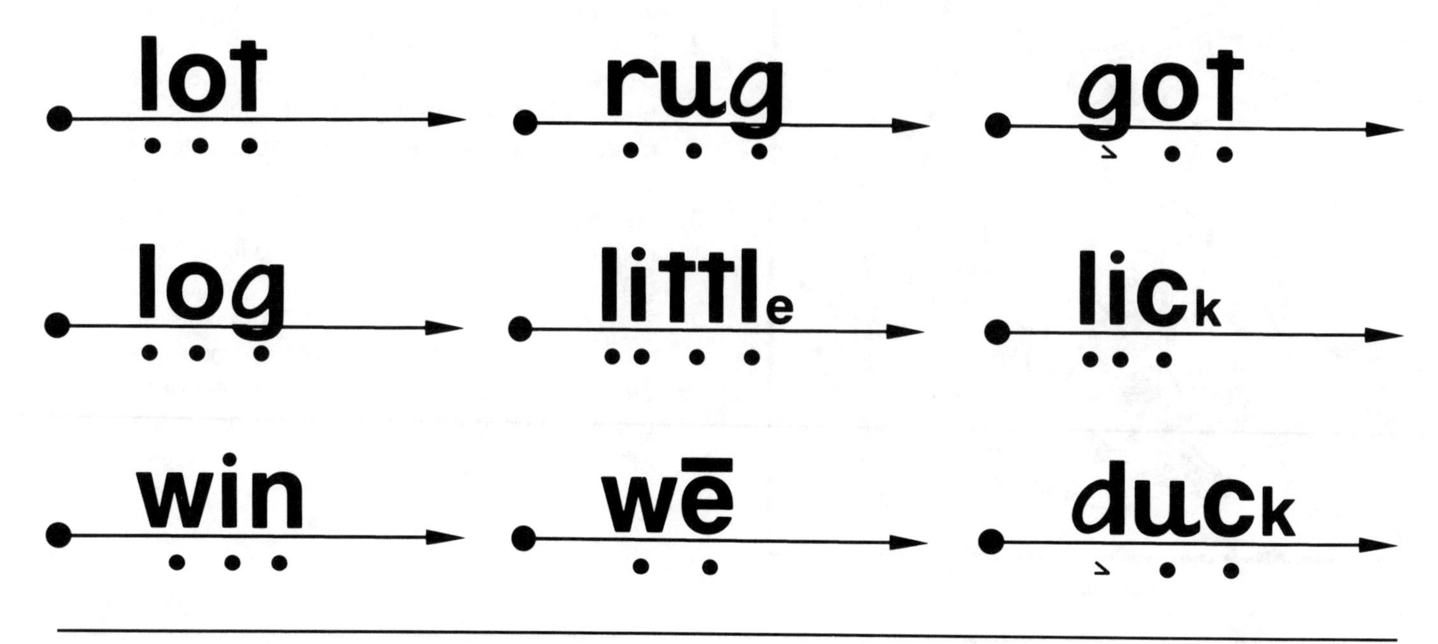

TASK 4 WORD READING

(Point to **I.**) I'll tell you this word: **I.** What word? "I." Remember this word. You'll see it in the story.

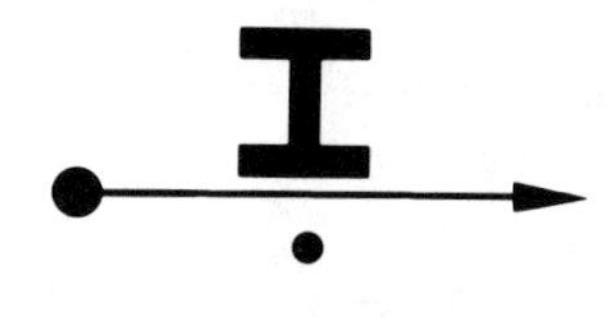

TASK 5 WORD READING

1 Now you get to read all the words on this page the fast way.
2. (Touch first ball for **lot.**) I'll go down the arrow one time and touch the sounds. Figure out the word. But don't say anything out loud until I tell you to read the fast way (Go down arrow, stopping at each ball. Return to first ball.) Read it the fast way. (Slide) "lot." Yes, **lot.**
3. (Repeat step 2 for each remaining word on page.)

TASK 6 SOUNDS

1. Take a good look at each sound. Say it slowly if you can. Don't get fooled.
2. (Touch first ball for **sh.**) Get ready. (Quickly move to second ball. Hold.) "shshsh."
3. (Repeat step 2 for **g, th, l, w,** and **u.** Remember to move quickly to end of arrow if there is no ball on arrow for sound.)

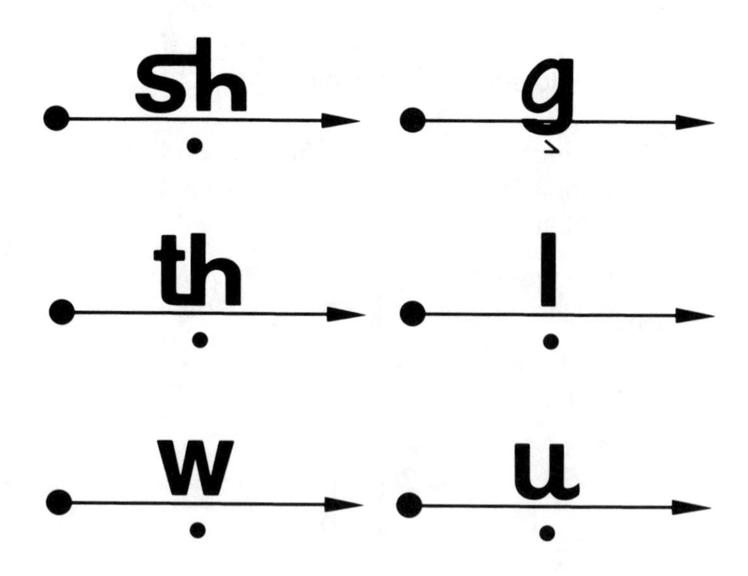

TASK 7 FIRST READING

1. Now you're going to read the story. Finger on the ball of the top line. Touch under the first word. What word? "uh."
2. Sound out the next word. (Child touches under and says:) "caaat." What word? "cat."
3. (Repeat step 2 for remaining words in story.)

TASK 8 SECOND READING

1. This time you read the story again and I'll ask questions. Touch the ball on the top line and get ready to read the words. (Repeat steps from first reading for each word. Ask following comprehension questions after child has read indicated sentences.)
2. (After child has read:) (You say:)

(After child has read:)	(You say:)
"A cat sat on a little rug."	Where did a cat sit?
"The cat got mud on that rug."	What did the cat do?
"Mom got mad at the cat."	How did Mom feel about the cat? I don't blame her.

TASK 9 READING THE FAST WAY

1. I'm going to read the first part of this story the fast way. Later, you'll get to read that part the fast way.
2. (Point to **a.** Pause.) **a.**
3. (Repeat step 2 for remaining words in first sentence: **cat, sat, on, a, little,** and **rug.**)

TASK 10 WORD FINDING

1. You're going to find words that are in the top line of the story.
2. Find the word (pause) **cat.**
3. (Repeat step 2 for **sat, cat, on, sat, on, cat, cat.**)
4. Good finding those words.

TASK 11 CHILD READS THE FAST WAY

1. Your turn to read the first part of the story the fast way.
   First word. "uh."
2. Next word. "cat."
3. (Repeat step 2 for **sat, on, a, little,** and **rug.**)
   Good reading the fast way.

a cat sat on a

little rug. thē

cat got mud on that

rug. mom got mad

at thē cat.

TASK 12 PICTURE COMPREHENSION

1. What will you see in the picture?
2. Look at the picture and get ready to answer some questions.
3. Look at Mom. How do you think she feels?
4. Why is she pointing her finger like that?
5. What do you think she is saying to the cat?
6. Where is the cat?
7. Why did the rug get so dirty?

TASK 13 SOUNDS WRITING

1. (Write **g** at beginning of first line. Point to **g.**) What sound? "g."
2. First trace the **g** that I made. Then make more of them on this line. (After tracing **g** several times, child is to make three to five **g**'s. Help child if necessary. For each acceptable letter say:) Good writing **g.**
3. Here's the next sound you're going to write. (Write **d** at beginning of second line. Point to **d.**) What sound? "d."
4. First trace the **d** that I made. Then make more of them on this line. (After tracing **d** several times, child is to make three to five **d**'s. Help child if necessary. For acceptable letters say:) Good writing **d.**

LESSON 36

TASK 1 SOUNDS

1. Take a good look at each sound. Say it slowly if you can. Don't get fooled.
2. (Touch ball for **g.**) Get ready. (Quickly move to end of arrow.) "g."
3. (Repeat step 2 for **sh, th, f, l,** and **w.** Remember to move quickly to end of arrow if there is no ball on arrow for sound.)

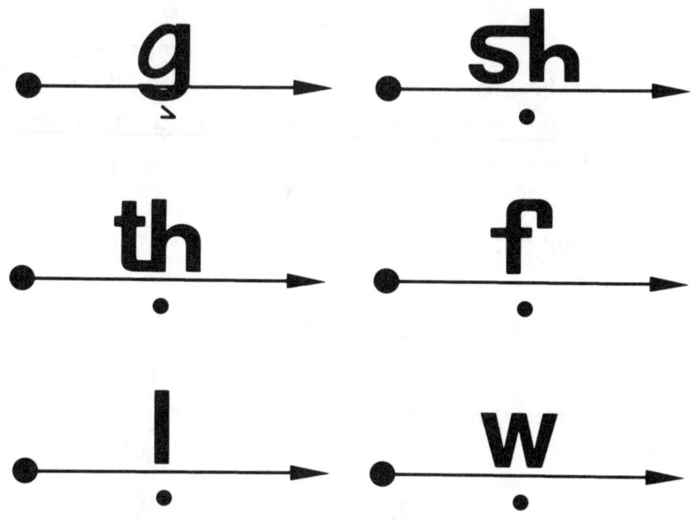

TASK 2 WORD READING

1. (Touch first ball for **said.**) Here's a new word. Sound it out. (Touch balls for sounds as child says:) "sssaaaiiid" (not "ssseeed").

(**To correct** if child says "ssseeed," touch under **a.**) This sound is **aaa.** You've got to say the sounds I touch. (Repeat sounding out.)

2. That's how we **sound out** the word. Here's how we **say** the word. (Pause.) **Said (sed).** How do we **say** the word? "said." Yes, **said**—it's a funny word.
3. (Return to first ball.) Sound it out again. (Touch balls for sounds as child says:) "sssaaaiiid." Now **say** the word "said." Yes, **said.** She **said** hello.

TASK 3 WORD READING

1. (Touch arrow under **g** in **got.**) Remember, I can't stop under this sound, but you have to say the sound with the next sound I stop at.
2. (Touch first ball for **got.**) Sound it out. Get ready. (Slide past **g.** Touch balls for other sounds.) "gooot." (Repeat until firm.) What word? "got." Yes, **got.**
3. (Touch first ball for **rug.**) Sound it out. (Touch balls for sounds.) "rrruuug." (Repeat until firm.) What word? "rug."
4. (Repeat step 3 for **log, she, shot, shack, we, run,** and **sick.**)
5. Now you get to read all these words the fast way.
6. (Touch first ball for **got.** Pause three seconds.) Read it the fast way. (Slide.) "got." Yes, **got.**
7. (Repeat step 6 for remaining words on this page.)

TASK 4 SOUNDS

1. Take a good look at each sound. Say it slowly if you can. Don't get fooled.
2. (Touch first ball for **th.**) Get ready. (Quickly move to second ball. Hold.) "ththth."
3. (Repeat step 2 for **sh, l, i, u,** and **ē.** Remember to move quickly to end of arrow if there is no ball on arrow for sound.)

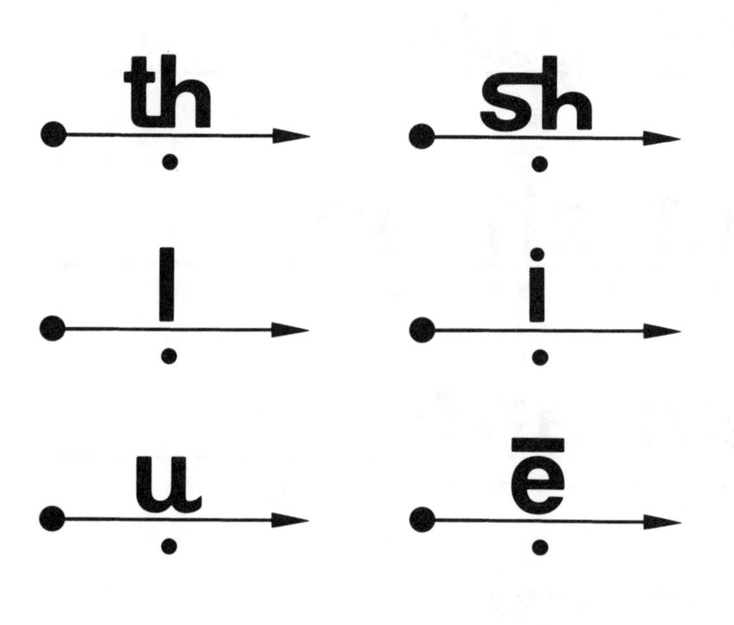

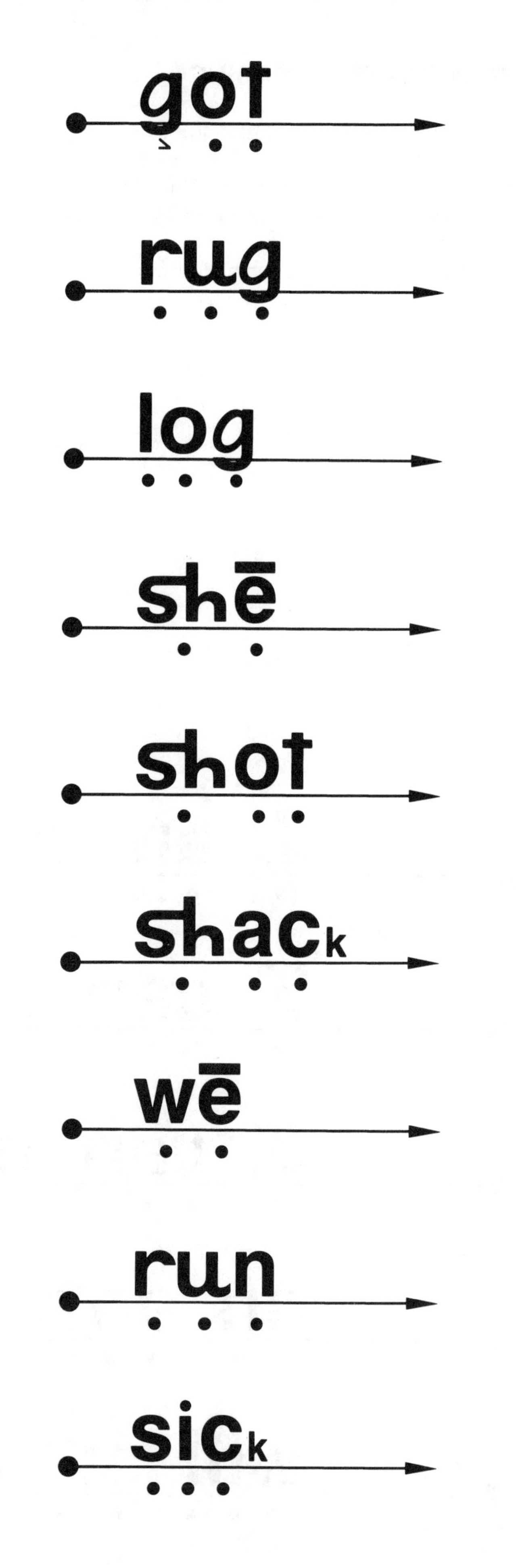

TASK 5 FIRST READING

1. Now you're going to read the story. Finger on the ball of the top line. What word? "I."
2. Sound out the next word. **(Child touches under and says:)** "aaammm." What word? "am."
3. **(Repeat step 2 for remaining words in story.)**

TASK 6 SECOND READING

1. You're going to read the story again. This time I'll ask a question each time you come to a period. **(Touch period after log.)** Here's the first period. It's a little ball that comes after a word. When you get to this period, stop and I'll ask a question. Sound out each word and then tell me the word. Read all the words to the period.
2. **(After child reads "I am a log," ask:)** Who am I? Yes, a log is telling this story. Do you know what a log is?
3. **(Touch period after run.)** Now read the next word and keep reading all the way to this period. Then I'll ask another question. **(After child reads "I can not run," ask:)** What did the log say?
4. **(Touch period after ant.)** Now read the next word and keep reading all the way to this period. **(After child reads "I can not sit on an ant," ask:)** Can this log sit on an ant?
5. **(Touch period after me.)** Now read the next word and keep reading all the way to this period. **(After child reads "An ant will sit on me," ask:)** What will an ant do to this log?

I am a log.

I can not run.

I can not sit on

an ant. an ant

will sit on mē.

TASK 7 PICTURE COMPREHENSION

1. What will you see in this picture?
2. Look at the picture and get ready to answer some questions.
3. Show me the log.
4. What do you see on that log?
5. What is that ant going to do?
6. Why are all those animals sitting on the log? Yes, they're watching a parade.

TASK 8 READING THE FAST WAY

1. I'm going to read the first part of this story the fast way. Later, you'll get to read that part the fast way.
2. (Point to **I.** Pause.) **I.**
3. (Repeat step 2 for remaining words in first sentence: **am, a,** and **log.**)

TASK 9 WORD FINDING

1. You're going to find words that are in the top line of the story.
2. Find the word (pause) **log.**
3. (Repeat step 2 for **am, log, I, log, I, am, log.**)
4. Good finding those words.

TASK 10 CHILD READS THE FAST WAY

1. Your turn to read the first part of the story the fast way. First word. "I."
2. Next word. "am."
3. (Repeat step 2 for **a** and **log.**) Good reading the fast way.

TASK 11 SOUNDS WRITING

1. Here's the first sound you're going to write. (Write **s** at beginning of first line. Point to **s.**) What sound? "sss."
2. First trace the **sss** that I made. Then make more of them on this line. (After tracing **s** several times, child is to make three to five **s**'s. Help child if necessary. For acceptable letters say:) Good writing **sss.**
3. Here's the next sound you're going to write. (Write **u** at beginning of second line. Point to **u.**) What sound? "uuu."
4. First trace the **uuu** that I made. Then make more of them on this line. (After tracing **u** several times, child is to make three to five **u**'s. Help child if necessary. For acceptable letters say:) Good writing **uuu.**

LESSON 37

TASK 1 SOUNDS INTRODUCTION

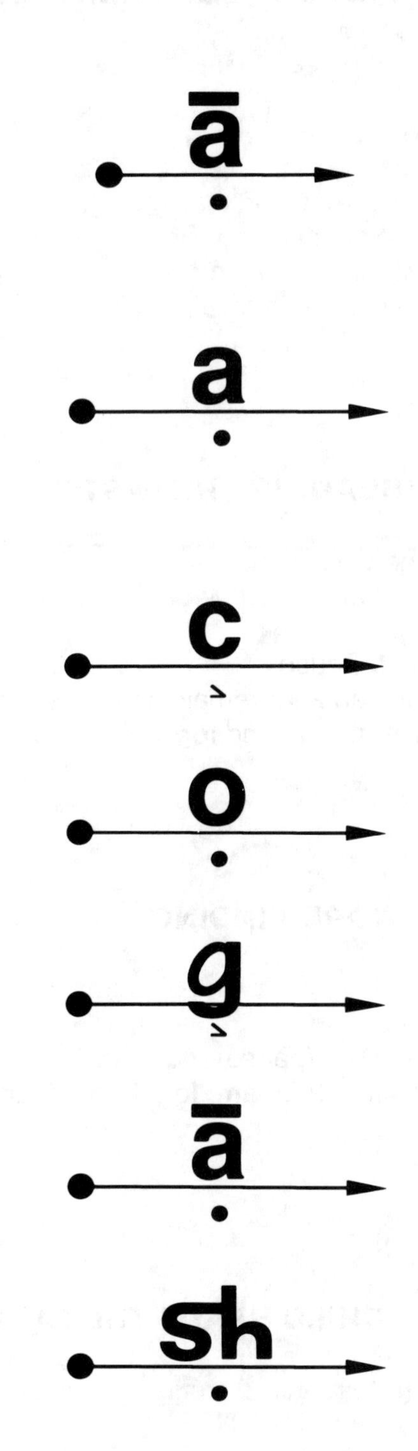

1. (Point to **ā**.) Here's a new sound. I'm going to touch under this sound and say the sound. (Touch first ball of arrow. Move quickly to second ball. Hold.) **āāā.**
2. Your turn to say the sound when I touch under it. (Touch first ball.) Get ready. (Move quickly to second ball. Hold.) "āāā."

(**To correct** child saying a wrong sound or not responding:) The sound is **āāā.** (Repeat step 2.)

3. (Touch first ball.) Again. Get ready. (Move quickly to second ball. Hold.) "āāā."

TASK 2 SOUNDS

1. Take a good look at each sound. Say it slowly if you can. Don't get fooled.
2. (Touch first ball for **a.**) Get ready. (Quickly move to second ball. Hold.) "aaa."
3. (Repeat step 2 for **c, o, g, ā,** and **sh.** Remember to move quickly to end of arrow if there is no ball on arrow for sound.)

TASK 3 WORD READING

1. (Touch first ball for **said.**) Here's that new word again. Sound it out. (Touch balls for sounds as child says:) "sssaaaiiid."
2. That's how we **sound out** the word. Here's how we **say** the word. (Pause.) **said.** How do we **say** the word? "said." Yes, **said**—it's a funny word.
3. (Return to first ball.) Sound it out again. (Touch balls for sounds as child says:) "sssaaaiiid." Now **say** the word. "said." Yes, **said.** (Repeat until firm.)

TASK 4 WORD READING

1. (Touch first ball for **shack.**) Sound it out. (Touch balls for sounds.) "shshshaaak." (Repeat until firm.) What word? "shack."
2. (Repeat step 1 for **she, we, fill, will, shot, got, lot, not,** and **feel.**)
3. Now you get to read all these words the fast way.
4. (Touch first ball for **shack.** Pause three seconds.) Read it the fast way. (Slide.) "shack." Yes, **shack.**
5. (Repeat step 4 for remaining words on this page.)

TASK 5 SOUNDS

1 Take a good look at each sound. Say it slowly if you can. Don't get fooled.
2. (Touch first ball for **a.**) Get ready. (Quickly move to second ball. Hold.) "aaa."
3. (Repeat step 2 for **ā, ē, u, n,** and **sh.** Remember to move quickly to end of arrow if there is no ball on arrow for sound.)

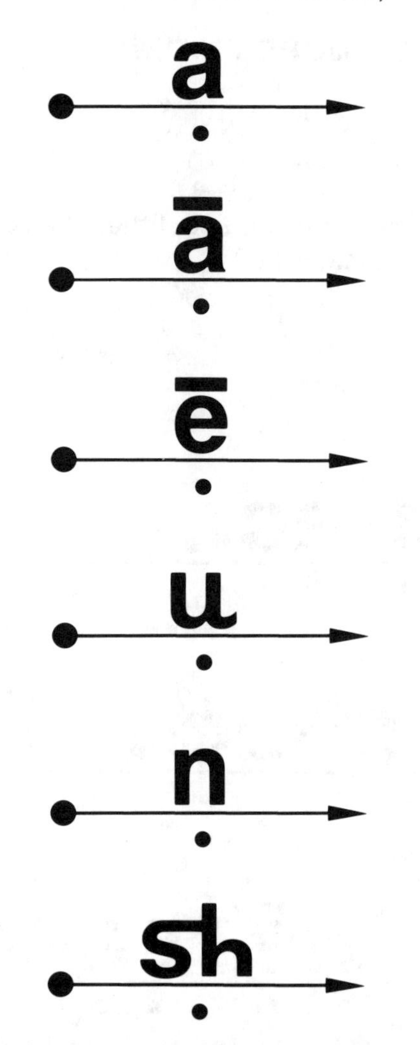

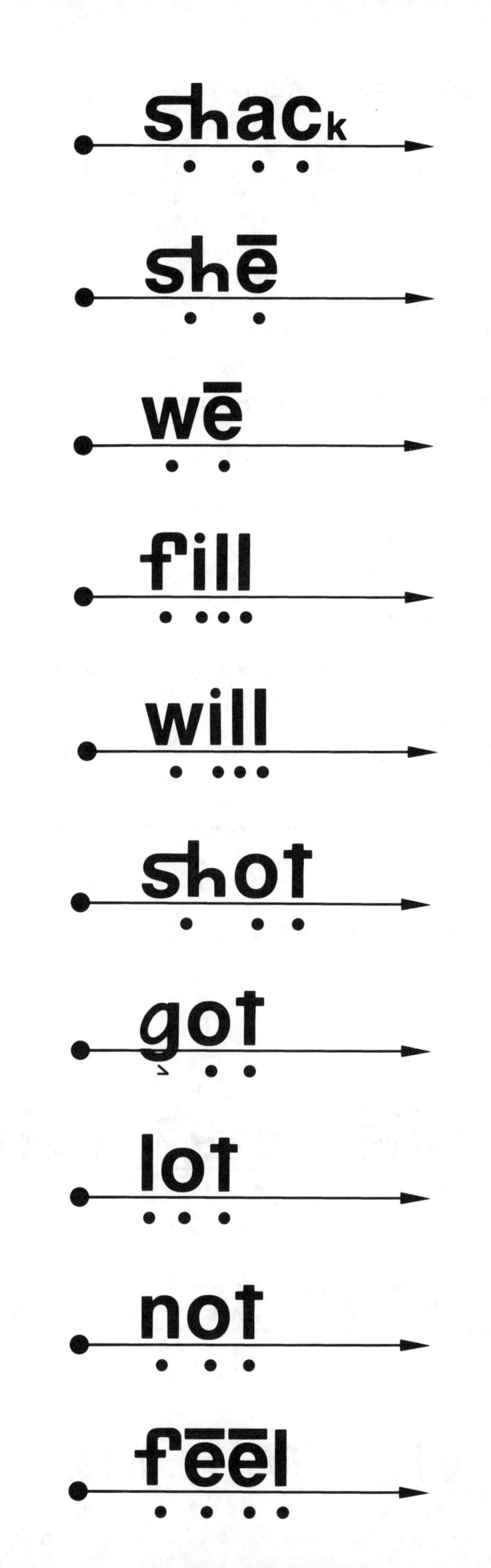

TASK 6 FIRST READING

1. Now you're going to read the story. Finger on the ball of the top line. Sound out the first word. (Child touches under and says:) "sssēēē." What word? "see."
2. Sound out the next word. (Child touches under and says:) "thththaaat." What word? "that."
3. (Repeat step 2 for remaining words in story.)

TASK 7 SECOND READING

1. You're going to read the story again. This time I'll ask a question each time you come to a period. (Touch period after **shack.**) Here's the first period. It's a little ball that comes after a word. When you get to this period, stop and I'll ask a question. Sound out each word and then tell me the word. Read all the words to the period.
2. (After child reads "See that little shack," ask:) What's this story about? Yes, a shack is a little house.
3. (Touch period after **shack** in second line.) Now read the next word and keep reading all the way to this period. Then I'll ask another question. (After child reads "Sand is in the shack," ask:) What is in the shack?
4. (Touch period after **sand.**) Now read the next word and keep reading all the way to this period. (After child reads "We will run in the sand," ask:) What are we going to do?

TASK 8 PICTURE COMPREHENSION

1. Tell me some things you'll see in the picture.
2. Look at the picture and get ready to answer some questions.
3. Show me the shack.
4. What do you see in the shack? This shack could be on the beach.
5. And who is coming up to the shack?
6. What will the children do in the shack?
7. What would you do if you were one of those children?

TASK 9 READING THE FAST WAY

1. I'm going to read the first part of this story the fast way. Later, you'll get to read that part the fast way.
2. (Point to **sēē.** Pause.) **see.**
3. (Repeat step 2 for remaining words in first sentence: **that, little,** and **shack.**)

TASK 10 WORD FINDING

1. You're going to find words that are in the top line of the story.
2. Find the word (pause) **little.**
3. (Repeat step 2 for **see, little, shack, little, see, shack, little.**)
4. Good finding those words.

sēē that little shack.

sand is in thē shack.

wē will run in thē sand.

TASK 11 CHILD READS THE FAST WAY

1. Your turn to read the first part of the story the fast way. First word. "see."
2. Next word. "that."
3. (Repeat step 2 for **little** and **shack.**) Good reading the fast way.

TASK 12 SOUNDS WRITING

1. Here's the first sound you're going to write. (Write **f** at beginning of first line. Point to **f.**) What sound? "fff."
2. First trace the **fff** that I made. Then make more of them on this line. (After tracing **f** several times, child is to make three to five **f**'s. Help child if necessary. For acceptable letters say:) Good writing **fff.**
3. Here's the next sound you're going to write. (Write **g** at beginning of second line. Point to **g.**) What sound? "g."
4. First trace the **g** that I made. Then make more of them on this line. (After tracing **g** several times, child is to make three to five **g**'s. Help child if necessary. For acceptable letters say:) Good writing **g.**

LESSON 38

TASK 1 SOUNDS

1. Take a good look at each sound. Say it slowly if you can. Don't get fooled.
2. (Touch first ball for **sh.**) Get ready. (Quickly move to second ball. Hold.) "shshsh."
3. (Repeat step 2 for **ā, u, i, ē,** and **o.** Remember to move quickly to end of arrow if there is no ball on arrow for sound.)

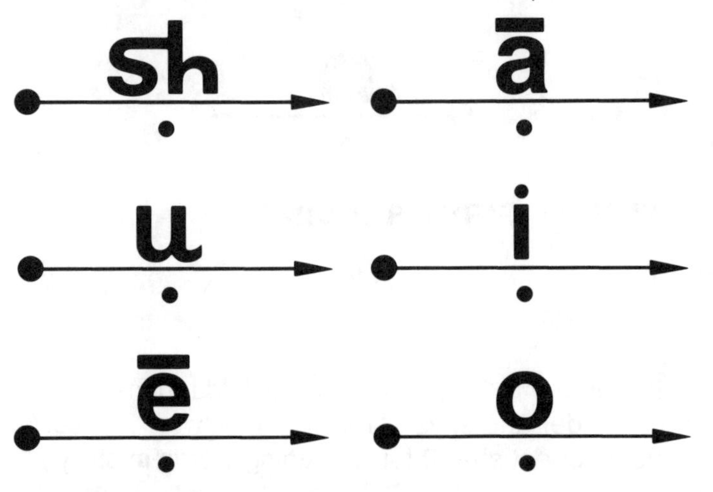

TASK 2 WORD READING

1. (Touch first ball for **said.**) Sound it out. (Touch under sounds as child says:) "sssaaaiiid." Again. (Return to first ball.) Sound it out. (Touch balls for sounds as child says:) "sssaaaiiid."
2. That's how we **sound out** the word. Now **say** the word. "said." Yes, **said.**

(**To correct** if child says "sa—id" for "said":) Here's how you say the word: **said.** How do you say it? "said." (Return to step 1.)

3. Let's do it again. (Return to first ball.) Sound it out. (Touch balls for sounds as child says:) "sssaaaiiid." Now say the word. "said." Yes, **said.**

TASK 3 WORD READING

1. (Touch first ball for **at.**) Sound it out. (Touch balls for sounds.) "aaat." (Repeat until firm.) What word? "at."
2. (Repeat step 1 for **ate, made, she, seat, wish, fish, late, tail, rug,** and **got.**)
3. Now you get to read all these words the fast way.
4. (Touch first ball for **at.** Pause three seconds.) Read it the fast way. (Slide.) "at." Yes, **at.**
5. (Repeat step 4 for remaining words on this page.)

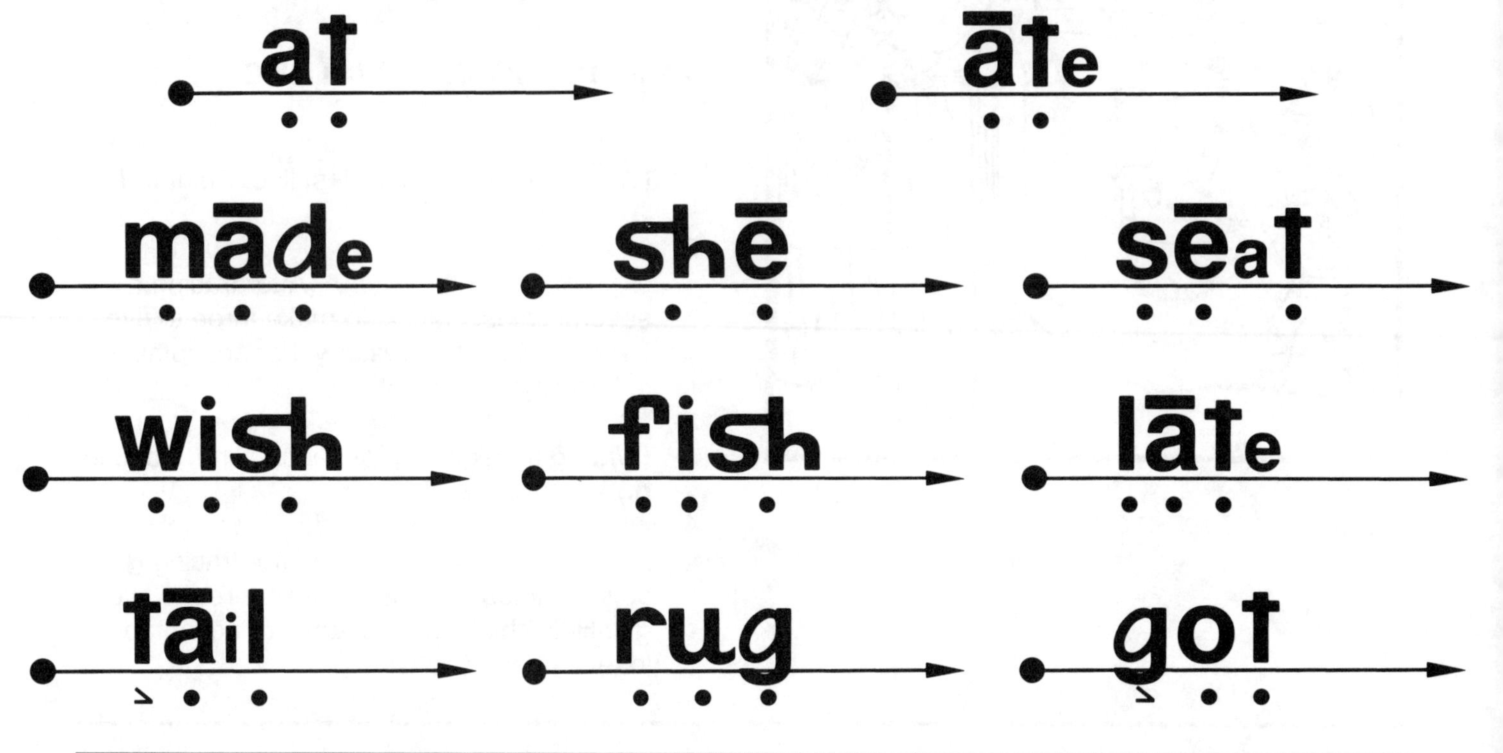

TASK 4 SOUNDS

1. Take a good look at each sound. Say it slowly if you can. Don't get fooled.
2. (Touch first ball for **ā.**) Get ready. (Quickly move to second ball. Hold.) "āāā."
3. (Repeat step 2 for **a, ē, i, u,** and **o.** Remember to move quickly to end of arrow if there is no ball on arrow for sound.)

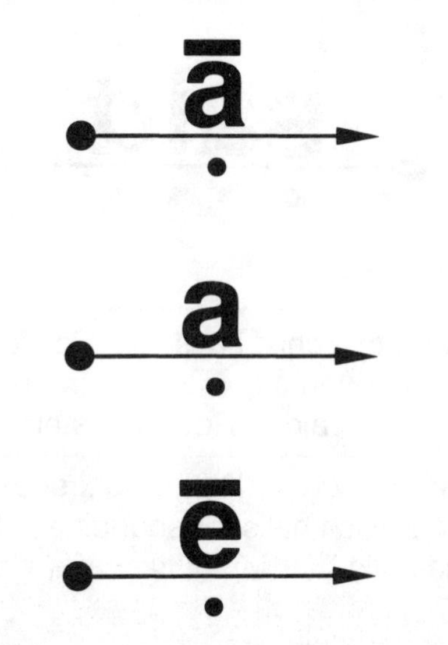

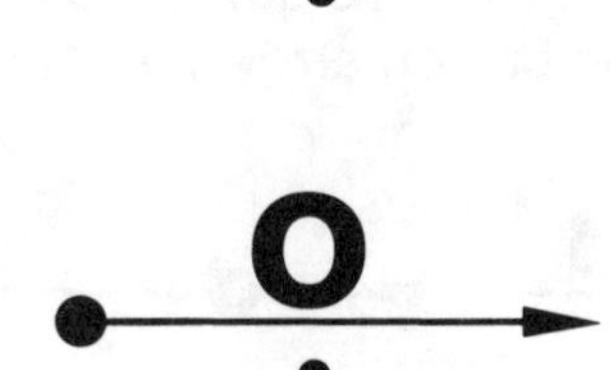

TASK 5 FIRST READING

1. Now you're going to read the story. Finger on the ball of the top line. Touch under the first word. What word? "uh."
2. Sound out the next word. (Child touches under and says:) "llliiitlll." What word? "little."
3. (Repeat step 2 for remaining words in story.)

a littl_e cat can sit on

a rug. shē can run in

thē sand. shē can lic_k

a man. shē will lic_k mē.

TASK 6 SECOND READING

1. You're going to read the story again. Find the first period. Read all the way to that period and stop. Sound out each word and tell me the word. When you get to the period, I'll ask a question.
2. (After child reads:) (You say:)

(After child reads:)	(You say:)
"A little cat can sit on a rug."	What can a cat do?
"She can run in the sand."	What else can she do?
"She can lick a man."	Cats like to lick.
"She will lick me."	What will this cat do?

3. I'll read to the first period of this story the fast way. Later on you'll get to read to that period the fast way.
4. (Point to first word of first sentence. Pause. Say word. Repeat for remaining words in sentence.)

TASK 7 WORD FINDING

1 You're going to find words that are in the top line of the story.
2. Find the word (pause) **on. on.**
3. (Repeat step 2 for **on, little, can, little, can, on, can.**)
4. Good finding those words.

TASK 8 CHILD READS THE FAST WAY

Your turn to read to the first period of this story the fast way. Find the period. Then read each word the fast way.

TASK 9 PICTURE COMPREHENSION

1. What will you see in the picture?
2. Look at the picture and get ready to answer some questions.
3. What is the man doing?
4. What is the cat looking at?
5. Would you like that cat to lick you?

TASK 10 SOUNDS WRITING

1. Here's the first sound you're going to write. (Write **i** at beginning of first line. Point to **i.**) What sound? "iii."
2. First trace the **iii** that I made. Then make more of them on this line. (After tracing **i** several times, child is to make three to five **i**'s. Help child if necessary. For acceptable letters say:) Good writing **iii.**
3. Here's the next sound you're going to write. (Write **u** at beginning of second line. Point to **u.**) What sound? "uuu."
4. First trace the **uuu** that I made. Then make more of them on this line. (After tracing **u** several times, child is to make three to five **u**'s. Help child if necessary. For acceptable letters say:) Good writing **uuu.**

LESSON 39

TASK 1 SOUNDS INTRODUCTION

1. (Touch ball for **h.**) We always have to say this sound fast. My turn to say it fast. (Quickly move to end of arrow as you say sound.) **h.**
2. My turn to say it fast again. (Touch ball for **h.**) Say it fast. (Quickly move to end of arrow.) **h.**
3. (Touch ball.) Your turn. (Pause.) Say it fast. (Quickly move to end of arrow.) "h."

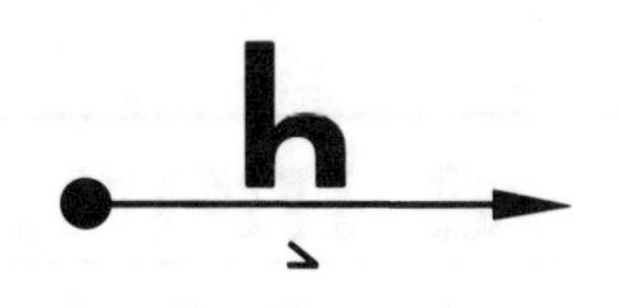

(**To correct** if child says "huh," "hah," or "hih":) Listen: **h.** Say it fast. "h." Yes, **h.**

TASK 2 SOUNDS

1. Take a good look at each sound. Say it slowly if you can. Don't get fooled.
2. (Touch first ball for **ā.**) Get ready. (Quickly move to second ball. Hold.) "āāā."
3. (Repeat step 2 for **c, g, w, h,** and **l.** Remember to move quickly to end of arrow if there is no ball on arrow for sound.)

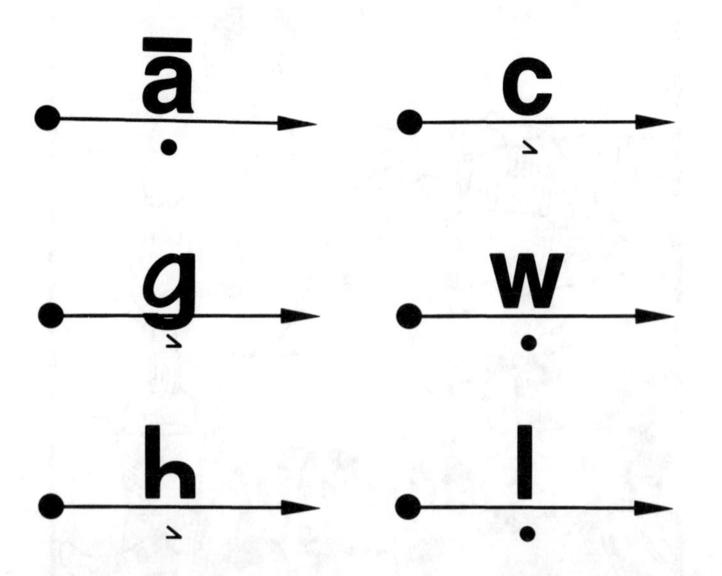

TASK 3 WORD READING

1. (Touch first ball for **said.**) Sound it out. (Touch under sounds as child says:) "sssaaaiiid." Again. (Return to first ball.) Sound it out. (Touch balls for sounds as child says:) "sssaaaiiid."
2. That's how we **sound out** the word. Now **say** the word. "said." Yes, **said.**
3. Let's do it again. (Return to first ball.) Sound it out. (Touch balls for sounds as child says:) "sssaaaiiid." Now say the word. "said." Yes, **said.**

TASK 4 WORD READING

1. (Touch first ball for **wish.**) Sound it out. (Touch balls for sounds.) "wwwiiishshsh." (Repeat until firm.) What word? "wish."

wish

2. (Repeat step 1 for **fish, made, game, dish, did,** and **now.**)
3. Now you get to read all these words the fast way.
4. (Touch first ball for **wish.** Pause three seconds.) Read it the fast way. (Slide.) "wish." Yes, **wish.**
5. (Repeat step 4 for remaining words.)

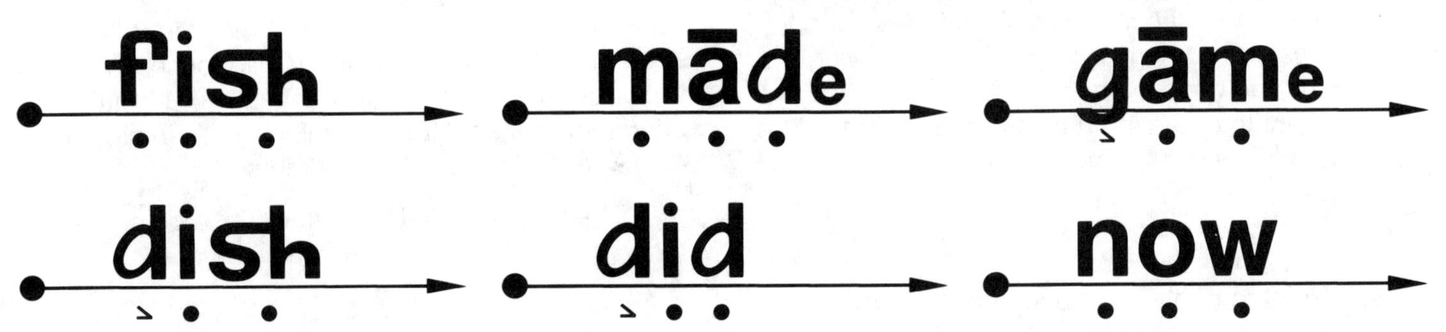

TASK 5 WORD READING

1. (Touch first ball for **wow.**) Sound it out. (Touch balls for sounds.) "wwwooowww." What word? "wow." Yes, **wow.**
2. (Return to first ball. Pause.) This word rhymes with (pause) **ow.** Read it the fast way. (Slide.) "wow."
3. (Touch ball for **cow.**) This word also rhymes with (pause) **ow.** Read it the fast way. (Slide.) "cow." Yes, **cow.** Good rhyming.
4. (Touch first ball for **ate.**) Sound it out. (Touch ball for sounds.) "āāā." What word? "ate." Yes, **ate.**
5. (Touch ball for **hate.**) This word rhymes with (pause) **ate.** Read it the fast way. (Slide.) "hate." Yes, **hate.** Good rhyming.
6. (Touch ball of **gate.**) This word also rhymes with (pause) **ate.** Read it the fast way. (Slide.) "gate." Yes, **gate.** Good rhyming.

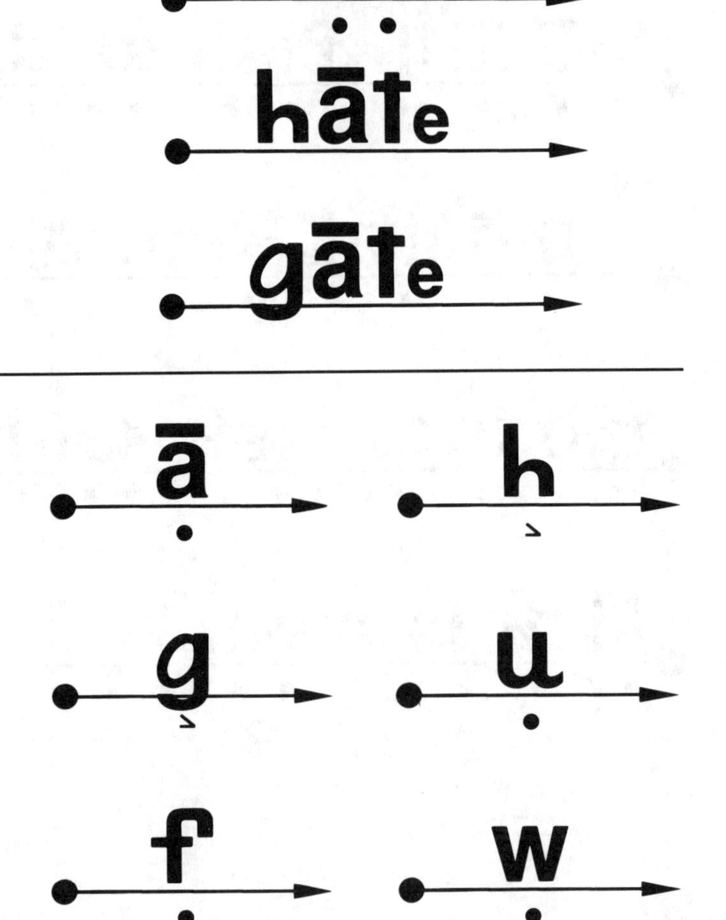

TASK 6 SOUNDS

1. Take a good look at each sound. Say it slowly if you can. Don't get fooled.
2. (Touch first ball for **ā.**) Get ready. (Quickly move to second ball. Hold.) "āāā."
3. (Repeat step 2 for **h, g, u, f,** and **w.** Remember to move quickly to end of arrow if there is no ball on arrow for sound.)

TASK 7 QUOTATION FINDING

1. (Point to quotation marks around **wow** in second sentence.) These are quotation marks. Quotation marks show that somebody is saying something. Somebody is saying the word between these marks.
2. (Point to quotation marks around **that fat fish is mom** in last sentence.) These marks show that somebody is saying something. Somebody's saying all the words between these marks.
3. (Point to quotation marks around **wow.**) Touch these quotation marks. Somebody is saying the word between those marks.
4. (Point to quotation marks around **that fat fish is mom.**) Touch these marks. Somebody is saying all the words between those marks.
5. (Repeat steps 3 and 4 until firm.)

TASK 8 FIRST READING

1. Now you're going to read the story and I'll ask questions. Finger on the ball of the top line. Touch under the first word. What word? "uh."
2. Sound out the next word. (Child touches under and says:) "lllliiitlll." What word? "little."
3. (Repeat step 2 for remaining words in story.)
4. (After child reads:) (You say:)

(After child reads:)	(You say:)
"The little fish said,"	Now we're going to read what he said.
" 'Wow.' "	What did the little fish say?
"The little fish said,"	Now we're going to read what he said.
" 'That fat fish is Mom.' "	What did he say?

a little fish sat on a fat fish.

thē little fish said, "wow."

thē little fish did not fēēl sad.

thē little fish said, "that fat

fish is mom."

TASK 9 SECOND READING

1. You're going to read the story again. Find the first period. Read all the way to that period and stop. Sound out each word and tell me the word. When you get to the period, I'll ask a question.
2. (After child reads:) (You say:)

(After child reads:)	(You say:)
"A little fish sat on a fat fish."	Who sat on whom?
"The little fish said, 'Wow.' "	What did he say?
"The little fish did not feel sad."	Did the little fish feel sad?
"The little fish said, 'That fat fish is Mom.' "	What did he say? Who said, "That fat fish is Mom"?

3. I'll read to the first period of this story the fast way. Later on you'll get to read to that period the fast way.
4. (Point to first word of first sentence. Pause. Say word. Repeat for remaining words in sentence.)

TASK 10 CHILD READS THE FAST WAY

Your turn to read to the first period of this story the fast way. Find the period. Then read each word the fast way.

TASK 11 PICTURE COMPREHENSION

1. What will you see in the picture?
2. Look at the picture and get ready to answer some questions.
3. What's the little fish doing?
4. Which fish is Mom?
5. What would you do if a little fish sat on you?

TASK 12 SOUNDS WRITING

1. Here's the first sound you're going to write. (Write **o** at beginning of first line. Point to **o.**) What sound? "ooo."
2. First trace the **ooo** that I made. Then make more of them on this line. (After tracing **o** several times, child is to make three to five **o**'s. Help child if necessary. For acceptable letters say:) Good writing **ooo.**
3. Here's the next sound you're going to write. (Write **m** at beginning of second line. Point to **m.**) What sound? "mmm."
4. First trace the **mmm** that I made. Then make more of them on this line. (After tracing **m** several times, child is to make three to five **m**'s. Help child if necessary. For acceptable letters say:) Good writing **mmm.**

LESSON 40

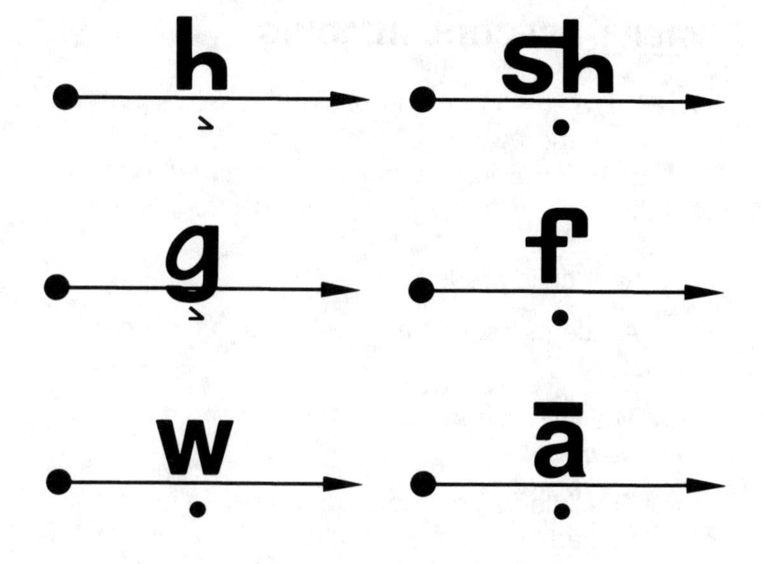

TASK 1 SOUNDS

1. Take a good look at each sound. Say it slowly if you can. Don't get fooled.
2. (Touch ball for **h.**) Get ready. (Quickly move to end of arrow.) "h."
3. (Repeat step 2 for **sh, g, f, w,** and **ā.** Remember to move quickly to end of arrow if there is no ball on arrow for sound.)

TASK 2 WORD READING

was

1. (Touch first ball for **was.**) Here's a new word. Sound it out. (Touch balls for sounds as child says:) "wwwaaasss" (not "wwwuuuzzz").
2. That's how we **sound out** the word. Here's how we **say** the word. (Pause.) (**wuz**) **was.** How do we say the word? "was." Yes, **was**—it's a funny word.
3. (Return to first ball.) Sound it out again. (Touch balls for sounds as child says:) "wwwaaasss." Now **say** the word. "was." Yes, **was.** A man **was** late.

TASK 3 WORD READING

1. (Touch first ball for **āte.**) Sound it out. (Touch balls for sounds.) "āāāt." What word? "ate." Yes, **ate.**
2. (Touch ball for **lāte.**) This word rhymes with (pause) **ate.** Read it the fast way. (Slide.) "late." Yes, **late.** Good rhyming.
3. (Touch ball for **hāte.**) This word also rhymes with (pause) **ate.** Read it the fast way. (Slide.) "hate." Yes, **hāte.** Good rhyming.

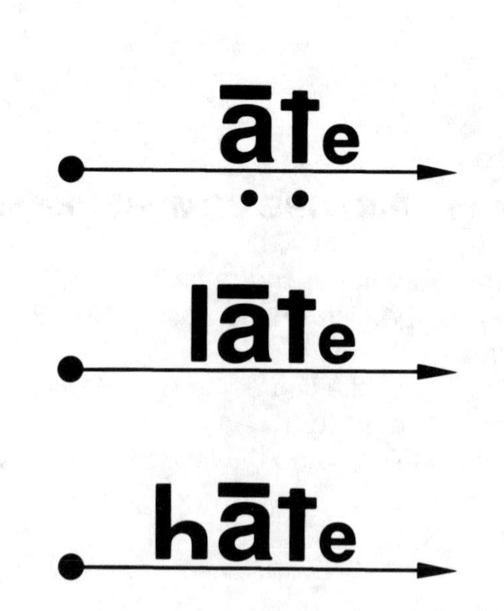

TASK 7 PICTURE COMPREHENSION

1. What will you see in the picture?
2. Look at the picture and get ready to answer some questions.
3. Can a cat lick a kitten?
4. Why is that mother cat licking the kitten?
5. How do you get clean when you're dirty?

TASK 8 SOUNDS WRITING

1. Here's the first sound you're going to write. (Write **k** at beginning of first line. Point to **k.**) What sound? "k."
2. First trace the **k** that I made. Then make more of them on this line. (After tracing **k** several times, child is to make three to five **k**'s. Help child if necessary. For acceptable letters say:) Good writing **k.**
3. Here's the next sound you're going to write. (Write **g** at beginning of second line. Point to **g.**) What sound? "g."
4. First trace the **g** that I made. Then make more of them on this line. (After tracing **g** several times, child is to make three to five **g**'s. Help child if necessary. For acceptable letters say:) Good writing **g.**

LESSON 46

TASK 1 SOUNDS

1. Take a good look at each sound. Say it slowly if you can. Don't get fooled.
2. (Touch first ball for **w.**) Get ready. (Quickly move to second ball. Hold.) "www."
3. (Repeat step 2 for **v, ā, k, h,** and **ō.** Remember to move quickly to end of arrow if there is no ball on arrow for sound.)

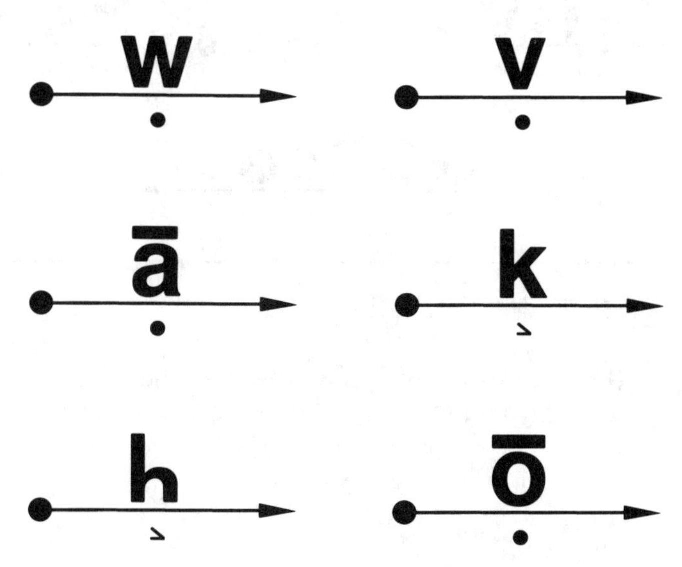

TASK 2 WORD READING

1. (Touch first ball for **of.**) Here's a new word. Sound it out. (Touch balls for sounds as child says:) "ooofff" (not "uuuvvv").
2. That's how we **sound out** the word. Here's how we **say** the word (Pause.) **of (uv).** How do we **say** the word? "of." Yes, **of**—it's a funny word.
3. (Return to first ball.) Sound it out again. (Touch balls for sounds as child says:) "ooofff." Now **say** the word. "of." Yes, **of.** Cups **of** cocoa.

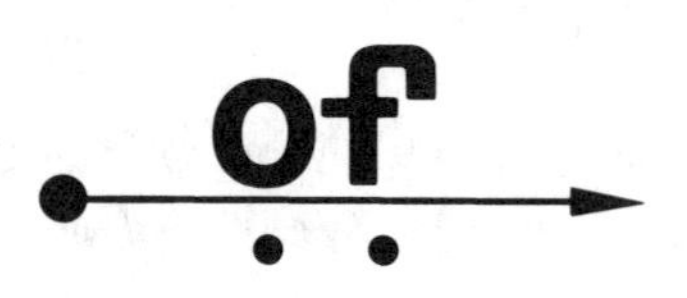

TASK 3 WORD READING

1. (Touch first ball for **māke.**) Sound it out. (Touch balls for sounds.) "mmmāāāk." (Repeat until firm.) What word? "make."
2. (Repeat step 1 for **sāme, sāve, give, have, lots, sacks,** and **nōse.**)
3. Now you get to read all these words the fast way.
4. (Touch first ball for **māke.** Pause three seconds.) Read it the fast way. (Slide.) "make." Yes, **māke.**
5. (Repeat step 4 for remaining words on this page.)

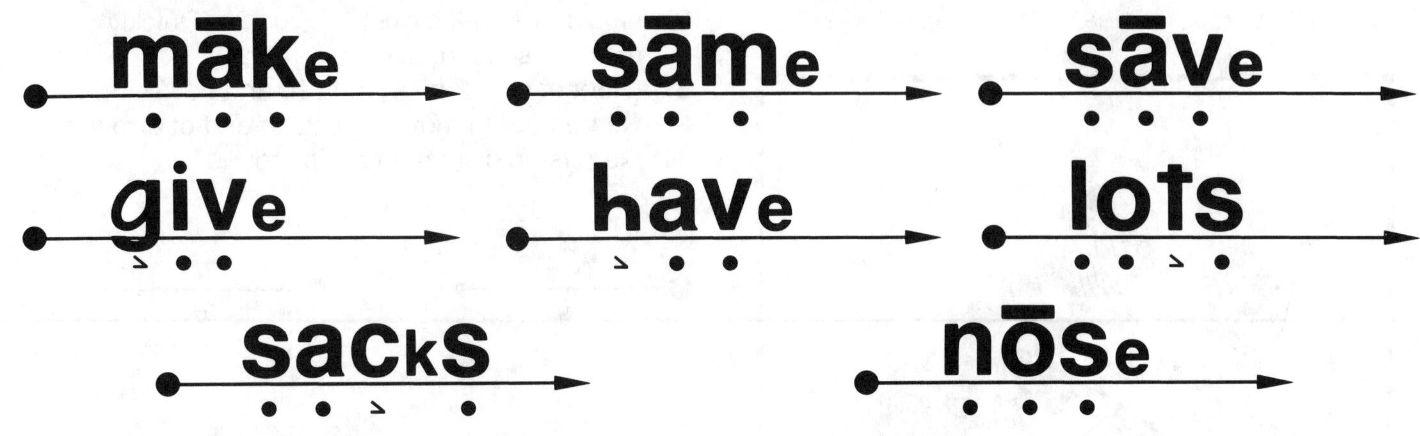

TASK 4 WORD READING

1. (Point to **rocks, wē, shē, thē, hē,** and **nō.**) You're going to read all these words the fast way. I'll go down the arrow one time for each word. Figure out the word. But don't say anything out loud until I tell you to read it the fast way.
2. (Touch ball for **rocks.** Touch under sounds. Return to ball.) Read it the fast way. (Slide.) "rocks." Yes, **rocks.**
3. (Repeat step 2 for remaining words.)

rocks wē shē
the hē nō

TASK 5 READING THE FAST WAY

1. Now you get to read all these words the fast way. (Touch first ball for **māke.** Pause three seconds.) Read it the fast way. (Slide.) "make." Yes, **make.**
2. (Repeat step 1 for remaining words on this page.)

TASK 6 SOUNDS

1. You're going to say all these sounds fast.
2. (Touch ball for **v.**) Say it fast. (Move to end of arrow.) "v."
3. (Repeat step 2 for each sound.)

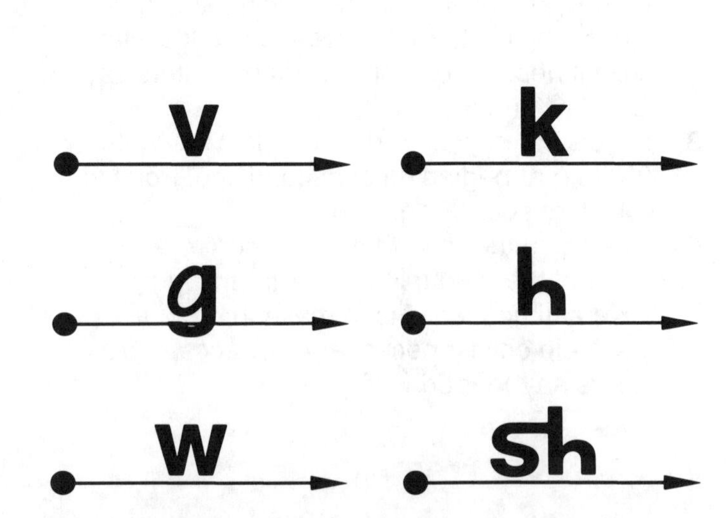

wē sāve rocks. wē sāve sacks

and sacks of rocks. wē sāve

lots and lots of rocks.

wē have lots of little rocks. can

wē sit on rocks? and wē give

an ōld man lots of rocks.

TASK 7 FIRST READING

You're going to read this story by sounding out each word. Then you get to read the whole story the fast way. First, sound out each word and tell me the word.

TASK 8 SECOND READING

1. You're going to read the story the fast way.
2. Find the first period or question mark. Then read the whole sentence the fast way.
3. Find the next period or question mark and read the next sentence.
4. (Repeat step 3 for each remaining sentence. Ask specified questions.)

(After child reads:)	(You say:)
"We save lots and lots of rocks."	What do we do?
"We have lots of little rocks."	What do we have?
"And we give an old man lot of rocks."	What can we do?

TASK 9 PICTURE COMPREHENSION

1. What will you see in the picture?
2. Look at the picture and get ready to answer some questions.
3. Show me the sacks.
4. What are the children doing with the rocks?
5. What would you do with a sack of rocks?

TASK 10 SOUNDS WRITING

1. (Write **v** at beginning of first line. Point to **v.**) What sound? "vvv."
2. First trace the **vvv** that I made. Then make more of them on this line. (After tracing **v** several times, child is to make three to five **v**'s. Help child if necessary. For each acceptable letter say:) Good writing **vvv.**
3. Here's the next sound you're going to write. (Write **h** at beginning of second line. Point to **h.**) What sound? "h."
4. First trace the **h** that I made. Then make more of them on this line. (After tracing **h** several times, child is to make three to five **h**'s. Help child if necessary. For acceptable letters say:) Good writing **h.**

LESSON 47

TASK 1 SOUNDS

1. Take a good look at each sound. Say it slowly if you can. Don't get fooled.
2. (Touch first ball for **v.**) Get ready. (Quickly move to second ball. Hold.) "vvv."
3. (Repeat step 2 for **ō, n, u, h,** and **w.** Remember to move quickly to end of arrow if there is no ball on arrow for sound.)

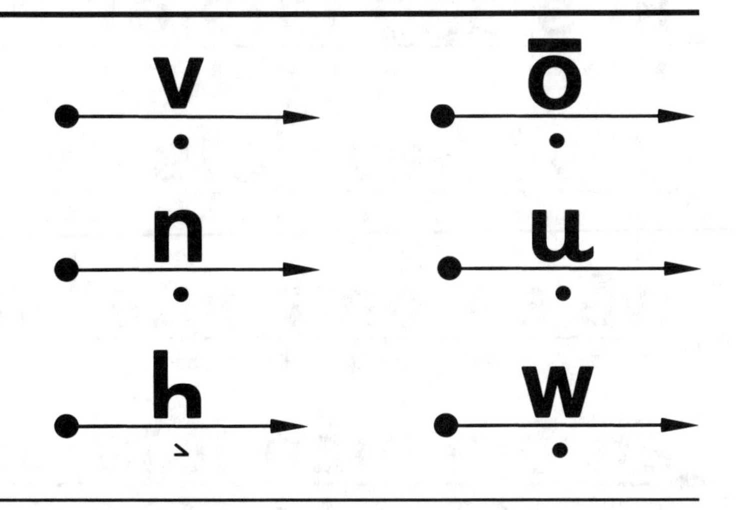

TASK 2 WORD READING

1. (Touch first ball for **of.**) Sound it out. (Touch balls for sounds as child says:) "ooofff."
2. That's how we **sound out** the word. Here's how we **say** the word (pause) **of.** How do we **say** the word? "of." Yes, **of**—it's a funny word.
3. (Return to first ball.) Sound it out again. (Touch balls for sounds as child says:) "ooofff." Now **say** the word. "of." Yes, **of.** (Repeat until firm.)

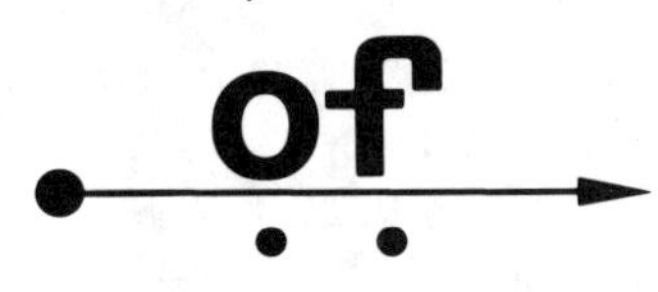

TASK 3 WORD READING

1. (Touch first ball for **or.**) Sound it out. (Touch balls for sounds.) "ōōōrrr." (Repeat until firm.) What word? "or."
2. (Repeat step 1 for **fōr, gōat, cōat, nēēd, have, socks, cōld, give,** and **gāve.**)

ōr

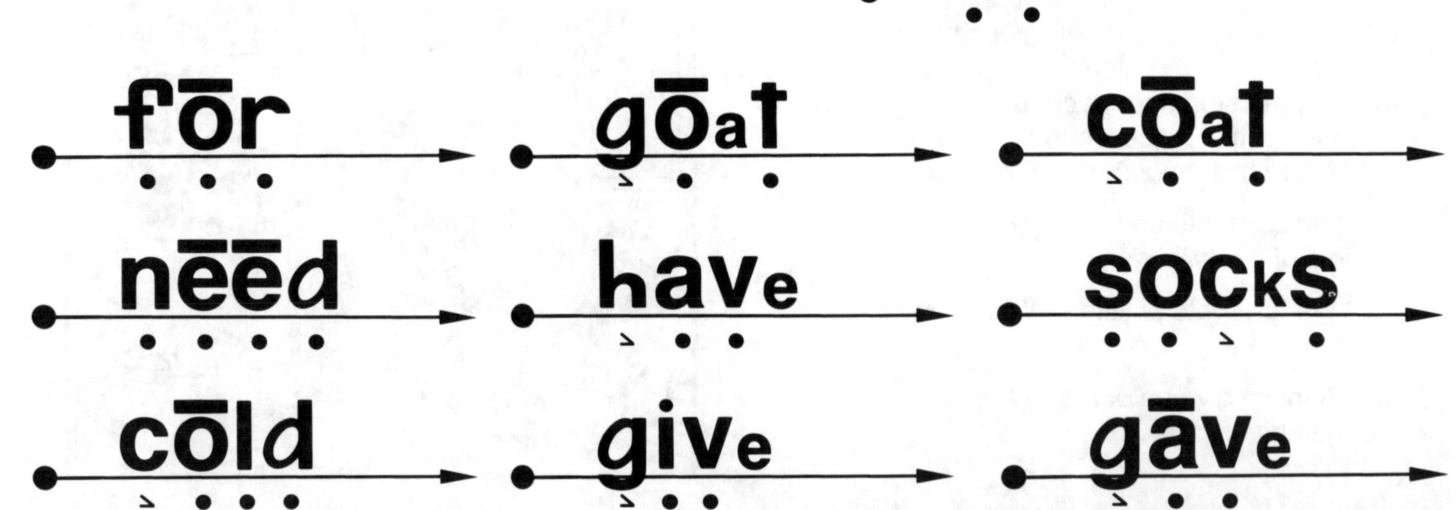

TASK 4 WORD READING

1. (Point to **sō, nōse, him, has, ōld,** and **said.**) You're going to read all these words the fast way. I'll go down the arrow one time for each word. Figure out the word. But don't say anything out loud until I tell you to read it the fast way.
2. (Touch ball for **sō.** Touch under sounds. Return to first ball.) Read it the fast way. (Slide.) "so." Yes, **so.**
3. (Repeat step 2 for remaining words.)
4. Read all these words again, the fast way.
5. (Touch ball for **ōr.** Pause three seconds.) Read it the fast way. (Slide.) "or." Yes, **or.**
6. (Repeat step 5 for remaining words.)

sō

nōse

him

has

ōld

said

TASK 5 SOUNDS

1. Take a good look at each sound. Say it slowly if you can. Don't get fooled.
2. (Touch first ball for **f.**) Get ready. (Quickly move to second ball. Hold.) "fff."
3. (Repeat step 2 for **v, ō, sh, g,** and **ā.** Remember to move quickly to end of arrow if there is no ball on arrow for sound.)

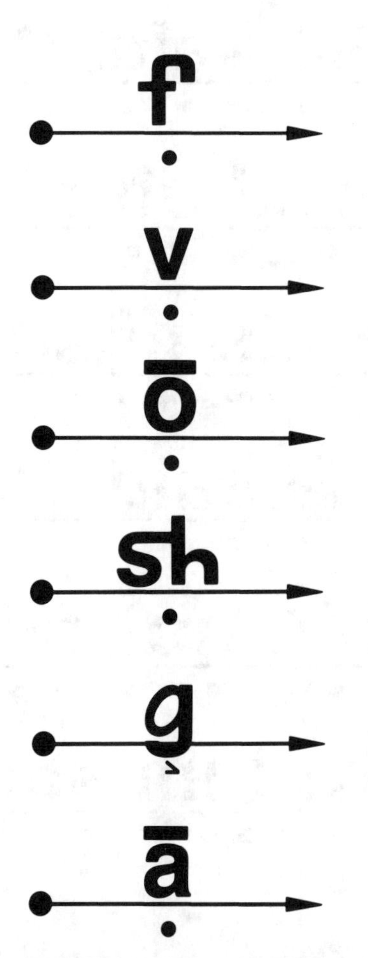

TASK 6 FIRST READING

You're going to read this story by sounding out each word. Then you get to read the whole story the fast way. First, sound out each word and tell me the word.

TASK 7 SECOND READING

1. You're going to read the story the fast way.
2. Find the first period or question mark. Then read the whole sentence the fast way.
3. Find the next period or question mark and read the next sentence.
4. (Repeat step 3 for each remaining sentence. Ask specified questions.)

(After child reads:)	(You say:)
" 'Give me a rock or a sock.' "	What did he want?
"So she gave him a sock on his nose."	What did she give him? She must have hit him on his nose. Is that what he wanted? Nobody wants to get socked on the nose.
"He said, 'I need socks on the feet, not on the nose.' "	What did he say?
"So she gave him socks for his feet."	What did she do?

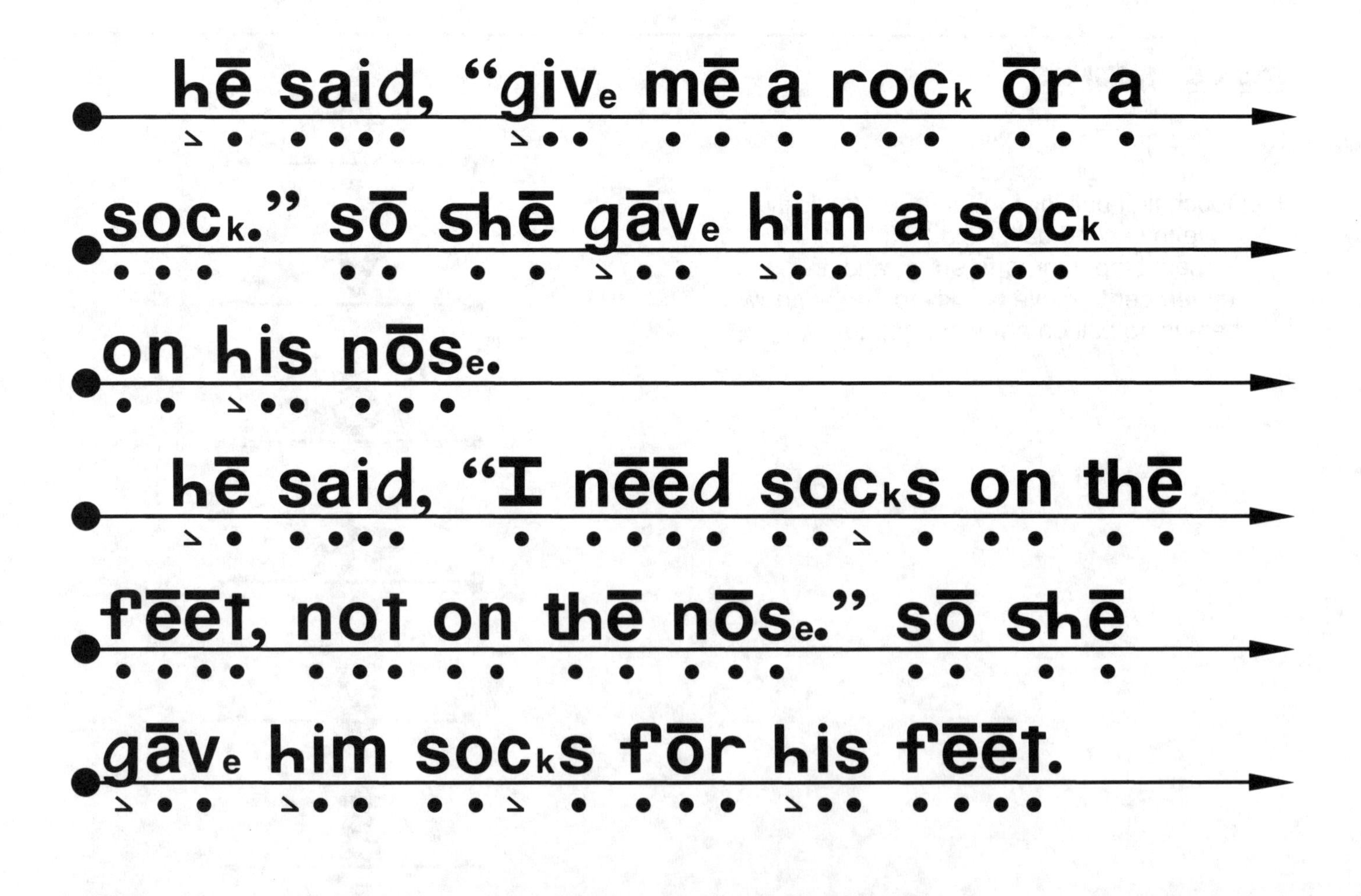

TASK 8 PICTURE COMPREHENSION

1. I wonder what kind of socks she gave him.
2. Look at the picture and get ready to answer some questions.
3. Did she give him socks for his feet?
4. What is he doing with those striped socks?

TASK 9 SOUNDS WRITING

1. Here's the first sound you're going to write. (Write **s** at beginning of first line. Point to **s.**) What sound? "sss."
2. First trace the **sss** that I made. Then make more of them on this line. (After tracing **s** several times, child is to make three to five **s**'s. Help child if necessary. For acceptable letters say:) Good writing **sss.**
3. Here's the next sound you're going to write. (Write **h** at beginning of second line. Point to **h.**) What sound? "h."
4. First trace the **h** that I made. Then make more of them on this line. (After tracing **h** several times, child is to make three to five **h**'s. Help child if necessary. For acceptable letters say:) Good writing **h.**
5. Here's the next sound you're going to write. (Write **v** at beginning of third line. Point to **v.**) What sound? "vvv."
6. First trace the **vvv** that I made. Then make more of them on this line. (After tracing **v** several times, child is to make three to five **v**'s. Help child if necessary. For acceptable letters say:) Good writing **vvv.**

LESSON 48

TASK 1 SOUNDS INTRODUCTION

p

1. (Touch ball for **p.**) We always have to say this sound fast. My turn to say it fast. (Quickly move to end of arrow as you say sound.) **p.**
2. My turn to say it fast again. (Touch ball for **p.**) Say it fast. (Quickly move to end of arrow.) **p.**
3. (Touch first ball.) Your turn. (Pause.) Say it fast. (Quickly move to end of arrow.) "p."

(To correct if child says "puh," "pah," or "pih":) Listen: **p.** Say it fast. "p." Yes, **p.**

TASK 2 SOUNDS

1. Take a good look at each sound. Say it slowly if you can. Don't get fooled.
2. (Touch first ball for **v.**) Get ready. (Quickly move to second ball. Hold.) "vvv."
3. (Repeat step 2 for **d, t, th, h,** and **p.** Remember to move quickly to end of arrow if there is no ball on arrow for sound.)

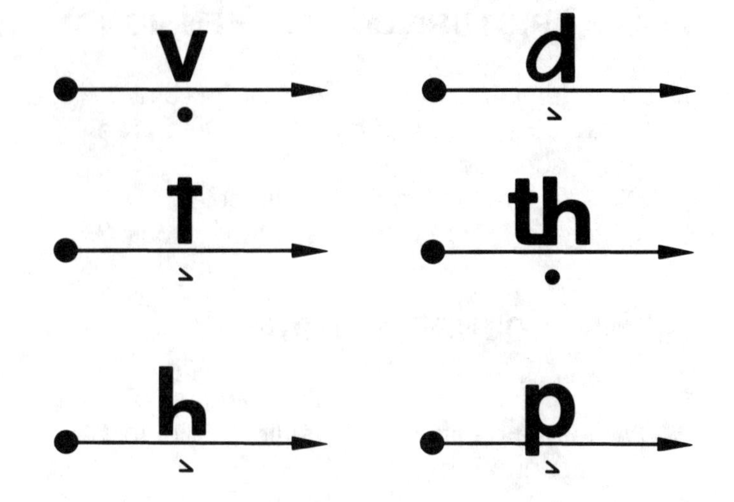

TASK 3 WORD READING

1. (Touch first ball for **to.**) Sound it out. (Touch under sounds as child says:) "tŏŏŏ."
2. That's how we **sound out** the word. Here's how we **say** the word. (Pause.) **to (too).** How do we **say** the word? "to." Yes, **to**—it's a funny word.
3. (Return to first ball.) Sound it out again. (Touch under sounds as child says:) "tooo." Now **say** the word. "to." Yes, **to.** Go **to** school.

to

TASK 4 WORD READING

1. (Touch first ball for **gōats.**) Sound it out. (Touch under sounds.) "gōōōtsss." (Repeat until firm.) What word? "goats."
2. (Repeat step 1 for **cōats, sāve, ōr, fōr,** and **hats.**)

gōats

cōats

sāve

ōr

fōr

hats

TASK 5 WORD READING

1. (Point to **was, old, cold, said, make, socks, lots,** and **have.**) You're going to read all these words the fast way. I'll go down the arrow one time for each word. Figure out the word. But don't say anything out loud until I tell you to read it the fast way.
2. (Touch ball for **was.** Touch under sounds. Return to ball.) Read it the fast way. (Slide.) "was." Yes, **was.**
3. (Repeat step 2 for remaining words.)
4. Read all these words again, the fast way.
5. (Touch first ball for **gōats.** Pause three seconds.) Read it the fast way. (Slide.) "goats." Yes, **goats.**
6. (Repeat step 5 for remaining words.)

was

ōld

cōld

said

māke

socks

lots

have

TASK 6 WORD READING

1. (Touch first ball for **of.**) Sound it out. (Touch under sounds as child says:) "ooofff." Again. (Return to first ball.) Sound it out. (Touch balls for sounds as child says:) "ooofff."
2. That's how we **sound out** the word. Now **say** the word. "of." Yes, **of.**
3. Let's do it again. (Return to first ball.) Sound it out. (Touch balls for sounds as child says:) "ooofff." Now **say** the word. "of." Yes, **of.**

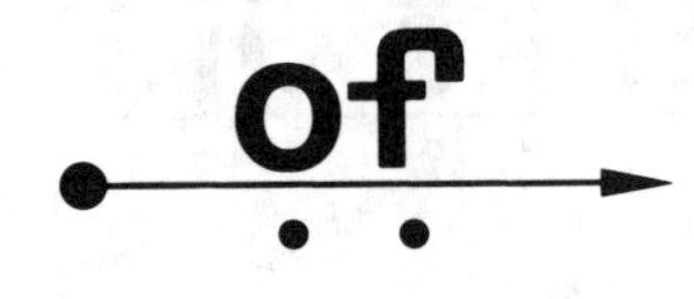

TASK 7 SOUNDS

1. Take a good look at each sound. Say it slowly if you can. Don't get fooled.
2. (Touch first ball for **v.**) Get ready. (Quickly move to second ball. Hold.) "vvv."
3. (Repeat step 2 for **p, d, ō,** and **k.** Remember to move quickly to end of arrow if there is no ball on arrow for sound.)

v p

d ō

k

TASK 8 FIRST READING

You're going to read this story by sounding out each word. Then you get to read the whole story the fast way. First, sound out each word and tell me the word.

TASK 9 SECOND READING

1. You're going to read the story the fast way.
2. Find the first period or question mark. Then read the whole sentence the fast way.
3. Find the next period or question mark and read the next sentence.
4. (Repeat step 3 for each remaining sentence. Ask specified questions.)

(After child reads:)	(You say:)
"The old man was cold."	How did he feel?
"He did not have a hat or a coat or socks."	Tell me what he didn't have.
"So he got a goat with lots of hats and coats and socks."	What did he get? What did the goat have?
"Now the old man is not cold."	Is the old man cold now?
"And the goat is not cold."	Is the goat cold?

TASK 10 PICTURE COMPREHENSION

1. What will you see in the picture?
2. Look at the picture and get ready to answer some questions.
3. Show me the goat's hats.
4. Show me the goat's coats.
5. Show me the goat's socks.
6. Why is that goat giving the old man a coat? Yes, the man is cold.
7. What would you do if you were that goat?

TASK 11 SOUNDS WRITING

1. (Write **w** at beginning of first line. Point to **w.**) What sound? "www."
2. First trace the **www** that I made. Then make more of them on this line. (After tracing **w** several times, child is to make three to five **w**'s. Help child if necessary. For each acceptable letter say:) Good writing **www.**
3. Here's the next sound you're going to write. (Write **v** at beginning of second line. Point to **v.**) What sound? "vvv."
4. First trace the **vvv** that I made. Then make more of them on this line. (After tracing **v** several times, child is to make three to five **v**'s. Help child if necessary. For acceptable letters say:) Good writing **vvv.**

thē ōld man was cōld. hē did

not have a hat ōr a cōat ōr socks.

sō hē got a gōat with lots of

hats and cōats and socks.

now thē ōld man is not cōld.

and thē gōat is not cōld.

LESSON 49

TASK 1 SOUNDS

1. Take a good look at each sound. Say it slowly if you can. Don't get fooled.
2. (Touch ball for **g.**) Get ready. (Quickly move to end of arrow.) "g."
3. (Repeat step 2 for **p, h, d, sh,** and **ā.** Remember to move quickly to end of arrow if there is no ball on arrow for sound.)

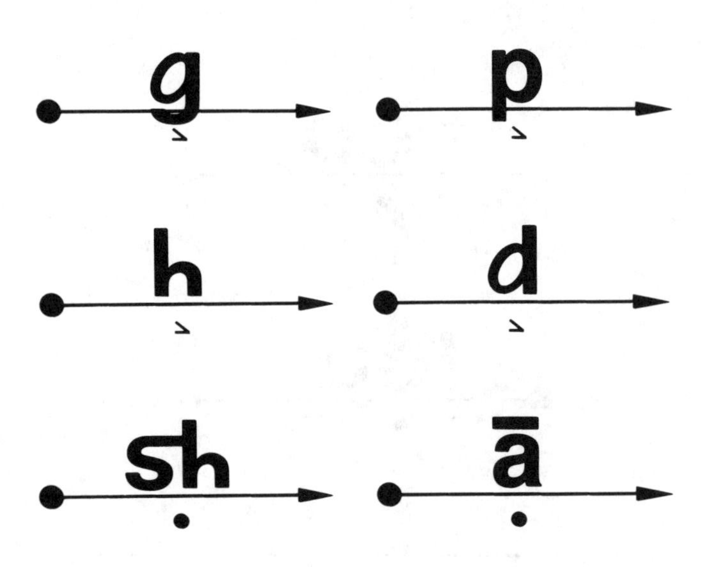

TASK 2 WORD READING

1. (Touch first ball for **to.**) Sound it out. (Touch under sounds as child says:) "tooo."
2. That's how we **sound out** the word. Here's how we **say** the word (pause) **to.** How do we **say** the word? "to." Yes, **to**—it's a funny word.
3. (Return to first ball.) Sound it out again. (Touch balls for sounds as child says:) "tooo." Now **say** the word. "to." Yes, **to.** (Repeat until firm.)

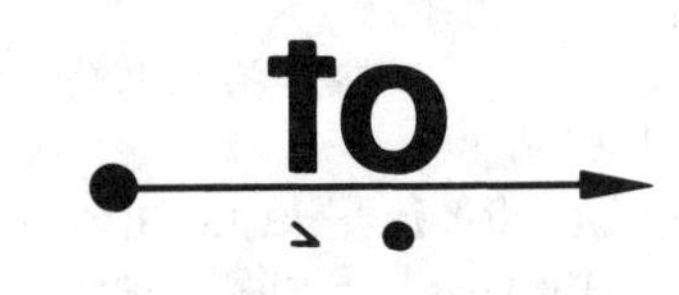

TASK 3 WORD READING

1. (Touch first ball for **mop.**) Sound it out. (Touch balls for sounds.) "mmmooop." (Repeat until firm.) What word?"mop."
2. (Repeat step 1 for **cop, top, hop, give, gāve,** and **ēars.**)

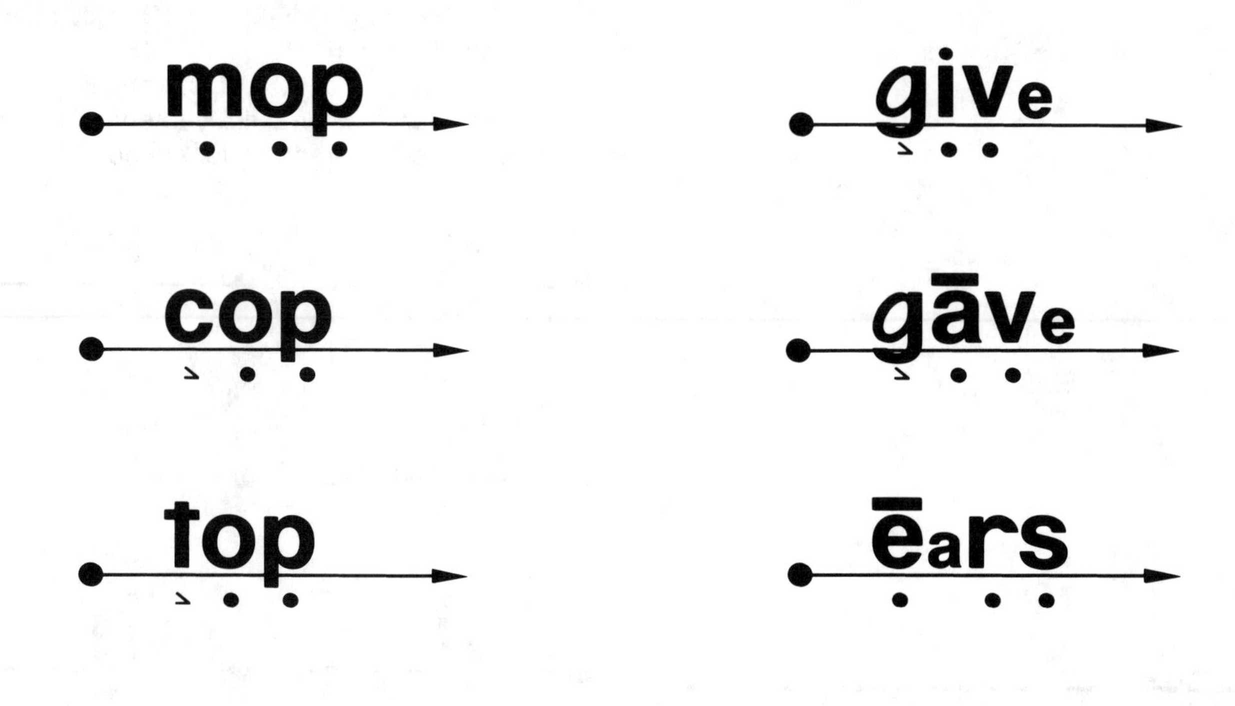

TASK 4 WORD READING—ar

1. (Touch ball for **ar.**) When these sounds are together, they usually say (pause) **are.** What do they say? "are."
2. (Touch ball for **ar** in **far.**) What do these sounds say? "are." Yes, **are.** (Touch first ball for **far.**) Sound it out. (Touch balls for sounds.) "fffŏrrr." (Repeat until firm.) What word? "far." Yes, **far.**
3. (Touch ball for **ar** in **car.**) What do these sounds say? "are." Yes, **are.** (Touch first ball for **car.**) Sound it out. (Slide past **c.** Touch ball for **ar.**) "cŏrrr." (Repeat until firm.) What word? "car." Yes, **car.**
4. (Touch ball for **ar** in **tar.**) What do these sounds say? "are." Yes, **are.** (Touch first ball for **tar.**) Sound it out. (Slide past **t.** Touch ball for **ar.**) "tŏrrr." (Repeat until firm.) What word? "tar." Yes, **tar.**
5. Now you're going to read all those words again, the fast way.
6. (Touch first ball for **far.** Pause three seconds.) Read it the fast way. (Slide.) "far." Yes, **far.**
7. (Repeat step 6 for **car** and **tar.**)

ar

far

car

tar

TASK 5 WORD READING

1. (Point to **was, did, of, gōat,** and **kitten.**) You're going to read all these words the fast way. I'll go down the arrow one time for each word. Figure out the word. But don't say anything out loud until I tell you to read it the fast way.
2. (Touch ball for **was.** Touch under sounds. Return to ball.) Read it the fast way. (Slide.) "was." Yes, **was.**
3. (Repeat step 2 for remaining words.)
4. Read all these words again, the fast way.
5. (Touch first ball for **mop.** Pause three seconds.) Read it the fast way. (Slide.) "mop." Yes, **mop.**
6. (Repeat step 5 for remaining words.)

TASK 6 SOUNDS

1. You're going to say all these sounds fast.
2. (Touch ball for **p.**) Say it fast. (Move to end of arrow.) "p."
3. (Repeat step 2 for each sound.)

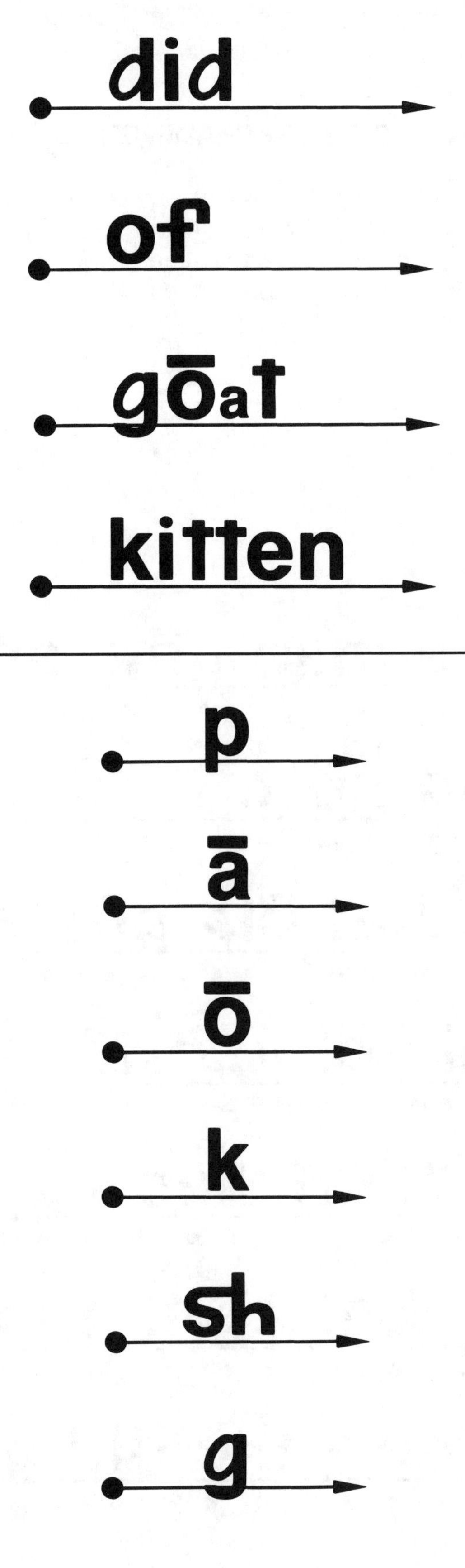

TASK 7 FIRST READING

You're going to read this story by sounding out each word. Then you get to read the whole story the fast way. First, sound out each word and tell me the word.

TASK 8 SECOND READING

1. You're going to read the story the fast way.
2. Find the first period or question mark. Then read the whole sentence the fast way.
3. Find the next period or question mark and read the next sentence.
4. (Repeat step 3 for each remaining sentence. Ask specified questions.)

(After child reads:)	(You say:)
"A man gave an old coat to an old goat."	What did the man give to the old goat?
"That old goat said, 'I will eat this old coat.' "	What did the goat say?
"So he did."	What did he do?
" 'That was fun,' he said."	What did he say?
" 'I ate an old coat.' "	What did the goat say?
" 'And now I am cold.' "	What did he say?
"Now the old goat is sad."	How does he feel? Why?

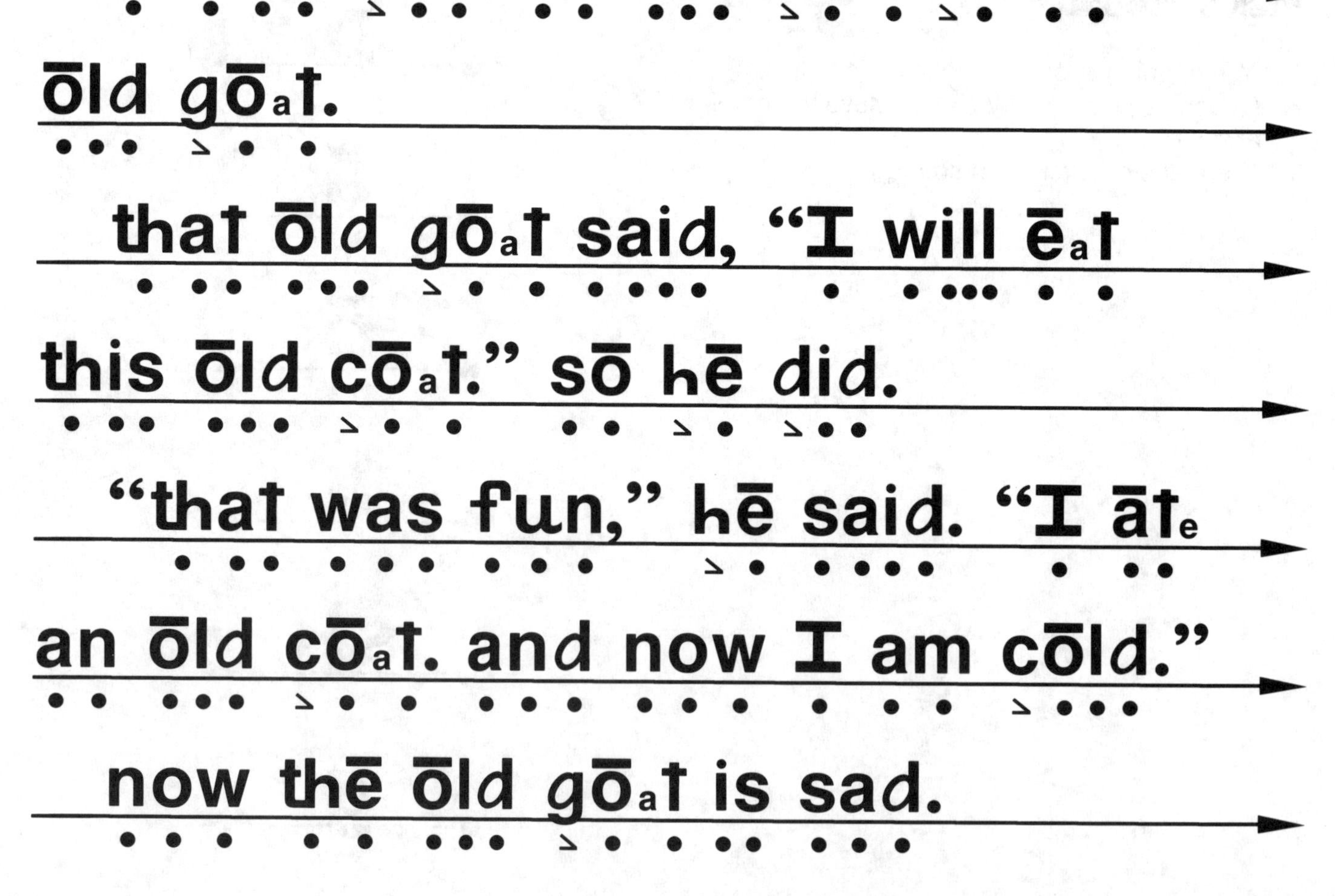

TASK 9 PICTURE COMPREHENSION

1. What will you see in the picture?
2. Look at the picture and get ready to answer some questions.
3. How does that goat feel?
4. Why is he out in the cold without a coat?
5. Did you ever go outside without a coat when it was cold?

TASK 10 SOUNDS WRITING

1. (Write **th** at beginning of first line. Point to **th.**) What sound? "thththth."
2. First trace the **thththth** that I made. Then make more of them on this line. (After tracing **th** several times, child is to make three to five **th**'s. Help child if necessary. For each acceptable letter say:) Good writing **thththth.**
3. (Write **sh** at beginning of second line. Point to **sh.**) What sound? "shshsh."
4. First trace the **shshsh** that I made. Then make more of them on this line. (After tracing **sh** several times, child is to make three to five **sh**'s. Help child if necessary. For each acceptable letter say:) Good writing **shshsh.**

LESSON 50

TASK 1 SOUNDS INTRODUCTION

1. (Touch ball for **ch.**) We always have to say this sound fast. My turn to say it fast. (Quickly move to end of arrow as you say sound.) **ch.**
2. My turn to say it fast again. (Touch ball for **ch.**) Say it fast. (Quickly move to end of arrow.) **ch.**
3. (Touch ball.) Your turn. (Pause.) Say it fast. (Quickly move to end of arrow.) "ch."

> **(To correct** if child says "chuh," "chah," or "chih":) Listen: **ch.** Say it fast. "ch." Yes, **ch.**

ch

TASK 2 SOUNDS

1. Take a good look at each sound. Say it slowly if you can. Don't get fooled.
2. (Touch first ball for **p.**) Get ready. (Quickly move to end of arrow.) "p."
3. (Repeat step 2 for **sh, th, ch, f,** and **h.** Remember to move quickly to end of arrow if there is no ball on arrow for sound.)

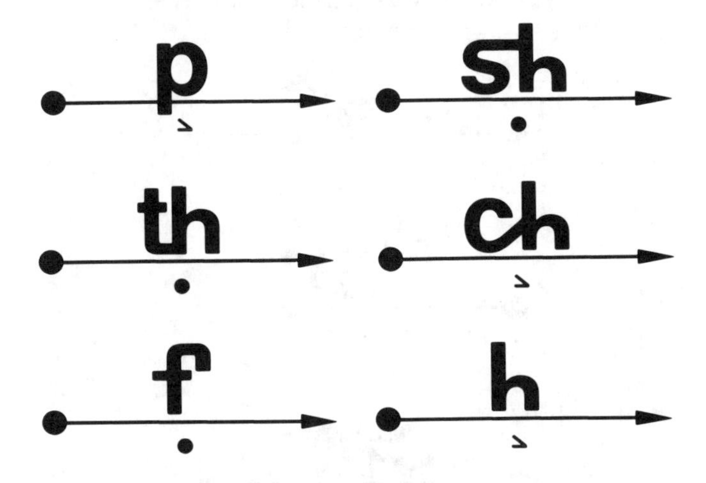

TASK 3 WORD READING

1. (Touch first ball for **to.**) Sound it out. (Touch under sounds as child says:) "tooo." Again. (Return to first ball.) Sound it out. (Touch balls for sounds as child says:) "tooo."
2. That's how we **sound out** the word. Now **say** the word. "to." Yes, **to.**
3. Let's do it again. (Return to first ball.) Sound it out (Touch balls for sounds as child says:) "tooo." Now say the word. "to." Yes, **to.**

to

TASK 4 WORD READING

1. (Touch first ball for **us.**) Sound it out. (Touch balls for sounds.) "uuusss." (Repeat until firm.) What word? "us."
2. (Repeat step 1 for **sēat, hēar, ran, sand, hōpe, pot,** and **dog.**)

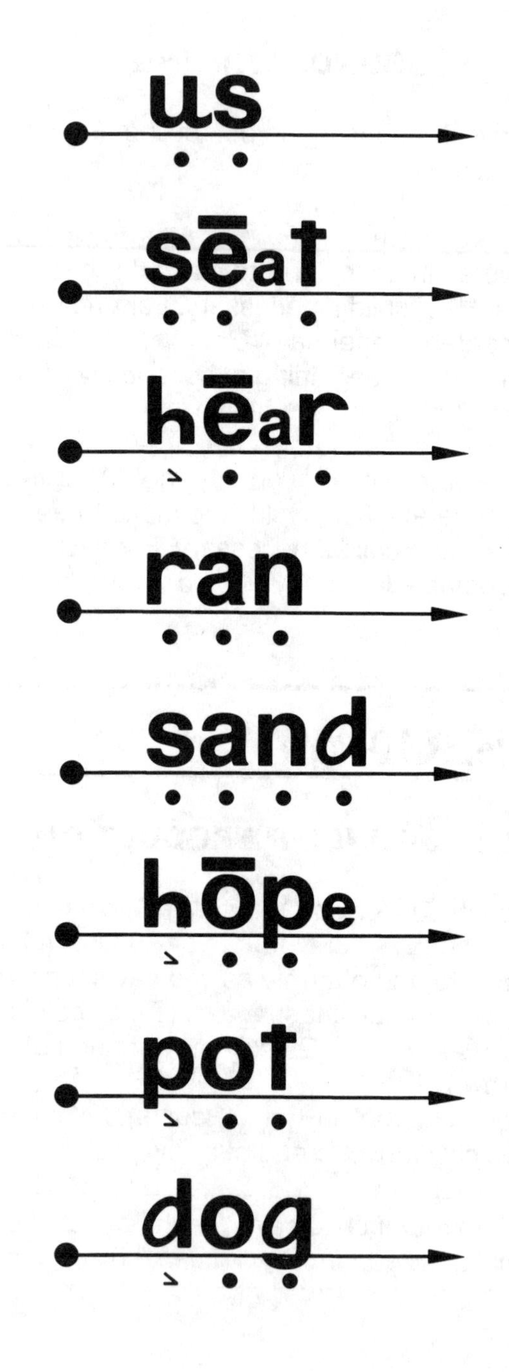

TASK 5 WORD READING

1. (Touch ball for **ar.**) When these sounds are together, they usually say (pause) **are.** What do they say? "are."
2. (Touch ball for **ar** in **far.**) What do these sounds say? "are." Yes, **are.** (Touch first ball for **far.**) Sound it out. (Touch balls for sounds.) "fffŏrrr." (Repeat until firm.) What word? "far." Yes, **far.**
3. (Touch ball for **ar** in **car.**) What do these sounds say? "are." Yes, **are.** (Touch first ball for **car.**) Sound it out. (Slide past **c.** Touch ball for art.) "cŏrrr." (Repeat until firm.) What word? "car." Yes, **car.**
4. Now you're going to read those words again, the fast way.
5. (Touch first ball for **far.** Pause three seconds.) Read it the fast way. (Slide.) "far." Yes, **far.**
6. (Repeat step 5 for **car.**)

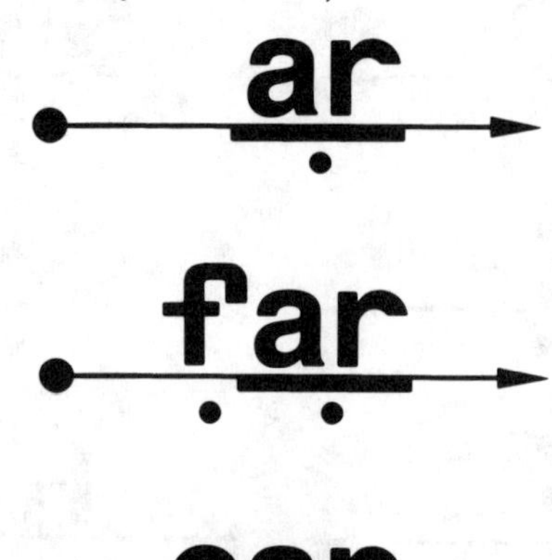

TASK 6 WORD READING

1. (Point to **lots, have, his, nēar,** and **ēars.**) You're going to read all these words the fast way. I'll go down the arrow one time for each word. Figure out the word. But don't say anything out loud until I tell you to read it the fast way.
2. (Touch ball for **lots.** Touch under sounds. Return to ball.) Read it the fast way. (Slide.) "lots." Yes, **lots.**
3. (Repeat step 2 for remaining words.)
4. Read all these words again, the fast way.
5. (Touch first ball for **to.** Pause three seconds.) Read it the fast way. (Slide.) "to." Yes, **to.**
6. (Repeat step 5 for remaining words.)

lots

have

his

nēar

ēars

TASK 7 SOUNDS

1. Take a good look at each sound. Say it slowly if you can. Don't get fooled.
2. (Touch first ball for **sh.**) Get ready. (Quickly move to second ball. Hold.) "shshsh."
3. (Repeat step 2 for **ch, g, d, p,** and **ō.** Remember to move quickly to end of arrow if there is no ball on arrow for sound.)

sh

ch

g

d

p

ō

shē said, "I have a fan."

hē said, "I have lots of sand."

shē said, "wē can run thē sand in that fan." sō hē ran thē fan nēar thē sand.

hē had sand in his ēars. hē said, "I can not hēar."

hē had sand on his sēat. shē said, "wē have sand on us."

TASK 8 FIRST READING

You're going to read this story by sounding out each word. Then you get to read the whole story the fast way. First, sound out each word and tell me the word.

TASK 9 SECOND READING

1. You're going to read the story the fast way.
2. Find the first period or question mark. Then read the whole sentence the fast way.
3. Find the next period or question mark and read the next sentence.
4. (Repeat step 3 for each remaining sentence. Ask specified questions.)

(After child reads:)	(You say:)
"She said, 'I have a fan.' "	Who said that?
"He said, 'I have lots of sand.' "	Who had the sand?
"She said, 'We can run the sand in that fan.' "	What did she say?
"So he ran the fan near the sand."	What did he do?
"He had sand in his ears."	Where did he have sand?
"He said, 'I can not hear.' "	What did he say? Why couldn't he hear?
"He had sand on his seat."	Where did he have sand?
"She said, 'We have sand on us.' "	Who said that?

TASK 10 PICTURE COMPREHENSION

1. What will you see in the picture?
2. Look at the picture and get ready to answer some questions.
3. Why do they have their hands over their faces?
4. Does that look like fun to you?
5. I wonder where they plugged that fan in.

TASK 11 SOUNDS WRITING

1. Here's the first sound you're going to write. (Write **w** at beginning of first line. Point to **w.**) What sound? "www."
2. First trace the **www** that I made. Then make more of them on this line. (After tracing **w** several times, child is to make three to five **w**'s. Help child if necessary. For acceptable letters say:) Good writing **www.**
3. Here's the next sound you're going to write. (Write **th** at beginning of second line. Point to **th.**) What sound? "ththth."
4. First trace the **ththth** that I made. Then make more of them on this line. (After tracing **th** several times, child is to make three to five **th**'s. Help child if necessary. For acceptable letters say:) Good writing **ththth.**

LESSON 51

TASK 1 SOUNDS

1. You're going to say all these sounds fast.
2. (Touch ball for **ch.**) Say it fast. (Move to end of arrow.) "ch."
3. (Repeat step 2 for each sound.)

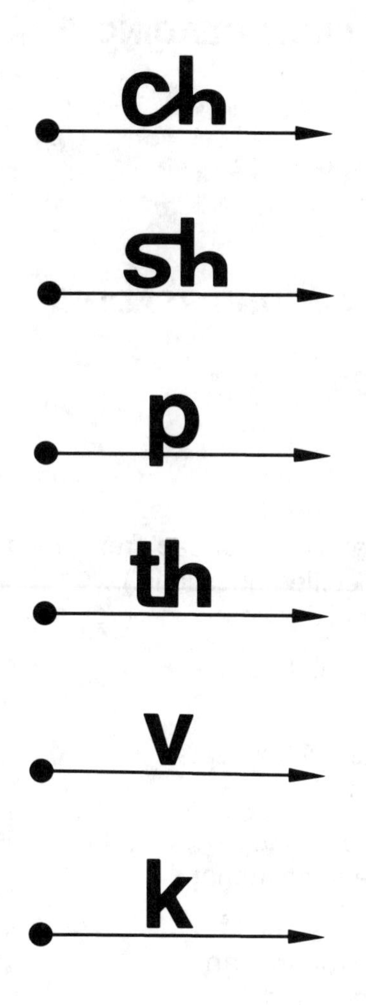

TASK 2 WORD READING

1. (Touch first ball for **to.**) Sound it out. (Touch under sounds as child says:) "tooo." Again. (Return to first ball.) Sound it out. (Touch balls for sounds as child says:) "tooo."
2. That's how we **sound out** the word. Now **say** the word. "to." Yes, **to.**
3. Let's do it again. (Return to first ball.) Sound it out. (Touch balls for sounds as child says:) "tooo." Now say the word. "to." Yes, **to.**

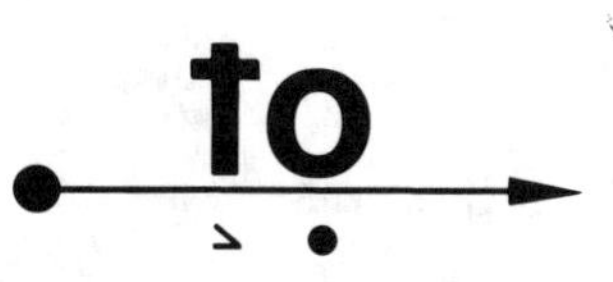

TASK 3 WORD READING

1. (Slide under **o** and **g** in **fog.**) This part says **og.**
2. (Touch first ball for **fog.**) This word rhymes with (pause) **og.** Read it the fast way. (Slide.) "fog." Yes, **fog.** Good rhyming.
3. (Slide under **o** and **g** in **log.**) This part says **og.**
4. (Touch first ball for **log.**) This word rhymes with (pause) **og.** Read it the fast way. (Slide.) "log." Yes, **log.** Good rhyming.

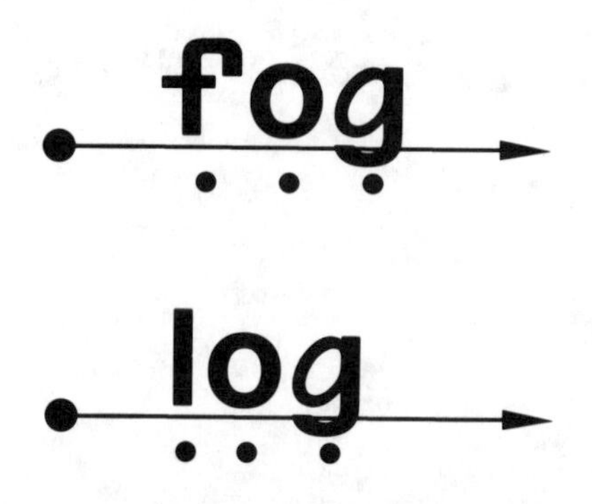

TASK 4 WORD READING

1. (Touch ball for **ar.**) Tell me what these sounds usually say when they are together. "are." Yes, **are.**
2. (Point to **car, tar,** and **park.**) Get ready to read these words the fast way.
3. (Touch first ball for **car.** Pause three seconds.) Read it the fast way. (Slide.) "car." Yes, **car.** (Touch ball for **ar** in **car.**) What do these sounds say? "are." Yes, **are.** (Touch first ball for **car.**) Sound it out. (Slide past **c.** Touch ball for **ar.**) "cŏrrr." What word? "car." Yes, **car.**
4. (Touch first ball for **tar.**) Figure it out. (Pause three seconds.) Read it the fast way. (Slide.) "tar." Yes, **tar.** (Touch ball for **ar** in **tar.**) What do these sounds say? "are." Yes, **are.** (Touch first ball for **tar.**) Sound it out. (Slide past **t.** Touch ball for **ar.**) "tŏrrr." What word? "tar." Yes, **tar.**
5. (Touch first ball for **park.**) Figure it out. (Pause three seconds.) Read it the fast way. (Slide.) "park." Yes, **park.** (Touch ball for **ar** in **park.**) What do these sounds say? "are." Yes, **are.** (Touch first ball for **park.**) Sound it out. (Slide past **p.** Touch balls for sounds.) "pŏrrrk." What word? "park." Yes, **park.**

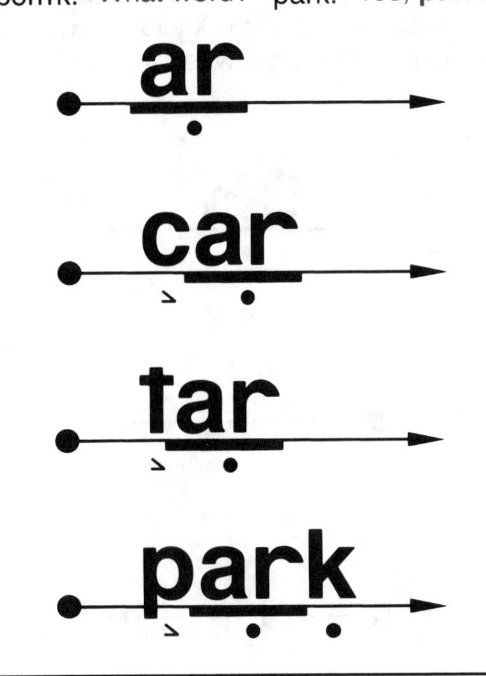

TASK 5 WORD READING

1. (Point to **of, sō, wē, cops, ōld, fōr, pot, dog, us, kick, shēēp,** and **gāve.**) You're going to read all these words the fast way. I'll go down the arrow one time for each word. Figure out the word. But don't say anything out loud until I tell you to read it the fast way.
2. (Touch ball for **of.** Touch under sounds. Return to ball.) Read it the fast way. (Slide.) "of." Yes, **of.**
3. (Repeat step 2 for remaining words.)
4. Read all these words again, the fast way.
5. (Touch first ball for **fog.** Pause three seconds.) Read it the fast way. (Slide.) "fog." Yes, **fog.**
6. (Repeat step 5 for remaining words.)

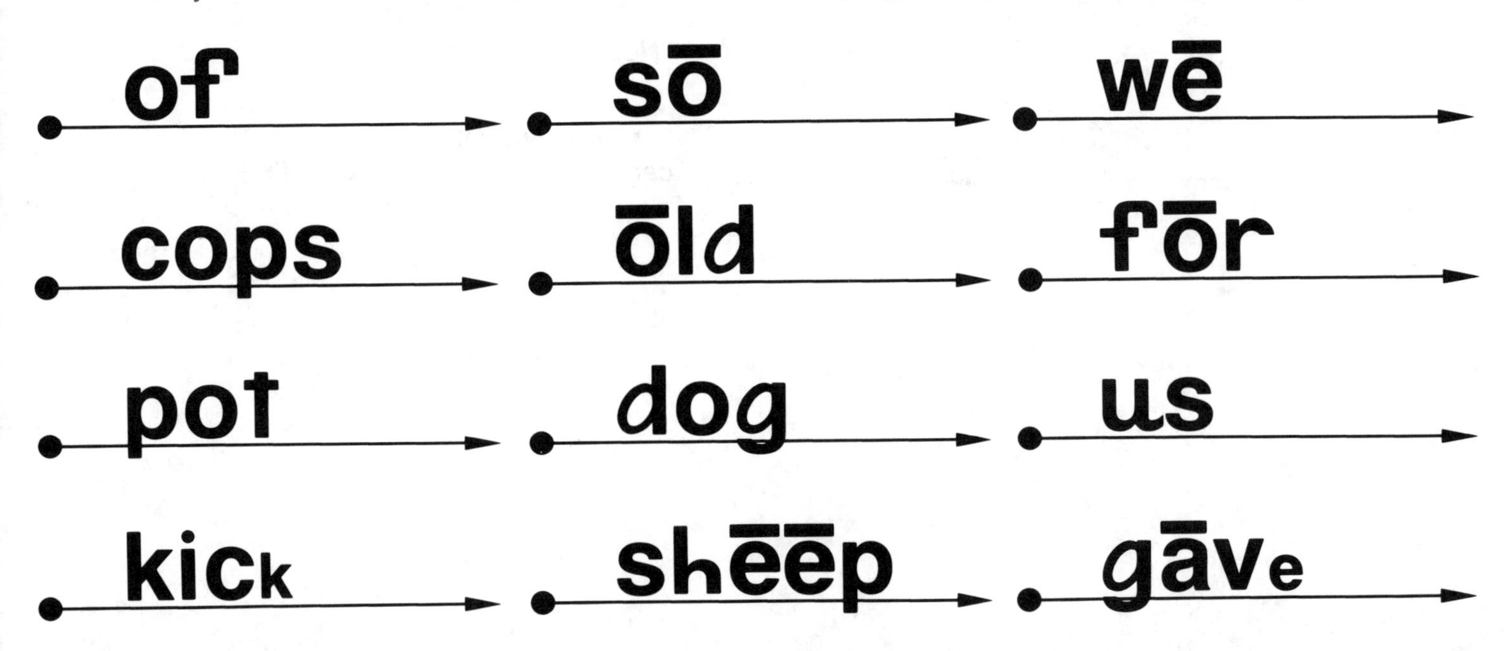

TASK 6 SOUNDS

1. Take a good look at each sound. Say it slowly if you can. Don't get fooled.
2. (Touch first ball for **ch.**) Get ready. (Quickly move to end of arrow.) "ch."
3. (Repeat step 2 for **v, p, h, k,** and **a.** Remember to move quickly to end of arrow if there is no ball on arrow for sound.)

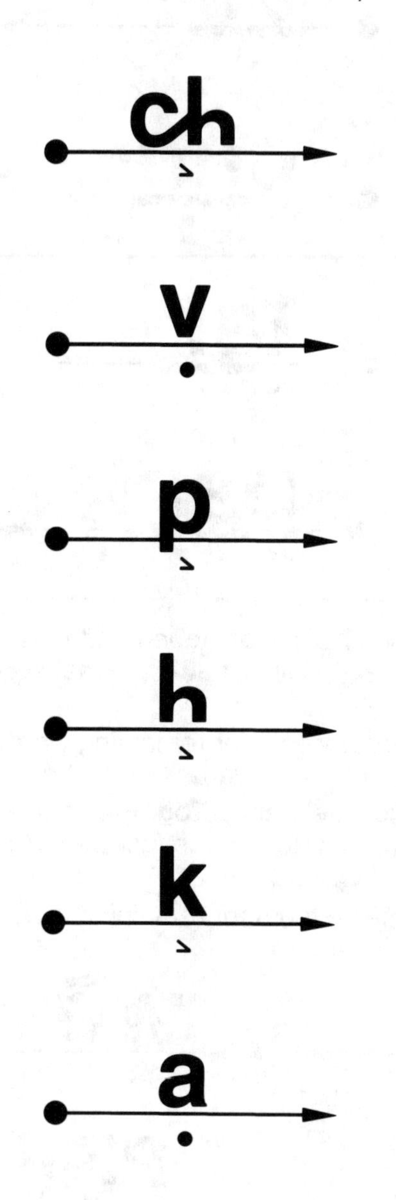

TASK 7 FIRST READING

You're going to read this story by sounding out each word. Then you get to read the whole story the fast way. First, sound out each word and tell me the word.

TASK 8 SECOND READING

1. You're going to read the story the fast way.
2. Find the first period or question mark. Then read the whole sentence the fast way.
3. Find the next period or question mark and read the next sentence.
4. (Repeat step 3 for each remaining sentence. Ask specified questions.)

(After child reads:)	(You say:)
"A dog sat in his little car."	What did the dog do?
"The dog said, 'I need to eat.' "	What did he say?
"Will this dog eat a fish?"	What do you think? Let's read and find out.
"No."	Will he eat a fish?
"Will this dog eat a log?"	What do you think? Let's read and find out.
"No."	Will he eat a log?
"Will he eat a pot of tar?"	What's a pot of tar? Let's see if he'll eat that.
"No."	Will he eat a pot of tar?
"The dog will eat his car."	What will he do? That's silly.

a dog sat in his little car.

thē dog said, "I nēēd to ēat."

will this dog ēat a fish? nō.

will this dog ēat a log? nō. will

hē ēat a pot of tar? nō.

thē dog will ēat his car.

TASK 9 PICTURE COMPREHENSION

1. What will you see in the picture?
2. Look at the picture and get ready to answer some questions.
3. Is he eating part of the car? What part?
4. Do you think that silly dog will eat the whole car? I don't think a car would taste very good.

TASK 10 SOUNDS WRITING

1. (Write **p** at beginning of first line. Point to **p.**) What sound? "p."
2. First trace the **p** that I made. Then make more of them on this line. (After tracing **p** several times, child is to make three to five **p**'s. Help child if necessary. For each acceptable letter say:) Good writing **p.**
3. Here's the next sound you're going to write. (Write **th** at beginning of second line. Point to **th.**) What sound? "thth."
4. First trace the **ththth** that I made. Then make more of them on this line. (After tracing **th** several times, child is to make three to five **th**'s. Help child if necessary. For acceptable letters say:) Good writing **ththth.**

LESSON 52

TASK 1 SOUNDS INTRODUCTION

1. (Point to **e.**) Here's a new sound. I'm going to touch under this sound and say the sound. (Touch first ball of arrow. Move quickly to second ball. Hold.) **ĕĕĕ.**
2. Your turn to say the sound when I touch under it. (Touch first ball.) Get ready. (Move quickly to second ball. Hold.) "ĕĕĕ."

> **(To correct** child saying a wrong sound or not responding:) The sound is **ĕĕĕ.** (Repeat step 2.)

3. (Touch first ball.) Again. Get ready. (Move quickly to second ball. Hold.) "ĕĕĕ."

e

TASK 2 SOUNDS

1. Take a good look at each sound. Say it slowly if you can. Don't get fooled.
2. (Touch first ball for **ē.**) Get ready. (Quickly move to second ball. Hold.) "ēēē."
3. (Repeat step 2 for **ch, p, v, e, ō,** and **k.** Remember to move quickly to end of arrow if there is no ball on arrow for sound.)

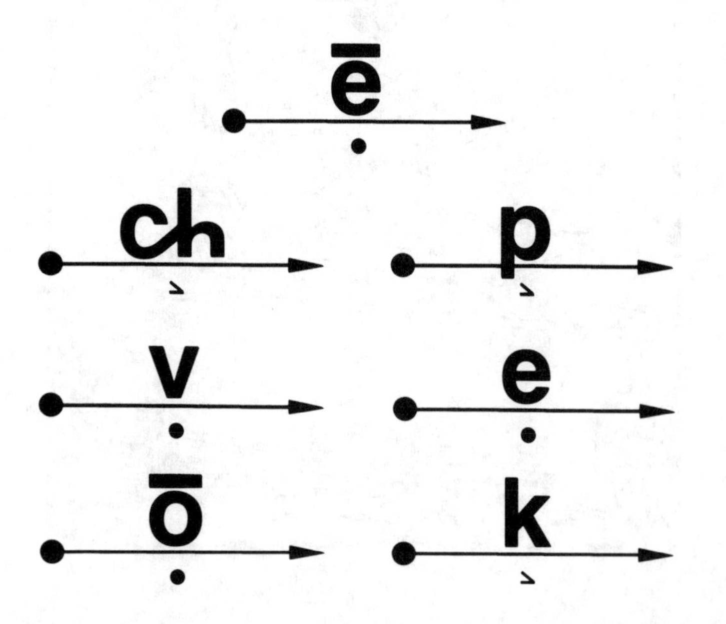

TASK 3 WORD READING

1. Here are some new words. (Touch first ball for **shop.**) Sound it out. (Touch balls for sounds.) "shshshooop." (Repeat until firm.) What word? "shop."
2. (Repeat step 1 for **chop** and **cāme.**)

TASK 4 WORD READING

1. Get ready to read these words the fast way.
2. (Touch ball for **ar** in **cars.**) What do these sounds say? "are." (Touch first ball for **cars.** Pause three seconds.) Read this word the fast way. (Slide.) "cars." Yes, **cars.**
3. (Repeat step 2 for **pa.'k** and **are.**)
4. (Touch ball for **dog.** Pause three seconds.) Read it the fast way. (Slide.) "dog." Yes, **dog.**
5. (Repeat step 4 for remaining words.)
6. Read each word again, the fast way.
7. (Touch first ball for **shop.** Pause three seconds.) What word? "shop."
8. (Repeat step 7 for remaining words.) Good reading those words.

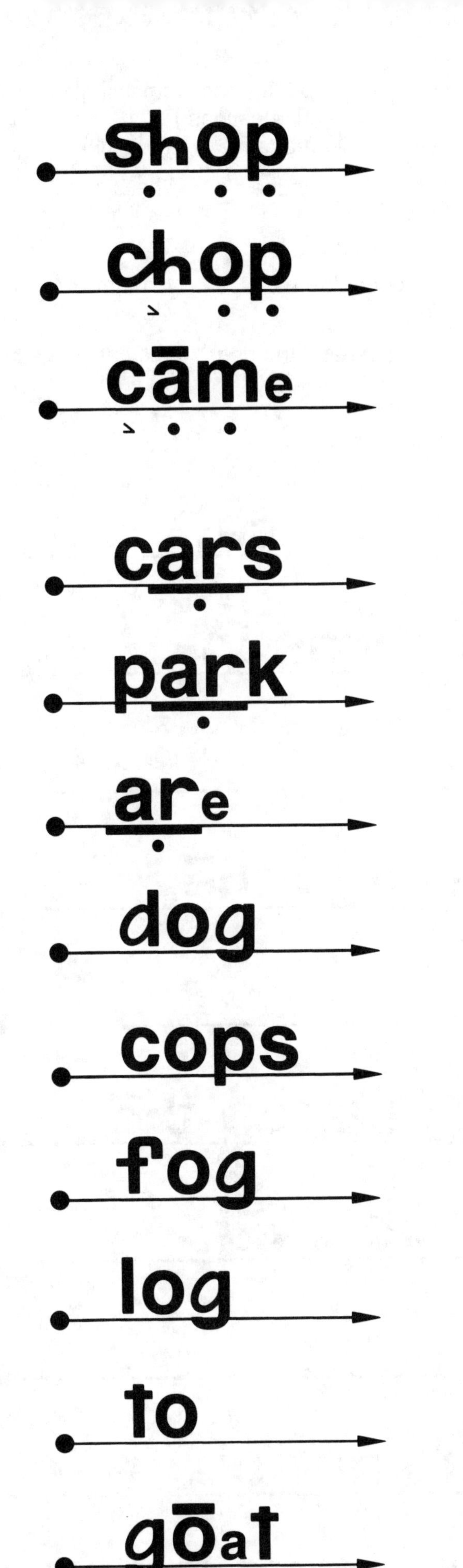

TASK 5 SOUNDS

1. Take a good look at each sound. Say it slowly if you can. Don't get fooled.
2. (Touch first ball for **e.**) Get ready. (Quickly move to second ball. Hold.) "eee."
3. (Repeat step 2 for **ō, k, p, o,** and **v.** Remember to move quickly to end of arrow if there is no ball on arrow for sound.)

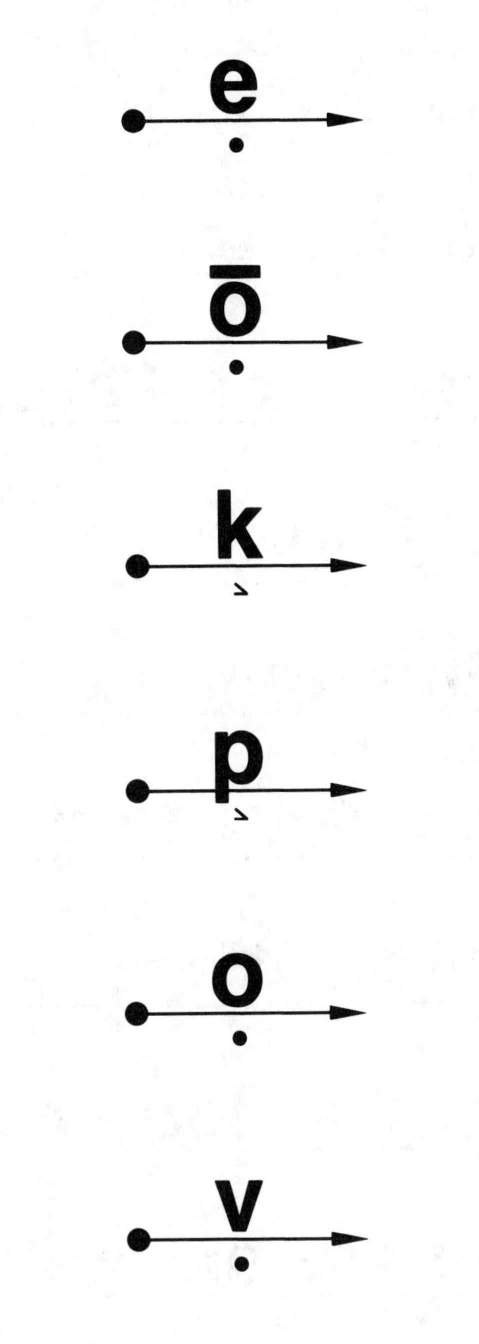

TASK 6 FIRST READING

You're going to read this story by sounding out each word. Then you get to read the whole story the fast way. First, sound out each word and tell me the word.

TASK 7 SECOND READING

1. You're going to read the story the fast way.
2. Find the first period or question mark. Then read the whole sentence the fast way.
3. Find the next period or question mark and read the next sentence.
4. (Repeat step 3 for each remaining sentence. Ask specified questions.)

(After child reads:)	(You say:)
"A dog was in the fog."	What's a fog? Yes, it's hard to see in fog.
"A goat was in the fog."	Name everybody who was in the fog.
"The cat and the dog sat on the log."	Who sat on the log? Who didn't sit on the log?
" 'He he.' "	Why is he laughing and saying **he he**?

a dog was in thē fog. a cat was in thē fog. a gōat was in thē fog.

thē dog and thē cat and thē gōat cāme to a log.

thē cat and thē dog sat on thē log. thē dog and thē cat said, "wē are on thē log."

thē gōat said, "I am not on thē log. I am in thē log. hē hē."

TASK 8 PICTURE COMPREHENSION

1. What will you see in the picture?
2. Look at the picture and get ready to answer some questions.
3. Is the goat in the log? Yes, that log is hollow.
4. Did you ever see a hollow log?
5. Did you ever see an animal go into a hollow log?
6. Who's on that log?

TASK 9 SOUNDS WRITING

1. (Write **ch** at beginning of first line. Point to **ch**.) What sound? "ch."
2. First trace the **ch** that I made. Then make more of them on this line. (After tracing **ch** several times, child is to make three to five **ch**'s. Help child if necessary. For each acceptable letter say:) Good writing **ch**.
3. Here's the next sound you're going to write. (Write **p** at beginning of second line. Point to **p**.) What sound? "p."
4. First trace the **p** that I made. Then make more of them on this line. (After tracing **p** several times, child is to make three to five **p**'s. Help child if necessary. For acceptable letters say:) Good writing **p**.

LESSON 53

TASK 1 SOUNDS

1. Take a good look at each sound. Say it slowly if you can. Don't get fooled.
2. (Touch first ball for **ē**.) Get ready. (Quickly move to second ball. Hold.) "ēēē."
3. (Repeat step 2 for **e, ā, a, ō, o.** Remember to move quickly to end of arrow if there is no ball on arrow for sound.)

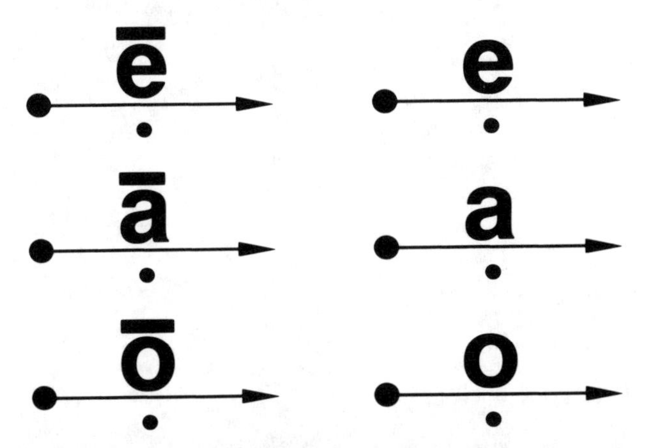

TASK 2 WORD READING

1. (Touch first ball for **girl**.) Sound it out. (Touch balls for sounds as child says:) "giiirrrlll" (not "gurrrlll").
2. That's how we **sound out** the word. Here's how we **say** the word. (Pause.) **girl (gurl).** How do we **say** the word? "girl." Yes, **girl**—it's a funny word.
3. (Return to first ball.) Sound it out again. (Touch balls for sounds as child says:) "giiirrrlll." Now **say** the word. "girl." Yes, **girl**. Annie is a **girl**.

TASK 3 WORD READING

1. (Touch first ball for **ēach.**) Sound it out. (Touch balls for sounds.) "ēēēch." (Repeat until firm.) What word? "each."
2. (Repeat step 1 for **cākes, hōme, ship, shop,** and **chop.**)

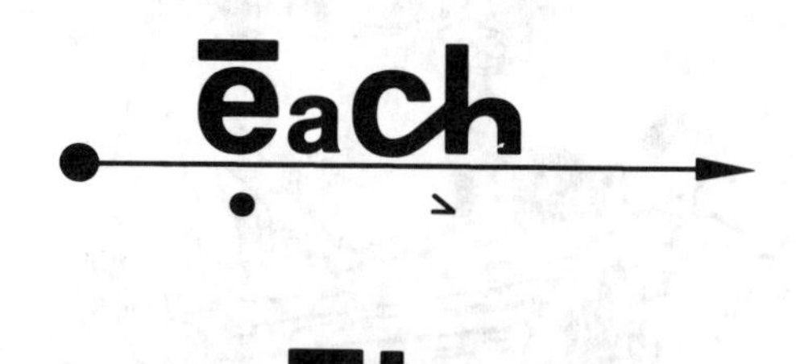

cākes

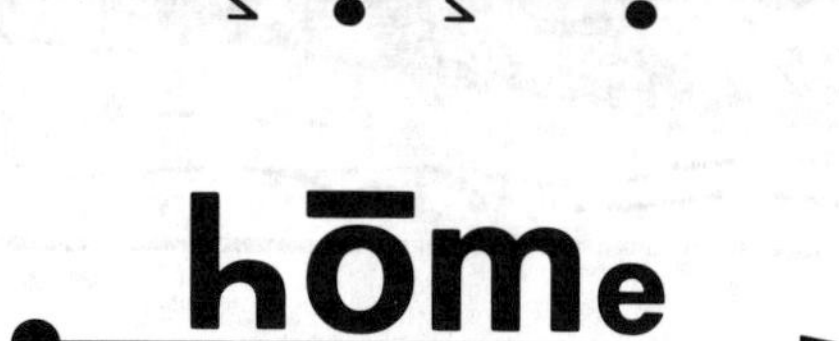

ship

shop

chop

TASK 4 WORD READING

1. Get ready to read these words the fast way.
2. (Touch **ar** in **farm.**) What do these sounds say? "are." (Touch first ball for **farm.** Pause three seconds.) Read this word the fast way. (Slide.) "farm." Yes, **farm.**
3. (Repeat step 2 for **are** and **cars.**)
4. (Touch ball for **lots.** Pause three seconds.) Read it the fast way (Slide.) "lots." Yes, **lots.**
5. (Repeat step 4 for remaining words.)
6. Now you're going to read these words again, the fast way.
7. (Touch first ball for **ēach.** Pause three seconds.) What word? "each."
8. (Repeat step 7 for remaining words.) Good reading those words.

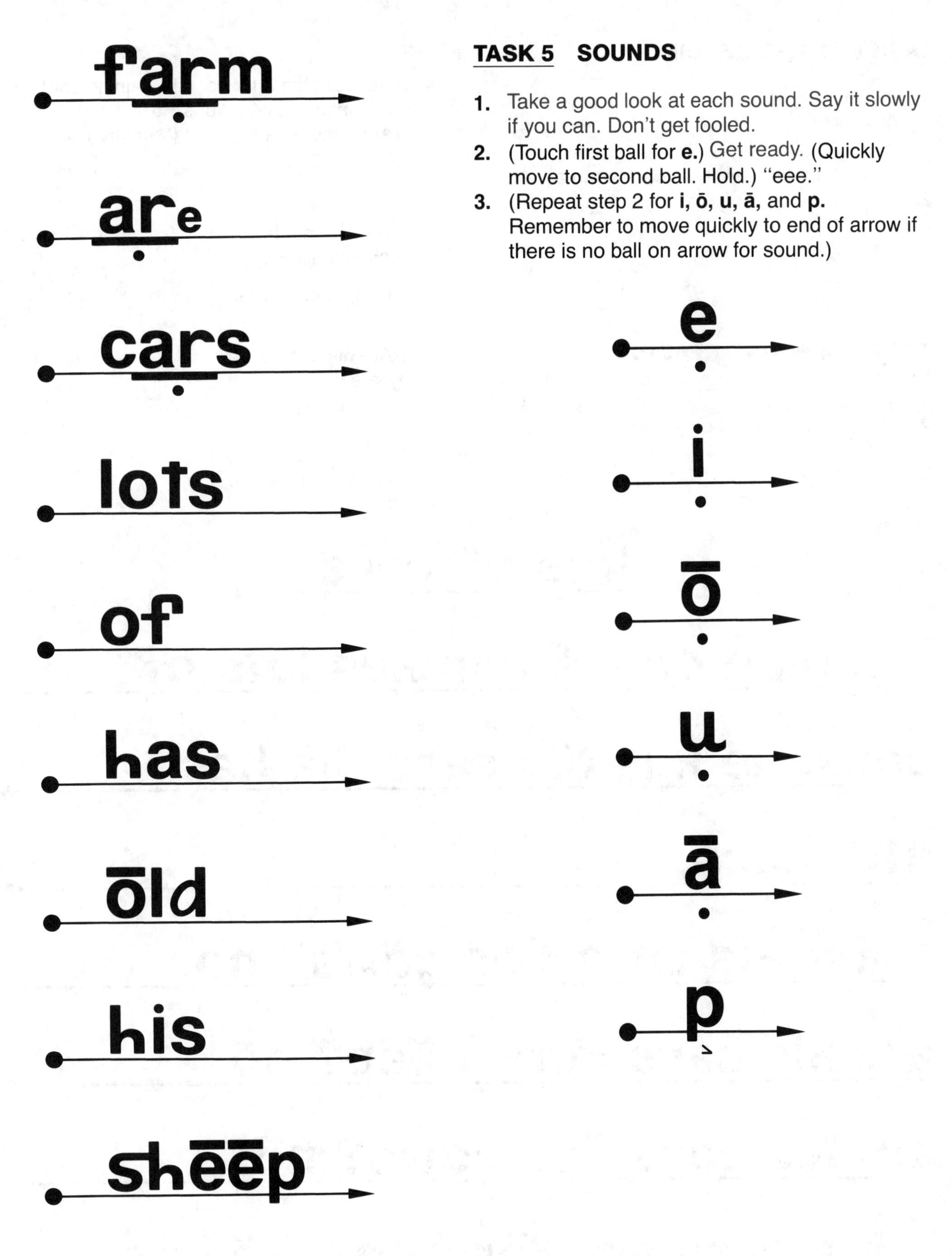

TASK 5 SOUNDS

1. Take a good look at each sound. Say it slowly if you can. Don't get fooled.
2. (Touch first ball for **e.**) Get ready. (Quickly move to second ball. Hold.) "eee."
3. (Repeat step 2 for **i, ō, u, ā,** and **p.** Remember to move quickly to end of arrow if there is no ball on arrow for sound.)

TASK 6 FIRST READING

1. (Point to title.) These words are called **the title of the story.** The title tells what the story is about.
   I'll read the title. (Point to each word as you
2. read.) **lots . . . of . . . cars.** What's this story about? "lots of cars." Yes, lots of cars. You're going to read this story. Point to each word, starting with the title. Sound it out and tell me the word.

TASK 7 SECOND READING

1. You're going to read the story the fast way.
2. Find the first period or question mark. Then read the whole sentence the fast way.
3. Find the next period or question mark and read the next sentence.
4. (Repeat step 3 for each remaining sentence. Ask specified questions.)

(After child reads:)	(You say:)
"Lots of cars."	What's this story about?
"A man on a farm has lots of cars."	What does he have?
"He has little cars."	What kinds of cars does he have?
"Are his cars for goats?"	What do you think? Let's read and find out.
"No."	Are they for goats?
"He has lots of cop cars."	What kinds of cars does he have?

lots of cars

a man on a farm has lots of cars. hē has ōld cars. hē has little cars.

are his cars fōr gōats? nō.

are his cars fōr shēēp? nō.

are his cars fōr cows? nō.

his cars are fōr cops. hē has lots of cop cars.

TASK 8 PICTURE COMPREHENSION

1. What will you see in the picture?
2. Look at the picture and get ready to answer some questions.
3. Do you see lots of cop cars? Yes, police cars look like that.
4. What would you do if you had all those cop cars?

TASK 9 SOUNDS WRITING

1. Here's the first sound you're going to write. (Write **w** at beginning of first line. Point to **w.**) What sound? "www."
2. First trace the **www** that I made. Then make more of them on this line. (After tracing **w** several times, child is to make three to five **w**'s. Help child if necessary. For acceptable letters say:) Good writing **www.**
3. Here's the next sound you're going to write. (Write **v** at beginning of second line. Point to **v.**) What sound? "vvv."
4. First trace the **vvv** that I made. Then make more of them on this line. (After tracing **v** several times, child is to make three to five **v**'s. Help child if necessary. For acceptable letters say:) Good writing **vvv.**
5. Here's the next sound you're going to write. (Write **p** at beginning of third line. Point to **p.**) What sound? "p."
6. First trace the **p** that I made. Then make more of them on this line. (After tracing **p** several times, child is to make three to five **p**'s. Help child if necessary. For acceptable letters say:) Good writing **p.**

LESSON 54

TASK 1 SOUNDS INTRODUCTION

1. (Touch ball for **b.**) We always have to say this sound fast. My turn to say it fast. (Quickly move to end of arrow as you say sound.) **b.**
2. My turn to say it fast again. (Touch ball for **b.**) Say it fast. (Quickly move to end of arrow.) **b.**
3. (Touch ball.) Your turn. (Pause.) Say it fast. (Quickly move to end of arrow.) "b."

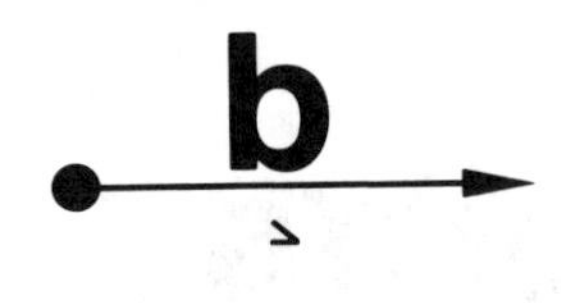

(**To correct** if child says "buh," "bah," or "bih":) Listen: **b.** Say it fast. "b." Yes, **b.**

TASK 2 SOUNDS

1. Take a good look at each sound. Say it slowly if you can. Don't get fooled.
2. (Touch first ball for **e.**) Get ready. (Quickly move to second ball. Hold.) "eee."
3. (Repeat step 2 for **ch, p, ō, b,** and **v.** Remember to move quickly to end of arrow if there is no ball on arrow for sound.)

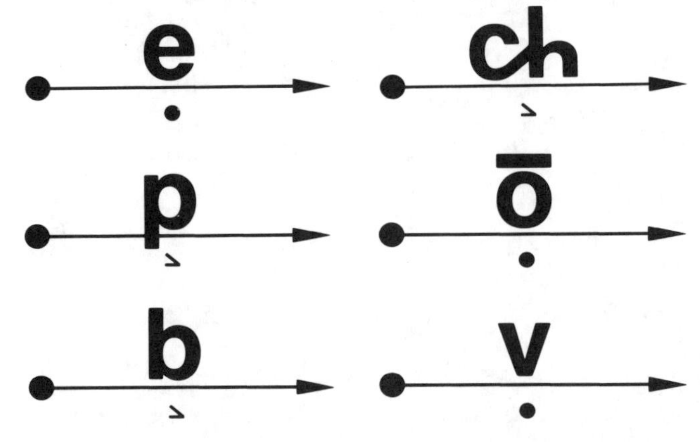

TASK 3 WORD READING

1. (Touch first ball for **girl.**) Sound it out. (Touch balls for sounds as child says:) "giiirrrlll."
2. That's how we **sound out** the word. Here's how we **say** the word. (Pause.) **girl.** How do we **say** the word? "girl." Yes, **girl**—it's a funny word.
3. (Return to first ball.) Sound it out again. (Touch balls for sounds as child says:) "giiirrrlll." Now **say** the word. "girl." Yes, **girl.** (Repeat until firm.)

TASK 4 WORD READING

1. (Touch first ball for **arm.**) Sound it out. (Touch balls for sounds.) "ŏrrrmmm." (Repeat until firm.) What word? "arm."
2. (Repeat step 1 for **charm, tāke, rāin, met, wet, pots,** and **tops.**)
3. Now you get to read all these words the fast way.
4. (Touch first ball for **arm.** Pause three seconds.) Read it the fast way. (Slide.) "arm." Yes, **arm.**
5. (Repeat step 4 for remaining words on this page.)

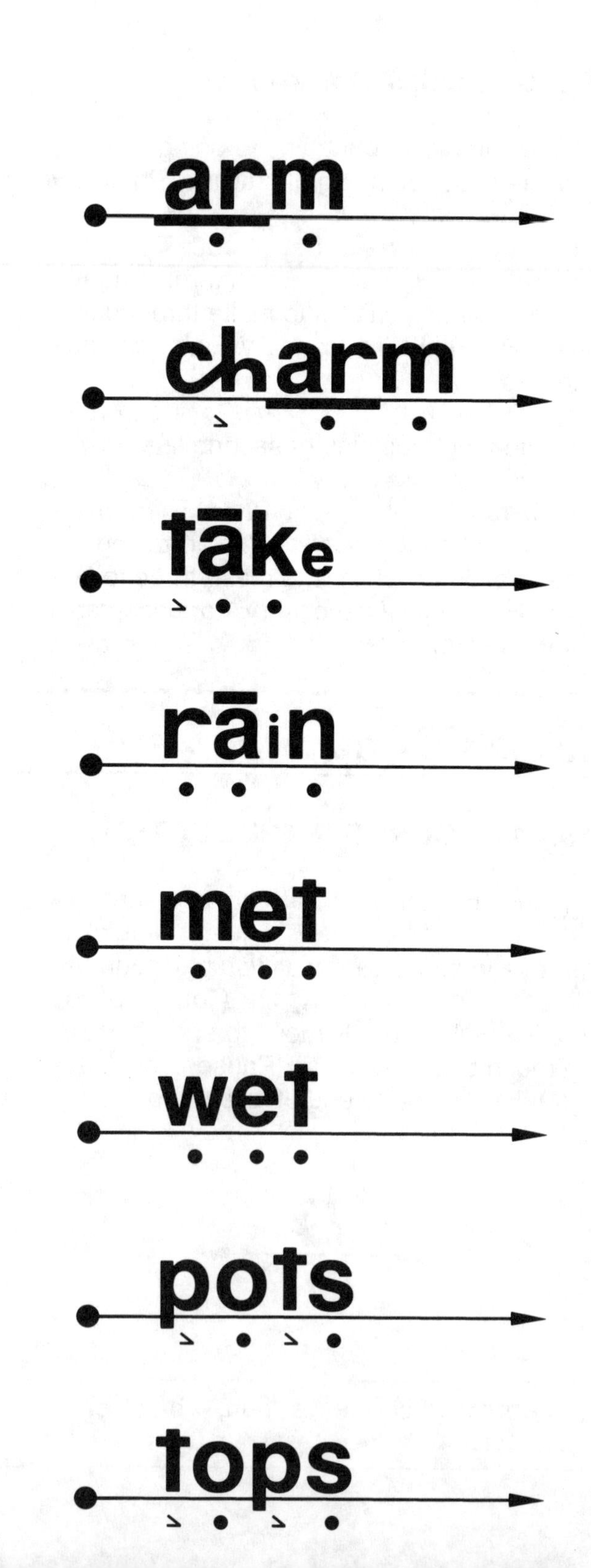

TASK 5 WORD READING

1. (Point to **to** and **do.**) These words rhyme with **oo.**
2. (Touch first ball for **to.**) This word rhymes with (pause) **oo.** Read it the fast way. (Slide.) "to." Yes, **to.**
3. (Touch first ball for **do.**) This word rhymes with (pause) **oo.** Read it the fast way. (Slide.) "do." Yes, **do.**
   Good rhyming.

to

do

TASK 6 WORD READING

1. Get ready to read these words the fast way.
2. (Touch ball for **with.** Pause three seconds.) Read it the fast way (Slide.) "with." Yes, **with.**
3. (Repeat step 2 for remaining words.)
4. Read these words again, the fast way.
5. (Touch ball for **with.** Pause three seconds.) What word? "with."
6. (Repeat step 5 for remaining words.) Good reading those words.

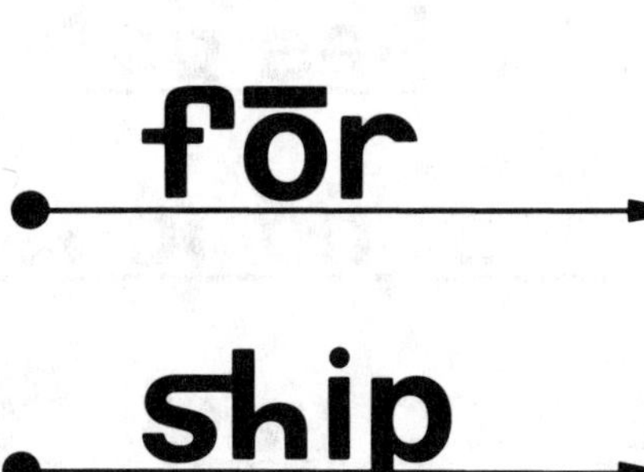

ship

hōme

TASK 7 SOUNDS

1. Take a good look at each sound. Say it slowly if you can. Don't get fooled.
2. (Touch first ball for **e.**) Get ready. (Quickly move to second ball. Hold.) "eee."
3. (Repeat step 2 for **b, p, k, h,** and **ch.** Remember to move quickly to end of arrow if there is no ball on arrow for sound.)

e

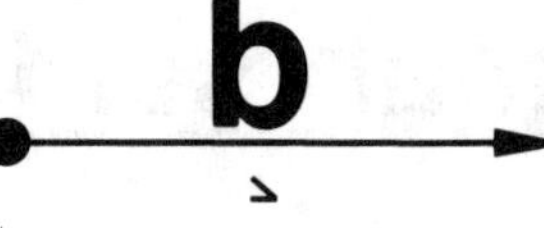

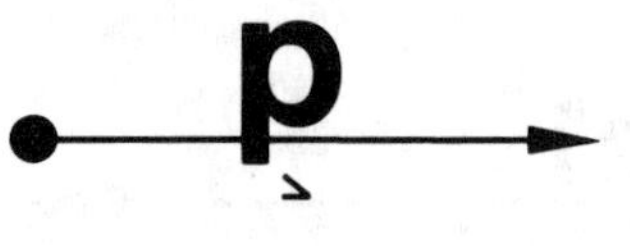

k

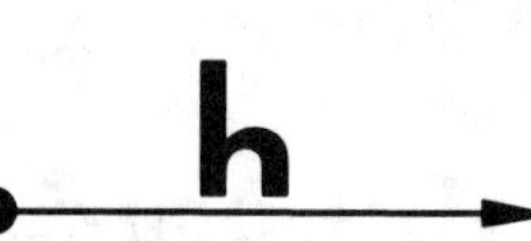

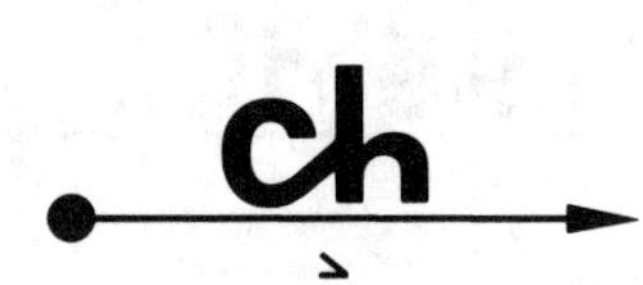

TASK 8 FIRST READING

1. (Point to title.) These words are called **the title of the story.** The title tells what the story is about.

2. I'll read the title. (Point to each word as you read.) **lots** . . . **of** . . . **pots.** What's this story about? "lots of pots." Yes, lots of pots. You're going to read this story. Point to each word. Sound it out and tell me the word.

lots of pots

a girl said, "that man has lots of pots. hē has pots with tops. hē has pots with nō tops."

the man said, "I have lots of cākes in pots. I have a pot with a ship in it. I have fish in pots."

the girl said, "can I have a pot fōr a little fish?"

the man said, "this is a pot fōr a little fish."

the girl said, "I will tāke this pot hōme with mē." and shē did.

TASK 9 SECOND READING

1. You're going to read the story the fast way.
2. Find the first period or question mark. Then read the whole sentence the fast way.
3. Find the next period or question mark and read the next sentence.
4. (Repeat step 3 for each remaining sentence. Ask specified questions.)

(After child reads:)	(You say:)
"Lots of pots."	What's this story about?
" 'He has pots with no tops.' "	What kind of pots did the man have?
" 'I have fish in pots.' "	What did the man say?
"The girl said, 'Can I have a pot for a little fish?' "	What did the girl want?
"The man said, 'This is a pot for a little fish.' "	Did the man have a pot for a little fish?
"And she did."	Did the girl take the pot home with her?

TASK 10 PICTURE COMPREHENSION

1. What will you see in the picture?
2. Look at the picture and get ready to answer some questions.
3. Look at all those pots. Which pot do you think is for a little fish?
4. Have you ever had a pet fish?

TASK 11 SOUNDS WRITING

1. Here's the first sound you're going to write. (Write **w** at beginning of first line. Point to **w.**) What sound? "www."
2. First trace the **www** that I made. Then make more of them on this line. (After tracing **w** several times, child is to make three to five **w**'s. Help child if necessary. For acceptable letters say:) Good writing **www.**
3. Here's the next sound you're going to write. (Write **p** at beginning of second line. Point to **p.**) What sound? "p."
4. First trace the **p** that I made. Then make more of them on this line. (After tracing **p** several times, child is to make three to five **p**'s. Help child if necessary. For acceptable letters say:) Good writing **p.**

LESSON 55

TASK 1 SOUNDS

1. Take a good look at each sound. Say it slowly if you can. Don't get fooled.
2. (Touch ball for **ch.**) Get ready. (Quickly move to end of arrow.) "ch."
3. (Repeat step 2 for **b, v, p, k,** and **ō.** Remember to move quickly to end of arrow if there is no ball on arrow for sound.)

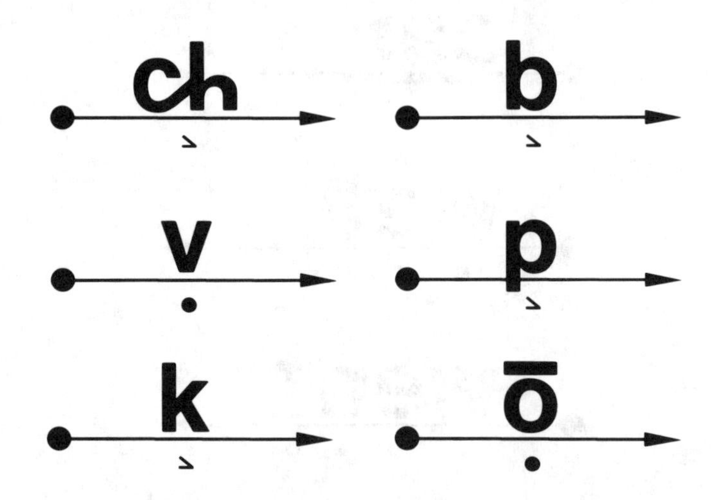

TASK 2 WORD READING

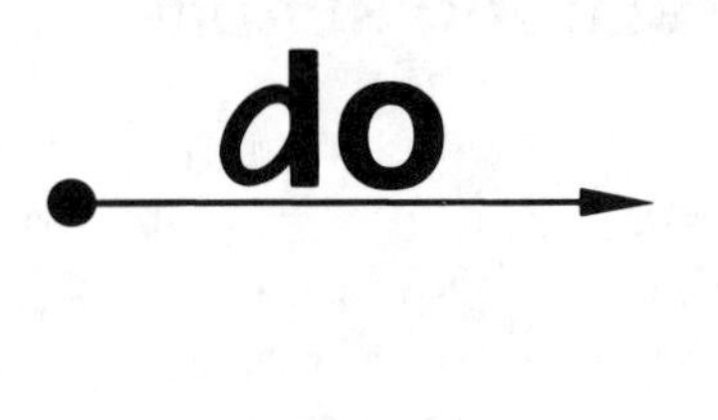

1. (Point to **do** and **to.**) These words rhyme with **oo.**
2. (Touch ball for **do.**) This word rhymes with (pause) **oo.**
   Read it the fast way. (Slide.) "do." Yes, **do.**
3. (Touch ball for **to.**) This word rhymes with (pause) **oo.** Read it the fast way. (Slide.) "to." Yes, **to.** Good rhyming.

TASK 3 WORD READING

1. (Touch first ball for **girl.**) Sound it out. (Touch under sounds as child says:) "giiirrrlll." Again. (Return to first ball.) Sound it out. (Touch balls for sounds as child says:) "giiirrrlll."
2. That's how we sound out the word. Now say the word. "girl." Yes, **girl.**
3. Let's do it again. (Return to first ball.) Sound it out. (Touch balls for sounds as child says:) "giiirrrlll." Now say the word. "girl." Yes, **girl.**

TASK 4 WORD READING

1. (Touch first ball for **are.**) Sound it out. (Touch ball for sound.) "ŏrrr." (Repeat until firm.) What word? "are."
2. (Repeat step 1 for **car, wet, went, met, hāte, if, thōse, down,** and **rōad.**)

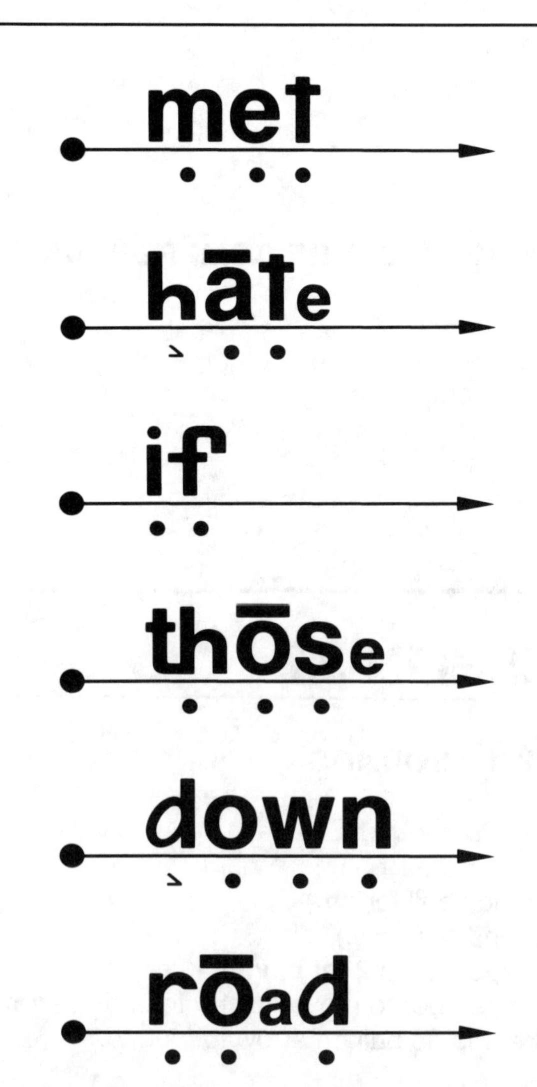

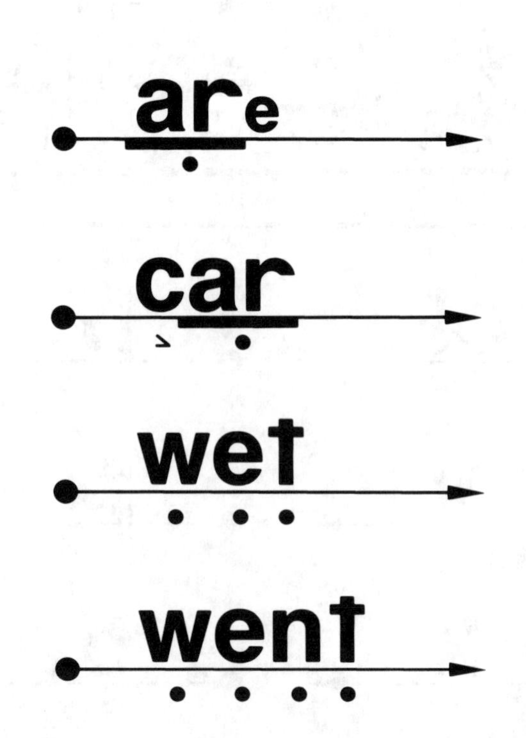

TASK 5 WORD READING

1. Get ready to read these words the fast way.
2. (Touch ball for **rāin.** Pause three seconds.) Read it the fast way. (Slide.) "rain." Yes, **rain.**
3. (Repeat step 2 for remaining words.)
4. Read these words again, the fast way.
5. (Touch first ball for **are.** Pause three seconds.) What word? "are."
6. (Repeat step 5 for remaining words.) Good reading those words.

rāin

get

shop

hōme

gāve

TASK 6 SOUNDS

1. You're going to say all these sounds fast.
2. (Touch ball for **b.**) Say it fast. (Move to end of arrow.) "b."
3. (Repeat step 2 for each sound.)

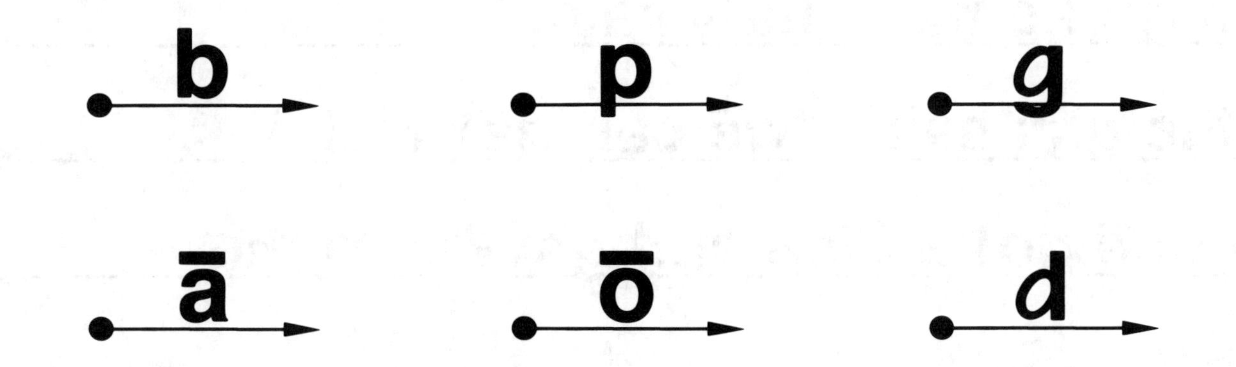

TASK 7 FIRST READING

1. You're going to read this story the fast way the first time you read it. But if you come to a word that you can't read the fast way, sound it out and then tell me the word.
2. Touch the title. Remember, the title of a story tells what the story is about. Read the title the fast way. "a fish in the rain." What is this story going to tell about? "a fish in the rain."
3. Read the first sentence the fast way. (Child reads first sentence.)
4. Read the next sentence the fast way. (Child reads second sentence.)
5. (Repeat step 4 for remaining sentences in story.)

TASK 8 SECOND READING

1. You're going to read the story again the fast way. This time I'll ask questions. Start with the title again. (Ask questions as child reads.)
2. (After child reads:) (You say:)

(After child reads:)	(You say:)
"A fish in the rain."	What's this story about?
"The man said, 'This is not fun.' "	What did the man say?
"The girl said, 'This is fun.' "	Did the girl like getting wet?
"So she got a fish and gave it to the man."	What did she do?

a fish in the rāin

a girl met a man in the rāin. that man got wet. that girl got wet.

the man said, "this is not fun."

the girl said, "this is fun."

the man said, "I have wet fēēt. sō I will gō hōme. I hāte rāin."

the girl said, "wē can get fish."

sō shē got a fish and gāve it to the man.

TASK 9 PICTURE COMPREHENSION

1. What will you see in the picture?
2. Look at the picture and get ready to answer some questions.
3. Who is in the rain?
4. What's that girl doing?
5. Do you like to wear boots and walk through puddles when it's raining?

TASK 10 SOUNDS WRITING

1. Here's the first sound you're going to write. (Write **ch** at beginning of first line. Point to **ch.**) What sound? "ch."
2. First trace the **ch** that I made. Then make more of them on this line. (After tracing **ch** several times, child is to make three to five **ch**'s. Help child if necessary. For acceptable letters say:) Good writing **ch.**
3. Here's the next sound you're going to write. (Write **sh** at beginning of second line. Point to **sh.**) What sound? "shshsh."
4. First trace the **shshsh** that I made. Then make more of them on this line. (After tracing **sh** several times, child is to make three to five **sh**'s. Help child if necessary. For acceptable letters say:) Good writing **shshsh.**

LESSON 56

TASK 1 SOUNDS INTRODUCTION

1. (Point to **ing.**) Here's a new sound. I'm going to touch under this sound and say the sound. (Touch first ball of arrow. Move quickly to second ball. Hold for only one second.) **iiing.** (Release.)
2. Your turn to say the sound when I touch under it. (Touch first ball.) Get ready. (Move quickly to second ball. Hold for only one second.) "iiing." (Release.)

> (**To correct** child saying a wrong sound or not responding:) The sound is **iiing.** (Repeat step 2.)

3. (Touch first ball.) Again. Get ready. (Move quickly to second ball. Hold for only one second.) "iiing." (Release.)

TASK 2 SOUNDS

1. Take a good look at each sound. Say it slowly if you can. Don't get fooled.
2. (Touch ball for **b.**) Get ready. (Quickly move to end of arrow.) "b."
3. (Repeat step 2 for **e, ch, ing, p,** and **v.** Remember to move quickly to end of arrow if there is no ball on arrow for sound.)

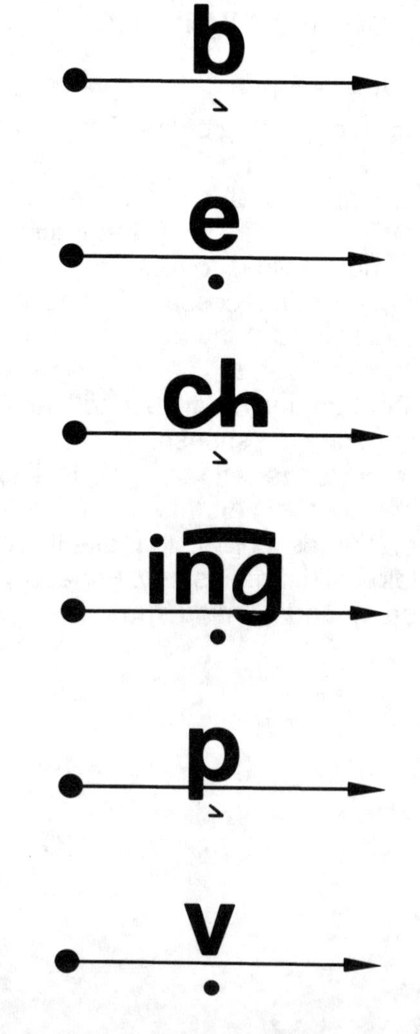

TASK 3 WORD READING

1. Get ready to read these words the fast way.
2. (Touch ball for **red.** Pause three seconds.) Read it the fast way. (Slide.) "red." Yes, **red.**
3. (Repeat step 2 for remaining words.)
4. Read these words again, the fast way.
5. (Touch ball for **red.** Pause three seconds.) What word? "red."
6. (Repeat step 5 for remaining words.) Good reading those words.

TASK 4 SOUNDS

1. Take a good look at each sound. Say it slowly if you can. Don't get fooled.
2. (Touch ball for **b.**) Get ready. (Quickly move to end of arrow.) "b."
3. (Repeat step 2 for **ing, v, k, e,** and **p.** Remember to move quickly to end of arrow if there is no ball on arrow for sound.)

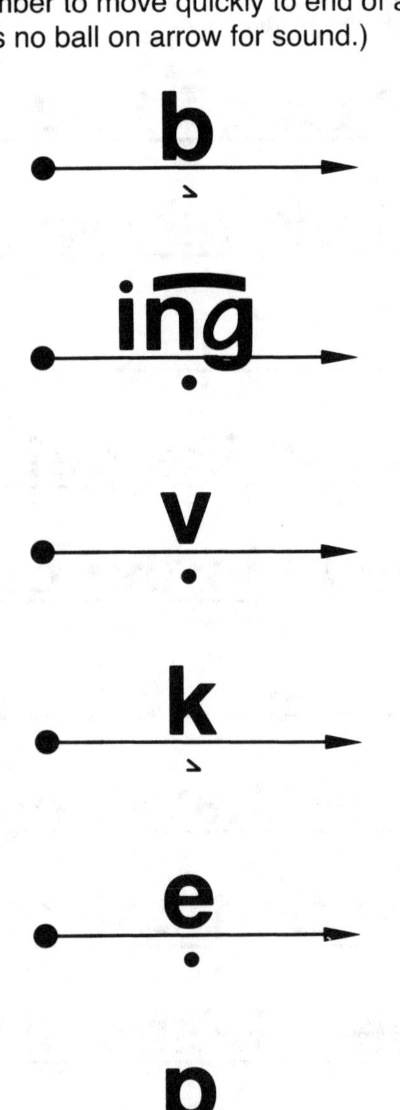

red

rēad

then

nēēd

went

let

them

dogs

do

pet

duck

down

rōad

hāte

girl

1. You're going to read this story the fast way the first time you read it. But if you come to a word that you can't read the fast way, sound it out and then tell me the word.
2. Touch the title. Remember, the title of a story tells what the story is about. Read the title the fast way. "the pet shop." What is this story going to tell about? "the pet shop."
3. Read the first sentence the fast way. (Child reads first sentence.)
4. Read the next sentence the fast way. (Child reads second sentence.)
5. (Repeat step 4 for remaining sentences in story.)

the pet shop

a girl said to a man, "let us gō to the pet shop." sō the man and the girl went down the rōad.

the man and the girl went in the pet shop. the girl said to the man in the pet shop, "I nēēd a dog."

the man said, "nō. I do not have dogs. I have a red cat. let mē get that cat."

sō hē did. and the girl went hōme with the red cat.

TASK 6 SECOND READING

1. You're going to read the story again the fast way. This time I'll ask questions. Start with the title again. (Ask questions as child reads.)
2. (After child reads:) (You say:)

(After child reads:)	(You say:)
"The pet shop."	What's this story about?
"A girl said to a man, 'Let us go to the pet shop.' "	Who said that? Whom was she talking to?
"The girl said to the man in the pet shop, 'I need a dog.' "	What did she say? Whom did she say that to?
" 'Let me get that cat.' "	What cat is he going to get?
"And the girl went home with the red cat."	What did the girl do with the cat?

TASK 7 PICTURE COMPREHENSION

1. What will you see in the picture?
2. Look at the picture and get ready to answer some questions.
3. Why are those hearts all around that girl? Yes, they mean that she loves the cat.
4. Do you think she'll take good care of that cat?
5. What would you do with a red cat?

TASK 8 SOUNDS WRITING

1. (Write **b** at beginning of first line. Point to **b.**) What sound? "b."
2. First trace the **b** that I made. Then make more of them on this line. (After tracing **b** several times, child is to make three to five **b**'s. Help child if necessary. For each acceptable letter say:) Good writing **b.**
3. Here's the next sound you're going to write. (Write **ch** at beginning of second line. Point to **ch.**) What sound? "ch."
4. First trace the **ch** that I made. Then make more of them on this line. (After tracing **ch** several times, child is to make three to five **ch**'s. Help child if necessary. For acceptable letters say:) Good writing **ch.**

LESSON 57

TASK 1 SOUNDS

1. Take a good look at each sound. Say it slowly if you can. Don't get fooled.
2. (Touch ball for **g.**) Get ready. (Quickly move to end of arrow.) "g."
3. (Repeat step 2 for **ing, v, ch, k,** and **b.** Remember to move quickly to end of arrow if there is no ball on arrow for sound.)

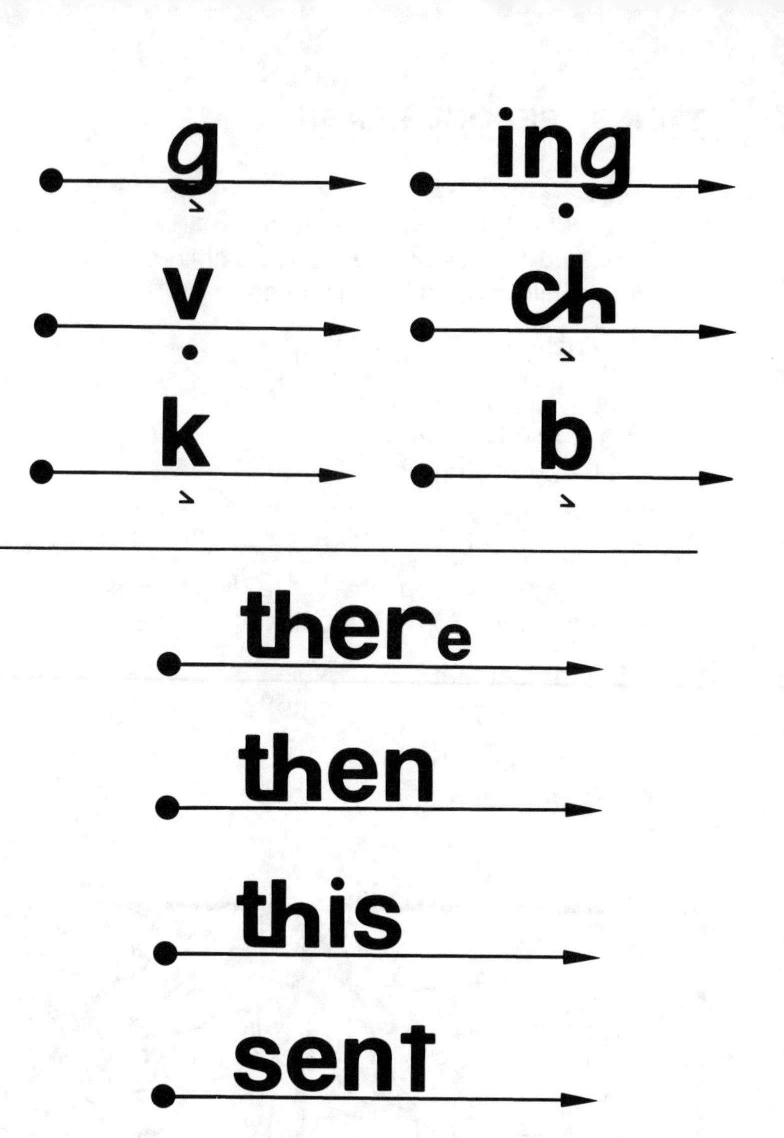

TASK 2 WORD READING

1. Get ready to read these words the fast way.
2. (Touch ball for **there.** Pause three seconds.) Read it the fast way. (Slide.) "there." Yes, **there.**
3. (Repeat step 2 for remaining words.)

farm

pet

duck

girl

TASK 3 WORD READING

1. (Touch arrow under **b** in **big.**) Remember, I can't stop under this sound, but you have to say the sound with the next sound I stop at.
2. (Touch first ball for **big.**) Sound it out. Get ready. (Slide past **b.**) Touch balls for other sounds.) "biiig." (Repeat until firm.) What word? "big." Yes, **big.**
3. (Touch first ball for **bug.**) Sound it out. (Touch under sounds.) "buuug." (Repeat until firm.) What word? "bug."
4. (Repeat step 3 for **pig, bit,** and **chicks.**)
5. Now you get to read all these words the fast way.
6. (Touch ball for **there.** Pause three seconds.) Read it the fast way. (Slide.) "there." Yes, **there.**
7. (Repeat step 6 for remaining words on this page.)

big

bug

pig

bit

chicks

TASK 4 SOUNDS

1. Take a good look at each sound. Say it slowly if you can. Don't get fooled.
2. (Touch first ball for **ing.**) Get ready. (Quickly move to second ball. Hold.) "iiing."
3. (Repeat step 2 for **i, ō, e, h,** and **l.** Remember to move quickly to end of arrow if there is no ball on arrow for sound.)

ing

i

ō

e

h

l

1. You're going to read this story the fast way the first time you read it. But if you come to a word that you can't read the fast way, sound it out and then tell me the word.
2. Touch the title. Remember, the title of a story tells what the story is about. Read the title the fast way "a girl and a man." What is this story going to tell about? "a girl and a man."
3. Read the first sentence the fast way. (Child reads first sentence.)
4. Read the next sentence the fast way (Child reads second sentence.)
5. (Repeat step 4 for remaining sentences in story.)

a girl and a man

a girl was on the rōad to a farm. shē met a man. shē said, "gō with mē to the farm. then wē will pet a pig."

the man said, "I pet ducks and I pet chicks. I do not pet pigs."

the girl said, "it is fun to pet pigs. pigs are fat."

the man said, "I will not pet them. I will gō to the park and pet a duck."

sō the man went to the park to pet a duck. then the girl went to the farm to pet a pig.

TASK 6 SECOND READING

1. You're going to read the story again the fast way. This time I'll ask questions. Start with the title again. (Ask questions as child reads.)
2. (After child reads:) (You say:)

(After child reads:)	(You say:)
"A girl and a man."	What's this story about?
"She met a man."	Whom did she meet? Where was she going?
" 'Then we will pet a pig.' "	What did she say?
" 'I do not pet pigs.' "	What did the man say?
" 'I will go to the park and pet a duck.' "	What did he say? Is he going to the farm? Where's he going? What did the man do?
"Then the girl went to the farm to pet a pig."	What did the girl do?

TASK 7 PICTURE COMPREHENSION

1. What will you see in the picture?
2. Look at the picture and get ready to answer some questions.
3. Where is the girl?
4. What is she doing?
5. Did you ever pet a pig?

TASK 8 SOUNDS WRITING

1. Here's the first sound you're going to write. (Write **p** at beginning of first line. Point to **p.**) What sound? "p."
2. First trace the **p** that I made. Then make more of them on this line (After tracing **p** several times, child is to make three to five **p**'s. Help child if necessary. For acceptable letters say:) Good writing **p.**
3. Here's the next sound you're going to write. (Write **b** at beginning of second line. Point to **b.**) What sound? "b."
4. First trace the **b** that I made. Then make more of them on this line. (After tracing **b** several times, child is to make three to five **b**'s. Help child if necessary. For acceptable letters say:) Good writing **b.**

LESSON 58

TASK 1 SOUNDS INTRODUCTION

1. (Point to ī.) Here's a new sound. I'm going to touch under this sound and say the sound. (Touch first ball of arrow. Move quickly to second ball. Hold.) **īīī.**
2. Your turn to say the sound when I touch under it. (Touch first ball.) Get ready. (Move quickly to second ball. Hold.) "īīī."

(**To correct** child saying a wrong sound or not responding:) The sound is **īīī.** (Repeat step 2.)

3. (Touch first ball.) Again. Get ready. (Move quickly to second ball. Hold.) "īīī."

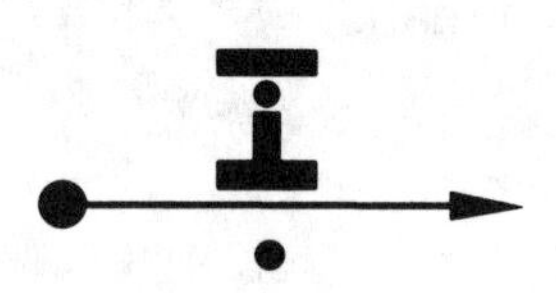

TASK 2 SOUNDS

1. Take a good look at each sound. Say it slowly if you can. Don't get fooled.
2. (Touch first ball for **i.**) Get ready. (Quickly move to second ball. Hold.) "iii."
3. (Repeat step 2 for **b, e, ī, ch,** and **ō.** Remember to move quickly to end of arrow if there is no ball on arrow for sound.)

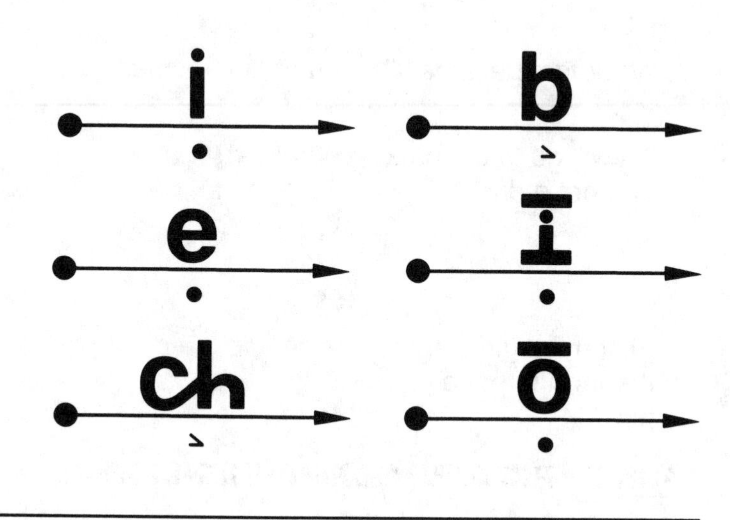

TASK 3 WORD READING

1. (Touch first ball for **bē.**) Sound it out. Get ready. (Slide past **b.** Touch ball for other sound.) "bēēē." (Repeat until firm.) What word? "be." Yes, **be.**
2. (Touch first ball for **big.**) Sound it out. (Touch under sounds.) "biiig." (Repeat until firm.) What word? "big."
3. (Repeat step 2 for **getting, bit, lēaf, ēating,** and **bugs.**)

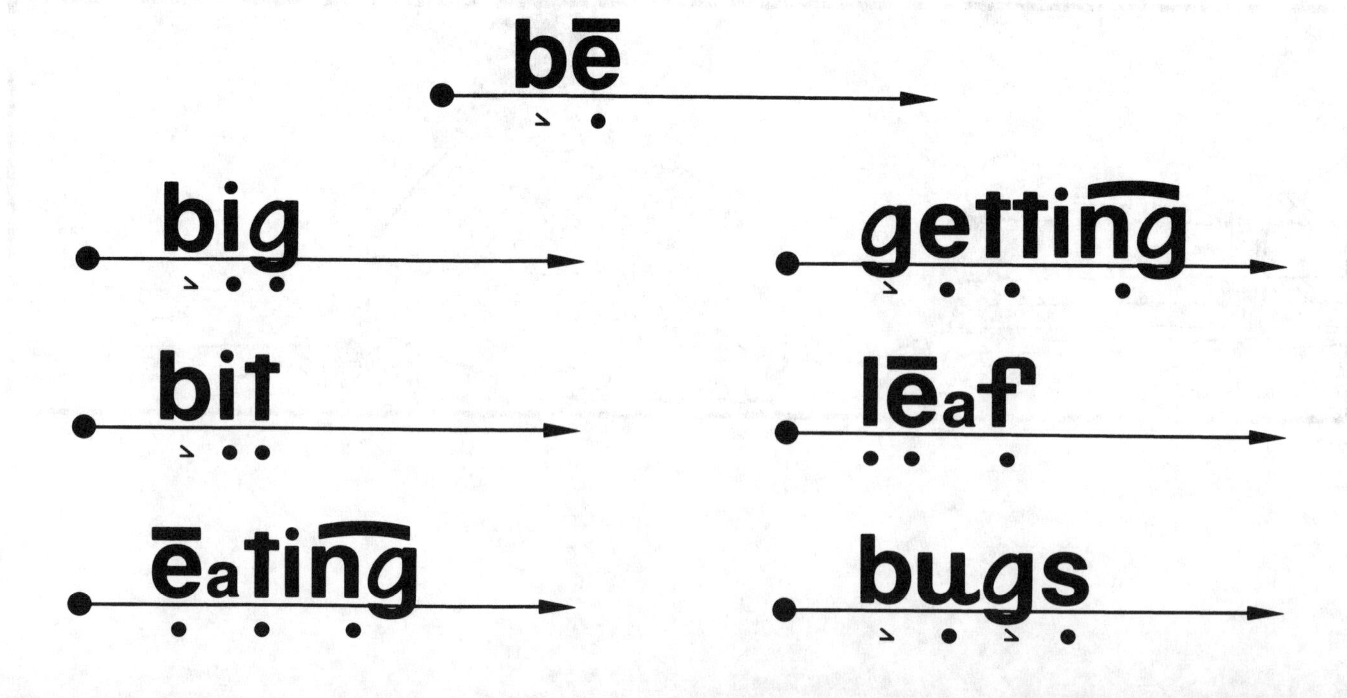

TASK 4 WORD READING

1. Get ready to read these words the fast way.
2. (Touch ball for **did.** Pause three seconds.) Read it the fast way. (Slide.) "did." Yes, **did.**
3. (Repeat step 2 for remaining words.)
4. Read these words again, the fast way.
5. (Touch first ball for **be.** Pause three seconds.) What word? "be."
6. (Repeat step 5 for remaining words.) Good reading those words.

did

hit

then

dog

log

him

now

how

TASK 5 SOUNDS

1. Take a good look at each sound. Say it slowly if you can. Don't get fooled.
2. (Touch ball for **b.**) Get ready. (Quickly move to end of arrow.) "b."
3. (Repeat step 2 for **ī, u, e, o,** and **a.** Remember to move quickly to end of arrow if there is no ball on arrow for sound.)

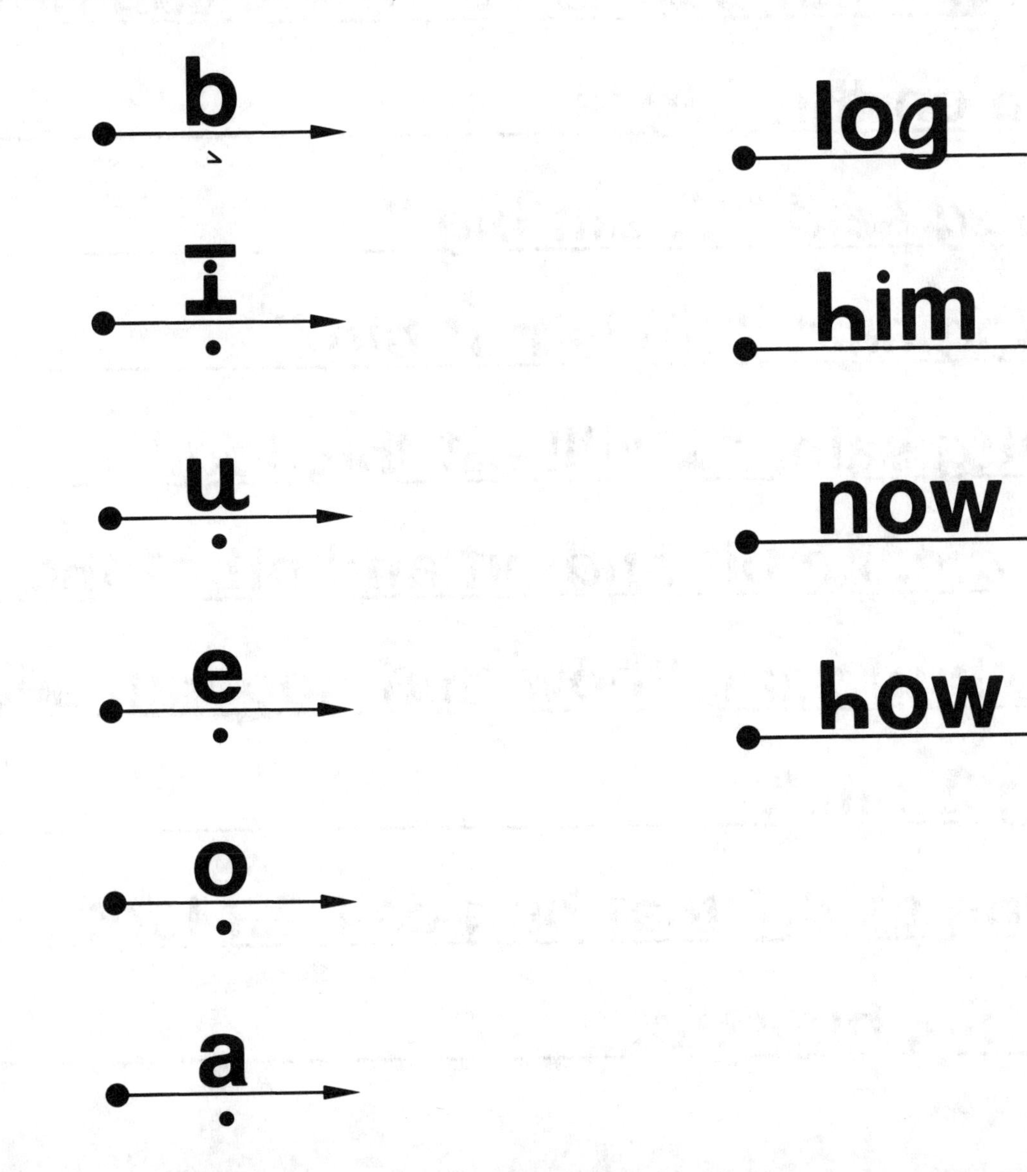

1. You're going to read this story the fast way the first time you read it. But if you come to a word that you can't read the fast way, sound it out and then tell me the word.
2. Touch the title. Remember, the title of a story tells what the story is about. Read the title the fast way. "a bug and a dog." What is this story going to tell about? "a bug and a dog."
3. Read the first sentence the fast way. (Child reads first sentence.)
4. Read the next sentence the fast way. (Child reads second sentence.)
5. (Repeat step 4 for remaining sentences in story.)

a bug and a dog

a bug and a dog sat on a log. the dog said, "that bug is sō little I can not sēē him on this log."

the bug said, "I am big."

the dog said, "hē is not big."

the bug said, "I will ēat this log." and hē did. hē bit and bit and bit at the log. the bug said, "now that dog can sēē how big I am."

the dog said, "that bug can ēat logs. hē is a big, big bug."

TASK 7 SECOND READING

1. You're going to read the story again the fast way. This time I'll ask questions. Start with the title again. (Ask questions as child reads.)
2. (After child reads:) (You say:)

(After child reads:)	(You say:)
"A bug and a dog."	What's this story about?
"The dog said, 'That bug is so little I can not see him on this log.' "	Why couldn't the dog see the bug?
"The bug said, 'I will eat this log.' "	What did the bug say?
"He bit and bit and bit at the log."	What did the bug do?
"The dog said, 'That bug can eat logs. He is a big, big bug.' "	Why did the dog say, **He is a big, big bug?**

TASK 8 PICTURE COMPREHENSION

1. What will you see in the picture?
2. Look at the picture and get ready to answer some questions.
3. Is that a big bug?
4. What's the little bug doing with the log?
5. Do you think a little bug can eat a log?

TASK 9 SOUNDS WRITING

1. Here's the first sound you're going to write. (Write **d** at beginning of first line. Point to **d.**) What sound? "d."
2. First trace the **d** that I made. Then make more of them on this line. (After tracing **d** several times, child is to make three to five **d**'s. Help child if necessary. For acceptable letters say:) Good writing **d.**
3. Here's the next sound you're going to write. (Write **b** at beginning of second line. Point to **b.**) What sound? "b."
4. First trace the **b** that I made. Then make more of them on this line. (After tracing **b** several times, child is to make three to five **b**'s. Help child if necessary. For acceptable letters say:) Good writing **b.**

LESSON 59

TASK 1 SOUNDS

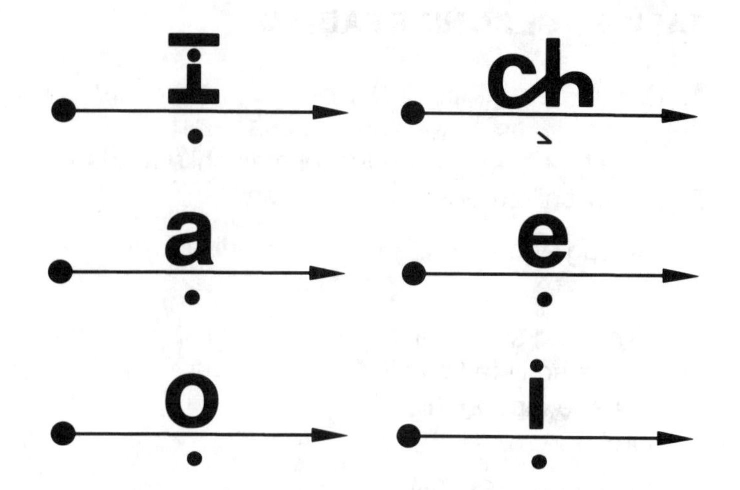

1. Take a good look at each sound. Say it slowly if you can. Don't get fooled.
2. (Touch first ball for **ī.**) Get ready. (Quickly move to second ball. Hold.) "īīī."
3. (Repeat step 2 for **ch, a, e, o,** and **i.** Remember to move quickly to end of arrow if there is no ball on arrow for sound.)

TASK 2 WORD READING

1. (Touch first ball for **fishing.**) Sound it out. (Touch balls for sounds.) "fffiiishshshiiing." (Repeat until firm.) What word? "fishing."
2. (Repeat step 1 for **bed, tub, but, bīte, slēēp,** and **līke.**)

fishing

bed

tub

but

bīte

slēēp

līke

TASK 3 WORD READING

1. Get ready to read these words the fast way
2. (Touch ball for **lēaf.** Pause three seconds.) Read it the fast way. (Slide.) "leaf." Yes, **leaf.**
3. (Repeat step 2 for remaining words.)
4. Read these words again, the fast way.
5. (Touch first ball for **fishing.** Pause three seconds.) What word? "fishing."
6. (Repeat step 5 for remaining words.) Good reading those words.

lēaf

ten

let's

TASK 4 SOUNDS

1. Take a good look at each sound. Say it slowly if you can. Don't get fooled.
2. (Touch first ball for **ī.**) Get ready. (Quickly move to second ball. Hold.) "īīī."
3. (Repeat step 2 for **i, e, b, ch,** and **p.** Remember to move quickly to end of arrow if there is no ball on arrow for sound.)

ī

i

e

b

ch

p

1. You're going to read this story the fast way the first time you read it. But if you come to a word that you can't read the fast way, sound it out and then tell me the word.
2. Touch the title. Remember, the title of a story tells what the story is about. Read the title the fast way. "the bugs." What is this story going to tell about? "the bugs."
3. Read the first sentence the fast way. (Child reads first sentence.)
4. Read the next sentence the fast way. (Child reads second sentence.)
5. (Repeat step 4 for remaining sentences in story.)

the bugs

a big bug met a little bug. the big bug said, "let's gō ēat." sō the big bug āte a lēaf and a nut and a rock. the big bug said, "that is how big bugs ēat."

the little bug said, "now I will ēat." sō the little bug āte a lēaf and a nut and a rock. then the little bug went to a log and āte the log. then shē āte ten mōre logs.

"wow," the big bug said. "that little bug can ēat a lot."

the little bug said, "now let's ēat mōre."

TASK 6 SECOND READING

1. You're going to read the story again the fast way. This time I'll ask questions. Start with the title again. (Ask questions as child reads.)
2. (After child reads:) (You say:)

(After child reads:)	(You say:)
"The bugs."	What's this story about?
"The big bug said, 'Let's go eat.' "	Did the big bug want to eat?
"So the big bug ate a leaf and a nut and a rock."	What did the big bug eat?
"So the little bug ate a leaf and a nut and a rock."	What did the little bug eat?
"Then the little bug went to a log and ate the log."	Did she eat the log?
"Then she ate ten more logs."	Then what did she eat?
"The little bug said, 'Now let's eat more.' "	What did the little bug say?

TASK 7 PICTURE COMPREHENSION

1. What will you see in the picture?
2. Look at the picture and get ready to answer some questions.
3. What is the little bug eating?
4. Do you think the big bug is surprised to see what the little bug can eat?

TASK 8 SOUNDS WRITING

1. Here's the first sound you're going to write. (Write **g** at beginning of first line. Point to **g.**) What sound? "g."
2. First trace the **g** that I made. Then make more of them on this line. (After tracing **g** several times, child is to make three to five **g**'s. Help child if necessary. For acceptable letters say:) Good writing **g.**
3. Here's the next sound you're going to write. (Write **b** at beginning of second line. Point to **b.**) What sound? "b."
4. First trace the **b** that I made. Then make more of them on this line. (After tracing **b** several times, child is to make three to five **b**'s. Help child if necessary. For acceptable letters say:) Good writing **b.**

LESSON 60

TASK 1 SOUNDS INTRODUCTION

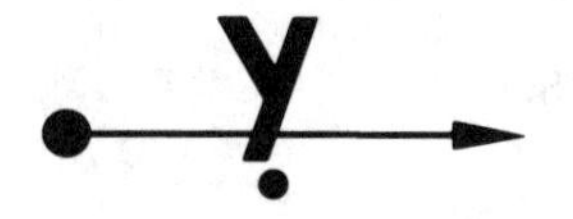

1. (Point to **y.**) Here's a new sound. I'm going to touch under this sound and say the sound. (Touch first ball of arrow. Move quickly to second ball. Hold.) **yyy** (**yyyē** as in **yard**).
2. Your turn to say the sound when I touch under it. (Touch first ball.) Get ready. (Move quickly to second ball. Hold.) "yyy."

> (**To correct** child saying "yah," "yih," or "yuh" or not responding:) The sound is **yyy.** (Repeat step 2.)

3. (Touch first ball.) Again. Get ready. (Move quickly to second ball. Hold.) "yyy."

TASK 2 SOUNDS

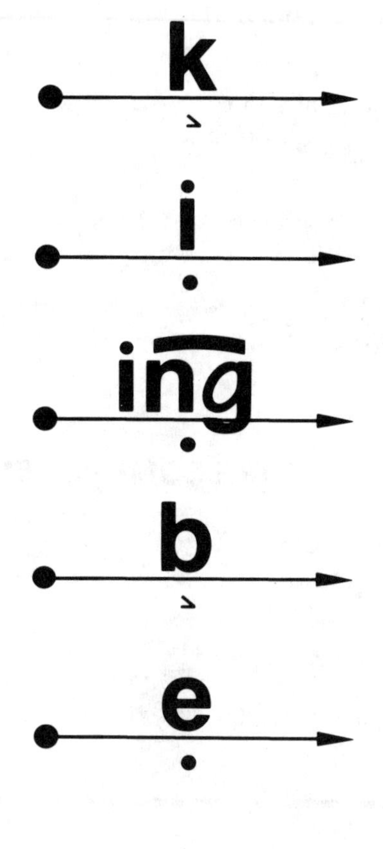

1. Take a good look at each sound. Say it slowly if you can. Don't get fooled.
2. (Touch ball for **k.**) Get ready. (Quickly move to end of arrow.) "k."
3. (Repeat step 2 for **i, ing, b,** and **e.** Remember to move quickly to end of arrow if there is no ball on arrow for sound.)

TASK 3 WORD READING

walk

talk

1. (Touch first ball for **walk.**) Sound it out. (Touch balls for sounds as child says:) "wwwaaalllk" (not "wwwoook").
2. That's how we **sound out** the word. Here's how we **say** the word. (Pause.) **Walk (wok).** How do we **say** the word? "walk." Yes, **walk**—it's a funny word.
3. (Return to first ball.) Sound it out again. (Touch balls for sounds as child says:) "wwwaaalllk." Now **say** the word. "walk." Yes, **walk.** (Repeat until firm.)
4. (Touch first ball for **talk.**) Sound it out. (Touch under sounds as child says:) "taaalllk" (not "toook").
5. That's how we **sound out** the word. Here's how we **say** the word. (Pause.) **talk (tok).** How do we **say** the word? "talk." Yes, **talk**—it's a funny word.
6. (Return to first ball.) Sound it out again. (Touch under sounds as child says:) "taaalllk." Now **say** the word. "talk." Yes, **talk.** (Repeat until firm.)

TASK 4 WORD READING

1. (Touch first ball for **stop.**) Sound it out. Get ready. (Touch **s.** Slide past **t.** Touch balls for other sounds.) "ssstooop." (Repeat until firm.) What word? "stop." Yes, **stop.**
2. (Repeat step 2 for **big, slēēp, bed, bīte, rub, fishing, līkes,** and **fīve.**)

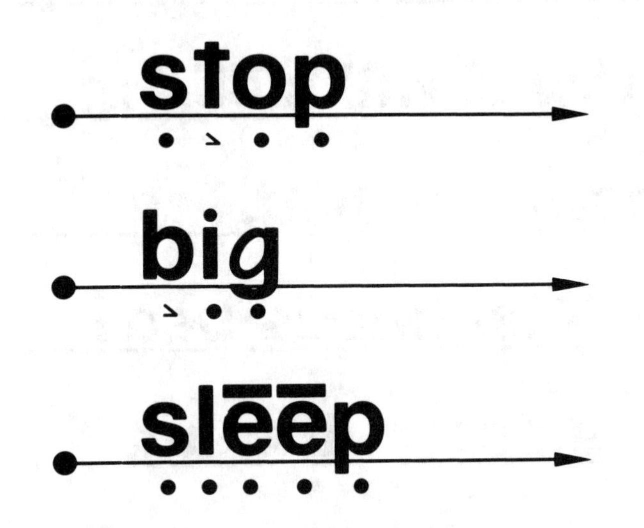

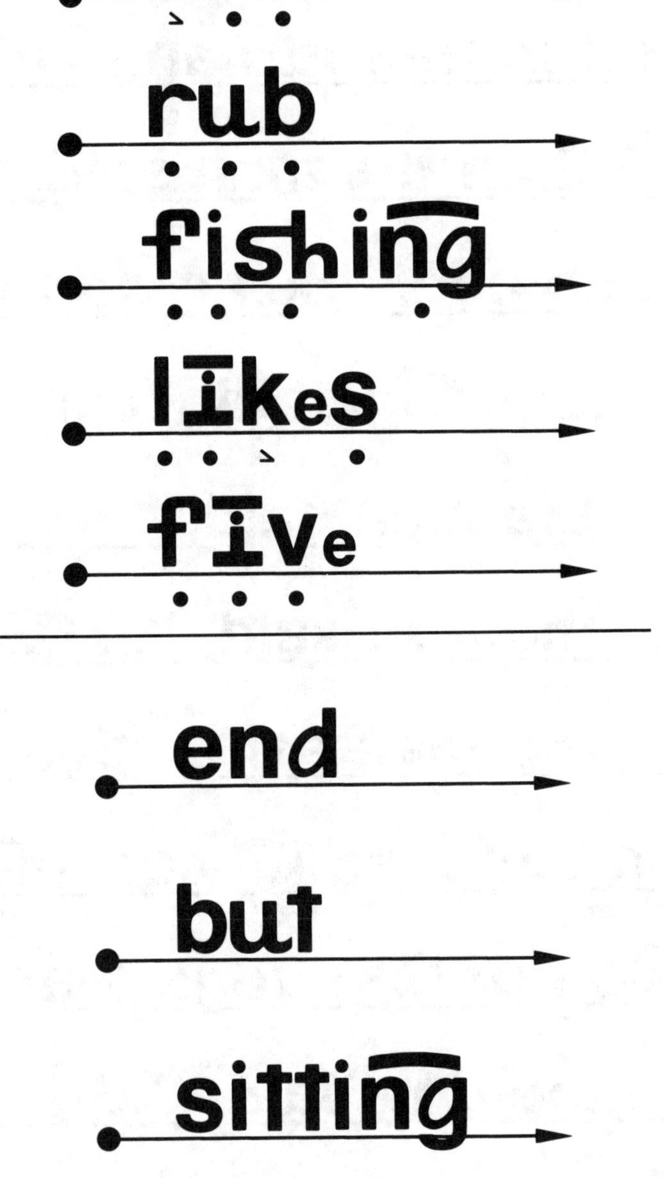

TASK 5 WORD READING

1. Get ready to read these words the fast way.
2. (Touch ball for **his.** Pause three seconds.) Read it the fast way. (Slide.) "his." Yes, **his.**
3. (Repeat step 2 for remaining words.)
4. Read these words again, the fast way.
5. (Touch first ball for **stop.** Pause three seconds.) What word? "stop."
6. (Repeat step 5 for remaining words.) Good reading those words.

end

but

sitting

TASK 6 SOUNDS

1. Take a good look at each sound. Say it slowly if you can. Don't get fooled.
2. (Touch first ball for **ī.**) Get ready. (Quickly move to second ball. Hold.) "īīī."
3. (Repeat step 2 for **y, e, ō, ā,** and **ē.** Remember to move quickly to end of arrow if there is no ball on arrow for sound.)

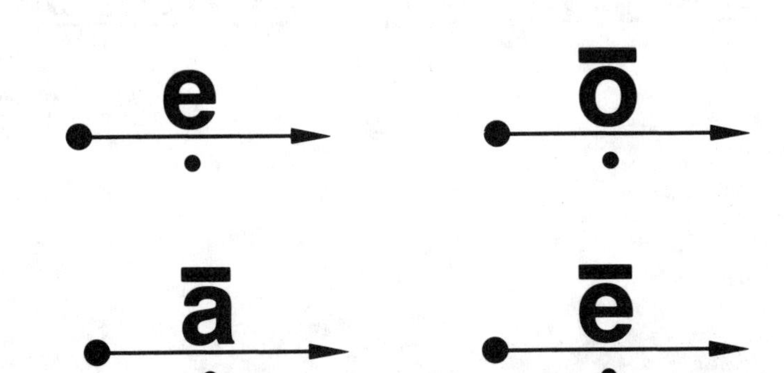

ī

y

the man and his bed

a man had a tub. hē said, "I like to sit in this tub and rub, rub, rub."

then the man said, "now I will slēēp in this bed." but a dog was in his bed.

the dog said, "can I slēēp in this bed?"

the man said, "nō. gō slēēp in the tub."

the dog said, "I like to slēēp in beds."

the man said, "this dog likes to slēēp in beds. sō hē can slēēp with mē. but I do not like dogs that bite."

the dog said, "I do not like to bite."

sō the man and the dog went to slēēp. and the dog did not bite the man.

TASK 7 FIRST READING

1. You're going to read this story the fast way the first time you read it. But if you come to a word that you can't read the fast way, sound it out and then tell me the word.
2. Touch the title. Remember, the title of a story tells what the story is about. Read the title the fast way. **"the man and his bed."** What is this story going to tell about? **"the man and his bed."**
3. Read the first sentence the fast way. **(Child reads first sentence.)**
4. Read the next sentence the fast way. **(Child reads second sentence.)**
5. **(Repeat step 4 for remaining sentences in story.)**

TASK 8 SECOND READING

1. You're going to read the story again the fast way. This time I'll ask questions. Start with the title again. **(Ask questions as child reads.)**
2. **(After child reads:)** **(You say:)**

(After child reads:)	(You say:)
"The man and his bed."	What's this story about?
"He said, 'I like to sit in this tub and rub, rub, rub.' "	What did the man say?
"Then the man said, 'Now I will sleep in this bed.' "	What did the man say?
"But a dog was in his bed."	What was in his bed?
" 'So he can sleep with me.' "	Will the man let the dog sleep in the bed?
"And the dog did not bite the man."	Does the dog like to bite? Did he bite the man?

TASK 9 PICTURE COMPREHENSION

1. What will you see in the picture?
2. Look at the picture and get ready to answer some questions.
3. What is in the man's bed?
4. What would you do if a dog wanted to sleep in your bed?

TASK 10 SOUNDS WRITING

1. Here's the first sound you're going to write. **(Write v at beginning of first line. Point to v.)** What sound? **"vvv."**
2. First trace the **vvv** that I made. Then make more of them on this line. **(After tracing v several times, child is to make three to five v's. Help child if necessary. For acceptable letters say:)** Good writing **vvv.**
3. Here's the next sound you're going to write. **(Write g at beginning of second line. Point to g.)** What sound? **"g."**
4. First trace the **g** that I made. Then make more of them on this line. **(After tracing g several times, child is to make three to five g's. Help child if necessary. For acceptable letters say:)** Good writing **g.**

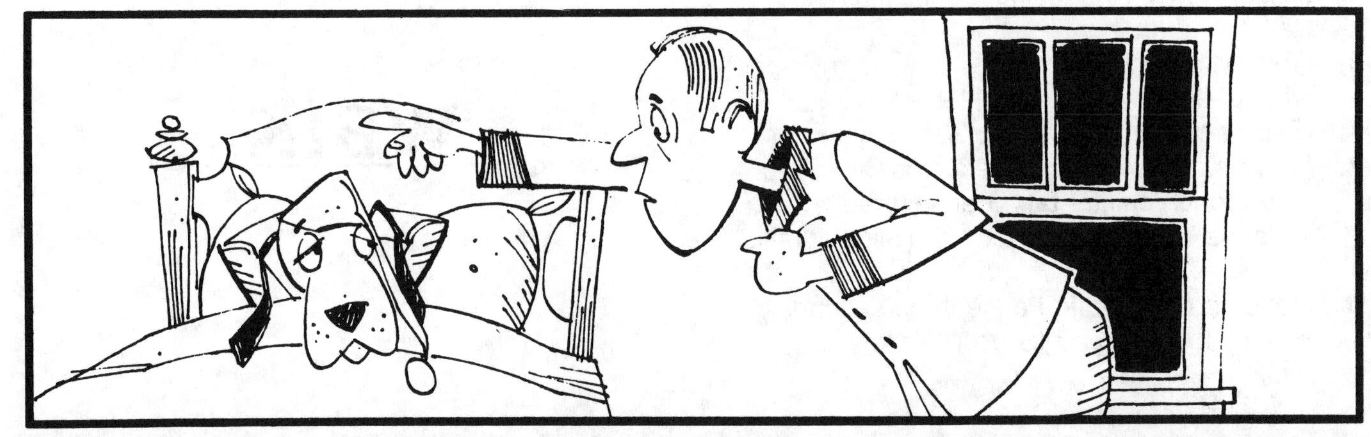

LESSON 61

TASK 1 SOUNDS

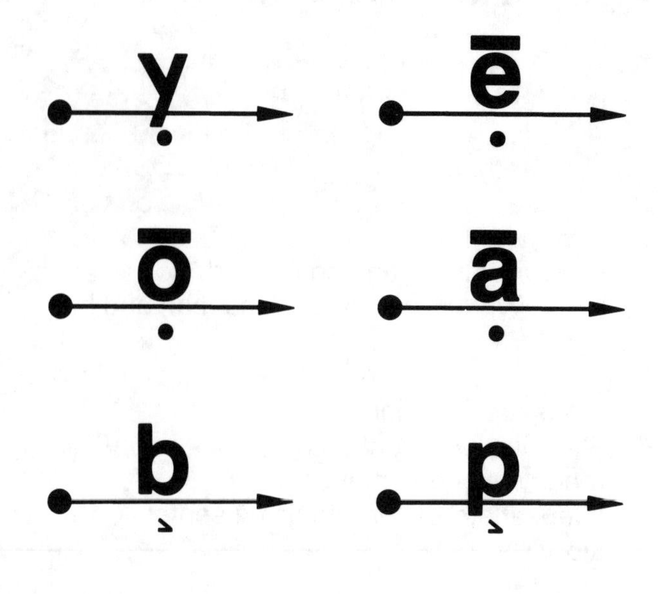

1. Take a good look at each sound. Say it slowly if you can. Don't get fooled.
2. (Touch first ball for **y.**) Get ready. (Quickly move to second ball. Hold.) "yyy."
3. (Repeat step 2 for **ē, ō, ā, b,** and **p.** Remember to move quickly to end of arrow if there is no ball on arrow for sound.)

TASK 2 WORD READING

1. (Touch first ball for **you.**) Sound it out. (Touch balls for sounds as child says:) "yyyooouuu" (not "ūūū").
2. That's how we **sound out** the word. Here's how we **say** the word. (Pause.) **you** (ū). How do we **say** the word? "you." Yes, **you**—it's a funny word.
3. (Return to first ball.) Sound it out again. (Touch balls for sounds as child says:) "yyyooouuu." Now **say** the word. "you." Yes, **you. You** are smart.

TASK 3 WORD READING

1. (Point to **talk** and **walk.**) These words rhyme with **awk.**
2. (Touch ball for **talk.**) This word rhymes with (pause) **awk.** Read it the fast way. (Slide.) "talk." Yes, **talk.**
3. (Touch first ball for **walk.**) This word rhymes with (pause) **awk.** Read it the fast way. (Slide.) "walk." Yes, **walk.** Good rhyming.
4. Now you get to read these words the fast way. (Touch ball for **talk.** Pause three seconds.) Read it the fast way. (Slide.) "talk." Yes, **talk.**
5. (Touch ball for **walk.** Pause three seconds.) Read it the fast way. (Slide.) "walk." Yes, **walk.**

TASK 4 WORD READING

1. Get ready to read these words the fast way.
2. (Touch ball for **rich.** Pause three seconds.) Read it the fast way. (Slide.) "rich." Yes, **rich.**
3. (Repeat step 2 for remaining words.)

lāke

live

them

thōse

slēēping

dark

TASK 5 WORD READING

1. (Touch first ball for **fīve.**) Sound it out. (Touch balls for sounds.) "fffīīīvvv." (Repeat until firm.) What word? "five."
2. (Repeat step 1 for **dīme** and **dīve.**)
3. Now you get to read these words the fast way.
4. (Touch ball for **rich.** Pause three seconds.) Read it the fast way. (Slide.) "rich." Yes, **rich.**
5. (Repeat step 4 for remaining words on this page.)

fīve

dīme

dīve

TASK 6 SOUNDS

1. Take a good look at each sound. Say it slowly if you can. Don't get fooled.
2. (Touch first ball for **i.**) Get ready. (Quickly move to second ball. Hold.) "iii."
3. (Repeat step 2 for **y, ch, p, e,** and **b.** Remember to move quickly to end of arrow if there is no ball on arrow for the sound.)

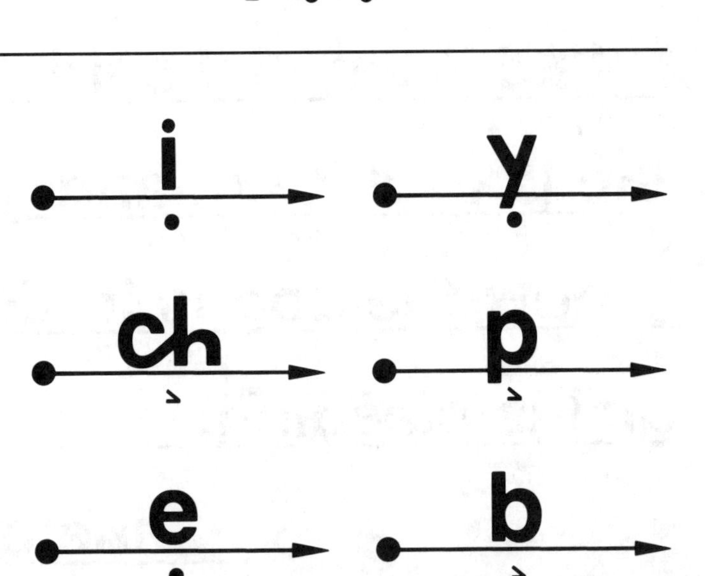

TASK 7 FIRST READING

1. You're going to read this story the fast way the first time you read it. But if you come to a word that you can't read the fast way, sound it out and then tell me the word.
2. Touch the title. Remember, the title of a story tells what the story is about. Read the title the fast way. "the dog that ate fish." What is this story going to tell about? "the dog that ate fish."
3. Read the first sentence the fast way. (Child reads first sentence.)
4. Read the next sentence the fast way. (Child reads second sentence.)
5. (Repeat step 4 for remaining sentences in story.)
6. (Point to **the end.**) Read the words on this arrow. "the end."

the dog that āte fish

a girl went fishing with a dog. that dog āte fish. the girl did not līke the dog to ēat fish. "do not ēat the fish," shē said.

the girl went fishing and the dog went to slēēp. the girl got fīve fish.

"give mē thōse fīve fish," the dog said.

"nō," the girl said. "mōre fish are in the lāke. dīve in and get them."

now the dog is in the lāke. and the girl is slēēping.

the end

TASK 8 SECOND READING

1. You're going to read the story again the fast way. This time I'll ask questions. Start with the title again. (Ask questions as child reads.)
2. (After child reads:) (You say:)

(After child reads:)	(You say:)
"The dog that ate fish."	What's this story about?
"The girl did not like the dog to eat fish."	Who went fishing? Did the dog eat fish? How did the girl feel about the dog's eating fish?
" 'Give me those five fish,' the dog said."	What did the dog say? How many fish did the girl catch? Do you think the girl will give the fish to the dog?
" 'No,' the girl said."	What did the girl say? Did she want to give the fish to the dog?
" 'Dive in and get them.' "	What did the girl say? She said, **More fish are in the lake. Dive in and get them.** Do you think the dog will do that?
"And the girl is sleeping."	Did the dog go in the lake? What is the girl doing now?
"The end."	Yes, that was the end of the story.

TASK 9 PICTURE COMPREHENSION

1. What will you see in the picture?
2. Look at the picture and get ready to answer some questions.
3. How many fish does the girl have?
4. What do you think she's saying to that dog?
5. I wonder what's in that can near the girl. Yes, worms.
6. Did you ever go fishing and catch five fish?

TASK 10 SOUNDS WRITING

1. Here's the first sound you're going to write. (Write **th** at beginning of first line. Point to **th.**) What sound? "ththth."
2. First trace the **ththth** that I made. Then make more of them on this line. (After tracing **th** several times, child is to make three to five **th**'s. Help child if necessary. For acceptable letters say:) Good writing **ththth.**
3. Here's the next sound you're going to write. (Write **b** at beginning of second line. Point to **b.**) What sound? "b."
4. First trace the **b** that I made. Then make more of them on this line. (After tracing **b** several times, child is to make three to five **b**'s. Help child if necessary. For acceptable letters say:) Good writing **b.**

LESSON 62

TASK 1 SOUNDS INTRODUCTION

1. (Point to **er.**) Here's a new sound. I'm going to touch under this sound and say the sound. (Touch first ball of arrow. Move quickly to second ball. Hold.) **urrr.**
2. Your turn to say the sound when I touch under it. (Touch first ball.) Get ready. (Move quickly to second ball. Hold.) "urrr."

(**To correct** child saying a wrong sound or not responding:) The sound is **urrr.** (Repeat step 2.)

3. (Touch first ball.) Again. Get ready. (Move quickly to second ball. Hold.) "urrr."

TASK 2 SOUNDS

1. Take a good look at each sound. Say it slowly if you can. Don't get fooled.
2. (Touch first ball for **y.**) Get ready. (Quickly move to second ball. Hold.) "yyy."
3. (Repeat step 2 for **sh, th, ch, ing,** and **er.** Remember to move quickly to end of arrow if there is no ball on arrow for sound.)

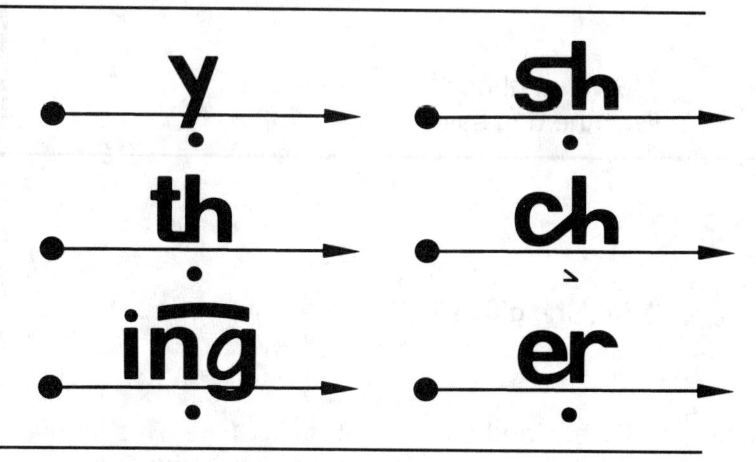

TASK 3 WORD READING

1. (Point to **walk** and **talk.**) These words rhyme with **awk.**
2. (Touch ball for **walk.**) This word rhymes with (pause) **awk.** Read it the fast way. (Slide.) "walk." Yes, **walk.**
3. (Touch ball for **talk.**) This word rhymes with (pause) **awk.** Read it the fast way. (Slide.) "talk." Yes, **talk.** Good rhyming.
4. Now you get to read these words again the fast way. (Touch ball for **walk.** Pause three seconds.) Read it the fast way. (Slide.) "walk." Yes, **walk.**
5. (Touch ball for **talk.** Pause three seconds.) Read it the fast way. (Slide.) "talk." Yes, **talk.**

TASK 4 WORD READING

1. (Touch first ball for **you.**) Sound it out. (Touch balls for sounds as child says:) "yyyooouuu."
2. That's how we **sound out** the word. Here's how we **say** the word. (Pause.) **you.** How do we **say** the word? "you." Yes, **you**—it's a funny word.
3. (Return to first ball.) Sound it out again. (Touch balls for sounds as child says:) "yyyooouuu." Now **say** the word. "you." Yes, **you.** (Repeat until firm.)

you

TASK 5 WORD READING

1. This word is made of two small words stuck together. You're going to read both small words the fast way.
2. (Point to ball for **in.**) Read this small word the fast way. (Touch ball.) "in."
3. (Point to ball for **to.**) Read this small word the fast way. (Touch ball.) "to."
4. (Touch first ball for **into.**) Read both small words the fast way. (Slide.) "into." Yes, **into.**

TASK 6 WORD READING

1. Get ready to read these words the fast way.
2. (Touch ball for **live.** Pause three seconds.) Read it the fast way. (Slide.) "live." Yes, **live.**
3. (Repeat step 2 for remaining words.)

live

led · māde · dark

park · farms · rich

līke · gun · dēēr

wāves · tāke · into

TASK 7 WORD READING

1. (Touch first ball for **hunting.**) Sound it out. Get ready. (Slide past **h.** Touch under other sounds.) "huuunnntiiing." (Repeat until firm.) What word? "hunting." Yes, **hunting.**
2. (Touch first ball for **stopping.**) Sound it out. (Touch under sounds.) "ssstooopiiing." (Repeat until firm.) What word? "stopping."
3. (Repeat step 1 for **yēar, yes,** and **bōy.**)
4. Now you get to read all these words the fast way.
5. (Touch ball for **live.** Pause three seconds.) Read it the fast way. (Slide.) "live." Yes, **live.**
6. (Repeat step 5 for remaining words on this page.)

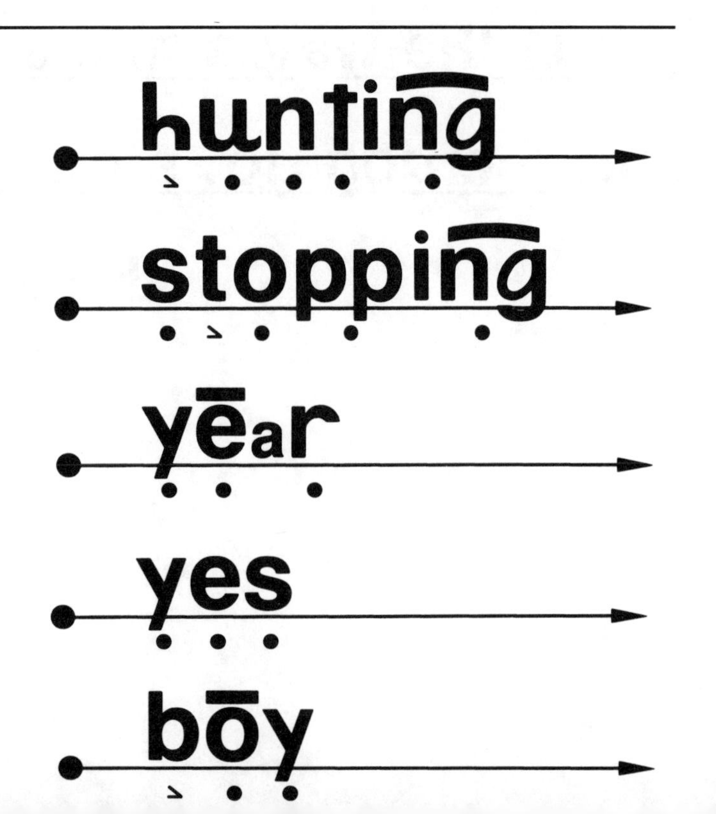

the rich pig

a dog was in the park. it was dark in the park.

the dog ran into a pig. the dog said, "pigs can not gō in this park. pigs live on farms."

the pig said, "not this pig. I live on a ship. I am a rich pig."

the dog said, "tāke mē to the ship." sō the pig did.

but the wāves māde the ship rock. and the dog got sick.

the end

TASK 8 SOUNDS

1. Take a good look at each sound. Say it slowly if you can. Don't get fooled.
2. (Touch first ball for **er.**) Get ready. (Quickly move to second ball. Hold.) "urrr."
3. (Repeat step 2 for **r, e, y, i,** and **ing.** Remember to move quickly to end of arrow if there is no ball on arrow for sound.)

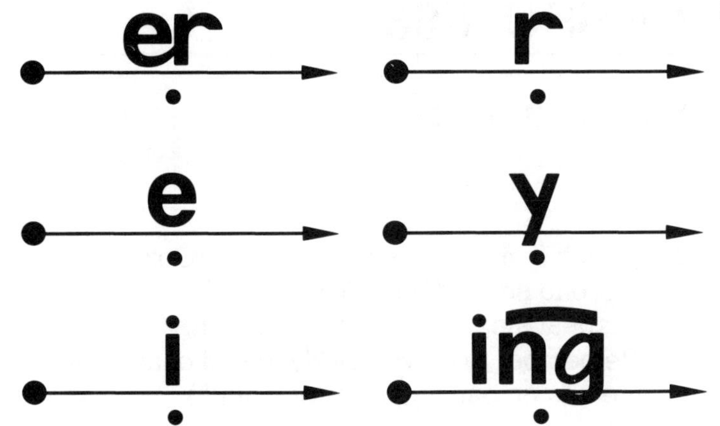

TASK 9 FIRST READING

1. You're going to read this story the fast way the first time you read it. But if you come to a word that you can't read the fast way, sound it out and then tell me the word.
2. Touch the title. Remember, the title of a story tells what the story is about. Read the title the fast way. "the rich pig." What is this story going to tell about? "the rich pig."
3. Read the first sentence the fast way. (Child reads first sentence.)
4. Read the next sentence the fast way. (Child reads second sentence.)
5. (Repeat step 4 for remaining sentences in story.)

TASK 10 SECOND READING

1. You're going to read the story again the fast way. This time I'll ask questions. Start with the title again. (Ask questions as child reads.)
2. (After child reads:) (You say:)

(After child reads:)	(You say:)
"The rich pig."	What's this story about?
"It was dark in the park."	Where was the dog? What was it like in the park?
"The dog ran into a pig."	Whom did the dog run into?
" 'Pigs live on farms.' "	What did the dog say?
" 'I am a rich pig.' "	What did the pig say?
"But the waves made the ship rock."	What happened to the ship? Show me how a ship rocks.
"And the dog got sick."	What happened to the dog? Why?

TASK 11 PICTURE COMPREHENSION

1. What will you see in the picture?
2. Look at the picture and get ready to answer some questions.
3. Who's on that ship?
4. What is the ship doing?
5. What's making the ship rock? Show me the waves.
6. Do you want to go on a boat or a ship?

TASK 12 SOUNDS WRITING

1. (Write **y** at beginning of first line. Point to **y.**) What sound? "yyy."
2. First trace the **yyy** that I made. Then make more of them on this line. (After tracing **y** several times, child is to make three to five **y**'s. Help child if necessary. For each acceptable letter say:) Good writing **yyy.**
3. Here's the next sound you're going to write. (Write **w** at beginning of second line. Point to **w.**) What sound? "www."
4. First trace the **www** that I made. Then make more of them on this line. (After tracing **w** several times, child is to make three to five **w**'s. Help child if necessary. For acceptable letters say:) Good writing **www.**

LESSON 63

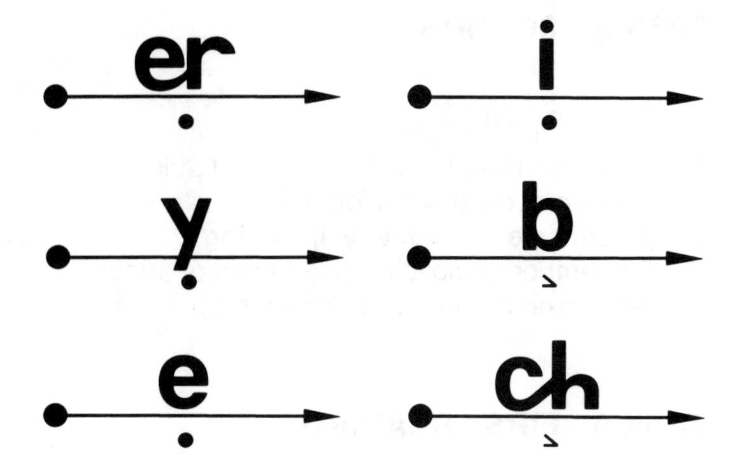

TASK 1 SOUNDS

1. Take a good look at each sound. Say it slowly if you can. Don't get fooled.
2. (Touch first ball for **er.**) Get ready. (Quickly move to second ball. Hold.) "urrr."
3. (Repeat step 2 for **i, y, b, e,** and **ch.** Remember to move quickly to end of arrow if there is no ball on arrow for sound.)

TASK 2 WORD READING

1. (Touch first ball for **you.**) Sound it out. (Touch under sounds as child says:) "yyyooouuu." Again. (Return to first ball.) Sound it out. (Touch balls for sounds as child says:) "yyyooouuu."
2. That's how we **sound out** the word. Now **say** the word. "you." Yes, **you.**
3. Let's do it again. (Return to first ball.) Sound it out. (Touch balls for sounds as child says:) "yyyooouuu." Now say the word. "you." Yes, **you.**

you

TASK 3 WORD READING

1. (Point to **other.**) This word is (pause) **other.** What word? "other."
2. (Touch first ball.) Sound it out. (Touch balls for sounds.) "ŏŏŏththththurrr." What word? "other."
3. (Touch ball for **mother.**) This word rhymes with (pause) **other.** Read it the fast way. (Slide.) "mother." Yes, **mother.** Good rhyming.

other

mother

TASK 4 WORD READING

1. (Touch ball for **love.**) This word is **love.** You can't hear the sound on the end of the word when you say it. Read this word the fast way. (Slide.) "love."
2. Yes, **love.** I **love** you.

love

TASK 5 WORD READING

1. Get ready to read these words the fast way.
2. (Touch ball for **seen.** Pause three seconds.) Read it the fast way. (Slide.) "seen." Yes, **seen.**
3. (Repeat step 2 for remaining words.)

TASK 6 WORD READING

1. (Touch first ball for **yes.**) Sound it out. (Touch balls for sounds.) "yyyeeesss." (Repeat until firm.) What word? "yes."
2. (Repeat step 1 for **they** and **her.**)
3. Now you get to read all these words the fast way.
4. (Touch ball for **sēēn.** Pause three seconds.) Read it the fast way. (Slide.) "seen." Yes, **seen.**
5. (Repeat step 4 for remaining words on this page.)

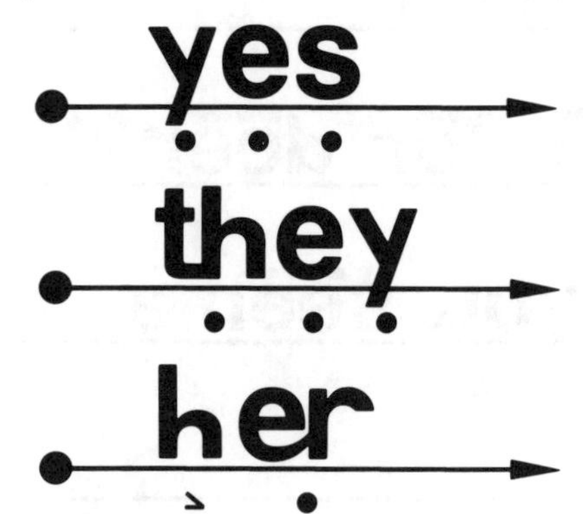

TASK 7 SOUNDS

1. Take a good look at each sound. Say it slowly if you can. Don't get fooled.
2. (Touch first ball for **ī.**) Get ready. (Quickly move to second ball. Hold.) "īīī."
3. (Repeat step 2 for **er, p, e, b,** and **y.** Remember to move quickly to end of arrow if there is no ball on arrow for sound.)

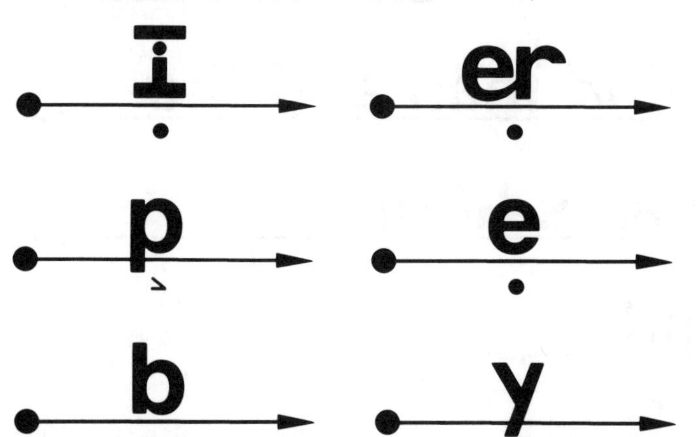

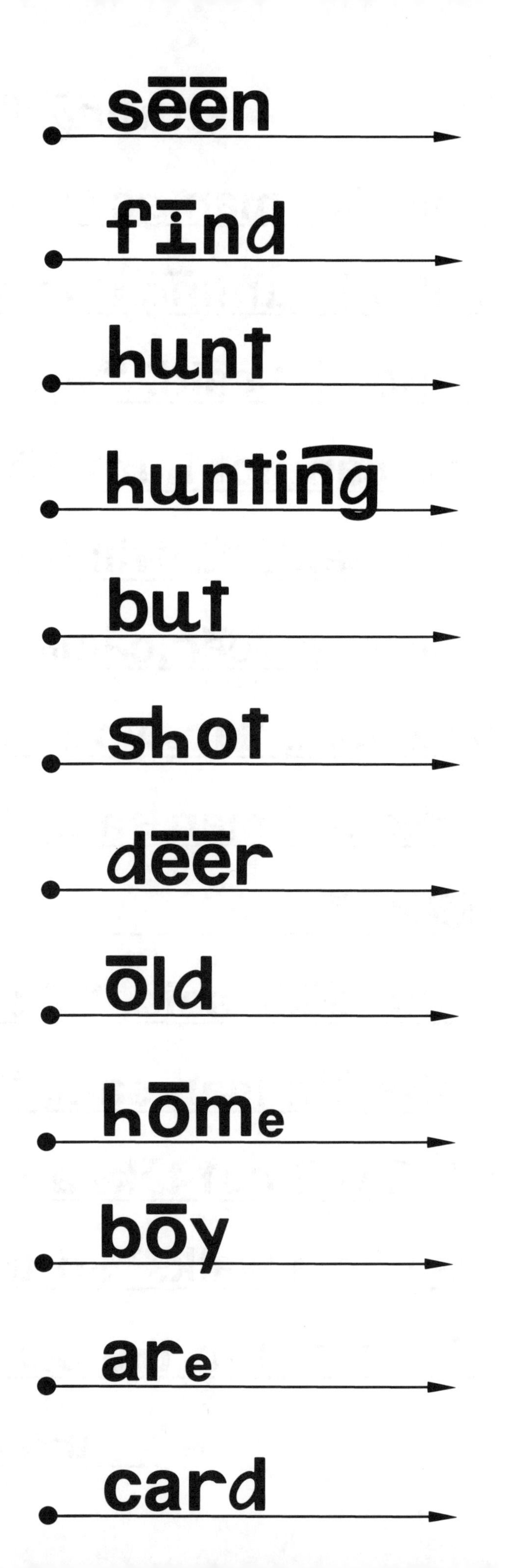

hunting fōr a dēēr

an ōld man got his gun. hē said, "I will gō hunting fōr dēēr."

the girl said, "you can not sēē. sō you can not hunt fōr dēēr."

hē said, "I will hunt fōr dēēr."

then a dēēr cāme to the man and said, "are you hunting fōr dēēr?"

the ōld man said, "have you sēēn a dēēr?"

the dēēr said, "I am a dēēr."

the ōld man said, "I can not sēē you. sō I will not tāke a shot at you. wē will gō fōr a walk." sō the ōld man and the dēēr went to the ōld man's hōme.

the end

TASK 8 FIRST READING

1. You're going to read this story the fast way the first time you read it. But if you come to a word that you can't read the fast way, sound it out and then tell me the word.
2. Touch the title. Remember, the title of a story tells what the story is about. Read the title the fast way. **"hunting for a deer."** What is this story going to tell about? **"hunting for a deer."**
3. Read the first sentence the fast way. **(Child reads first sentence.)**
4. Read the next sentence the fast way. **(Child reads second sentence.)**
5. **(Repeat step 4 for remaining sentences in story.)**

TASK 9 SECOND READING

1. You're going to read the story again the fast way. This time I'll ask questions. Start with the title again. **(Ask questions as child reads.)**
2. **(After child reads:)** **(You say:)**

(After child reads:)	(You say:)
"Hunting for a deer."	What's this story about?
"He said, 'I will go hunting for a deer.' "	Who said that? How will he hunt for deer?
" 'So you can not hunt for deer.' "	What did she say? That old man is in trouble. He can't see. So he can't hunt for deer.
"Then a deer came to the man and said, 'Are you hunting for deer?' "	Who said that? Do you think that the old man knows that a deer is talking to him? Why not?
" 'So I will not take a shot at you.' "	What did the old man say?
"So the old man and the deer went to the old man's home."	Where did the old man and the deer go?

TASK 10 PICTURE COMPREHENSION

1. What will you see in the picture?
2. Look at the picture and get ready to answer some questions.
3. What's the old man doing?
4. Have you ever seen a deer?

TASK 11 SOUNDS WRITING

1. Here's the first sound you're going to write. **(Write y at beginning of first line. Point to y.)** What sound? **"yyy."**
2. First trace the **yyy** that I made. Then make more of them on this line. **(After tracing y several times, child is to make three to five y's. Help child if necessary. For acceptable letters say:)** Good writing **yyy.**
3. Here's the next sound you're going to write. **(Write b at beginning of second line. Point to b.)** What sound? **"b."**
4. First trace the **b** that I made. Then make more of them on this line. **(After tracing b several times, child is to make three to five b's. Help child if necessary. For acceptable letters say:)** Good writing **b.**

LESSON 64

TASK 1 SOUNDS

1. Take a good look at each sound. Say it slowly if you can. Don't get fooled.
2. (Touch first ball for **i.**) Get ready. (Quickly move to second ball. Hold.) "iii."
3. (Repeat step 2 for **ī, e, ō, ā,** and **u.** Remember to move quickly to end of arrow if there is no ball on arrow for sound.)

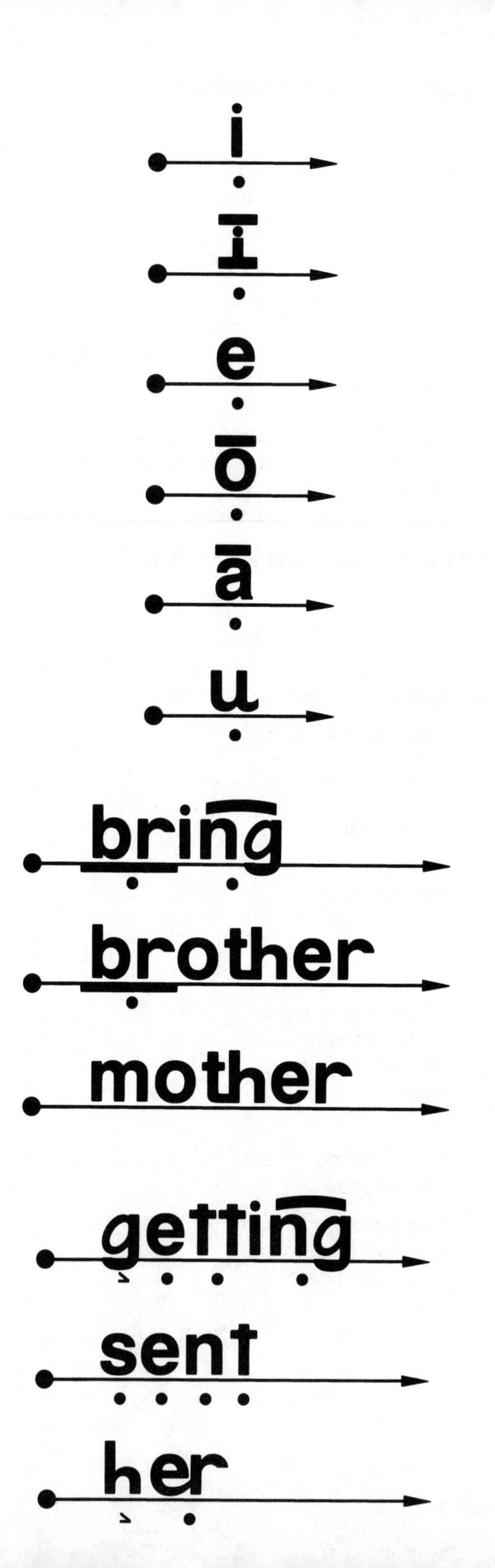

TASK 2 WORD READING

1. (Touch ball for **br** in **bring.**) These sounds are hard to say when they are together. Listen: **brrr.** Sounds as if I'm cold. **brrr.** Say that. "brrr."
2. (Touch first ball for **bring.**) Sound out this word. (Touch balls for sounds.) "brrriiing." What word? "bring."
3. (Touch first ball for **brother.**) This word also starts with **brrr.** And it rhymes with **other.** Read it the fast way. "brother." Yes, **brother.**
4. (Touch ball for **mother.**) This word rhymes with **other.** Read it the fast way. (Slide.) "mother." Yes, **mother.**

TASK 3 WORD READING

1. (Touch first ball for **getting.**) Sound it out. Get ready. (Slide past **g.** Touch under other sounds.) "geeetiiing." (Repeat until firm.) What word? "getting." Yes, **getting.**
2. (Touch first ball for **sent.**) Sound it out. (Touch balls for sounds.) "ssseeennnt." (Repeat until firm.) What word? "sent."
3. (Repeat step 2 for **her.**)

TASK 4 WORD READING

1. Get ready to read these words the fast way.
2. (Touch ball for **love.** Pause three seconds.) Read it the fast way. (Slide.) "love." Yes, **love.**
3. (Repeat step 2 for remaining words.)
4. Read all these words again, the fast way.
5. (Touch first ball for **bring.** Pause three seconds.) What word? "bring."
6. (Repeat step 5 for remaining words.) Good reading those words.

love

fīnd

give

gāve

up

bōy

got

tāil

they

TASK 5 SOUNDS

1. Take a good look at each sound. Say it slowly if you can. Don't get fooled.
2. (Touch first ball for **o.**) Get ready. (Quickly move to second ball. Hold.) "ooo."
3. (Repeat step 2 for **er, ō, e, ē,** and **ī.** Remember to move quickly to end of arrow if there is no ball on arrow for sound.)

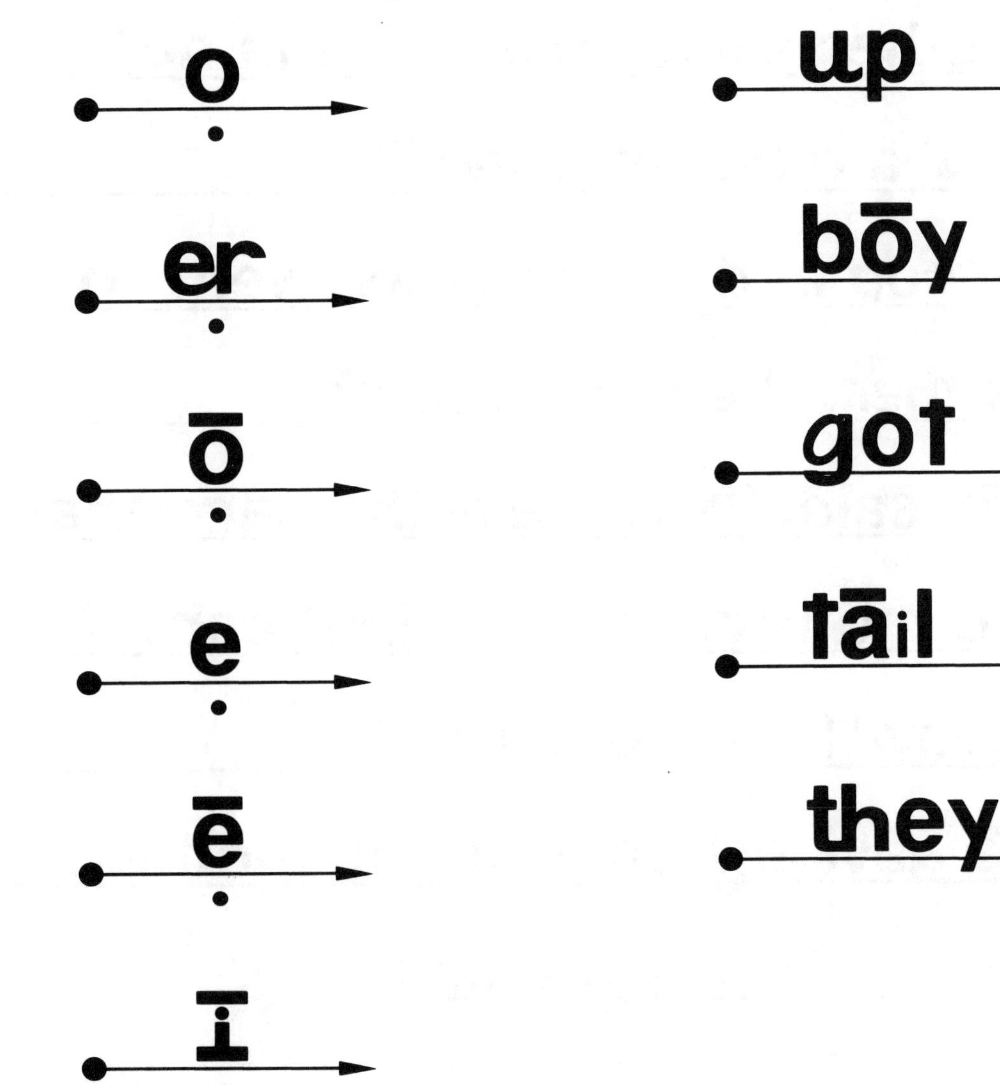

a card fōr mother

a boy sent a card to his mother. the card said, "mother, I love you." but his mother did not get the card.

a cop got the card. hē said, "I am not mother." sō hē gāve the card to his brother.

his brother said, "this card is not fōr mē. I am not mother."

sō the cop and his brother went to fīnd mother. they met the bōy.

the bōy said, "you have the card that I sent to mother. give mē that card."

sō they gāve him the card.

and hē gāve the card to his mother.

this is the end.

TASK 6 FIRST READING

1. You're going to read this story the fast way the first time you read it. But if you come to a word that you can't read the fast way, sound it out and then tell me the word.
2. Touch the title. Remember, the title of a story tells what the story is about. Read the title the fast way. "a card for mother." What is this story going to tell about? "a card for mother."
3. Read the first sentence the fast way. (Child reads first sentence.)
4. Read the next sentence the fast way. (Child reads second sentence.)
5. (Repeat step 4 for remaining sentences in story.)

TASK 7 SECOND READING

1. You're going to read the story again the fast way. This time I'll ask questions. Start with the title again. (Ask questions as child reads.)
2. (After child reads:) (You say:)

(After child reads:)	(You say:)
"A card for mother."	What's this story about?
"But his mother did not get the card."	What did the card say? Did his mother get the card?
"A cop got the card."	Who got the card?
"They met the boy."	Whom did they meet? Whom were they looking for?
" 'Give me that card.' "	What did the boy say? Do you think the cop and his brother will give the boy the card? Let's read and find out.
"So they gave him the card."	Did they give the boy the card?
"And he gave the card to his mother."	What did the boy do?

TASK 8 PICTURE COMPREHENSION

1. What will you see in the picture?
2. Look at the picture and get ready to answer some questions.
3. Who is that in the picture?
4. What do you think that card says?
5. Did you ever send a pretty card to your mother?

TASK 9 SOUNDS WRITING

1. (Write **er** at beginning of first line. Point to **er.**) What sound? "urrr."
2. First trace the **er (urrr)** that I made. Then make more of them on this line. (After tracing **er** several times, child is to make three to five **er**'s. Help child if necessary. For each acceptable letter say:) Good writing **er (urrr).**
3. Here's the next sound you're going to write. (Write **w** at beginning of second line. Point to **w.**) What sound? "www."
4. First trace the **www** that I made. Then make more of them on this line. (After tracing **w** several times, child is to make three to five **w**'s. Help child if necessary. For acceptable letters say:) Good writing **www.**

LESSON 65

TASK 1 SOUNDS INTRODUCTION

1. (Point to **oo.**) Here's a new sound. I'm going to touch under this sound and say the sound. (Touch first ball of arrow. Move quickly to second ball. Hold.) **pooooo** (as in **boo**).
2. Your turn to say the sound when I touch under it. (Touch first ball.) Get ready. (Move quickly to second ball. Hold.) "oooooo."

> (**To correct** child saying a wrong sound or not responding:) The sound is **oooooo.** (Repeat step 2.)

3. (Touch first ball.) Again. Get ready. (Move quickly to second ball. Hold.) "oooooo."

TASK 2 SOUNDS

1. Take a good look at each sound. Say it slowly if you can. Don't get fooled.
2. (Touch first ball for **er.**) Get ready. (Quickly move to second ball. Hold.) "urrr."
3. (Repeat step 2 for **y, i, ē,** and **ch.** Remember to move quickly to end of arrow if there is no ball on arrow for sound.)

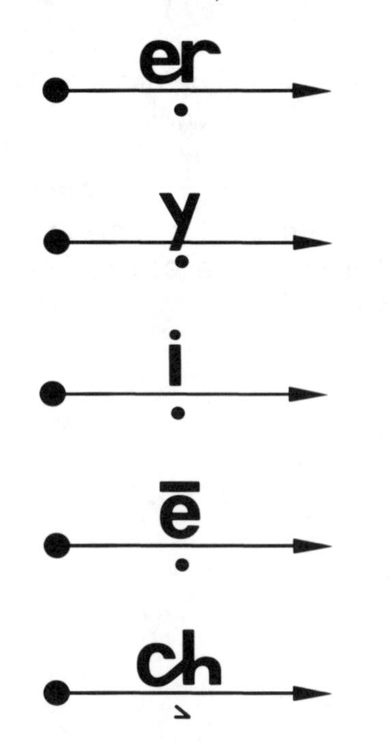

TASK 3 WORD READING

1. (Touch first ball for **you.**) Sound it out. (Touch under sounds as child says:) "yyyooouuu." Again. (Return to first ball.) Sound it out. (Touch balls for sounds as child says:) "yyyooouuu."
2. That's how we **sound out** the word. Now **say** the word. "you." Yes, **you.**
3. Let's do it again. (Return to first ball.) Sound it out. (Touch balls for sounds as child says:) "yyyooouuu." Now say the word. "you." Yes, **you.**

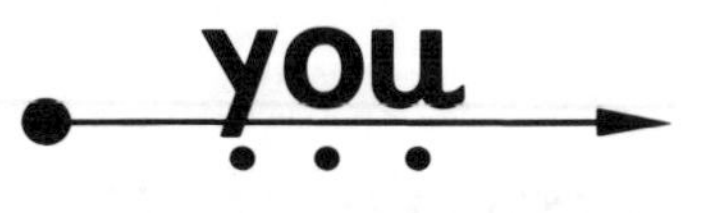

TASK 4 WORD READING

1. Get ready to read these words the fast way.
2. (Touch ball for **over.** Pause three seconds.) Read it the fast way. (Slide.) "over." Yes, **over.**
3. (Repeat step 2 for remaining words.)
4. Read these words again, the fast way.
5. (Touch ball for **over.** Pause three seconds.) What word? "over."
6. (Repeat step 5 for remaining words.) Good reading those words.

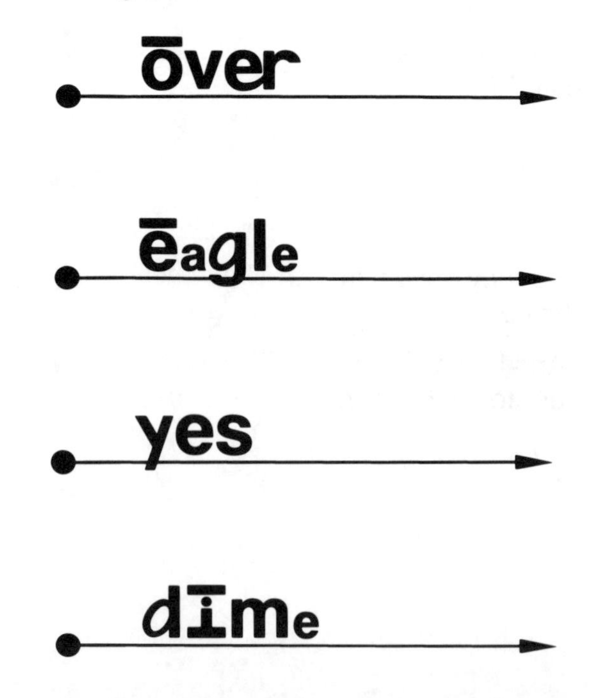

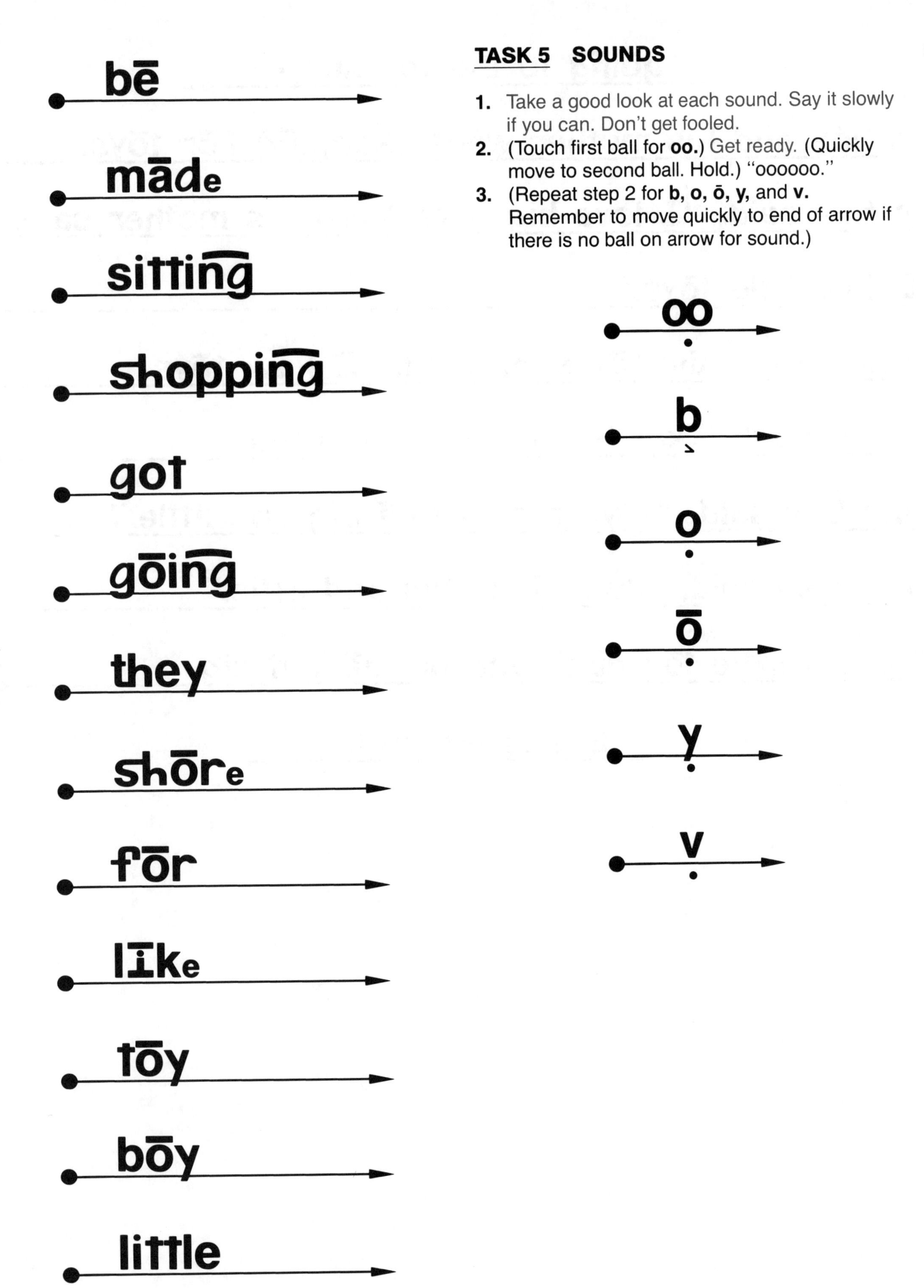

TASK 5 SOUNDS

1. Take a good look at each sound. Say it slowly if you can. Don't get fooled.
2. (Touch first ball for **oo.**) Get ready. (Quickly move to second ball. Hold.) "oooooo."
3. (Repeat step 2 for **b, o, ō, y,** and **v.** Remember to move quickly to end of arrow if there is no ball on arrow for sound.)

gōing to the tōy shop

a bōy and his mother went shopping fōr tōys.

the bōy said, "I love big tōys." but his mother said,

"I lIke little tōys."

the man in the tōy shop said, "I have tōys

that you will lIke. they are big and little."

the bōy said, "tōys can not bē big and little."

the man said, "this tōy is big and little."

hē got a little tōy duck and hē māde it big.

this is the end.

TASK 6 FIRST READING

1. You're going to read this story the fast way the first time you read it. But if you come to a word that you can't read the fast way, sound it out and then tell me the word.
2. Touch the title. Remember, the title of a story tells what the story is about. Read the title the fast way. "**going to the toy shop.**" What is this story going to tell about? "**going to the toy shop.**"
3. Read the first sentence the fast way. **(Child reads first sentence.)**
4. Read the next sentence the fast way. **(Child reads second sentence.)**
5. **(Repeat step 4 for remaining sentences in story.)**

TASK 7 SECOND READING

1. You're going to read the story again the fast way. This time I'll ask questions. Start with the title again. **(Ask questions as child reads.)**
2. **(After child reads:)** **(You say:)**

(After child reads:)	(You say:)
" 'They are big and little.' "	What did the man say? I wonder how toys can be big and little. Let's read and find out.
"He got a little toy duck and he made it big."	I wonder how he did that.

TASK 8 PICTURE COMPREHENSION

1. What will you see in the picture?
2. Look at the picture and get ready to answer some questions.
3. Now I see how he made the little duck big. How did he do that?
4. Is that duck big and little?
5. When is it big? After it's blown up.
6. When is it little? Before it's blown up.
7. Did you ever have a toy that you could blow up and make big?

TASK 9 SOUNDS WRITING

1. Here's the first sound you're going to write. **(Write d at beginning of first line. Point to d.)** What sound? "d."
2. First trace the **d** that I made. Then make more of them on this line. **(After tracing d several times, child is to make three to five d's. Help child if necessary. For acceptable letters say:)** Good writing **d.**
3. Here's the next sound you're going to write. **(Write er at beginning of second line. Point to er.)** What sound? "urrr."
4. First trace the **er (urrr)** that I made. Then make more of them on this line. **(After tracing er several times, child is to make three to five er's. Help child if necessary. For acceptable letters say:)** Good writing **er (urrr).**

LESSON 66

TASK 1 SOUNDS

1. Take a good look at each sound. Say it slowly if you can. Don't get fooled.
2. (Touch first ball for **oo.**) Get ready. (Quickly move to second ball. Hold.) "oooooo."
3. (Repeat step 2 for **ō, b, ī, p,** and **e.** Remember to move quickly to end of arrow if there is no ball on arrow for sound.)

TASK 2 WORD READING

1. Get ready to read these words the fast way.
2. (Touch ball for **you.** Pause three seconds.) Read it the fast way. (Slide.) "you." Yes, **you.**
3. (Repeat step 2 for remaining words.)
4. Read these words again, the fast way.
5. (Touch ball for **you.** Pause three seconds.) What word? "you."
6. (Repeat step 5 for remaining words.) Good reading those words.

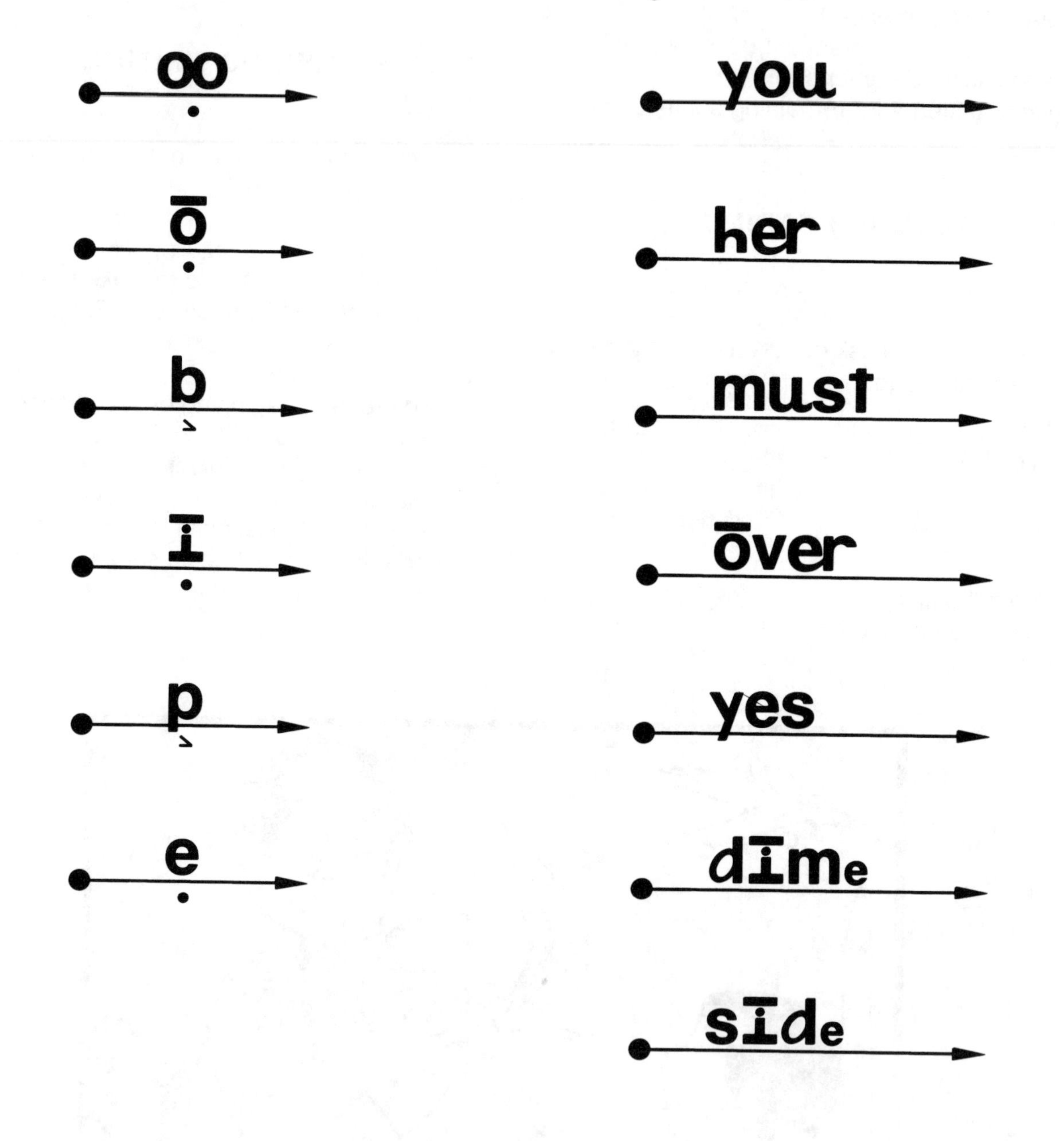

TASK 3 SOUNDS

1. Take a good look at each sound. Say it slowly if you can. Don't get fooled.
2. (Touch first ball for **oo.**) Get ready. (Quickly move to second ball. Hold.) "oooooo."
3. (Repeat step 2 for **o, ō, y, ī,** and **b.** Remember to move quickly to end of arrow if there is no ball on arrow for sound.)

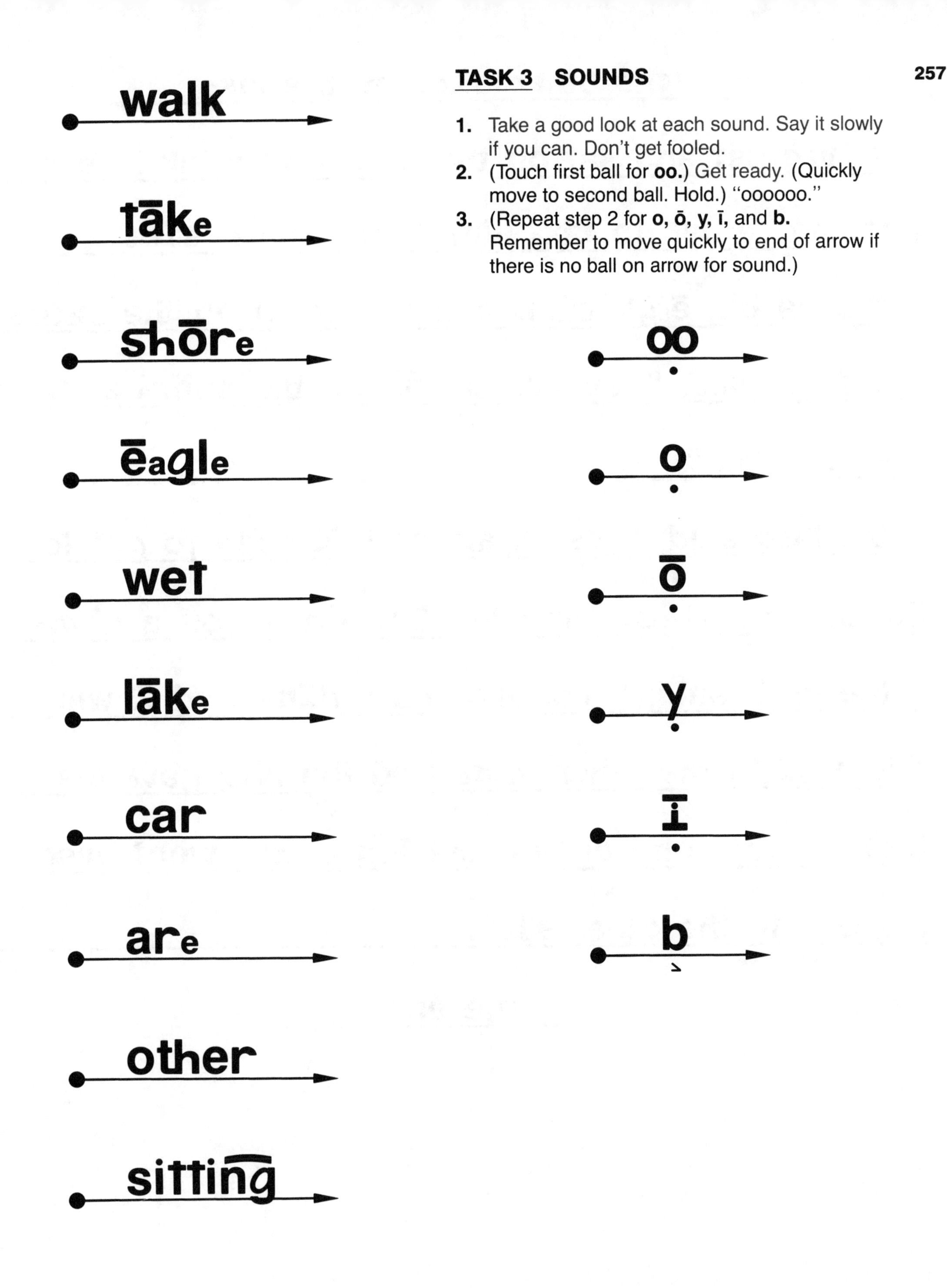

the other sīde of the lāke

a bug sat and sat on the shōre of a lāke. hē did not have a car to tāke him to the other sīde.

then a big ēagle cāme and sat down on the shōre. the ēagle said, "you are sitting on the shōre and you are sad."

the bug said, "yes. I am sad. I nēēd to get to the other sīde of the lāke. I will give you a dīme."

the ēagle said, "yes. give mē a dīme and I will tāke you to the other sīde." sō the bug gāve the ēagle a dīme and got on the ēagle. they went ōver the lāke to the other sīde.

the end

TASK 4 FIRST READING

1. You're going to read this story the fast way the first time you read it. But if you come to a word that you can't read the fast way, sound it out and then tell me the word.
2. Touch the title. Remember, the title of a story tells what the story is about. Read the title the fast way. **"the other side of the lake."** What is this story going to tell about? **"the other side of the lake."**
3. Read the first sentence the fast way. **(Child reads first sentence.)**
4. Read the next sentence the fast way. **(Child reads second sentence.)**
5. **(Repeat step 4 for remaining sentences in story.)**

TASK 5 SECOND READING

1. You're going to read the story again the fast way. This time I'll ask questions. Start with the title again. **(Ask questions as child reads.)**
2. **(After child reads:)**

(After child reads:)	(You say:)
"The other side of the lake."	What's this story about?
" 'I need to get to the other side of the lake.' "	What did the bug say? Where was he?
" 'Give me a dime and I will take you to the other side.' "	What did the eagle say?
"They went over the lake to the other side."	Did the bug get to the other side of the lake? How did the bug get to the other side?

TASK 6 PICTURE COMPREHENSION

1. What will you see in the picture?
2. Look at the picture and get ready to answer some questions.
3. What does that bug have in his hand? Yes, a dime.
4. What will he do with the dime?
5. I wonder why he doesn't take a car to the other side.
6. What would you do if you were that bug?

TASK 7 SOUNDS WRITING

1. Here's the first sound you're going to write. **(Write sh at beginning of first line. Point to sh.)** What sound? **"shshsh."**
2. First trace the **shshsh** that I made. Then make more of them on this line. **(After tracing sh several times, child is to make three to five sh's. Help child if necessary. For acceptable letters say:)** Good writing **shshsh.**
3. Here's the next sound you're going to write. **(Write y at beginning of second line. Point to y.)** What sound? **"yyy."**
4. First trace the **yyy** that I made. Then make more of them on this line. **(After tracing y several times, child is to make three to five y's. Help child if necessary. For acceptable letters say:)** Good writing **yyy.**

LESSON 67

TASK 1 SOUNDS INTRODUCTION

1. (Touch ball for **j.**) We always have to say this sound fast. My turn to say it fast. (Quickly move to end of arrow as you say sound.) **j.**
2. My turn to say it fast again. (Touch ball for **j.**) Say it fast. (Quickly move to end of arrow.) **j.**
3. (Touch ball.) Your turn. (Pause.) Say it fast. (Quickly move to end of arrow.) "j."

(**To correct** if child says "juh," "jah," or "jih":) Listen: **j.** Say it fast. "j." Yes, **j.**

TASK 2 SOUNDS

1. Take a good look at each sound. Say it slowly if you can. Don't get fooled.
2. (Touch first ball for **oo.**) Get ready. (Quickly move to second ball. Hold.) "oooooo."
3. (Repeat step 2 for **er, y, j, i,** and **ing.** Remember to move quickly to end of arrow if there is no ball on arrow for sound.)

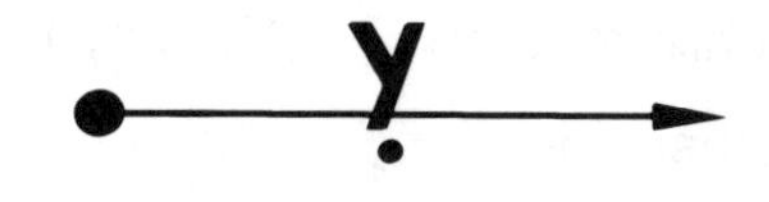

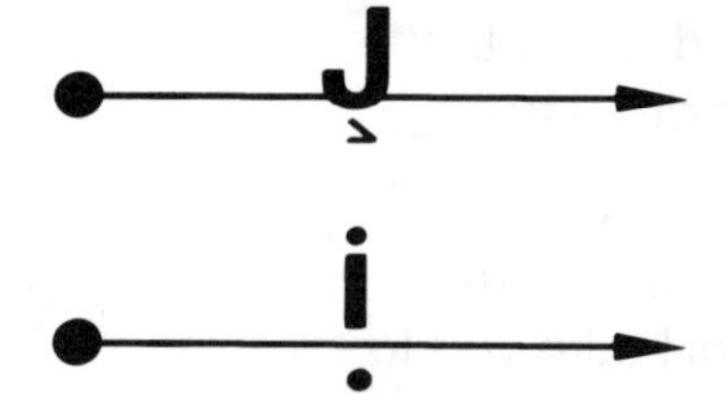

TASK 3 WORD READING

1. (Touch first ball for **some.**) Sound it out. (Touch balls for sounds—but not **o**—as child says:) "sssooommm" (not "sssuuummm").
2. That's how we **sound out** the word. Here's how we **say** the word. (Pause.) **some (sum).** How do we **say** the word? "some." Yes, **some**—it's a funny word.
3. (Return to first ball.) Sound it out again. (Touch balls for sounds as child says:) "sssooommm." Now **say** the word. "some." Yes, **some.** I have **some** money.

TASK 4 WORD READING

(Touch ball for **come.**) This word rhymes with **some.** Read it the fast way. (Slide.) "come."

TASK 5 WORD READING

1. Get ready to read these words the fast way.
2. (Touch **ar** in **park.**) What do these sounds say? "are."
3. (Touch first ball for **park.** Pause three seconds.) Read this word the fast way. (Slide.) "park." Yes, **park.**
4. Get ready to read these words the fast way.
5. (Touch ball for **ever.** Pause three seconds.) Read it the fast way. (Slide.) "ever." Yes, **ever.**
6. (Repeat step 5 for remaining words.)

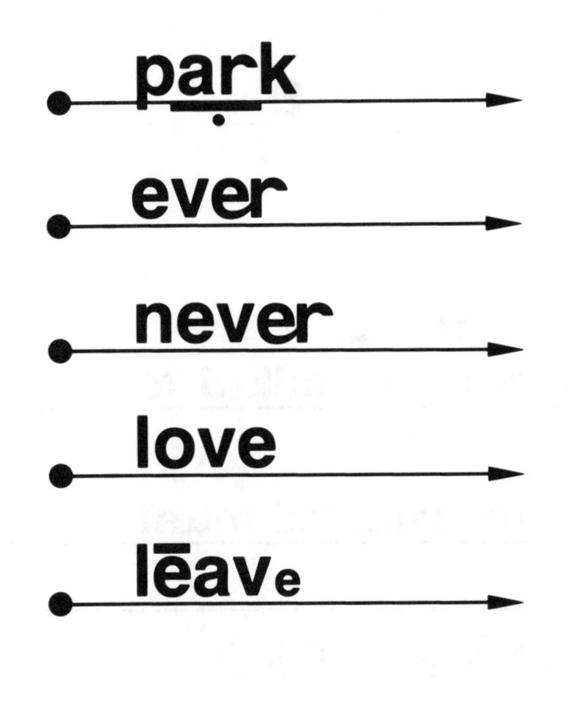

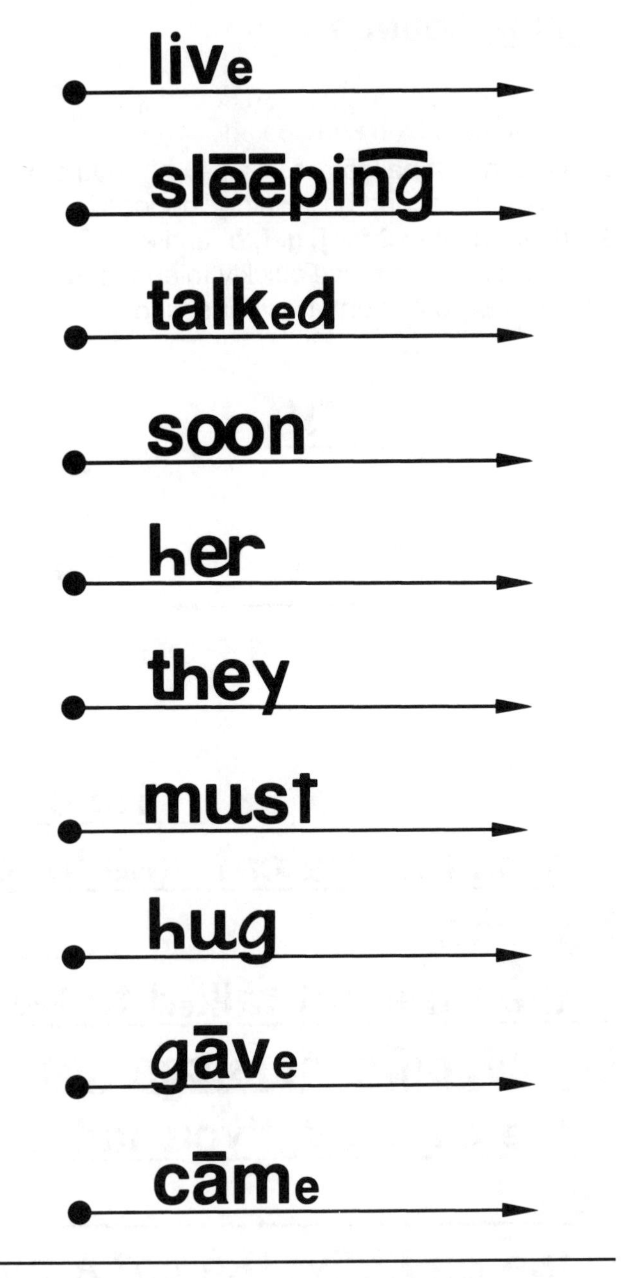

TASK 6 WORD READING

1. (Touch first ball for **jump.**) Sound it out. Get ready. (Slide past **j.** Touch balls for other sounds.) "juuummmp." (Repeat until firm.) What word? "jump." Yes, **jump.**
2. (Touch first ball for **pool.**) Sound it out. (Touch under sounds.) "poooooolll." (Repeat until firm.) What word? "pool."
3. (Repeat step 3 for **moon, swim,** and **lived.**) Now you get to read all these words the fast way.
4. (Touch first ball for **some.** Pause three seconds.) Read it the fast way. (Slide.) "some." Yes, **some.**
5. (Repeat step 4 for remaining words on this page.)

moon swim lived

1. Take a good look at each sound. Say it slowly if you can. Don't get fooled.
2. (Touch first ball for **oo.**) Get ready. (Quickly move to second ball. Hold.) "oooooo."
3. (Repeat step 2 for **j, g, f, b,** and **e.** Remember to move quickly to end of arrow if there is no ball on arrow for sound.)

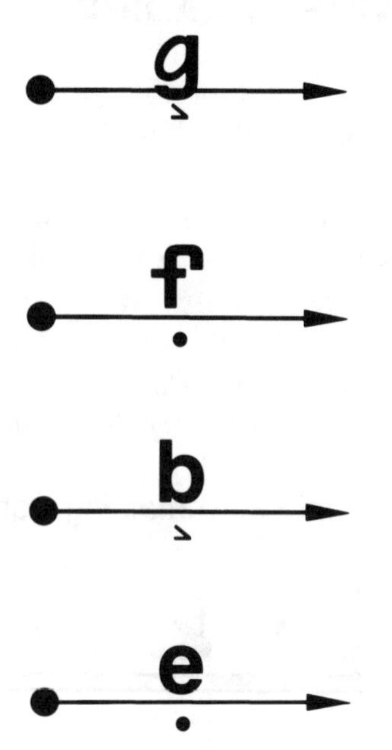

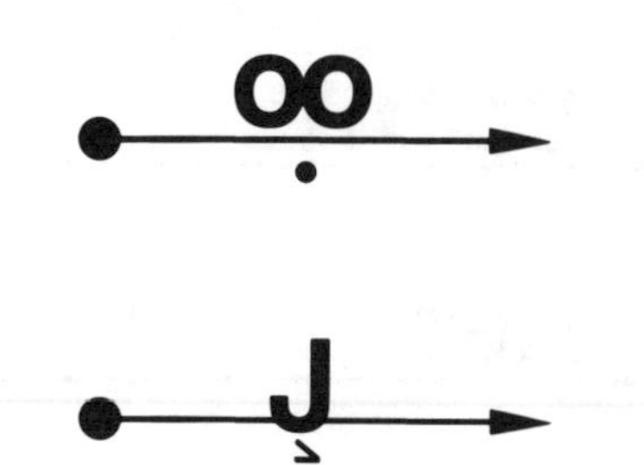

the cat that talked

a girl had a cat. shē loved her cat. shē talked to her cat.

then the cat talked to her. the girl said, "I must bē slēēping. cats can not talk."

the cat said, "you talk to mē. sō I can talk to you."

the girl gāve the cat a big hug. "I never had a cat that talked."

the cat said, "I never had a cat that talked." the girl and the cat talked and talked.

then a man cāme to the park. hē went up to the girl and said, "can I have that cat?"

the cat said, "I will not gō with you."

the man said, "I must bē slēēping. cats do not talk. I will lēave this park." and hē did.

the end

TASK 8 FIRST READING

1. You're going to read this story the fast way the first time you read it. But if you come to a word that you can't read the fast way, sound it out and then tell me the word.
2. Touch the title. Remember, the title of a story tells what the story is about. Read the title the fast way. **"the cat that talked."** What is this story going to tell about? **"the cat that talked."**
3. Read the first sentence the fast way. **(Child reads first sentence.)**
4. Read the next sentence the fast way. **(Child reads second sentence.)**
5. **(Repeat step 4 for remaining sentences in story.)**

TASK 9 SECOND READING

1. You're going to read the story again the fast way. This time I'll ask questions. Start with the title again. **(Ask questions as child reads.)**
2. **(After child reads:)** **(You say:)**

(After child reads:)	(You say:)
" 'Cats can not talk.' "	What did the girl say? Why did she say that?
"The girl gave the cat a big hug."	Show me how you give a big hug.
"The cat said, 'I never had a cat that talked.' "	What did the cat say? That's silly.
"He went up to the girl and said, 'Can I have that cat?' "	What did he say? Who said that? What do you think will happen?
"The cat said, 'I will not go with you.' "	What did the cat say? What do you think the man will do now?
" 'I will leave this park.' "	What did the man say? I'll bet he was surprised to hear that cat talk.
"And he did."	What did he do?

TASK 10 PICTURE COMPREHENSION

1. What will you see in the picture?
2. Look at the picture and get ready to answer some questions.
3. Why does that man look so surprised?
4. What's the cat saying? Yes, **I will not go with you.** I bet it would be a lot of fun to have a talking cat.

TASK 11 SOUNDS WRITING

1. Here's the first sound you're going to write. **(Write b at beginning of first line. Point to b.)** What sound? "b."
2. First trace the **b** that I made. Then make more of them on this line. **(After tracing b several times, child is to make three to five b's. Help child if necessary. For acceptable letters say:)** Good writing **b.**
3. Here's the next sound you're going to write. **(Write p at beginning of second line. Point to p.)** What sound? "p."
4. First trace the **p** that I made. Then make more of them on this line. **(After tracing p several times, child is to make three to five p's. Help child if necessary. For acceptable letters say:)** Good writing **p.**

LESSON 68

TASK 1 SOUNDS

1. You're going to say all these sounds fast.
2. (Touch ball for **j.**) Say it fast. (Move to end of arrow.) "j."
3. (Repeat step 2 for each sound.)

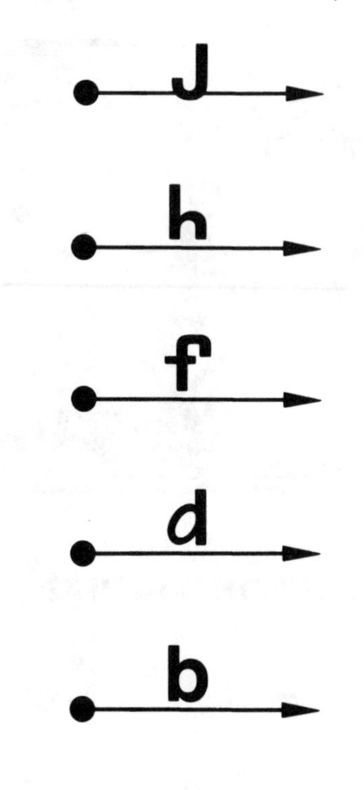

TASK 2 WORD READING

1. (Point to **o** in **some.**) In all these words, this sound is funny. It says **ŭŭŭ.** Get ready to read all these words the fast way.
2. (Touch ball for **some.** Pause three seconds.) Read it the fast way. (Slide.)
3. (Repeat step 2 for **come, love, other, mother,** and **brother**.)

TASK 3 WORD READING

1. (Touch first ball for **every.**) Sound it out. (Touch balls for sounds.) "eeevvvurrryyy." (Repeat until firm.) What word? "every."
2. (Repeat step 1 for **soon, never, pool, brōke, swimming, jumps, jumped,** and **start.**)

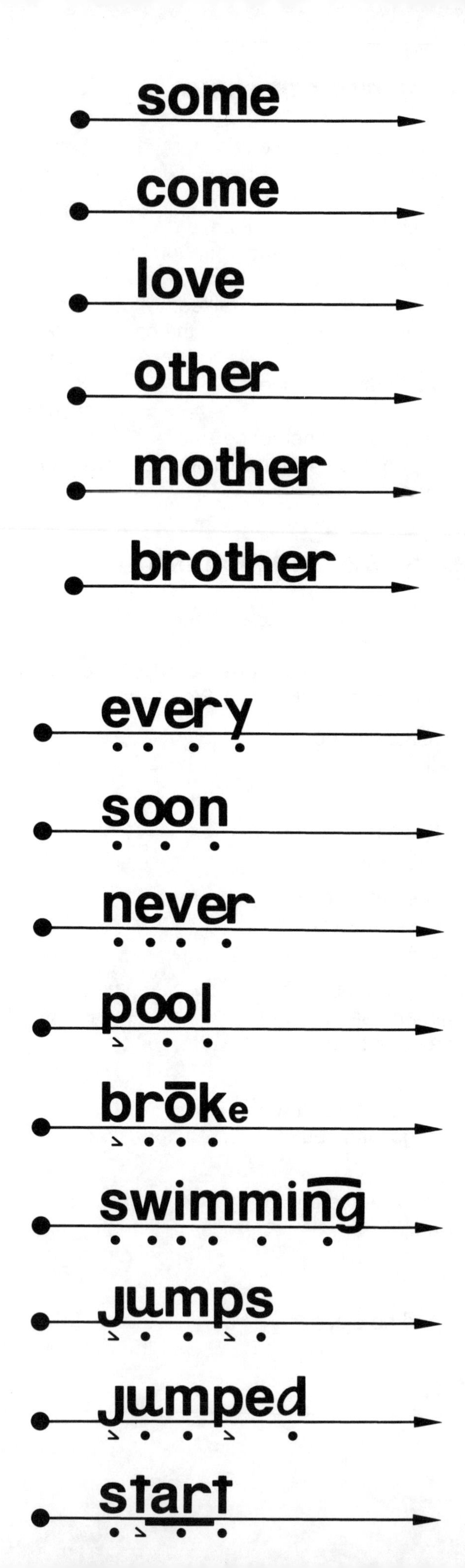

TASK 4 WORD READING

1. Get ready to read these words the fast way.
2. (Touch ball for **men.** Pause three seconds.) Read it the fast way. (Slide.) "men." Yes, **men.**
3. (Repeat step 2 for remaining words.)
4. Read these words again, the fast way.
5. (Touch first ball for **every.** Pause three seconds.) What word? "every."
6. (Repeat step 5 for remaining words.) Good reading those words.

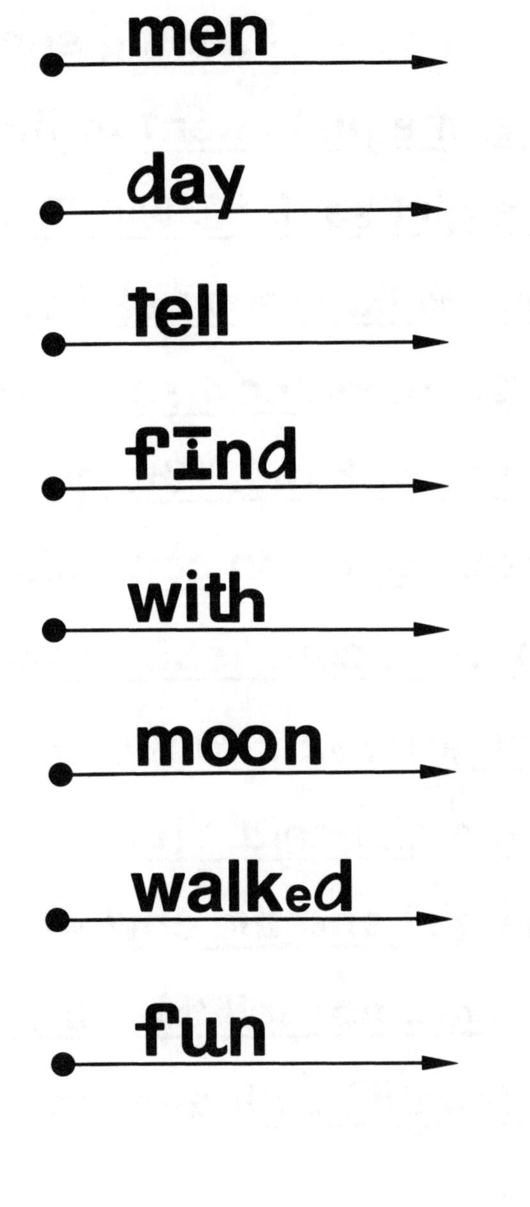

TASK 5 SOUNDS

1. You're going to say all these sounds fast.
2. (Touch ball for **j.**) Say it fast. (Move to end of arrow.) "j."
3. (Repeat step 2 for each sound.)

j

g

f

d

k

finding some fun on the moon

some girls went to the moon in a moon ship.

a girl said, "I will find some fun." shē walked and walked. soon shē cāme to a cow.

the moon cow said, "wē can have lots of fun. come with mē." the girl went with the moon cow to a pool. the moon cow said, "this is how wē have fun on the moon." shē jumped into the pool. and the girl jumped into the pool.

the girl said, "it is fun to swim on the moon." sō the girl and the cow went swimming every dāy. the girl did not tell the other girls that shē went swimming with a moon cow.

the end

TASK 6 FIRST READING

1. You're going to read this story the fast way the first time you read it. But if you come to a word that you can't read the fast way, sound it out and then tell me the word.
2. Touch the title. Remember, the title of a story tells what the story is about. Read the title the fast way. "finding some fun on the moon." What is this story going to tell about? "finding some fun on the moon."
3. Read the first sentence the fast way. (Child reads first sentence.)
4. Read the next sentence the fast way. (Child reads second sentence.)
5. (Repeat step 4 for remaining sentences in story.)

TASK 7 SECOND READING

1. You're going to read the story again the fast way. This time I'll ask questions. Start with the title again. (Ask questions as child reads.)
2. (After child reads:) (You say:)

(After child reads:)	(You say:)
"Finding some fun on the moon."	What's this story about?
"A girl said, 'I will find some fun.' "	What did she say? Where was she? How did the girls get to the moon?
" 'Come with me.' "	What did the cow say? I wonder what kind of fun they have. Let's read and find out.
"She jumped into the pool."	What did the cow do? How do they have fun on the moon?
"The girl did not tell the other girls that she went swimming with a moon cow."	I wonder why she didn't tell the girls about the pool.

TASK 8 PICTURE COMPREHENSION

1. What will you see in the picture?
2. Look at the picture and get ready to answer some questions.
3. What's happening in the picture?
4. Does that look like fun to you?
5. Would you like to swim with a moon cow?

TASK 9 SOUNDS WRITING

1. (Write **j** at beginning of first line. Point to **j.**) What sound? "j "
2. First trace the **j** that I made. Then make more of them on this line. (After tracing **j** several times, child is to make three to five **j**'s. Help child if necessary. For each acceptable letter say:) Good writing **j.**
3. Here's the next sound you're going to write. (Write **er** at beginning of second line. Point to **er.**) What sound? "urrr."
4. First trace the **er (urrr)** that I made. Then make more of them on this line. (After tracing **er** several times, child is to make three to five **er**'s. Help child if necessary. For acceptable letters say:) Good writing **er (urrr).**

side

take

smile

bite

lake

five

nine

fine

late

TASK 4 WORD READING

1. Get ready to read these words the fast way.
2. (Touch ball for **road.** Pause three seconds.) Read it the fast way. (Slide.) "road." Yes, **road.**
3. (Repeat step 2 for remaining words.)

road

stopped

came

near

over

back

start

started

come

town

sick

makes

my

then

away

gas

TASK 5 WORD READING THE FAST WAY

1. Now you get to read all the words the fast way.
2. (Touch first ball for first word of lesson. Pause three seconds.) Read it the fast way. (Slide. Child reads word.) Yes, good reading.
3. (Repeat step 2 for remaining words of lesson.)

1. There are circled letters in this story. Touch circled letter **a.** Touch circled letter **b.**
2. After you read the story, you'll read it again and I'll ask questions when you read to the circled letters.
3. First read the story the fast way. Start with the words in the title and read it the fast way. (Child reads title.)
4. What's this story going to tell about? "the fat man coming back."
5. Read the first sentence the fast way. (Child reads first sentence.)
6. Read the next sentence the fast way. (Child reads second sentence.)
7. (Repeat step 6 for remaining sentences in story.)

the fat man came back

the fat man was in the old car. he went far, far down the road.ⓐ he had told the other man, "I will never come back." but the road came to a town. then the road started to go this way and that way.ⓑ

the road went near a pool and near a cow. it went near a rat and near five farms. that road went under trees and over barns. the fat man said, "the way this road is going it will take me to the moon."ⓒ

as the road came near a man, the old car stopped. the fat man said, "this car has no more gas."ⓓ

the man on the road said, "I see you came back with my car."ⓔ

the fat man said, "I did not come back. the road came back." then the fat man said, "I must get away. but I will not take that road. I will go to the lake and start swimming."

and he did.ⓕ

this is the end.

TASK 7 SECOND READING

1. Now you're going to read the story again. This time start with the title and read until you get to the first circled letter. Then stop.
2. (Ask following questions when child reaches each letter.)
   - ⓐ Where did he go? What was the fat man in?
   - ⓑ What does that mean: **the road went this way and that way?** (Idea: all over the place.)
   - ⓒ What did he say? Does he like that road? Why not?
   - ⓓ Why did the car stop?
   - ⓔ Whom does the car belong to?
   - ⓕ How did he get away? Why didn't he want to take the road again?

TASK 8 PICTURE COMPREHENSION

Look at the picture. Follow that road and tell me what it goes over and under. Name some things the road goes near. Why is the fat man kicking that car?

TASK 9 WRITING LETTERS

1. You're going to write the letters that I write. Here's what you're going to write first. Watch. (Write **u** at beginning of first line. Point to **u.**) What's the **name** of this letter? "ū." What **sounds** does that letter make? "ŭŭŭ, ŭŭŭ." We're going to write **u** without a line.
2. First trace the **u** that I made. Then make more of them on this line.
3. (After tracing **u** several times, child is to make three to five **u**'s. Help child if necessary. For acceptable letters say:) Good writing **u.**
4. Here's the next letter you're going to write. Watch (Write **b** at beginning of second line. Point to **b.**) What's the **name** of this letter? "b." What **sound** does that letter make? "b."
5. First trace the **b** that I made. Then make more of them on this line.
6. (After tracing **b** several times, child is to make three to five **b**'s. Help child if necessary. For acceptable letters say:) Good writing **b.**

LESSON 78

TASK 1 WORD READING

1. (Point to words.) Here are the words you're going to read.
(Touch first ball for **black.**) Sound it out. Get ready. (Slide past **b.** Touch balls for other sounds.) "blllaaak." (Repeat until firm.) What word? "black." Yes, **black.**
2. (Touch first ball for sleep.) Sound it out. (Touch balls for sounds.) "ssslllēēēp." (Repeat until firm.) What word? "sleep."
3. (Repeat step 2 for **having, meets,** and **sing.**)

black   sleep   having

meets   sing

TASK 2 LONG VOWEL

1. These words have an **e** on the end. The **e** doesn't make a sound. But you can tell how to say the rest of the word by saying the letter names. The letter names tell you the sounds to make.
2. (Point to **take.**) Say all the letter names for this word. "t-a-k-e." Good. Now listen to the letter names without the **e.** (Pause, then exaggerate **ā** as you say letter names.) **t-āāā-k.** The word is **take.** What word? "take."
3. (Point to **bite.**) Say all the letter names for this word. "b-i-t-e." Listen to the letter names without the **e.** (Pause.) **b-īīī-t.** What word? "bite."
4. (Point to **late.**) Say all the letter names for this word. "l-a-t-e." Listen to the letter names without the **e.** (Pause.) **l-āāā-t.** What word? "late."
5. (Point to **time.**) Say all the letter names for this word. "t-i-m-e." Listen to the letter names without the **e.** (Pause.) **t-īīī-m.** What word? "time."
6. (Point to **side.**) Say all the letter names for this word. "s-i-d-e." Listen to the letter names without the **e.** (Pause.) **s-īīī-d.** What word? "side."
7. (Point to **smile.**) Say all the letter names for this word. "s-m-i-l-e." Listen to the letter names without the **e.** (Pause.) **s-m-īīī-l.** What word? "smile."
8. (Point to **home.**) Say all the letter names for this word. "h-o-m-e." Listen to the letter names without the **e.** (Pause.) **h-ōōō-m.** What word? "home."
9. (Point to **nine.**) Say all the letter names for this word. "n-i-n-e." Listen to the letter names without the **e.** (Pause.) **n-īīī-n.** What word? "nine."
10. (Point to **like.**) Say all the letter names for this word. "l-i-k-e." Listen to the letter names without the **e.** (Pause.) **l-īīī-k.** What word? "like."
11. Get ready to read all those words the fast way.
12. (Touch first ball for **take.** Pause three seconds.) Read it the fast way. (Slide.) "take."
13. (Repeat step 12 for remaining words that end in **e.**)

side

home   nine   like

TASK 3 WORD READING

1. You're going to read these words the fast way. (Touch ball for **look.** Pause three seconds.) Read it the fast way. (Slide.) "look." Yes, **look.**
2. The rest of the words rhyme with **look.** (Touch ball for **took.** Pause three seconds.) Read it the fast way. (Slide.) "took." Yes, **took.**
3. (Touch ball for **book.** Pause three seconds.) Read it the fast way. (Slide.) "book." Yes, **book.** Remember those words.

look

took

book

TASK 4 WORD READING

1. Get ready to read these words the fast way.
2. (Touch ball for **girl.** Pause three seconds.) Read it the fast way. (Slide.) "girl." Yes, **girl.**
3. (Repeat step 2 for remaining words.)

TASK 5 WORD READING THE FAST WAY

1. Now you get to read all the words the fast way.
2. (Touch ball for first word of lesson. Pause three seconds.) Read it the fast way. (Slide. Child reads word.) Yes, good reading.
3. (Repeat step 2 for remaining words of lesson.)

girl

talked

talks

love

other

gold

jumped

things

started

singing

the gold cat and the black cat

a girl had a cat that talked. her cat was big and black. she loved her cat, but when it was time to sleep, the cat talked and talked and talked.[a] the girl said, "I must get some sleep."

then she said, "I will get a cat that can not talk. when my black cat is having fun with the other cat, my black cat will not talk, talk, talk."[b]

so the girl got a cat. this cat was little and gold. she said to the little gold cat, "when my black cat meets you, she will like you."[c]

the black cat did like the gold cat.[d] they ran and they jumped. they bit socks and bit cat tails.[e] then they sat. but the black cat did not stop talking.[f]

the black cat said to the other cat, "how are things going with you?"[g]

but the gold cat did not talk back. the gold cat started to sing.[h] and that cat did not stop singing.

so now the girl has 2 cats that do not let her sleep. she has a cat that talks, talks, talks. and she has a cat that sings, sings, sings.[i]

the end

TASK 6 FIRST READING

1. There are circled letters in this story. Touch circled letter **a.** Touch circled letter **b.**
2. After you read the story, you'll read it again, and I'll ask questions when you read to the circled letters.
3. First read the story the fast way. Start with the words in the title and read it the fast way. (Child reads title.)
4. What's this story going to tell about? "the gold cat and the black cat."
5. Read the first sentence the fast way. (Child reads first sentence.)
6. Read the next sentence the fast way. (Child reads second sentence.)
7. (Repeat step 7 for remaining sentences in story.)

TASK 7 SECOND READING

1. Now you're going to read the story again. This time I'll ask questions when you read to the circled letters. Start with the title and read until you get to the first circled letter. Then stop.
2. (Ask following questions when child reaches each letter.)
   - ⓐ Was it easy for her to get to sleep? Why not?
   - ⓑ What was the girl going to do to stop her black cat from talking?
   - ⓒ Does the girl think the black cat will like the little gold cat? What do you think?
   - ⓓ Did the black cat like the gold cat?
   - ⓔ Whose cat tails did they bite?
   - ⓕ Did the black cat stop talking? So did the girl's plan work?
   - ⓖ What did the black cat say? Whom was the black cat talking to?
   - ⓗ Did the gold cat talk? What did the gold cat start doing?
   - ⓘ Which cat talks, talks, talks? Which cat sings, sings, sings? Does the girl get much sleep?

TASK 8 PICTURE COMPREHENSION

Look at the picture. What is that girl trying to do? Why does she have her hands over her ears? What is the black cat doing? What is the gold cat doing? How would you like to try sleeping with those cats in the room?

TASK 9 WRITING LETTERS

1. You're going to write the letters that I write. Here's what you're going to write first. Watch. (Write **x** at beginning of first line. Point to **x.**) What's the **name** of this letter? "x.' What **sound** does that letter make? "ksss."
2. First trace the **x** that I made. Then make more of them on this line.
3. (After tracing **x** several times, child is to make three to five **x**'s. Help child if necessary. For acceptable letters say:) Good writing **x.**
4. Here are the next letters you're going to write. Watch. (Write **er** at beginning of second line. Point to **er.**) What are the **names** of these letters? "e-r." What **sound** do these letters make? "urrr."
5. First trace the **er** that I made. Then make more of them on this line.
6. (After tracing **er** several times, child is to make three to five **er**'s. Help child if necessary. For acceptable letters say:) Good writing **er.**

LESSON 79

TASK 1 WORD READING

1. (Touch first ball for **fast.**) Sound it out. (Touch balls for sounds.) "fffaaassst." (Repeat until firm.) What word? "fast."
2. (Repeat step 1 for **part, big, very,** and **swam.**)

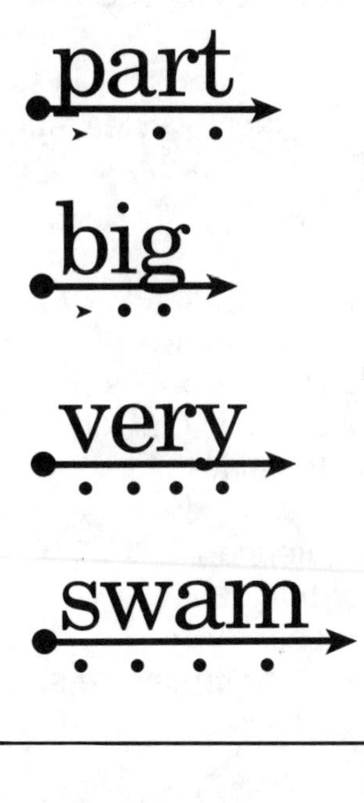

TASK 2 LONG VOWEL

1. These words have the letter **o.** The letter names for these words help you say the sounds.
2. (Point to **more.**) Say all the letter names for this word. "m-o-r-e." Yes, **m-ōōō-r-e.** What word? "more." Yes, **more.**
3. (Point to **sore.**) Say all the letter names for this word. "s-o-r-e." Yes, **s-ōōō-r-e.** What word? "sore." Yes, **sore.**
4. (Point to **shore.**) Say all the letter names for this word. "s-h-o-r-e." Yes, **s-h-ōōō-r-e.** What word? "shore." Yes, **shore.**
5. (Point to **nose.**) Say all the letter names for this word. "n-o-s-e." Yes, **n-ōōō-s-e.** What word? "nose." Yes, **nose.**
6. (Point to **note.**) Say all the letter names for this word. "n-o-t-e." Yes, **n-ōōō-t-e.** What word? "note." Yes, **note.**
7. (Point to **hope.**) Say all the letter names for this word. "h-o-p-e." Yes, **h-ōōō-p-e.** What word? "hope." Yes, **hope.**

more

sore

shore

nose

note

hope

TASK 3 WORD READING—ea

1. (Touch ball for **ea.**) When these sounds are together, they usually say (pause) **ēēē.** What do they say? "ēēē."
2. (Touch ball for **ea** in **near.**) What do these sounds say? "ēēē." (Touch first ball for **near.**) Sound it out. (Touch balls for sounds.) "nnnēēērrr." (Repeat until firm.) What word? "near." Yes, **near.**

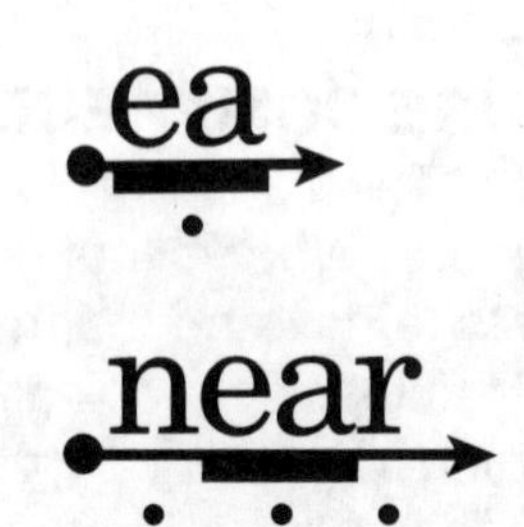

3. (Touch ball for **ea** in **leave.**) What do these sounds say? "ēēē." (Touch first ball for **leave.**) Sound it out (Touch balls for sounds.) "lllēēēvvv." (Repeat until firm.) What word? "leave." Yes, **leave.**
4. (Touch ball for **ea** in **mean.**) What do these sounds say? "ēēē." (Touch first ball for **mean.**) Sound it out. (Touch balls for sounds.) "mmmēēēnnn." (Repeat until firm.) What word? "mean." Yes, **mean.**

leave

mean

TASK 4 WORD READING

1. Get ready to read these words the fast way.
2. (Touch ball for **here.** Pause three seconds.) Read it the fast way. (Slide.) "here." Yes, **here.**
3. (Repeat step 2 for remaining words.)

TASK 5 WORD READING THE FAST WAY

1. Now you get to read all the words the fast way.
2. (Touch first ball for first word of lesson. Pause three seconds.) Read it the fast way. (Slide. Child reads word.) Yes, good reading.
3. (Repeat step 2 for remaining words of lesson.)

here

duck

started

love

same

made

come

the duck and the fish—part 1

a little fish was near the shore of a lake. a duck came near the fish. the duck said, "this is my part of the lake. you can not swim here." ⓐ

the fish said, "my mom said I can swim here." ⓑ

the duck got mad. "I told you that you must go. now leave this part of the lake."

"I will go," the fish said. "but I will come back with my mom." ⓒ

the duck started to swim for the fish so the fish started to swim away very fast. then the little fish looked back at the duck. the little fish said, "I will leave. but I will come back with my mom. when she talks with you, you will let me swim in this part of the lake." ⓓ

"ho, ho," the duck said. "you can't swim in this part of the lake if you have five moms or ten moms. this is my part of the lake."

the duck went for the little fish and the fish swam away from the duck. ⓔ

this is not the end.

TASK 6 FIRST READING

1. We'll read the first part of this story. In the next lesson we'll read the second part of this story. After you read this part of the story, you'll read it again and I'll ask questions.
2. Read the title the fast way. (Child reads title.)
3. Read the first sentence the fast way. (Child reads first sentence.)
4. Read the next sentence the fast way. (Child reads second sentence.)
5. (Repeat step 4 for remaining sentences in story.)

TASK 7 SECOND READING

1. Now you're going to read the story again. This time I'll ask questions when you read to the circled letters. Start with the title and read until you get to the first circled letter. Then stop.
2. (Ask following questions when child reaches each letter.)
   - ⓐ Did the duck want the fish to swim in this part of the lake? Why not?
   - ⓑ What did the fish say?
   - ⓒ Whom is the fish going to come back with?
   - ⓓ Did the little fish think his mom would talk the duck into letting the little fish swim near the shore? I wonder why that little fish is so sure that his mom will be able to fix things up.
   - ⓔ Does that duck want to be friends with the little fish?

TASK 8 PICTURE COMPREHENSION

Look at the picture. What do you think that duck is saying to the little fish? What do you think the little fish is saying to the duck? Show me the shore of the lake. The little fish wants to be near that shore.

TASK 9 WRITING LETTERS

1. You're going to write the letters that I write. Here's what you're going to write first. Watch. (Write **z** at beginning of first line. Point to **z.**) What's the **name** of this letter? "z." What **sound** does that letter make? "zzz."
2. First trace the **z** that I made. Then make more of them on this line.
3. (After tracing **z** several times, child is to make three to five **z**'s. Help child if necessary. For acceptable letters say:) Good writing **z.**
4. Here's the next letter you're going to write. Watch. (Write **s** at beginning of second line. Point to **s.**) What's the **name** of this letter? "s." What **sound** does that letter make? "sss."
5. First trace the **s** that I made. Then make more of them on this line.
6. (After tracing **s** several times, child is to make three to five **s**'s. Help child if necessary. For acceptable letters say:) Good writing **s.**

LESSON 80

TASK 1 WORD READING

1. (Touch first ball for **swim.**) Sound it out. (Touch balls for sounds.) "ssswwwiiimmm." (Repeat until firm.) What word? "swim."
2. (Repeat step 1 for **swam, let, left, went,** and **with.**)

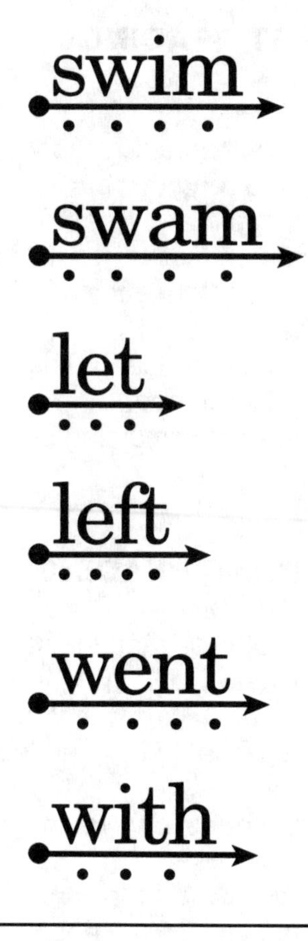

TASK 2 LONG VOWEL

1. These words have the letter **o.** The letter names for these words help you say the sounds.
2. (Point to **shore.**) Say all the letter names for this word. "s-h-o-r-e." Yes, **s-h-ōōō-r-e.** What word? "shore." Yes, **shore.**
3. (Point to **nose.**) Say all the letter names for this word. "n-o-s-e." Yes, **n-ōōō-s-e.** What word? "nose." Yes, **nose.**
4. (Point to **more.**) Say all the letter names for this word. "m-o-r-e." Yes, **m-ōōō-r-e.** What word? "more." Yes, **more.**
5. (Point to **hope.**) Say all the letter names for this word. "h-o-p-e." Yes, **h-ōōō-p-e.** What word? "hope." Yes, **hope.**
6. (Point to **no.**) Say all the letter names for this word. "n-o." Yes, **n-ōōō.** What word? "no." Yes, **no.**
7. (Point to **ho.**) Say all the letter names for this word. "h-o." Yes, **h-ōōō.** What word? "ho." Yes, **ho.**
8. (Point to **horse.**) Say all the letter names for this word. "h-o-r-s-e." Yes, **h-ōōō-r-s-e.** What word? "horse." Yes, **horse.**

TASK 3 WORD READING

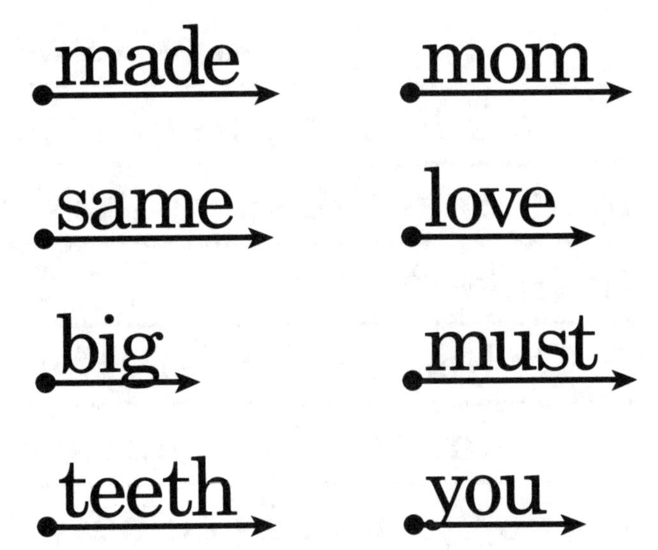

1. Get ready to read these words the fast way.
2. (Touch ball for **made.** Pause three seconds.) Read it the fast way. (Slide.) "made." Yes, **made.**
3. (Repeat step 2 for remaining words.)

TASK 4 WORD READING

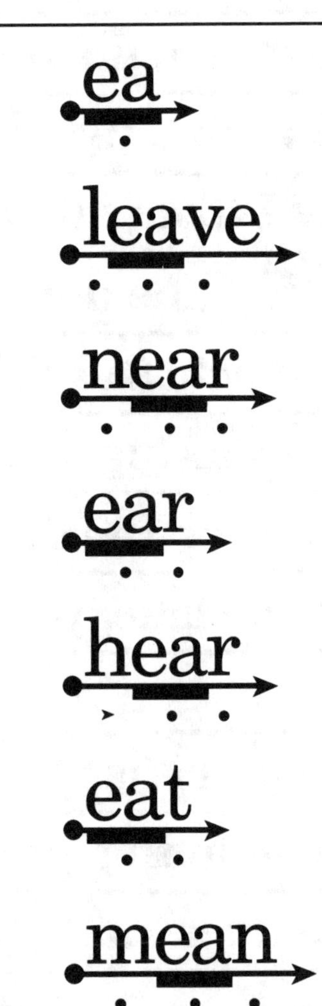

1. (Touch ball for **ea.**) When these sounds are together, they usually say (pause) **ēēē.** What do they say? "ēēē."
2. (Touch ball for **ea** in **leave.**) What do these sounds say? "ēēē." (Touch first ball for **leave.**) Sound it out. (Touch balls for sounds.) "lllēēēvvv." (Repeat until firm.) What word? "leave." Yes, **leave.**
3. (Touch ball for **ea** in **near.**) What do these sounds say? "ēēē." (Touch first ball for **near.**) Sound it out. (Touch balls for sounds.) "nnnēēērrr." (Repeat until firm.) What word? "near." Yes, **near.**
4. (Touch ball for **ea** in **ear.**) What do these sounds say? "ēēē." (Touch first ball for **ear.**) Sound it out. (Touch balls for sounds.) "ēēērrr." (Repeat until firm.) What word? "ear." Yes, **ear.**
5. (Touch ball for **ea** in **hear.**) What do these sounds say? "ēēē." (Touch first ball for **hear.**) Sound it out. (Touch balls for sounds.) "hēēērrr." (Repeat until firm.) What word? "hear." Yes, **hear.**
6. (Touch ball for **ea** in **eat.**) What do these sounds say? "ēēē." (Touch first ball for **eat.**) Sound it out. (Touch balls for sounds.) "ēēēt." (Repeat until firm.) What word? "eat." Yes, **eat.**
7. (Touch ball for **ea** in **mean.**) What do these sounds say? "ēēē." (Touch first ball for **mean.**) Sound it out. (Touch balls for sounds.) "mmmēēēnnn." (Repeat until firm.) What word? "mean." Yes, **mean.**

TASK 5 WORD READING THE FAST WAY

1. Now you get to read all the words the fast way.
2. (Touch first ball for first word of lesson. Pause three seconds.) Read it the fast way. (Slide. Child reads word.) Yes, good reading.
3. (Repeat step 2 for remaining words of lesson.)

the duck and the fish—part 2

a little fish was near the shore of a lake but a duck made that fish leave. the duck said, "this is my part of the lake."

when the fish left, the duck started to swim and have fun. the duck started to sing, "I made that fish go, go, go. now I can have fun. ho, ho, ho."

just then, the little fish came back. ⓐ the duck looked at that fish and started to get mad. the duck yelled, "I told you not to come back to this part of the lake." then the duck looked at the fish that was next to the little fish. this fish was as big as ten fish. this fish had teeth as big as the little fish. ⓑ the duck started to smile. ⓒ then the duck said, "I mean, if you like this part of the lake, you can come here for part of every day."

the mom fish smiled, then she said, "my little fish will swim in this part of the lake." ⓓ

the duck said, "yes, yes. that will be a lot of fun. I will love to swim with your little fish." ⓔ

so the little fish went swimming near the shore.

and the duck went swimming with the little fish. the

duck never got mad or said that the little fish must

leave that part of the lake.Ⓕ

this is the end.

TASK 6 FIRST READING

1. Last time you read the first part of the story about the duck and the fish. What happened at the end of that part of the story?
2. In this part of the story, we'll find out what happened to the duck and the fish. After you read this part of the story, you'll read it again and I'll ask questions.
3. Read the title the fast way. (Child reads title.)
4. Read the first sentence the fast way. (Child reads first sentence.
5. Read the next sentence the fast way. (Child reads second sentence.)
6. (Repeat step 5 for remaining sentences in story.)

TASK 7 SECOND READING

1. Now you're going to read the story again. This time I'll ask questions when you read to the circled letters. Start with the title and read until you get to the first circled letter. Then stop.
2. (Ask following questions when child reaches each letter.)
   - Ⓐ Do you think the little fish is alone? Who do you think is with the little fish?
   - Ⓑ Who is that big fish with big teeth?
   - Ⓒ Why is that duck smiling now?
   - Ⓓ What did mom fish say? Do you think the duck will listen to her?
   - Ⓔ Is that the way the duck talked before the mom came back with the little fish? Why is the duck being so friendly now?
   - Ⓕ Why didn't the duck get mad at the little fish?

TASK 8 PICTURE COMPREHENSION

Look at the picture. Touch the little fish. Does that mom fish look very friendly? What do you think the duck is saying? Look at how that duck is sweating.

TASK 9 WRITING LETTERS

1. You're going to write the letters that I write. Here's what you're going to write first. Watch. **(Write u at beginning of first line. Point to u.)** What's the name of this letter? "u." What sounds does that letter make? "ūūū, ŭŭŭ." We're going to write **u** without a line.
2. First trace the **u** that I made. Then make more of them on this line.
3. **(After tracing u several times, child is to make three to five u's. Help child if necessary. For acceptable letters say:)** Good writing **u.**
4. Here's the next letter you're going to write. Watch. **(Write z at beginning of second line. Point to z.)** What's the name of this letter? "z." What sound does that letter make? "zzz."
5. First trace the **z** that I made. Then make more of them on this line.
6. **(After tracing z several times, child is to make three to five z's. Help child if necessary. For acceptable letters say:)** Good writing **z.**

LESSON 81

TASK 1 CAPITAL LETTERS

1. The letters in the top line are capital letters. What kind of letters are they? "capitals."
2. The capitals are above the same smaller letters that you already know. Capital **A** is above the letter **a** you know. Capital **B** is above the **b** that you know. Touch capital letter **C.** It looks a lot like the **c** that you know, but it is bigger.
3. See if you can touch each capital letter and say its name, starting with **A. (Child reads each capital letter in alphabet.)**
4. I'll name some capital letters that are like the letters you know. See if you can find the capitals I name. Capital **I. (Child touches I.)** Good finding. Capital **J. (Child touches J.)** Good finding.
5. **(Repeat step 4 for capital O, capital F, capital S, capital T, capital U, capital W, capital X, capital Y, and capital Z.)**
6. There are other capitals that look something like the letters you know. See if you can find capital **E.**
7. **(Repeat step 6 for capital M.)**

A B C D E F G H I J K L M N O P Q R S T U V W X Y Z

a b c d e f g h i j k l m n o p q r s t u v w x y z

TASK 2 WORD READING

1. **(Touch first ball for zoom.)** Sound it out. **(Touch balls for sounds.)** "zzzoooooommm." **(Repeat until firm.)** What word? "zoom."
2. **(Repeat step 1 for hill, fast, went, did,** and **gas.)**

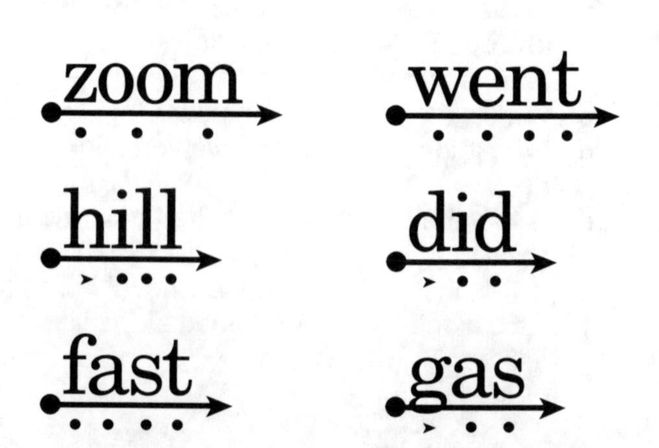

TASK 3 WORD READING

1. Get ready to read these words the fast way.
2. (Touch ball for **horse.** Pause three seconds.) Read it the fast way. (Slide.) "horse." Yes, **horse.**
3. (Repeat step 2 for remaining words.)

horse

stopped so

fast no

over nose

things has

go as

TASK 4 WORD READING

1. These words have two **o**'s in the middle. The **o**'s make the same sound in all these words. You're going to read the words the fast way.
2. (Touch ball for **look.** Pause.) Read it the fast way. (Slide.) "look." Yes, **look.**
3. (Repeat step 2 for **took** and **good.**)

look

TASK 5 WORD READING

1. (Touch ball for **ea** in **ear.**) What do these sounds say? "ēēē."
2. Get ready to read these words the fast way. (Touch first ball for **ear.** Pause three seconds.) Read it the fast way. (Slide.) "ear." Yes, **ear.**
3. (Touch first ball for **near.** Pause three seconds.) Read it the fast way. (Slide.) "near." Yes, **near.**
4. (Touch first ball for **deal.** Pause three seconds.) Read it the fast way. (Slide.) "deal." Yes, **deal.**

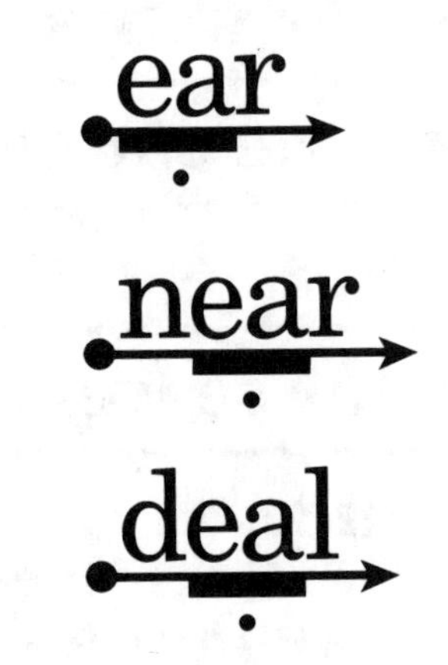

TASK 6 WORD READING THE FAST WAY

1. Now you get to read all the words the fast way.
2. (Touch first ball for first word of lesson. Pause three seconds.) Read it the fast way. (Slide. Child reads word.) Yes, good reading.
3. (Repeat step 2 for remaining words of lesson.)

do not make fun of a horse—part 1

a horse met a car. the car said, "look at you. you are not as good as I am."

the horse said, "I can do the things that you can do."

"you can not," the car said.

then the car said, "look at how fast I can go."

the car went down the road "zoom."

then the car stopped and said, "let me see you go that fast."[a]

the horse went down the road, but not as fast as the car did.

the car made fun of the horse.[b] then the horse said, "I can go far over that hill. but you can not do that."

"yes, I can," the car said.[c] the car went "zoom" up the road. but it did not go over the hill. it ran out of gas. so the car came to a stop.[d]

this is not the end.

TASK 7 FIRST READING

1. We'll read the first part of this story. In the next lesson we'll read the second part of this story. After you read this part of the story, you'll read it again and I'll ask questions.
2. Read the title the fast way. (Child reads title.)
3. Read the first sentence the fast way. (Child reads first sentence.)
4. Read the next sentence the fast way. (Child reads second sentence.)
5. (Repeat step 4 for remaining sentences in story.)

TASK 8 SECOND READING

1. Now you're going to read the story again. This time I'll ask questions when you read to the circled letters. Start with the title and read until you get to the first circled letter. Then stop.
2. (Ask following questions when child reaches each letter.)
   - ⓐ Can the horse go that fast?
   - ⓑ What would the car say when it made fun of the horse?
   - ⓒ What did the car say that it could do?
   - ⓓ Did the car go far over the hill? Why not?

TASK 9 PICTURE COMPREHENSION

Look at the picture. What is moving very fast in this picture? Where is all that dust coming from? What is the horse doing? What do you think that car is saying to the horse?

TASK 10 WRITING LETTERS

1. You're going to write the letters that I write. Here's what you're going to write first. Watch. (Write **x** at beginning of first line. Point to **x.**) What's the name of this letter? "x." What sound does that letter make? "ksss."
2. First trace the **x** that I made. Then make more of them on this line.
3. (After tracing **x** several times, child is to make three to five **x**'s. Help child if necessary. For acceptable letters say:) Good writing **x.**
4. Here are the next letters you're going to write. Watch. (Write **q** and **u** at beginning of second line. Point to **q, u.**) What are the names of these letters? "q-u." What sound do these letters make? "kwww."
5. First trace the **qu** that I made. Then make more of them on this line.
6. (After tracing **qu** several times, child is to make three to five **qu**'s. Help child if necessary. For acceptable letters say:) Good writing **qu.**

LESSON 82

TASK 1 CAPITAL LETTERS

1. These are capital letters. What kind of letters are they? "capitals."
2. Touch each capital letter and say its name, starting with **A.** (Child reads each capital letter in alphabet.)
3. I'll name capitals. See if you can find them. Capital **B.** (Child touches **B.**) Good finding.
4. (Repeat step 3 for capital **A,** capital **C,** capital **D,** capital **F,** capital **I,** capital **D,** capital **A,** capital **E,** capital **F,** capital **G,** capital **D,** capital **G.**)

A B C D E F G H I J K L M N O P Q R S T U V W X Y Z

TASK 2 WORD READING

1. (Touch first ball for **when.**) Sound it out. (Touch balls for sounds.) "wwweeennn." (Repeat until firm.) What word? "when."
2. (Repeat step 1 for **grass, then,** and **never.**)

TASK 3 WORD READING

1. Get ready to read these words the fast way.
2. (Touch ball for **made.** Pause three seconds.) Read it the fast way. (Slide.) "made." Yes, **made.**
3. (Repeat step 2 for remaining words.)

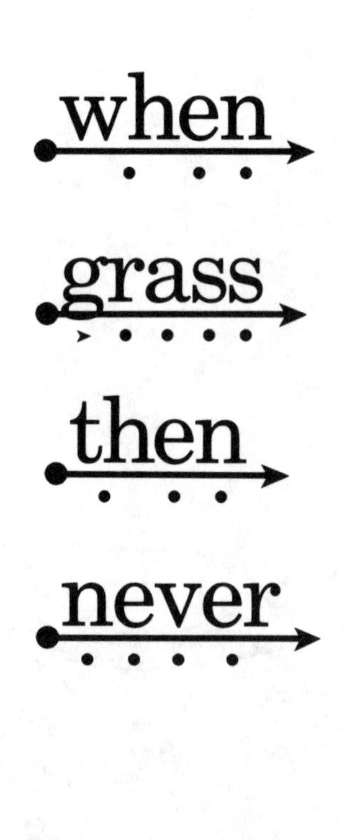

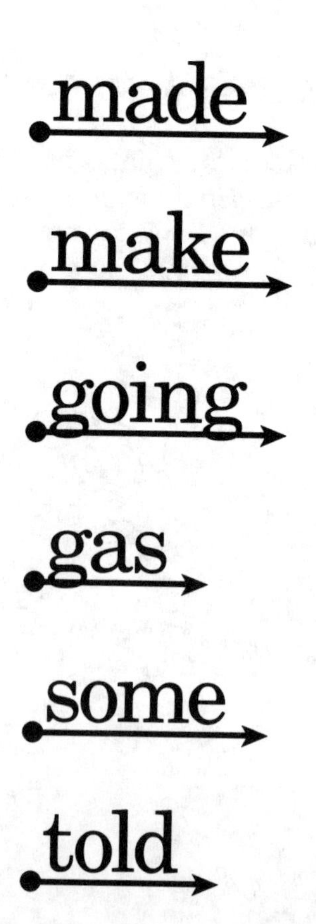

TASK 4 WORD READING—CAPITAL LETTERS

1. The stories that you will read from now on look different. The first letter of every sentence is written with a capital letter. (Point to words.) Here are some of the words that you will read in your story. Each word starts with a capital. See if you can read all the words the fast way.
2. (Touch ball for **When.** Pause.) Read it the fast way. (Slide.) "When." Yes, **When.**
3. (Repeat step 2 for remaining words.)

(**To correct,** say:) The word is (say word). Say all the letters for the word. (Child responds.) Now read the word the fast way. (Child responds.)

When

Do

The

Now

Let

Can

So

Horse

TASK 5 WORD READING THE FAST WAY

1. Now you get to read all the words the fast way.
2. (Touch first ball for first word of lesson. Pause three seconds.) Read it the fast way. (Slide. Child reads word.) Yes, good reading.
3. (Repeat step 2 for remaining words of lesson.)

Do Not Make Fun of a Horse—Part 2

A car made fun of a horse. The horse did not go as fast as the car. But the car did not make it to the other side of the hill. The car ran out of gas.

When the horse got to the car, the horse said, "I do not need gas. I eat grass." ⓐ The horse ate some grass. "Now I can keep on going. Let me see you do that." ⓑ

The car said, "I need gas, not grass. Can you get some for me?" ⓒ

The horse said, "I will get gas for you if you make a deal with me."

"Yes," the car said. "Just get me lots of gas so I can go home." ⓓ

So the horse went back and got gas for the car.

Then the horse told the car, "Here is the deal. I will give you gas if you do not make fun of me." ⓔ

So the car took the gas. Did the car keep his part of the deal?

The car never made fun of the horse. ⓕ

Stop—This Is the End.

TASK 6 CAPITAL LETTERS

Look at all the capital letters in your story. Remember, every sentence begins with a capital letter.

TASK 7 FIRST READING

1. Last time you read the first part of the story about a horse and a car. What happened at the end of that part of the story?
2. In this part of the story, we'll find out what happened when the car made fun of the horse. After you read this part of the story, you'll read it again and I'll ask questions.
3. Read the title the fast way. **(Child reads title.)**
4. Read the first sentence the fast way. **(Child reads first sentence.)**
5. Read the next sentence the fast way. **(Child reads second sentence.)**
6. **(Repeat step 5 for remaining sentences in story.)**

TASK 8 SECOND READING

1. Now you're going to read the story again. This time I'll ask questions when you read to the circled letters. Start with the title and read until you get to the first circled letter. Then stop.
2. **(Ask following questions when child reaches each letter.)**
   - ⓐ Does that horse need gas? What does the horse need? What does the car need?
   - ⓑ Do you think the car can do that?
   - ⓒ Will the horse get gas for the car?
   - ⓓ Did the car say that he would make a deal with the horse? I wonder what that deal is.
   - ⓔ What is the deal?
   - ⓕ Did the car keep his part of the deal?

TASK 9 PICTURE COMPREHENSION

Look at the picture. What does that horse have? What do you think the car is saying to the horse? What is the horse saying? Does it look as if that can hold lots of gas?

TASK 10 WRITING LETTERS

1. You're going to write the letters that I write. Here's what you're going to write first. Watch. **(Write v at beginning of first line. Point to v.)** What's the name of this letter? "v." What sound does that letter make? "vvv."
2. First trace the **v** that I made. Then make more of them on this line.
3. **(After tracing v several times, child is to make three to five v's. Help child if necessary. For acceptable letters say:)** Good writing **v.**
4. Here's the next letter you're going to write. Watch. **(Write w at beginning of second line. Point to w.)** What's the name of this letter? "w." What sound does that letter make? "www."
5. First trace the **w** that I made. Then make more of them on this line.
6. **(After tracing w several times, child is to make three to five w's. Help child if necessary. For acceptable letters say:)** Good writing **w.**

LESSON 83

TASK 1 CAPITAL LETTERS

1. These are capital letters. What kind of letters are they? "capitals."
2. Touch each capital letter and say its name, starting with **A.** (Child reads each capital letter in alphabet.)
3. I'll name capitals. See if you can find them. Capital **D.** (Child touches **D.**) Good finding.
4. Repeat step 3 for: capital **A,** capital **F,** capital **G,** capital **B,** capital **C,** capital **E,** capital **G,** capital **A,** capital **B,** capital **G,** capital **D.**)

A B C D E F G H I J K L M N O P Q R S T U V W X Y Z

TASK 2 WORD READING

1. (Touch first ball for **sing.**) Sound it out. (Touch balls for sounds.) "sssiiing." (Repeat until firm.) What word? "sing."
2. (Repeat step 1 for **but, bugs, bad, and, hand,** and **park.**)

TASK 3 WORD READING

1. Get ready to read these words the fast way.
2. (Touch ball for **girl.** Pause three seconds.) Read it the fast way. (Slide.) "girl." Yes, **girl.**
3. (Repeat step 2 for remaining words.)

sing

but

bugs

bad

and

hand

park

TASK 4 WORD READING—CAPITAL LETTERS

1. The stories that you will read from now on look different. The first letter of every sentence is written with a capital letter. (Point to words.) Here are some of the words that you will read in your story. Each words starts with a capital. See if you can read all the words the fast way.
2. (Touch ball for **She.** Pause.) Read it the fast way. (Slide.) "She." Yes, **She.**
3. (Repeat step 2 for remaining words.)

(**To correct,** say:) The word is (say word). Say all the letters for the word. (Child responds.) Now read the word the fast way. (Child responds.)

She

The

Then

So

But

Go

Bugs

That

TASK 5 WORD READING THE FAST WAY

1. Now you get to read all the words the fast way.
2. (Touch first ball for first word of lesson. Pause three seconds.) Read it the fast way. (Slide. Child reads word.) Yes, good reading.
3. (Repeat step 2 for remaining words of lesson.)

The Singing Bug—Part 1

A girl was going for a walk in a park. She sat down to eat some cake. A bug came up to her and said, "I like cake. Can I have some?" ⓐ

The girl looked at the bug. Then she looked back at the cake. Then she said, "Bugs do not talk. You are a bug. So you can not talk."

The bug said, "But I can talk." ⓑ

The girl said, "Go away. I do not talk to bugs. Bugs can not talk."

The bug said, "I can talk and I can sing." The bug started to sing. But the bug was not good at singing. "I wish that bug did not sing," the girl said.

"That singing is bad. I will have to hold my hands over my ears." ⓒ

So she did.

The bug said, "If you do not like my singing, give me some cake." ⓓ

More to Come

TASK 6 CAPITAL LETTERS

Look at all the capital letters in your story. Remember, every sentence begins with a capital letter.

TASK 7 FIRST READING

1. We'll read the first part of this story. In the next lesson we'll read the second part of this story. After you read this part of the story, you'll read it again and I'll ask questions.
2. Read the title the fast way. (Child reads title.)
3. Read the first sentence the fast way. (Child reads first sentence.)
4. Read the next sentence the fast way. (Child reads second sentence.)
5. (Repeat step 4 for remaining sentences in story.)

TASK 8 SECOND READING

1. Now you're going to read the story again. This time I'll ask questions when you read to the circled letters. Start with the title and read until you get to the first circled letter. Then stop.
2. (Ask following questions when child reaches each letter.)
   - ⓐ What did the bug say?
   - ⓑ Can that bug talk?
   - ⓒ What is she going to have to do? Why?
   - ⓓ Do you think the girl will give that bug some cake to stop the singing?

TASK 9 PICTURE COMPREHENSION

Look at the picture. What is that bug doing? How does the girl like that singing? Does she look as if she's having a good time eating cake? What do you think she should do to shut that bug up?

TASK 10 WRITING LETTERS

1. You're going to write the letters that I write. Here's what you're going to write first. Watch. (Write **qu** at beginning of first line. Point to **qu.**) What are the names of these letters? "q-u." What sound do these letters make? "kwww."
2. First trace the **qu** that I made. Then make more of them on this line.
3. (After tracing **qu** several times, child is to make three to five **qu**'s. Help child if necessary. For acceptable letters say:) Good writing **qu.**
4. Here's the next letter you're going to write. Watch. (Write **z** at beginning of second line. Point to **z.**) What's the name of this letter? "z." What sound does that letter make? "zzz."
5. First trace the **z** that I made. Then make more of them on this line
6. (After tracing **z** several times, child is to make three to five **z**'s. Help child if necessary. For acceptable letters say:) Good writing **z.**

LESSON 84

TASK 1 CAPITAL LETTERS

1. These are capital letters. What kind of letters are they? "capitals."
2. Touch each capital letter and say its name, starting with **A.** (Child reads each capital letter in alphabet.)
3. I'll name capitals. See if you can find them. Capital **G.** (Child touches **G.**) Good finding.
4. (Repeat step 3 for capital **H,** capital **D,** capital **B,** capital **A,** capital **K,** capital **L,** capital **D,** capital **L,** capital **H,** capital **B,** capital **G,** capital **J,** capital **K,** capital **L.**)

A B C D E F G H I J K L M N O P Q R S T U V W X Y Z

TASK 2 WORD READING

1. (Touch first ball for **were.**) Sound it out. (Touch balls for sounds.) "wwwurrr." (Repeat until firm.) What word? "were."
2. (Repeat step for **where, yell, lots,** and **sick.**)

were

where

yell

lots

sick

TASK 3 WORD READING

1. Get ready to read these words the fast way.
2. (Touch ball for **gave.** Pause three seconds.) Read it the fast way. (Slide.) "gave." Yes, **gave.**
3. (Repeat step 2 for remaining words.)

TASK 4 WORD READING THE FAST WAY

1. Now you get to read these words the fast way.
2. (Touch first ball for first word of lesson. Pause three seconds.) Read it the fast way. (Slide. Child reads word.) Yes, good reading.
3. (Repeat step 2 for remaining words of lesson.)

gave

singing

give

some

ate

eat

looked

hear

yelling

good

more

The Singing Bug—Part 2

A girl was with a bug. The bug was singing. The girl did not like that singing.

The bug did not stop singing. Then the girl said, "Eating cake is not fun with this bad singing."

Soon the girl said, "Stop singing, and I will give you some cake." ⓐ

So the girl gave some cake to the bug and the bug ate cake. Then the bug looked at the girl and said, "You were good to me. So I will be good to you. I will let you hear me yell." ⓑ So the bug started to yell. It was bad.

The girl said, "Stop that yelling and I will give you more cake." ⓒ

The bug stopped and the girl gave the bug a lot of cake.

The bug got sick. That bug said, "Now I can not sing and I can not yell."

The girl said, "That is good." Then she ate the rest of the cake. ⓓ

The End

TASK 5 FIRST READING

1. Last time you read the first part of the story about the singing bug. What happened at the end of that part of the story?
2. In this part of the story, we'll find out what happened to the singing bug. After you read this part of the story, you'll read it again and I'll ask questions.
3. Read the title the fast way. **(Child reads title.)**
4. Read the first sentence the fast way. **(Child reads first sentence.)**
5. Read the next sentence the fast way. **(Child reads second sentence.)**
6. **(Repeat Step 5 for remaining sentences in story.)**

TASK 6 SECOND READING

1. Now you're going to read the story again. This time I'll ask questions when you read to the circled letters. Start with the title and read until you get to the first circled letter. Then stop.
2. **(Ask following questions when child reaches each letter.)**
   - ⓐ What's the girl going to do? And what does the bug have to do?
   - ⓑ Do you think that will be fun for the girl?
   - ⓒ What deal did the girl make with the bug this time?
   - ⓓ Do you think she had more fun eating cake when the bug wasn't making noise?

TASK 7 PICTURE COMPREHENSION

Look at the picture. How does that bug feel? What do you think the bug is saying to the girl? What do you think the girl is saying to the bug?

TASK 8 WRITING LETTERS

1. You're going to write the letters that I write. Here's what you're going to write first. Watch. **(Write j at beginning of first line. Point to j.)** What's the name of this letter? "j." What sound does that letter make? "j."
2. First trace the **j** that I made. Then make some more of them on this line.
3. **(After tracing j several times, child is to make three to five j's. Help child if necessary. For acceptable letters say:)** Good writing **j.**
4. Here's the next letter you're going to write. Watch. **(Write t at beginning of second line. Point to t.)** What's the name of this letter? "t." What sound does that letter make? "t."
5. First trace the **t** that I made. Then make some more of them on this line.
6. **(After tracing t several times, child is to make three to five t's. Help child if necessary. For acceptable letters say:)** Good writing **t.**

LESSON 85

TASK 1 CAPITAL LETTERS

1. These are capital letters. What kind of letters are they? "capitals."
2. Touch each capital letter and say its name, starting with **A.** (Child reads each capital letter in alphabet.)
3. I'll name capitals. See if you can find them. Capital **G.** (Child touches **G.**) Good finding.
4. (Repeat step 3 for capital **H,** capital **P,** capital **Q,** capital **H,** capital **Q,** capital **B,** capital **D,** capital **Q,** capital **R,** capital **Q,** capital **S,** capital **G,** capital **D,** capital **B,** capital **A.**)

A B C D E F G H I J K L M N O P Q R S T U V W X Y Z

TASK 2 WORD READING

1. (Touch first ball for **digging.**) Sound it out. Get ready. (Slide past **d.** Touch under other sounds.) "diiigiiing." (Repeat until firm.) What word? "digging." Yes, **digging.**
2. (Touch first ball for **must.**) Sound it out. (Touch balls for sounds.) "mmmuuussst." (Repeat until firm.) What word? "must."
3. (Repeat step 2 for **dug, they, after,** and **yard.**)

digging

must

dug

they

after

yard

TASK 3 WORD READING

1. Get ready to read these words the fast way.
2. (Touch ball for **hole.** Pause three seconds.) Read it the fast way. (Slide.) "hole." Yes, **hole.**
3. (Repeat step 2 for remaining words.)

TASK 4 WORD READING THE FAST WAY

1. Now you get to read all the words the fast way.
2. (Touch first ball for first word of lesson. Pause three seconds.) Read it the fast way. (Slide. Child reads word.) Yes, good reading.
3. (Repeat step 2 for remaining words of lesson.)

hole

leave

five

into

every

dog

hold

away

stay

were

inside

The Dog That Dug—Part 1

An old dog liked to dig. That dog went digging on a farm. ⓐ The dog made hole after hole after hole. ⓑ A man on the farm said, "That dog must leave this farm."

So the dog went to a home to live with a boy and a girl. ⓒ But the dog did not stop digging. The dog went into the yard and dug five holes. Then the dog went into other yards and dug ten more holes.

Soon there were holes in every yard. ⓓ

The boy and the girl said, "That dog must stop digging holes."

They made the dog stay inside for five days. Then the dog went into the yard and dug five more holes.

The boy and the girl ran over to the dog. The dog was making a big, big hole. The boy said, "Get hold of that dog and we will stop this digging." ⓔ

Stop.

TASK 5 FIRST READING

1. We'll read the first part of this story. In the next lesson we'll read the second part of this story. After you read this part of the story, you'll read it again and I'll ask questions.
2. Read the title the fast way. (Child reads title.)
3. Read the first sentence the fast way. (Child reads first sentence.)
4. Read the next sentence the fast way. (Child reads second sentence.)
5. (Repeat step 5 for remaining sentences in story.)

TASK 6 SECOND READING

1. Now you're going to read the story again. This time I'll ask questions when you read to the circled letters. Start with the title and read until you get to the first circled letter. Then stop.
2. (Ask following questions when child reaches each letter.)
   - (a) Where did he go digging?
   - (b) What does that mean, **hole after hole after hole?**
   - (c) Where did the dog go now?
   - (d) Do you suppose that made people happy?
   - (e) What are they going to try to do?

TASK 7 PICTURE COMPREHENSION

Look at the picture. What is that dog doing? What are the boy and the girl trying to do? Does it look as if they are stopping that dog? Have you ever seen a dog dig a hole that big? That dog sure likes to dig.

TASK 8 WRITING LETTERS

1. You're going to write the letters that I write. Here's what you're going to write first. Watch. (Write **th** at beginning of first line. Point to **th.**) What are the names of these letters? "t-h." What sound do these letters make? "thththth."
2. First trace the **th** that I made. Then make more of them on this line.
3. (After tracing **th** several times, child is to make three to five **th**'s. Help child if necessary. For acceptable letters say:) Good writing **th.**
4. Here's the next letter you're going to write. Watch. (Write **d** at beginning of second line. Point to **d.**) What's the name of this letter? "d." What sound does that letter make? "d."
5. First trace the **d** that I made. Then make more of them on this line.
6. (After tracing **d** several times, child is to make three to five **d**'s. Help child if necessary. For acceptable letters say:) Good writing **d.**

LESSON 86

TASK 1 CAPITAL LETTERS

1. These are capital letters. What kind of letters are they? "capitals."
2. Touch each capital letter and say its name, starting with **A.** (Child reads each capital letter in alphabet.)
3. I'll name capitals. See if you can find them. Capital **S.** (Child touches **S.**) Good finding.
4. (Repeat step 3 for capital **R,** capital **H,** capital **G,** capital **B,** capital **A,** capital **D,** capital **Q,** capital **R,** capital **B,** capital **X,** capital **Y,** capital **Z,** capital **Q.**)

A B C D E F G H I J K L M N O P Q R S T U V W X Y Z

TASK 2 WORD READING—qu

1. The name for the letter **q** tells you the letter that always comes after the **q.** That letter is **u.** What letter always comes after **q?** "u."
2. You can hear the **u** in the name of the letter **q.** The **u** that comes after **q** does not make any sound. (Touch **qu** in **quick.**) The letters in **qu** make the sound **kwww.** What sound do these letters make? "kwww."
3. (Touch first ball for **quick.**) Sound it out. (Touch balls for sounds.) "kwwwiiik." What word? "quick."
4. (Touch **qu** in **quit.**) What sound do these letters make? "kwww." (Touch first ball for **quit.**) Sound it out. (Touch balls for sounds.) "kwwwiiit." What word? "quit."
5. You're going to read the next word the fast way. (Touch ball for **quitting.** Pause three seconds.) Read it the fast way. (Slide.) "quitting." Yes, **quitting.**

quick

quit

quitting

TASK 3 WORD READING

1. Get ready to read these words the fast way.
2. (Touch ball for **digging.** Pause three seconds.) Read it the fast way. (Slide.) "digging." Yes, **digging.**
3. (Repeat step 2 for remaining words.)

digging

holes

yard

told

hold

gold

mad

rich

were

TASK 4 WORD READING THE FAST WAY

1. Now you get to read all the words the fast way.
2. (Touch first ball for first word of lesson. Pause three seconds.) Read it the fast way. (Slide. Child reads word.) Yes, good reading.
3. (Repeat step 2 for remaining words of lesson.)

The Dog That Dug—Part 2

A girl and a boy had a dog that came from a farm. That dog had to leave the farm for digging holes. But now the dog was digging holes in the yard. The boy told the girl to get hold of that dog.

The girl got hold of the dog's tail. Then the girl looked in the hole. She said, "Take a look in that hole."

The boy took a look. Then he said, "Do I see gold in that hole?" ⓐ

The girl said, "Yes. That dog has dug up a lot of gold."

So the boy and the girl took the gold from the hole. They let the dog dig some more. And the dog dug up more gold. ⓑ

Now the boy and the girl are not mad at the digging dog. They like that dog. They are rich and the dog is rich, too. ⓒ The dog has five yards to dig in. ⓓ

This Is the End.

TASK 5 FIRST READING

1. Last time you read the first part of the story about the dog that dug. What happened at the end of that part of the story?
2. In this part of the story, we'll find out what happened when the girl got hold of the dog's tail. After you read this part of the story, you'll read it again and I'll ask questions.
3. Read the title the fast way. (Child reads title.)
4. Read the first sentence the fast way. (Child reads first sentence.)
5. Read the next sentence the fast way. (Child reads second sentence.)
6. (Repeat step 5 for remaining sentences in story.)

TASK 6 SECOND READING

1. Now you're going to read the story again. This time I'll ask questions when you read to the circled letters. Start with the title and read until you get to the first circled letter. Then stop.
2. (Ask following questions when child reaches each letter.)
   - ⓐ What was in the bottom of the hole?
   - ⓑ What did the dog dig up? That's a pretty good dog.
   - ⓒ Why is the dog rich?
   - ⓓ Do you think that dog is happy now?

TASK 7 PICTURE COMPREHENSION

Look at the picture. What is that dog digging? How do the boy and the girl feel? How would you feel if you had all that gold? If that dog doesn't stop digging, there will be gold all over the yard.

TASK 8 WRITING LETTERS

1. You're going to write the letters that I write. Here's what you're going to write first. Watch. (Write **b** at beginning of first line. Point to **b.**) What's the name of this letter? "b." What sound does that letter make? "b."
2. First trace the **b** that I made. Then make more of them on this line.
3. (After tracing **b** several times, child is to make three to five **b**'s. Help child if necessary. For acceptable letters say:) Good writing **b.**
4. Here's the next letter you're going to write. Watch. (Write **z** at beginning of second line. Point to **z.**) What's the name of this letter? "z." What sound does that letter make? "zzz."
5. First trace the **z** that I made. Then make more of them on this line.
6. (After tracing **z** several times, child is to make three to five **z**'s. Help child if necessary. For acceptable letters say:) Good writing **z.**

LESSON 87

TASK 1 WORD READING

1. You're going to read these words the fast way. (Touch ball for **eagle.** Pause three seconds.) Read it the fast way. (Slide.) "eagle." Yes, **eagle.**
2. This word rhymes with **eagle.** (Touch ball for **beagle.** Pause three seconds.) Read it the fast way. (Slide.) "beagle." Yes, **beagle.** Remember those words.

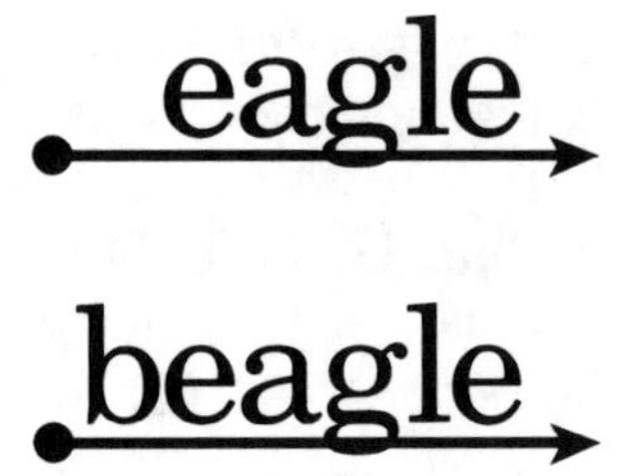

TASK 2 WORD READING

1. (Touch first ball for **hunt.**) Sound it out. Get ready. (Slide past **h.** Touch balls for other sounds.) "huuunnnt." (Repeat until firm.) What word? "hunt." Yes, **hunt.**
2. (Touch first ball for **Biff.**) Sound it out. (Touch under sounds.) "Biiifff." (Repeat until firm.) What word? "Biff."
3. (Repeat step 2 for **smell, sun,** and **held.**)

hunt

Biff

smell

sun

held

TASK 3 WORD READING

1. The name for the letter **q** tells you the letter that always comes after the **q.** That letter is **u.** What letter always comes after **q?** "u."
2. You can hear the **u** in the name of the letter **q.** The **u** that comes after **q** does not make any sound. (Touch **qu** in **quick.**) The letters in **qu** make the sound **kwww.** What sound do these letters make? "kwww."
3. (Touch first ball for **quick.**) Sound it out. (Touch balls for sounds.) "kwwwiiik." What word? "quick."
4. You're going to read the next word the fast way. (Touch ball for **quitting.** Pause three seconds.) Read it the fast way. (Slide.) "quitting." Yes, **quitting.**

quick

quitting

TASK 4 WORD READING

1. Get ready to read these words the fast way.
2. (Touch ball for **grass.** Pause three seconds.) Read it the fast way. (Slide.) "grass." Yes, **grass.**
3. (Repeat step 2 for remaining words.)

TASK 5 WORD READING THE FAST WAY

1. Now you get to read all the words the fast way.
2. (Touch ball for first word of lesson. Pause three seconds.) Read it the fast way. (Slide. Child reads word.) Yes, good reading.
3. (Repeat step 2 for remaining words of lesson.)

grass

nose

sleep

went

thing

tore

store

story

The Eagle Meets a Beagle—Part 1

A beagle is a dog. It has big ears. And it likes to hunt, hunt, hunt. (a) The beagle in this story liked to hunt more than other beagles. This beagle was Biff. Every day Biff went out hunting. She held her nose near the grass. "Booooooooooo, booooooo," she said when she got the smell of a deer, or a ram, or a cow, or a duck. (b)

When Biff came back from hunting, the sun was near the hills. So the dog went to sleep, "Zzzzzzzzzz, zzzzzzzz, zzzzz." (c) Then, when the sun got up, so did Biff. "Boooooo, booooo," she said as she smelled the grass. And away she went. (d)

On a day that was hot, she came to the shore of a lake. She smelled fish. "Boooooooo," she said, and went into the lake. But she did not get a fish. Then she went up the hill. She smelled some thing that was good, good, good. "Boooooo, booooo," she said, and up the hill she went. (e)

Stop.

TASK 6 FIRST READING

1. We'll read the first part of this story. In the next lesson we'll read the second part of this story. After you read this part of the story, you'll read it again and I'll ask questions.
2. Read the title the fast way. (Child reads title.)
3. Read the first sentence the fast way. (Child reads first sentence.)
4. Read the next sentence the fast way. (Child reads second sentence.)
5. (Repeat step 4 for remaining sentences in story.)

TASK 7 SECOND READING

1. Now you're going to read the story again. This time I'll ask questions when you read to the circled letters. Start with the title and read until you get to the first circled letter. Then stop.
2. (Ask following questions when child reaches each letter.)
   ⓐ What kind of animal is a beagle? What kind of ears does it have? What does it like to do?
   ⓑ What kind of animals did that beagle hunt? Make the kind of sound Biff made when she hunted.
   ⓒ What's making those **zzzzzz** sounds?
   ⓓ What was she doing?
   ⓔ I wonder what that beagle is after.

TASK 8 PICTURE COMPREHENSION

Look at the picture. What kind of dog is that in the picture? What's the dog saying? What kind of animal is that beagle after? How is she going to feel after she hunts all day long?

TASK 9 WRITING LETTERS

1. You're going to write the letters that I write. Here's what you're going to write first. Watch. (Write **x** at beginning of first line. Point to **x.**) What's the name of this letter? "x." What sound does that letter make? "ksss."
2. First trace the **x** that I made. Then make more of them on this line.
3. (After tracing **x** several times, child is to make three to five **x**'s. Help child if necessary. For acceptable letters say:) Good writing **x.**
4. Here's the next letter you're going to write. Watch. (Write **g** at beginning of second line. Point to **g.**) What's the name of this letter? "g." What sound does that letter make? "g."
5. First trace the **g** that I made. Then make more of them on this line.
6. (After tracing **g** several times, child is to make three to five **g**'s. Help child if necessary. For acceptable letters say:) Good writing **g.**

LESSON 88

TASK 1 WORD READING

1. (Touch first ball for **picked.**) Sound it out. Get ready. (Slide past **p.** Touch under other sounds.) "piiikd." (Repeat until firm.) What word? "picked." Yes, **picked.**
2. (Repeat step 1 for **hunting** and **stopped.**)

picked

hunting

stopped

TASK 2 WORD READING

1. Get ready to read these words the fast way.
2. (Touch ball for **into.** Pause three seconds.) Read it the fast way. (Slide.) "into." Yes, **into.**
3. (Repeat step 2 for remaining words.)

into

started

fly

good

LESSON 94

TASK 1 WORD READING—MODEL

1. (Point to **don't.**) This word is **don't.** What word? "don't."
2. (Touch first ball.) Sound it out. (Touch under sounds.) "dōōōnnnt."
3. And how do we say the word? "don't." Remember that word.

don't

TASK 2 WORD READING

(Touch first ball for **green.**) Sound it out. Get ready. (Slide past **g.** Touch balls for other sounds.) "grrrēēēnnn." (Repeat until firm.) What word? "green." Yes, **green.**

green

TASK 3 WORD READING

1. (Touch ball for **ai.**) When these sounds are together, they usually say **āāā.** What do they say? "āāā."
2. (Touch ball for **ai** in **pail.**) What do these sounds say? "āāā." (Touch first ball for **pail.**) Sound it out. (Touch under sounds.) "pāāālll." (Repeat until firm.) What word? "pail." Yes, **pail.**
3. (Touch ball for **ai** in **pain.**) What do these sounds say? "āāā." (Touch first ball for **pain.**) Sound it out. (Touch under sounds.) "pāāānnn." (Repeat until firm.) What word? "pain." Yes, **pain.**
4. (Touch ball for **ai** in **paint.**) What do these sounds say? "āāā." (Touch first ball for **paint.**) Sound it out. (Touch under sounds.) "pāāānnnt." (Repeat until firm.) What word? "paint." Yes, **paint.**

ai

pail

pain

paint

TASK 4 WORD READING THE FAST WAY

1. Now you get to read all the words the fast way.
2. (Touch first ball for first word of lesson. Pause three seconds.) Read it the fast way. (Slide. Child reads word.) Yes, good reading.
3. (Repeat step 2 for remaining words of lesson.)

The Pig That Liked to Hide—Part 2

There was a pig that was too big to hide. That pig was looking for something big.

The pig went to the lake. "No," the pig said. "A lake is big, but I can not hide in back of a lake." ⓐ

The pig went to a park. "No," the pig said. "A park is big, but I can not hide in back of a park." ⓑ

Then, that pig went to a hill. "No," the pig said. "That hill is big, but if those little pigs go to the top of the hill, they will see me on the other side." ⓒ

An eagle said to the pig, "You don't need a hill. You are a hill. Get some green paint and make every part of you green. Then you will look like a hill and you can hide." ⓓ

So the pig got cans and cans of green paint. The pig started painting. Soon every part of that pig was green. The pig went back to the farm and sat down near the barn.

"I am hiding," the pig shouted. "Come and get me."

The little pigs looked and looked. But they did not find the big pig. A little pig said, "I see a farm and I see a barn and I see a big green hill. But I do not see a fat pig." ⓔ

The End

TASK 5 FIRST READING

1. Last time you read the first part of the story about the pig that liked to hide. What happened at the end of that part of the story?
2. In this part of the story, we'll find out what happened to the pig when she looked for something big. After you read this part of the story, you'll read it again and I'll ask questions.
3. Read the title the fast way. **(Child reads title.)**
4. Read the first sentence the fast way. **(Child reads first sentence.)**
5. Read the next sentence the fast way. **(Child reads second sentence.)**
6. **(Repeat step 5 for remaining sentences in story.)**

TASK 6 SECOND READING

1. Now you're going to read the story again. This time I'll ask questions when you read to the circled letters. Start with the title and read until you get to the first circled letter. Then stop.
2. **(Ask following questions when child reaches each letter.)**
   - ⓐ Why couldn't that pig hide in back of a lake?
   - ⓑ Why couldn't the pig hide in back of a park?
   - ⓒ Why didn't the pig like the hill for hiding?
   - ⓓ Why will that pig be able to hide if she makes herself green?
   - ⓔ What things did the little pig see? Which of those things was the big pig hiding?

TASK 7 PICTURE COMPREHENSION

Look at the picture. Touch the thing the little pigs thought was a big green hill. Does that big pig look very happy? What are the little pigs trying to do? What are the little pigs saying?

TASK 8 WRITING LETTERS

1. You're going to write the letters that I write. Here's what you're going to write first. Watch. (Write **x** at beginning of first line. Point to **x.** What's the name of this letter? "x." What sound does that letter make? "ksss."
2. First trace the **x** that I made. Then make more of them on this line.
3. (After tracing **x** several times, child is to make three to five **x**'s. Help child if necessary. For acceptable letters say:) Good writing **x.**
4. Here are the next letters you're going to write. Watch. (Write **qu** at beginning of second line. Point to **qu.**) What are the names of these letters? "q-u." What sound do these letters make? "kwww."
5. First trace the **qu** that I made. Then make more of them on this line.
6. (After tracing **qu** several times, child is to make three to five **qu**'s. Help child if necessary. For acceptable letters say:) Good writing **qu.**

LESSON 95

TASK 1 WORD READING

1. (Touch first ball for **fog.**) Sound it out. (Touch balls for sounds.) "fffooog." (Repeat until firm.) What word? "fog."
2. (Repeat step 1 for **frog, spots, blap, loud, sound, ruck,** and **ding.**)

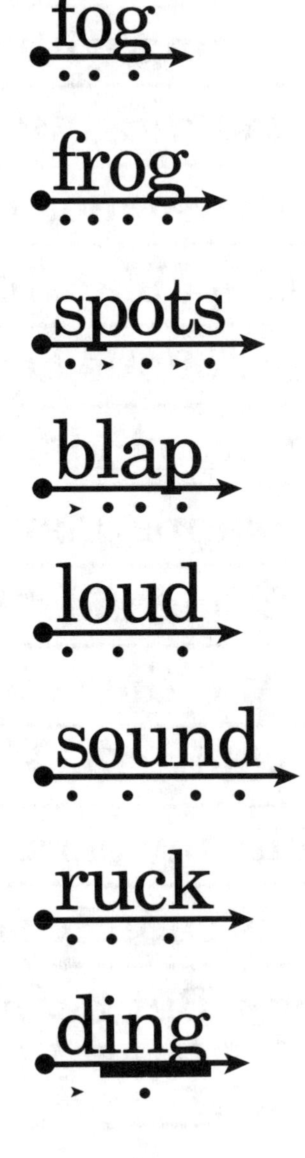

TASK 2 WORD READING

1. Get ready to read these words the fast way.
2. (Touch ball for **green.** Pause three seconds.) Read it the fast way. (Slide.) "green." Yes, **green.**
3. (Repeat step 2 for remaining words.)

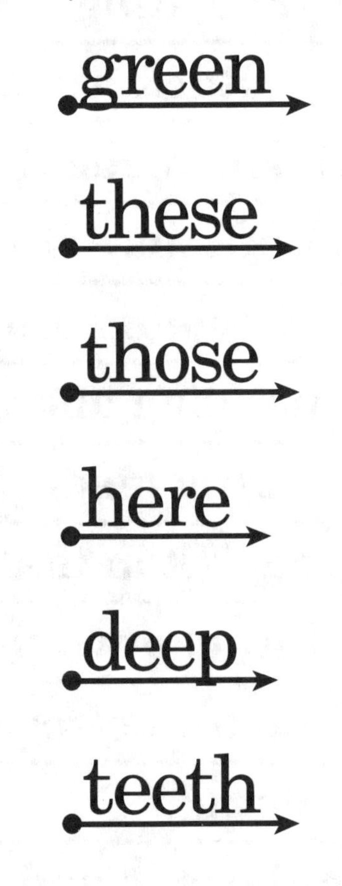

TASK 3 WORD READING THE FAST WAY

1. Now you get to read all the words the fast way.
2. (Touch first ball for first word of lesson. Pause three seconds.) Read it the fast way. (Slide. Child reads word.) Yes, good reading.
3. (Repeat step 2 for remaining words of lesson.)

The Frog That Made Big Sounds—Part 1

There was a little frog with green spots. That frog made very big sounds.ⓐ The other frogs in the lake got on the shore and made sounds. Some went "Ding, ding, ding." Some of the big frogs made deep sounds: "Ruck, ruck, ruck." But the little frog with green spots made this sound: "Blap, blap, blap."ⓑ The sound was very loud. Frogs like to sing with each other. They ding and ruck and ruck and ding. But the frogs that ding and ruck did not like the sounds that the little frog made. When he went, "Blap, blap, blap," they said, "Stop that blap, blap. Those sounds are too loud. How can we sing if you make loud sounds?"ⓒ

Then these frogs said, "Yes, stop blapping and start singing." Soon one of the other frogs said, "Let's dive in the lake and get out of here." And they did.

The little frog had a mother. She said, "You make sounds that are like big teeth. They bite my ears."ⓓ

The little frog with green spots was sad. He said, "I do not like to make those big sounds. But I can not sing the way the other frogs sing."ⓔ

More to Come

TASK 4 FIRST READING

1. We'll read the first part of this story. In the next lesson we'll read the second part of this story. After you read this part of the story, you'll read it again and I'll ask questions.
2. Read the title the fast way. (Child reads title.)
3. Read the first sentence the fast way. (Child reads first sentence.)
4. Read the next sentence the fast way. (Child reads second sentence.)
5. (Repeat step 4 for remaining sentences in story.)

TASK 5 SECOND READING

1. Now you're going to read the story again. This time I'll ask questions when you read to the circled letters. Start with the title and read until you get to the first circled letter. Then stop.
2. (Ask following questions when child reaches each letter.)
   - ⓐ What did that little frog do?
   - ⓑ What sound did the little frog make? That's a terrible sound for a little frog with green spots.
   - ⓒ Did the other frogs like the sounds the little frog made?
   - ⓓ Why does she think the little frog's sounds are like big teeth?
   - ⓔ How does that frog feel?

TASK 6 PICTURE COMPREHENSION

Look at the picture. What are the frogs in this picture doing? What sounds are the big frogs making? What sounds are most of the little frogs making? Which frog is the little frog with green spots? What sounds is that frog making? Do the other frogs look as if they like that **blap blap?**

TASK 7 WRITING LETTERS

1. You're going to write the letters that I write. Here's what you're going to write first. Watch. (Write **qu** at beginning of first line. Point to **qu.**) What are the names of these letters? "q-u." What sound do these letters make? "kwww."
2. First trace the **qu** that I made. Then make more of them on this line.
3. (After tracing **qu** several times, child is to make three to five **qu**'s. Help child if necessary. For acceptable letters say:) Good writing **qu.**
4. Here's the next letter you're going to write. Watch. (Write **g** at beginning of second line. Point to **g.**) What's the name of this letter? "g." What sound does that letter make? "g."
5. First trace the **g** that I made. Then make more of them on this line.
6. (After tracing **g** several times, child is to make three to five **g**'s. Help child if necessary. For acceptable letters say:) Good writing **g.**

LESSON 96

TASK 1 WORD READING

1. Get ready to read these words the fast way.
2. (Touch ball for **fog.** Pause three seconds.) Read it the fast way. (Slide.) "fog." Yes, **fog.**
3. (Repeat step 2 for remaining words.)

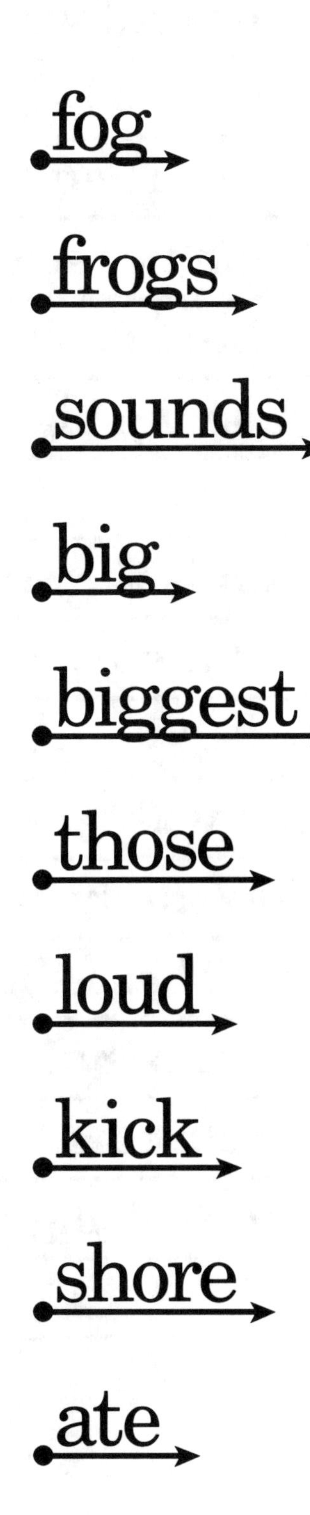

TASK 2 WORD READING

1. (Touch first ball for **room.**) Sound it out. (Touch balls for sounds.) "rrrooooooommm." (Repeat until firm.) What word? "room."
2. (Repeat step 1 for **dust, mouse, house, proud, found, around,** and **spring.**)

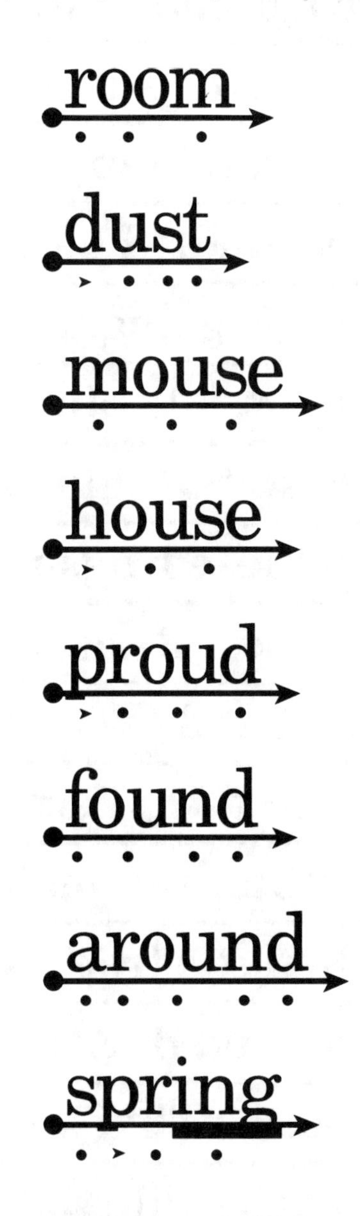

TASK 3 WORD READING THE FAST WAY

1. Now you get to read all the words the fast way.
2. (Touch ball for first word of lesson. Pause three seconds.) Read it the fast way. (Slide. Child reads word.) Yes, good reading.
3. (Repeat step 2 for remaining words of lesson.)

The Frog That Made Big Sounds—Part 2

A little frog with green spots made big sounds. The other frogs in the lake did not like those sounds.

On a spring day a big fog came over the lake. (a) The frogs said, "We can not see in this fog, but we can sit on the shore and sing." The fog was so bad that the sound of the frogs was not loud. (b) Then a big frog said, "I hear a ship. That ship can not see where it is going. It will run up on the shore if we do not stop it." Another frog said, "We will make big sounds so the ship will hear us."

So these frogs made the biggest sounds they had ever made. "Ruck, ding, ding, ruck." But the fog ate up the sounds. (c)

Then a big frog said to the little frog with green spots, "Can you make sounds that a ship can hear?"

The little frog shouted, "Blap, blap." These sounds were so loud that the other frogs jumped into the lake. (d) They said, "That sound is like a kick in the ears." (e)

But the ship did not run into the shore. A big frog said, "They can hear that loud sound." (f)

So now the other frogs like the little frog. When there is a big fog, go to the shore of a lake. You may hear that frog going, "Blap, blap."

This Is the End.

TASK 4 FIRST READING

1. Last time you read the first part of the story about the frog that made big sounds. What happened at the end of that part of the story?
2. In this part of the story, we'll find out what happened to the frog that made big sounds. After you read this part of the story, you'll read it again and I'll ask questions.
3. Read the title the fast way. (Child reads title.)
4. Read the first sentence the fast way. (Child reads first sentence.)
5. Read the next sentence the fast way. (Child reads second sentence.)
6. (Repeat step 5 for remaining sentences in story.)

TASK 5 SECOND READING

1. Now you're going to read the story again. This time I'll ask questions when you read to the circled letters. Start with the title and read until you get to the first circled letter. Then stop.
2. (Ask following questions when child reaches each letter.)
   - ⓐ What happened on that day?
   - ⓑ Why weren't their sounds loud?
   - ⓒ What happened to the sounds they made?
   - ⓓ What did they do? Why?
   - ⓔ How did that sound feel to their ears?
   - ⓕ Why didn't the ship run into the shore?

TASK 6 PICTURE COMPREHENSION

Look at the picture. What's that little frog shouting? What are the other frogs doing? Why do they have their hands over their ears? Why can you see only part of some frogs?

TASK 7 WRITING LETTERS

1. You're going to write the letters that I write. Here's what you're going to write first. Watch. (Write **z** at beginning of first line. Point to **z.**) What's the name of this letter? "z." What sound does that letter make? "zzz."
2. First trace the **z** that I made. Then make more of them on this line.
3. (After tracing **z** several times, child is to make three to five **z**'s. Help child if necessary. For acceptable letters say:) Good writing **z.**
4. Here's the next letter you're going to write. Watch. (Write **c** at beginning of second line. Point to **c.**) What's the name of this letter? "c." What sound does that letter make? "c."
5. First trace the **c** that I made. Then make more of them on this line.
6. (After tracing **c** several times, child is to make three to five **c**'s. Help child if necessary. For acceptable letters say:) Good writing **c.**

LESSON 97

TASK 1 WORD READING

1. Get ready to read these words the fast way.
2. (Touch ball for **mouse.** Pause three seconds.) Read it the fast way. (Slide.) "mouse." Yes, **mouse.**
3. (Repeat step 2 for remaining words.)

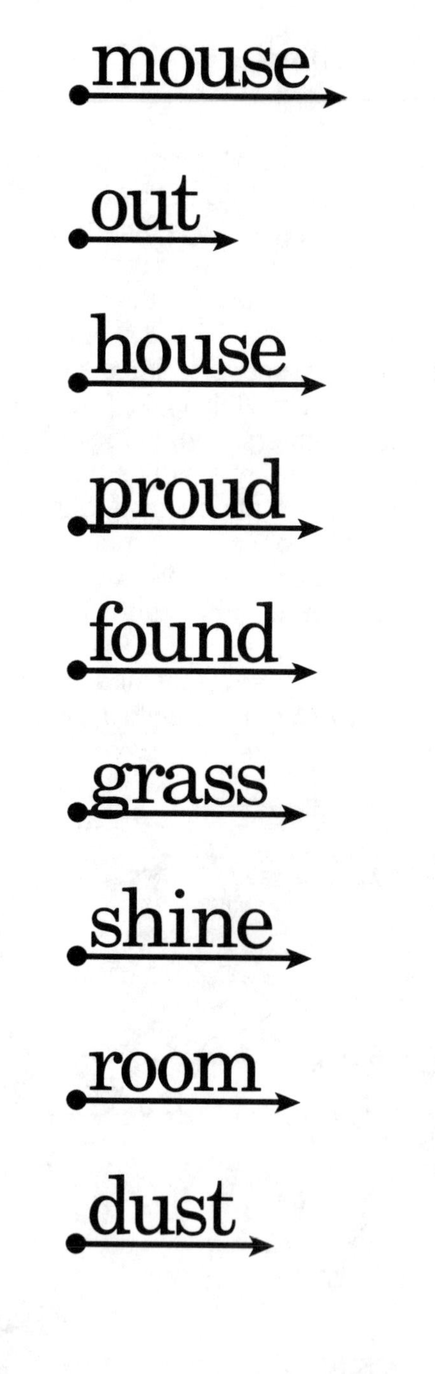

TASK 2 WORD READING THE FAST WAY

1. Now you get to read all the words the fast way again.
2. (Touch first ball for first word of lesson. Pause three seconds.) Read it the fast way. (Slide. Child reads word.) Yes, good reading.
3. (Repeat step 2 for remaining words of lesson.)

TASK 3 FIRST READING

1. We'll read the first part of this story. In the next lesson we'll read the second part of this story. After you read this part of the story, you'll read it again and I'll ask questions.
2. Read the title the fast way. (Child reads title.)
3. Read the first sentence the fast way. (Child reads first sentence.)
4. Read the next sentence the fast way. (Child reads second sentence.)
5. (Repeat step 4 for remaining sentences in story.)

TASK 4 SECOND READING

1. Now you're going to read the story again. This time I'll ask questions when you read to the circled letters. Start with the title and read until you get to the first circled letter. Then stop.
2. (Ask following questions when child reaches each letter.)
   - ⓐ What do you think that mouse will do with the rag?
   - ⓑ Does that mouse like a messy house?
   - ⓒ What was in the bed? How do you think that made the mouse feel?
   - ⓓ Why did they say they had to stay in the bed?
   - ⓔ Why can't they live in the grass? Why can't they live in a barn? I think that mouse has a real problem.

The Bed Bugs—Part 1

A mouse had a house that shined. Every day, that mouse got a rag and went from room to room.[a] The mouse picked up every bit of dust. The mouse was very proud. "This is how I like my house."[b]

But on a cold day that mouse found something bad. The mouse was going to dust in the bed room. The mouse looked at the bed and said, "I see bugs in that bed."[c] There were ten red bugs in the bed.

"Get out of that bed," the mouse yelled.

"No," a bug said. "We must stay in a bed. We are bed bugs."[d]

"My house shines," the mouse said. "I can not have bugs in here."

A bug came near the mouse. That bug said, "If we are bed bugs, we must live in beds. We are not grass bugs, so we can not live in the grass. We are not barn bugs, so we can not live in a barn."[e]

Stop.

TASK 5 PICTURE COMPREHENSION

Look at the picture. Count those bugs on the bed. Do they look as if they're ready to leave the bed? Does that mouse look very happy? What do you think the mouse is saying? What do you think the bed bugs are saying?

TASK 6 WRITING LETTERS

1. You're going to write the letters that I write. Here's what you're going to write first. Watch. **(Write b at beginning of first line. Point to b.)** What's the name of this letter? "b." What sound does that letter make? "b."
2. First trace the **b** that I made. Then make more of them on this line.
3. **(After tracing b several times, child is to make three to five b's. Help child if necessary. For acceptable letters say:)** Good writing **b.**
4. Here are the next letters you're going to write. Watch. **(Write qu at beginning of second line. Point to qu.)** What are the names of these letters? "q-u." What sound do these letters make? "kwww."
5. First trace the **qu** that I made. Then make more of them on this line.
6. **(After tracing qu several times, child is to make three to five qu's. Help child if necessary. For acceptable letters say:)** Good writing **qu.**

LESSON 98

TASK 1 WORD READING

1. Get ready to read these words the fast way.
2. (Touch ball for **other.** Pause three seconds.) Read it the fast way. (Slide.) "other." Yes, **other.**
3. (Repeat step 2 for remaining words.)

TASK 2 WORD READING THE FAST WAY

1. Now you get to read all the words the fast way again.
2. (Touch ball for first word of lesson. Pause three seconds.) Read it the fast way. (Slide. Child reads word.) Yes, good reading.
3. (Repeat step 2 for remaining words of lesson.)

other

another

around

bite

dust

from

too

smiled

bug

bed

grass

biting

room

The Bed Bugs—Part 2

A mouse found bed bugs in the bed. That mouse was very mad, but the bugs said that they had to live in beds. ⓐ

The mouse said, "Get out of this room or I will hit you with a dust rag."

"We are too fast for you," a bug said. The mouse hit the bed with the rag. But the rag did not hit bugs. It hit the bed. The bugs were on another part of the bed. They said, "If you do that, we will bite. And bed bugs are good at biting." ⓑ

"This is bad," the mouse said. The mouse walked from the bed room. "I must do something," the mouse said.

Soon the mouse came back into the bed room. The mouse was holding a little bed. That bed was made from a dish and a dust rag. ⓒ The mouse said to the bugs, "You are bed bugs. And this is a little bed. So hop out of my bed and get into this bed."

The bugs smiled. Then, hop, jump, they got into the little bed.

They ran around on the dust rag. Then a bug looked at the mouse and said, "This is a good bed. But a bed needs a bed room and a bed room needs a house."

So the mouse had to make a house with a bed room.ⓓ And now the bug bed is in the bed room and the bed bugs are in the bug bed.ⓔ

The End

TASK 3 FIRST READING

1. Last time you read the first part of the story about the bed bugs. What happened at the end of that part of the story?
2. In this part of the story, we'll find out what happened to the mouse and the bed bugs. After you read this part of the story, you'll read it again and I'll ask questions.
3. Read the title the fast way. (Child reads title.)
4. Read the first sentence the fast way. (Child reads first sentence.)
5. Read the next sentence the fast way. (Child reads second sentence.)
6. (Repeat step 5 for remaining sentences in story.)

TASK 4 SECOND READING

1. Now you're going to read the story again. This time I'll ask questions when you read to the circled letters. Start with the title and read until you get to the first circled letter. Then stop.
2. (Ask following questions when child reaches each letter.)
   - ⓐ Why did they say that they had to live in beds?
   - ⓑ What are they going to do if the mouse keeps trying to hit them with the dust rag?
   - ⓒ What was the bed made from? What is the mouse going to do with that tiny bed?
   - ⓓ What did the mouse have to build for those bed bugs?
   - ⓔ What is in the bed room? Where are the bed bugs?

TASK 5 PICTURE COMPREHENSION

Look at the picture. Where are the bed bugs in this picture? What are they doing? Do they look as if they're having a good time? What are they all on? Where is that bug bed?

TASK 6 WRITING LETTERS

1. You're going to write the letters that I write. Here's what you're going to write first. Watch. **(Write er at beginning of first line. Point to er.)** What are the names of these letters? "e-r." What sound do these letters make? "urrr."
2. First trace the **er** that I made. Then make more of them on this line.
3. **(After tracing er several times, child is to make three to five er's. Help child if necessary. For acceptable letters say:)** Good writing **er.**
4. Here's the next letter you're going to write. Watch. **(Write d at beginning of second line. Point to d.)** What's the name of this letter? "d." What sound does that letter make? "d."
5. First trace the **d** that I made. Then make more of them on this line.
6. **(After tracing d several times, child is to make three to five d's. Help child if necessary. For acceptable letters say:)** Good writing **d.**

LESSON 99

TASK 1 WORD READING

1. Get ready to read these words the fast way.
2. (Touch ball for **hear.** Pause three seconds.) Read it the fast way. (Slide.) "hear." Yes, **hear.**
3. (Repeat step 2 for remaining words.)

TASK 2 WORD READING THE FAST WAY

1. Now you get to read all the words the fast way again.
2. (Touch ball for first word of lesson. Pause three seconds.) Read it the fast way. (Slide. Child reads word.) Yes, good reading.
3. (Repeat step 2 for remaining words of lesson.)

hear

near

take

shot

blam

tiger

mouse

stopped

picked

Hunting for Tigers—Part 1

The old man said, "I need a tiger coat. So I will hunt for a tiger." ⓐ

The girl said, "But you can not see. How can you hunt for a tiger?" ⓑ

The old man said, "I can hear. Tigers make sounds. I will hear those sounds and take a shot."

The girl said, "The shot may miss."

"No," the old man said. "When I hear something I will take a good shot." ⓒ

So the man went out with his gun. He did not see well. So he fell over a log. Then he fell over a rock. Then he walked up a hill. When he got to the top he stopped. "I hear something," he said. "I have found a tiger."

The man did hear the sound of a tiger. It was a big tiger. And it was very near. The old man picked up his gun. "Blam." ⓓ

The shot did not hit the tiger. It hit a nut in a tree. The nut fell on a mouse.

The mouse yelled, "Stop hitting me with nuts." ⓔ

This Is Not the End.

TASK 3 FIRST READING

1. We'll read the first part of this story. In the next lesson we'll read the second part of this story. After you read this part of the story, you'll read it again and I'll ask questions.
2. Read the title the fast way. **(Child reads title.)**
3. Read the first sentence the fast way. **(Child reads first sentence.)**
4. Read the next sentence the fast way. **(Child reads second sentence.)**
5. **(Repeat step 4 for remaining sentences in story.)**

TASK 4 SECOND READING

1. Now you're going to read the story again. This time I'll ask questions when you read to the circled letters. Start with the title and read until you get to the first circled letter. Then stop.
2. **(Ask following questions when child reaches each letter.)**
   ⓐ Why did the old man want to hunt for a tiger?
   ⓑ Why didn't the girl think the old man should hunt for tigers?
   ⓒ Do you think the old man's plan will work?
   ⓓ What was the **blam** sound?
   ⓔ What did the shot hit? What did the nut fall on? What did the mouse say?

TASK 5 PICTURE COMPREHENSION

Look at the picture. Is the old man pointing his gun at the tiger? What did the old man shoot? Follow that nut down and see what it will hit. How will that mouse feel when it gets hit with a big nut?

TASK 6 WRITING LETTERS

1. You're going to write the letters that I write. Here's what you're going to write first. Watch. **(Write s at beginning of first line. Point to s.)** What's the name of this letter? "s." What sound does that letter make? "sss."
2. First trace the **s** that I made. Then make more of them on this line.
3. **(After tracing s several times, child is to make three to five s's. Help child if necessary. For acceptable letters say:)** Good writing **s.**
4. Here's the next letter you're going to write. Watch. **(Write r at beginning of second line. Point to r.)** What's the name of this letter? "r." What sound does that letter make? "rrr."
5. First trace the **r** that I made. Then make more of them on this line.
6. **(After tracing r several times, child is to make three to five r's. Help child if necessary. For acceptable letters say:)** Good writing **r.**

LESSON 100

TASK 1 WORD READING

1. Get ready to read these words the fast way.
2. (Touch ball for **sing.** Pause three seconds.) Read it the fast way. (Slide.) "sing." Yes, **sing.**
3. (Repeat step 2 for remaining words.)

TASK 2 WORD READING THE FAST WAY

1. Now you get to read all the words the fast way again.
2. (Touch ball for first word of lesson. Pause three seconds.) Read it the fast way. (Slide. Child reads word.) Yes, good reading.
3. (Repeat step 2 for remaining words of lesson.)

sing

back

shouted

sand

thank

kept

licked

nose

noses

home

bite

tame

house

Hunting for Tigers—Part 2

An old man was shooting at a tiger.

The tiger sat down and started to sing. The old man shot. This shot hit a rock. A bug was in back of that rock. "Stop making this rock jump," the bug shouted. ⓐ

But the old man did not stop shooting. The man shot a hole in the sand. An ant said, "Thank you. That is a good ant hole." ⓑ

The tiger kept singing and the man kept shooting. Then the man stopped. He said, "I am out of shots. So I must stop hunting."

The tiger came over and licked the old man on the nose. ⓒ The old man said, "You can not do that. Tigers do not lick. They bite."

The tiger said, "Not this tiger. I am a tame tiger." ⓓ Then the tiger said, "I love to lick noses and I love to sing."

The old man said, "I must get out of here. But I can not see. So I can not find my house."

The tiger said, "I will take you home if you give me a good coat." ⓔ

So now the tiger has a tiger coat and a coat from the old man. ⓕ **And the old man has no coats.** ⓖ

This Is the Last Ending.

TASK 3 FIRST READING

1. Last time you read the first part of the story about hunting for tigers. What happened at the end of that part of the story?
2. In this part of the story, we'll find out what happened to the old man shooting at the tiger. After you read this part of the story, you'll read it again and I'll ask questions.
3. Read the title the fast way. (Child reads title.)
4. Read the first sentence the fast way. (Child reads first sentence.)
5. Read the next sentence the fast way. (Child reads second sentence.)
6. (Repeat step 5 for remaining sentences in story.)

TASK 4 SECOND READING

1. Now you're going to read the story again. This time I'll ask questions when you read to the circled letters. Start with the title and read until you get to the first circled letter. Then stop.
2. (Ask following questions when child reaches each letter.)
   - ⓐ What did the bug shout?
   - ⓑ Did the ant like that hole in the sand? Why?
   - ⓒ What did the tiger do? Is that a very mean tiger?
   - ⓓ What did the tiger say it was?
   - ⓔ What did the tiger want for taking the man home? How many coats does the old man have?
   - ⓕ Which coat is the tiger coat? That's the coat the old man wanted.
   - ⓖ How many coats does the old man have? He's worse off than he was before he went hunting.

TASK 5 PICTURE COMPREHENSION

Look at the picture. How many coats is the tiger wearing? Touch the tiger coat. Touch the coat the tiger got from the old man. Who looks happier, the tiger or the old man?

TASK 6 WRITING LETTERS

1. You're going to write the letters that I write. Here's what you're going to write first. Watch. **(Write a at beginning of first line. Point to a.)** What's the name of this letter? "a." What sounds does that letter make? "ăăă, āāā." We're going to write **a** without a line.
2. First trace the **a** that I made. Then make more of them on this line.
3. **(After tracing a several times, child is to make three to five a's. Help child if necessary. For acceptable letters say:)** Good writing **a.**
4. Here's the next letter you're going to write. Watch. **(Write z at beginning of second line. Point to z.)** What's the name of this letter? "z." What sound does that letter make? "zzz."
5. First trace the **z** that I made. Then make more of them on this line.
6. **(After tracing z several times, child is to make three to five z's. Help child if necessary. For acceptable letters say:)** Good writing **z.**

WHAT NOW?

Your child has taken the biggest step in reading—that of learning what words are, how they work, and how written statements are the same as orally presented utterances. With the knowledge that your child has gained, reading comprehension is not a serious issue. If the child knows what something means when somebody says it verbally, the child knows what the written counterpart of that utterance means. Of course, your child may have trouble understanding some of the textbooks that will be presented in school, but this prediction says nothing about the adequacy of your child, merely about the adequacy of the textbooks.

As you know, your child is not yet sufficiently skilled in decoding to read (decode) many larger words and irregulars. The next steps in instruction should focus on the decoding skills the child has not yet mastered.

Here are some suggestions:

Teach new sound combinations. Teach new words that have the sound combination **al** (as in **also**), using a presentation that parallels the one presented in the program for teaching the sound combination **ar** in Lessons 49–51. (Present words; underline the part that contains the letters **al;** tell the sound; then require the child to identify the sound made by the underlined part and then read the word.) Use these words: **also, all, fall, call, ball, tall, always, almost.** Then mix the words in this list with other words the child has learned, particularly **ar** words: **tar, bar, car,** and so on. Give the child practice in saying the letter *names* for each word after reading a list of words.

Teach words that have the sound combination **ee.** The child already knows some of these words **(tree, see, feel).** Use the procedure described for teaching **al** words. Introduce **wheel, feed, need, indeed, speed,** and other **ee** words.

Teach other combinations such as **igh** (**night, right, sight, fight, fright, high,** and so on). Use the same basic procedure suggested for introducing the other combinations.

Introduce new reading material. It might seem that if your child has mastered the first steps in decoding, the child should easily be able to read other material that is ostensibly designed for beginning reading, such as the easy-to-read books that are advertised in stores and on TV. The problem is that your child probably reads at the second-grade level (if the child has completed the program successfully). Most of these books are written for the third-, fourth-, or fifth-grade level. Most of them contain an outrageous vocabulary. The best of them are good listening books, but not very good reading books for the neophyte reader.

However, of the incredibly large group of children's books that is available, there are a handful that can be presented with some preteaching to a child who reads at the second-grade level. Below is a list of twenty books that you can introduce. A list of the words that you should preteach before presenting the book is included for each book.

Title, author, (publisher) and *vocabulary words* to be taught before book is read:

1. **Have You Seen My Cat?** Eric Carle (Little Simon)

2. **Look What I Can Do,** Jose Aruego (Aladdin)
   what, too

3. **We Hide, You Seek,** Jose Aruego and Ariane Dewey (HarperFestival)
   ready, seek, turn, want, we'll

4. **I Love You, Dear Dragon,** Margaret Hillert and Carl Kock (Modern Curriculum Press)
   work, who, pretty, one, make, guess, father, dragon, dear

5. **If All the Seas Were One Sea,** Janina Domanska (Aladdin)
   ax, axes, great, sea, seas, splish, would

6. **Blue Sea,** Robert Kalan and Donald Crews (Scott Foresman)
   blue, goodbye, ouch, smaller

7. **Hop on Pop,** Dr. Seuss (Beginner Books)
   pup, tall, sad, cup, bee, Jim, Pat, Ted, wall, bat, dad, ball, fight

8. **Inside, Outside, Upside Down,** Stan and Jan Berenstain (Random House)
   coming, mama, outside, right, track, upside

9. **Green Eggs and Ham,** Dr. Seuss (Beginner Books)
   anywhere, boat, eggs, thank, train, would

10. **Go, Dog, Go,** P. D. Eastman (Beginner Books)
    all, around, black, hello, party, three, two, water, work, yellow

11. **Mine's the Best,** Crosby Bonsall (HarperTrophy)
    bigger, dead, does, fault, it's, mine, she's, smart, things, yours

12. **The Carrot Seed,** Ruth Krauss and Crockett Johnson (HarperFestival)
    ground, carrot, pulled, nothing, afraid, water, sprinkled, weeds, around, seeds

13. **Whose Mouse Are You?** Robert Kraus and Jose Aruego (Aladdin)
    inside, far, none, nobody's, whose, caught, trap, toe, new

14. **Home for a Bunny,** Margaret Wise Brown and Garth Williams (Golden)
    Spring, robin, bunny, groundhog, leaves, burst, would, drown, road, until, home

15. **Who Took the Farmer's Hat?** Joan L. Nodset and Fritz Siebel (HarperTrophy)
    goat, farmer, hill, flowerpot, nest, squirrel, wind, round, boat, nice, oh, new

16. **A Kiss for Little Bear,** Else Homelund Minarik and Maurice Sendak (HarperCollins)
    hi, glad, decided, bear, grandmother, kiss, skunk, pond, hen, wedding

17. Henry and Mudge, Cynthia Rylant and Sucie Stevenson (Aladdin)
searched, straight, weighed, drooled, tornadoes, whined, worry, worried, thought, chocolate, vanilla, silent, couldn't

18. Nate the Great, Marjorie Weinman Sharmat and Marc Simont (Young Yearling)
Nate, Great, detective, diamonds, pearls, searched, comfortable, monster, picture, Rosamond, kitchen, bury, yesterday, passages, trails, secret, breakfast, minutes, balloons, juice,

19. Magic Tree House #1: Dinosaurs Before Dark, Mary Pope Osborne and Sal Murdocca (Random House)
Pennsylvania, disappeared, neighbor, ancient, absolutely, volcanoes, cautiously, giant, weighed, incredibly, ignored, gigantic, enormous, miracle, engraving, tingle

20. Look Out, Washington, D.C.! Patricia Reilly Giff amd Blanche Sims (Pearson Learning)
famous, pioneers, cafeteria, comedy, garage, diaries, prairie, escalator, nerves, scrunched, dedication, Union Station, palace, Lincoln Memorial, Washington Monument, aisle, statue, breath, couple, shoulders, museum, ceiling, ordinary, souvenir

Present the books in the order of their appearance on the list. If you select books 3, 4, 9, 12, and 16, present them in that order. To present each book, follow these steps:

1. Read the book to your child at least one day before the child is to read it. Interpret the pictures and translate any funny wording that the child may not understand.

2. Teach the words that are specified for the book that you introduce. The simplest procedure is to write the words on a large sheet of paper, with the title of the book at the top. Point to each word and read it. After you have read the entire list, tell the child, "Your turn. Point to each word and read it." Direct the child to reread the list if any words are not firm on the first reading.

3. Tell the child, "First you're going to read the book to me. Then it's your book" (or "your book for a while"). "You can read it to yourself as many times as you wish." As the child reads, correct mistakes and ask questions about what is happening in the story and about the scenes depicted in the pictures.

4. Review the list of words from the story after about three or four days. Encourage the child to read the book independently and to read it to others (Daddy, sister, or other family members).

After the child completes ten or more of these books, you should be able to introduce most "kid" books. To present them, follow the steps specified: read the book at least a day before the child is to read it; present the words that the child needs to learn in order to read the book; direct the child to read the book to you; then permit the child to "keep" the book and read it independently. To find the words that should be pretaught in these books, read the book yourself. The more flagrant words that should be pretaught will jump out at you.

Don't enter this extended teaching with the idea that the task will be overwhelming for you or that it must be undertaken with the same amount of precision required for the teaching of skills presented early in the program. Your child now has a solid basis. You've undoubtedly discovered that your child generalizes to new words that you haven't taught, and you may have noticed how rapidly your child learns new words, even those that are irregular.

You have probably had the experience of identifying a new word to your child and later discovering that the child recalls the word. Remember, the more the child knows about reading, the easier it is to teach new skills. (In fact, the child will start to learn them even if you don't teach them directly.) So give the child practice. Make sure that reading continues to be an important activity. And have fun.

ACKNOWLEDGMENTS

Some books spring fully formed from the heads of their authors. Others do not. This one fits into the latter group, emerging slowly, growing organically bit by bit from notes on yellow pads. This product is the result of more than ten years of notes, expansion, refinement, and the formulation of a philosophy that integrates the parts into a cohesive whole. Many have been instrumental in my process. First, I acknowledge Jack Taylor, my mentor at Arizona State University, whose knowledge, wisdom, and high energy teaching inspired me to move beyond teaching at the K–12 level to become a trainer of teachers. Second, I acknowledge the many K–12 teachers who have modeled excellent practice in the classroom and helped me define my path. Third, viewing teaching as a dance in which teacher and student take turns leading and following, I acknowledge the hundreds of students who have served as teachers for me. Of course, there are also numerous art educators who have shaped the field. Those who have been most influential in my development are introduced in the text. Additionally, I acknowledge those who have been so supportive in the production of this work. They include my colleagues at Towson University and my student assistants, especially Jane Wynn, whose dedication and expertise were invaluable in the development of the final manuscript. And finally, for manifesting a vision in concrete form, I acknowledge the following people associated with Wadsworth Publishing Company: Dianne Lindsay, education editor; Trudy Brown, project editor; Dusty Friedman, production service; Linda Purrington, copy editor; Norman Baugher, designer; and David Ruppe, artist.

I especially want to thank reviewers of this edition: Lynda E. Andrus, Kansas State University; David W. Baker, University of Wisconsin, Milwaukee; Ann Beiersdorfer, Xavier University; Shauna Castellaw, Lewis-Clark State College; Cynthia Colbert, University of South Carolina; Carol Edwards, Kennesaw State University; Linda Ganstrom, Fort Hays State University; Jacqueline Golden, University of Arkansas; Eugene Harrison, Eastern Illinois University; Elisabeth Hartung, California State University, Long Beach; Gregory W. Hawkins, Eastern Washington University; Howard Hull, University of Tennessee; Erik Nielsen, Southwest Texas State University; Lee A. Ransaw, Morris Brown College; Ralph Raunft, Miami University; Susan Shoaff-Ballanger, Truman State University; Marcia F. Taylor, The College of New Jersey; Betty Tisinger (professor emeritus), Virginia Commonwealth University; and Randy L. Waln, Montana State University, Northern. To all of the above I extend my deepest appreciation and say thank you.

ABOUT THE AUTHOR

Growing up hasn't been easy. I was born and raised in Los Angeles, where I attended six elementary schools, two high schools, and two colleges, graduating from UCLA in 1964. The threads that connected the parts of my life were first my passion for art and then my passion for teaching art. I began teaching in 1965 in a high school thirty miles from where I lived.

After four years of driving to and from work on the freeway and totaling two Volkswagens in the process, I decided to explore life outside California. I applied to the Department of Defense and was sent to teach art in grades 7–12 on an army base in Würzburg, Germany. There I got married and the following year moved with my husband to his home in Rochester, New York, where I taught art in grades 7–12 in the inner city. After a year of serving as a "roving" teacher (transporting boxes of art supplies from the basement to the third floor), dealing with race riots, and driving in blizzards, we moved to someplace that was gentler, warmer, and had schools built on one level. I spent the next thirteen years in Scottsdale, Arizona, teaching art in grades 1–8. There I learned to avoid bats, earned a master's degree at Arizona State University, had two children, and eventually, tiring of telling children not to eat the paste, returned to Arizona State University for a doctoral degree. On graduation, I focused on my next goals: (1) going some place green, and (2) teaching on the college level. I began by accepting a position at Marshall University in West Virginia, where I stayed for two years. In 1986, I moved to Baltimore, Maryland, to teach at Towson University, my home today.

In support of my teaching, I regularly present at district, state, and national conferences; have written curriculum for the states of Arizona and Maryland; and have served as a consultant for museum education. I received awards as the Outstanding Art Educator of the Year in the state of Arizona and the Outstanding Art Educator of the Year in the Higher Education Division for the Eastern Region. At Towson University I direct the undergraduate and graduate programs in art education, mentor students through the writing of their master's theses, supervise student teachers, and teach the three-semester sequence of course work for which I wrote this text. As a teacher first and foremost, I welcome this opportunity to share in the becoming of those who have chosen art education as their field.

PART 1

PREPARING FOR TEACHING

1 Exploring Our Roots

2 Emphasizing Art Making

3 Planning Verbally and Visually

4 Progressing Through Planning Toward Teaching

PART I focuses on preparing for teaching. Chapter 1, "Exploring Our Roots," presents an introduction to philosophical and historical perspectives of art education, which provide a context for understanding issues and trends of today. A model of art education diagrams the philosophical stance embraced within this text. It is holistic in nature, integrating child- and subject-centered approaches, and presents art production at its core. Chapter 2, "Emphasizing Art Making," reflects the focus of our model and moves into the relationship between theory and practice. Models for teaching art production lay the foundation for teaching studio-centered units of study. Chapter 3, "Planning Verbally and Visually," moves into unit planning and support of written plans through visual planning. Chapter 4, "Progressing Through Planning Toward Teaching," illustrates how to move from the general in a unit plan to the specific, fleshed out in individual lesson plans, to teaching. These four chapters are intended to provide enough preparation for a student to walk into an introductory preservice experience and begin to teach.

C H A P T E R

EXPLORING OUR ROOTS

Recognizing bats and bat-making experiences is not difficult. Agreeing on what constitutes sound art education theory and practice can be much more challenging—especially now. Art education today is a result of what we have chosen to embrace or to react against in our past. Presented here is a brief introduction—art education's beginnings in the United States, rationales for its existence within the general curriculum, and influences leading to where we are today. At any given time in our history we can see a relationship among the needs and values of society, the direction of general education in response to those needs and values, and the focus of art education as a particular aspect of general education. As needs and values have changed, art education has changed. This chapter explores the relationship diagrammed in Figure 1.1 and the movements that have developed since art was introduced into the general curriculum in the mid 1800s. Sections discuss (1) art to support society, (2) art to enhance the individual child, (3) art as a curricular discipline, (4) art education of the 1980s and 1990s, and (5) a vision for art education today.

Needs and values of society
↓
General education fulfills needs and reflects values
↓
Art education refines goals of general education

FIGURE 1.1
Society, General Education, and Art Education Relationships

ART TO SUPPORT SOCIETY

In the 1800s the general curriculum was designed to support the well-being of the social order. As a new country, the United States was focused on developing a strong, economically independent nation. Draftspeople and designers were needed to promote our Industrial Revolution. To address this need, art was taught as mechanical drawing. Three educators were particularly influential in promoting society-centered art education during the nineteenth century: William Bentley Fowle, William Minifie, and Walter Smith. William Bentley Fowle was a general educator who published *Common Schools Journal* (1842–1852), through which he promoted art as useful in developing drawing skills. Because of his efforts, drawing was first introduced in 1847 as a permissible subject at Boston English High School.

William Minifie was an architect who was hired by the public commissioners of Baltimore to teach drawing at Boys' High School during the 1840s and 1850s. Through a textbook on geometric drawing, he promoted drawing as a science rather than as picture making. Walter Smith was brought to Boston from England to be the Director of Art Education for the city and the State Supervisor of Drawing. He provided leadership in the development of art education in Massachusetts, which in 1870 passed the first law making drawing a required high school subject. He saw art education as a sequence of drawing lessons that were so clear and precise that non-art specialists could teach students to draw. His book *Teacher's Manual for Freehand Drawing and Designing* (1876) consisted of a series of graduated exercises in which students were required to copy geometric patterns of lines and shapes. This type of teaching, reflected by these early art educators, is called *closed-ended* instruction. Its purpose is to develop skills in working with tools, materials, and techniques.

The society-centered orientation has continued to be a thread throughout our history. It has been most visible when our nation has been most challenged. For example, during the depression of the 1930s "art for daily living" became a rationale for art education. The Owattona Project reflected this rationale in a program designed to help community members of Owattona, Minnesota make aesthetic decisions relevant to their daily lives. In the 1940s art education was used to promote the war effort. In the 1950s art education was used to develop creative thinking skills necessary to compete with the Soviet Union in the space race. In the 1960s "art for the social order" reflected the civil rights movement. Today some of what we see in art education reflects our concern with issues such as conservation of natural resources.

ART TO ENHANCE THE INDIVIDUAL CHILD

The child-centered orientation developed in the 1920s as a reaction against the philosophy that education existed to serve the needs of the society at the expense of the individual. Goals and content for art education were derived from the developmental levels and needs of the child. The purpose of art education was seen at this time as promoting self-expression. Children were encouraged to experiment with materials and were allowed freedom to develop their intrinsic qualities through relatively unstructured art experiences.

One of the most influential and revolutionary educators supporting the child-centered orientation was John Dewey, the intellectual leader of the Progressive Movement from 1920 to 1940. Dewey believed the child was not merely a miniature adult in the process of becoming fully formed. He thought children needed types of experiences other than rote memorization of facts and closed-ended art instruction intended to develop mature artistic skills. He saw the task of education as providing environments that would encourage creativity and adaptation to real life situations. Dewey viewed the school as a place that allowed students freedom to make choices, to move around, and to solve problems.

Two important developments in art education grew out of Dewey's philosophy and the practices of the Progressive Movement—correlated art and art for self-expression. Correlated art activities were introduced in classrooms designed to reflect the outside world. Many teachers set up their rooms as small communities in which students were presented with problem situations to solve through cooperative efforts. Students produced murals, puppet shows, tabletop models, charts, displays, and bulletin boards. These activities all involved art. Art correlated with other subjects became a way of providing experiential learning, problem-solving opportunities, and freedom for self-expression.

During the Progressive Movement "art for self-expression" became the major rationale for art education. In seeking to provide experiences that encouraged problem-solving behavior and self-expression, educators replaced closed-ended instruction with other teaching strategies. The *open-ended* approach was used to develop skills in problem solving. Teachers presented a "problem" defined by a set of rules or criteria. Students were given opportunities to work within the criteria to solve the problem. Using this approach teachers recognized individual differences, a variety of problem-solving behaviors, and multiple "right" answers. An even less structured teaching strategy used to encourage self-expression was the *laissez-faire* approach. *Laissez-faire,* a French expression meaning "without interference or direction," is a teaching method that allows students maximum freedom to explore and experiment. Students are presented with a wide range of materials in order to discover how they can be used in self-expressive ways. The laissez-faire strategy was used to elicit the freshness and spontaneity intrinsic in children's artwork and to protect children from what was perceived as contamination by adult standards.

The child-centered orientation introduced by Dewey and practiced in the Progressive Movement has continued primarily through the work of another major figure in art education—Viktor Lowenfeld. Lowenfeld was an Austrian art educator who in 1939 fled before the Holocaust and came to the United States. Coming from a background in which he had contact with horrendous social conditions, Lowenfeld naturally aligned with the child-centered movement. He focused on the holistic nature of the child, considering physical, mental, emotional, and creative capacities. In *Creative and Mental Growth* (1947) Lowenfeld clearly reflected the philosophy of postwar times. Educators were concerned with making the world "safe for peace." Art was seen as a humanizing activity that was broadly therapeutic. Lowenfeld saw art as a vehicle for developing human creative capacities through freedom of expression. Through his teaching and writing, he has had an impact that endures to the present day.

ART AS A CURRICULAR DISCIPLINE

Not long after the return to peace after World War II, America was shaken by the Soviets' launch of *Sputnik.* The approach adopted by general education was "back to basics." Engineers and scientists needed to be trained to compete in the space race. Art education that focused on freedom for self-expression was perceived as "soft" and lacking in substance. Mirroring the academization occurring in general education, art education of the 1960s began a major movement in the direction of content and structure. The focus started to shift from art taught through experiential studio activities in child-centered approaches to art presented as a "body of knowledge." Curricula with specific concepts and content were designed in an effort to place art as a discipline alongside math and science. This approach, referred to as *subject centered, content centered,* or *discipline based,* grew gradually over a twenty-year period and was formalized in the 1980s as DBAE (discipline-based art education).

ART EDUCATION OF THE 1980s AND 1990s

DBAE developed into a major movement due in large part to the Getty Education Institute for the Arts. In the 1980s the institute, investigating art education practices throughout the country, found that despite the direction subject-centered approaches had begun to take, most programs remained heavily focused on studio production. One of its goals was to balance art making with the study of art in culture and as culture. This was accomplished by presenting art education as four interrelated domains or disciplines:

- *Art production*—focusing on art making
- *Art criticism*—focusing on perceiving and understanding visual qualities of art through the use of critical dialogue
- *Aesthetics*—focusing on the development of appreciation, personal taste, and knowledge of art's value as established within various times, places, and cultures
- *Art history*—focusing on art within the context of history and culture

The institute provided research, curriculum, and training to implement its philosophy and to fulfill what had become the number one goal of the National Art Education Association (NAEA): "All elementary and secondary schools shall require students to complete a sequential program of art instruction that integrates the study of art production, aesthetics, art criticism, and art history."

Although art educators in general may have supported this goal, many questioned implementation strategies. Educators critical of DBAE as it existed in practice made these observations:

- Some discipline-based approaches replaced art production as the primary focus with the study of art objects. This was referred to as *object-centered* art education because the main activity consisted of viewing and discussing objects, rather than making art. The approach was seen by some as a weakness, because studio experiences were viewed by many as the essence of art education.
- Some discipline-based programs were rigidly implemented through a formula in which domains were presented in a specific order with production addressed last. This structure restricted flexible integration and tended to de-emphasize art production.
- When art production was de-emphasized, students often created expressions modeled after the artwork they had studied, rather than exhibiting creative self-expression. Instead of making bat clones, they made Picasso, Matisse, or Mona Lisa clones.
- Art activities that were reduced to recreating expressions based on ideas of master artists tended to be product oriented. Rather than becoming involved in the experiential processes of art making, students were focused on producing end results. These were often judged on their resemblance to the original, rather than on the intrinsic worth of the experience.
- The majority of artwork presented for study when DBAE began was from Western cultures. Non-Western cultures were inadequately represented.
- When implementing DBAE, some school districts designed guides that specified particular artists to be presented at each grade level. This was seen as overly restrictive in program planning.
- Some advocates of DBAE avoided interdisciplinary planning, fearing integration with other subjects would diminish art education. Lack of connectedness was seen as a weakness.
- Some discipline-based art educators presented artwork and studio activities in ways that were inappropriate for the developmental levels of children and had little or no relevance to the lives of their students.

These criticisms were often well founded, well taken, and addressed. Art educators began experimenting with different ways to integrate child- and subject-centered approaches. A number of strategies were developed that shared these characteristics:

- They integrated art history, aesthetics, and art criticism with art production in ways that supported rather than devalued studio experiences.

- They addressed developmental levels and age appropriateness.
- They promoted self-expression and developed problem-solving skills.
- They were inclusive rather than exclusive, recognizing the connection of art to other subjects and to life in general.
- They developed reading, writing, and thinking skills.
- They provided a global perspective of art, presenting expressions representative of all cultures.
- They made connections between the values, ideas, experiences, and expressions of artists and of individual students.
- They were concerned with accountability and provided measures to assess learning in all domains of art education.

One way to gain an understanding of subject-centered art education and how it differs from child-centered is to compare texts in the field. Lowenfeld's *Creative and Mental Growth* is still popular today and considered by many to be the "bible" of child-centered art education. In contrast, a number of subject-centered student texts have been written in the last three decades of the twentieth century.

Selected examples, presented next, indicate the use of these texts at all grade levels:

elementary-level student texts
- *Adventures in Art* (a series of six texts) by Chapman
- *Art in Action* (a series of six texts) by Hubbard
- *Art: Meaning, Method and Media* (a series of six texts) by Hubbard and Rouse
- *Discover Art* (a series of six texts) by Chapman

middle-school–level student texts
- *A World of Images* by Chapman
- *Art: Images and Ideas* by Chapman
- *Art in Your Visual Environment* by Brommer and Horn
- *Art in Your World* by Brommer and Horn
- *Exploring Art* by Mittler and Ragans
- *Exploring Visual Design* by Gatto, Porter, and Sellack
- *Introducing Art* by Ragans, Mittler, Morman, Unsworth, and Scannell
- *Understanding and Creating Art* by Goldstein, Katz, Kowalchuk, and Saunders
- *Understanding Art* by Mittler and Ragans
- *The Visual Experience* by Hobbs and Salome

high-school–level texts
- *Art in Focus* by Mittler
- *Art Talk* by Ragans
- *Creating and Understanding Drawings* by Mittler and Howze
- *Discovering Art History* by Brommer
- *Themes and Foundations of Art* by Katz, Lankford, and Plank

The controversy over what to and what not to do increased significantly in the 1980s and 1990s with the emergence of DBAE. Teachers became consumed in healthy debate over purposes of art education, content of art education, and methods for delivering instruction. Some clung adamantly to child-centered art education, viewing DBAE as the enemy that substituted academic study of art for authentic self-expression. Others saw DBAE as offering much-needed content and structure. Still others adopted more holistic approaches, integrating positive aspects of both orientations. Regardless of where one stood along the child-subject–centered continuum, all were encouraged to move into the year 2000 providing opportunities for students at every grade level to connect with art through experiences in art production, art criticism, aesthetics, and art history.

This encouragement came in the form of the Goals 2000: Educate America Act, which identified the arts as core subjects equal in importance to the academics and mandated their teaching in grades K–12. The result of this law was the formulation of the National Visual Arts Standards (presented in full in Chapter 14). These identify what students should know and be able to do on completion of high school. They reflect the breadth of what is deemed important in art education today: ability to communicate through the arts, capacity to reflect on and assess art, knowledge of art within a variety of cultures and historical periods, and understanding of art's relevance to other subjects and life in general. Moving into the twenty-first century, we see as one of our strengths our diversity, the variety of voices and approaches addressing standards and demonstrating accountability in art education. The individuals introduced next illustrate this point.

ELLIOT EISNER

Elliot Eisner has been especially noteworthy as a supporter of DBAE. A writer, curriculum designer, and art educator at Stanford University, Eisner is an outspoken advocate for art as basic and provided us with a vision of what DBAE at its best might be. He has presented these rationales for teaching art:

- Art invites students to look carefully so that they might see.
- Art develops multiple forms of literacy that give students meaningful access to "cultural capital."
- Art provides children with opportunities to use their imaginations, to create multiple solutions to problems, and to rely on their own judgment to determine when a problem is solved.

In answer to the question posed in his 1987 article on DBAE, "Are the arts ornamental in our schools?" Eisner responded,

> *[Art] is only ornamental if meaningful access to some of our most significant cultural achievements is a marginal educational aim. It is only ornamental if the kinds of mental skills fostered by work in the arts are tangential to the kinds of problems both children and adults encounter outside school. . . . The arts represent a form of thinking and a way of knowing. Their presence in our schools is as basic as anything could be. (p. 10)*

HOWARD GARDNER

Eisner is not alone in his belief in the power of art education to develop multiple forms of literacy, encourage multiple solutions to problems, and pro- multiple forms of intelligence. Howard Gardner is a psychologist and ed- most noted for his research in multiple intelligences. Viewing human gs in a holistic way, Gardner identified eight forms of intelligence: (1) ver- linguistic, (2) logical/mathematical, (3) body/kinesthetic, (4) visual/spatial, musical/rhythmical, (6) interpersonal (person to person), (7) intrapersonal wareness of self), and (8) naturalistic (relating to the world of nature). His in- erest in going beyond "verbal ability," most characteristically identified as "in- telligence," led him into a long-term involvement: Project Zero. This was an investigation co-directed with David Perkins at Harvard University, studying the nature of understanding across disciplines, the origins of creativity, the development of thinking abilities, and the promotion of critical judgment. The project was inspired by and took its name from the answer to the question "What do we know about how humans learn in and through the arts?" (posed by the philosopher Nelson Goodman). The answer was "zero." Growing out of Project Zero, a group dealing specifically with the arts was developed—Arts PROPEL. This organization was formed to investigate, teach, and assess cognitive functioning through the arts. It is based in studio production and focuses on experiential processes of art making and performance. Emphasis is placed on creating and assessing a record of progress through the keeping of studio portfolios. This approach is significantly different from that of DBAE. However, many paths lead to common goals, as we may infer from this statement from Arts PROPEL:

> *The creation and production of art represents human achievement at its highest. Exercising hand, heart and mind together develops important mental skills such as symbol use, analysis, problem solving, invention and reflection . . . exactly the sort of independent intellectual activity that distinguishes thinkers, inventors and leaders.*

ELLEN DISSANAYAKE

In contrast to these two examples, consider the ideas of Ellen Dissanayake, an anthropologist who influenced the field with her view of art as "species centered." In *What Is Art For?* (1988), she presented art as a universal behavior and explored these ideas:

- Human beings have engaged in art behaviors since the earliest beginnings of our species.
- Art began when early humans were not only able to recognize something as "special," but deliberately set out to make something "special."
- "Making special" is behavior that elevates experiences and objects from the mundane, the everyday, and the ordinary.
- Our ancestors not only made "special" objects (such as tools) but also developed "special" or "controlled" behaviors (rituals) in order to ensure success.
- Because rituals have been and are still part of life in all cultures, we may view ritualistic objects not as examples of art for art's sake, but as *art for life's sake.*

Dissanayake also viewed art as basic, not so much because of its potential to teach about cultures or to develop intelligence, but because art making is intrinsic behavior of humankind. Delivering a keynote address at the 1991 convention of the NAEA, she stated,

> *Art is not confined to a small coterie of geniuses, visionaries, cranks and charlatans—indistinguishable from one another—but is instead a fundamental human species characteristic that demands and deserves to be promoted and nourished. . . . Art is a normal and necessary behavior of human beings that like talking, exercising, playing, working, socializing, learning, loving and nurturing should be encouraged and developed in everyone.*

PETER LONDON

Finally, let's turn to the work of Peter London—writer, art therapist, art educator, and a leading proponent of child-centered art education today. Much like Dissanayake, London defined art as "a category of human activity." In this process-centered orientation he urged art educators to go beyond "simply providing strategies to replicate, study, talk about and display . . . aesthetic amenities" (things in which we seek relief from or enhancement of everyday life). He viewed art education as a powerful instrument through which we may transform the quality of an individual's life from its current condition to a preferred and elevated one. In *No More Secondhand Art* (1989, p. 8), he described art in the service of transformation as functioning in these ways:

- Renewing and reaffirming the covenants between humankind and nature and between man and God
- Grappling with the ephemeral qualities of life and with our own mortality
- Marking significant times, places, and events
- Discovering the actual range of human possibilities
- Awakening us to higher levels of consciousness

In *Step Outside* (1994), London presented ways to translate these ideas into classroom practice. His approach, *community-based art education* (CBAE), begins with the experiences, knowledge, and curiosity the student brings into the classroom. From this central point in which interaction is based on what the student initially offers, the scope of experiences is widened to include the immediate environment outside the classroom, the larger school, the home and family, neighborhood, community, nation, and ultimately the globe.

These individuals were not selected because they represent all of art education. Some might argue that they may not even represent art education in the mainstream. Do we really have a "mainstream" today? Times have changed from the days in which art education was defined as drawing. As our profession has grown, we have become more inclusive and diversified. Today we are about many things. What Eisner, Gardner, Dissanayake, and London collectively represent is the richness of the tapestry. They were selected not only because each has delivered a significant message about the purpose and path of art education, but also because their messages are different.

The fabric of art education has been woven over a long period. At any given time those in the field have attempted to provide what was perceived as best within the context of general education and the larger society. These educators did not exist in a vacuum. Their ideas came from observations of human behaviors, perceptions of the world beyond the classroom, study of art and other fields, analyses of art education of the past, assessments of strengths and weaknesses of art education in the present, and visions of how we might guide individuals and society into the future. Table 1.1 on page 10 summarizes the development of art education, chronicling the progress of society-, child-, and subject-centered approaches.

A VISION OF ART EDUCATION TODAY

Progressing from an introduction to [illegible] consciousness" to knowledge of events in our history and resulting trends in art education, you may understand how a number of rationales for the teaching of art have emerged. They include

- To ensure economic security
- To develop connections among people
- To support the social order
- To promote appreciation
- To develop trade skills
- For leisure time
- To teach moral values
- To gain skills for careers
- To support war efforts
- For spiritual unfolding
- To enhance daily living
- For personal and planetary transformation

TABLE 1.1
Selected Examples of Three Orientations in Art Education

TIME	HISTORICAL EVENTS AND INFLUENCES OF GENERAL EDUCATION	SOCIETY-CENTERED ORIENTATION IN ART EDUCATION
1870s	The Industrial Revolution promotes economic competition with Europe.	Mechanical drawing is introduced as the first art education to train boys to be draftsmen and designers in the Industrial Revolution.
1890s	Schools include vocational training to develop skills useful for children of immigrants.	Crafts—woodwork, metal work, sewing, weaving—are introduced to provide training in trades.
1900s	Education includes training in morals and values.	Art appreciation called "picture study" involves discussing religious subject matter of "famous paintings" to transmit moral values.
1920s	The Progressive Movement embraces Dewey's views that education should be experiential and promote self-expression.	
1930s	The Depression leads to financial and emotional stress.	"Art for daily living" becomes a rationale. Children are taught to make decorative and practical items to brighten home environments.
1940s	America fights World War II.	Art education is seen as a vehicle to support the war effort and focuses on making patriotic posters and mementos.
	World War II ends. Education seeks to make the world "safe for peace" through the development of creative capacities.	
1950s	The Soviets launch *Sputnik,* leaping ahead in the race to control space.	"Art for creativity" becomes a rationale to promote creative problem-solving skills needed in the space race.
1960s	The reaction to the Soviet Union's achievements in space is a back-to-basics movement. Education stresses academic excellence.	
	The civil rights movement and women's liberation movement promote multicultural awareness.	Art for the social order becomes important. Courses in black and Hispanic art are added to programs. The work of women artists begins to be introduced into art education curricula.
1970s	A counterculture develops, protesting the values of the establishment and the war in Vietnam.	
1980s	*A Nation at Risk* calls for educational reform.	
1990s	Education emphasizes standards, assessment, and accountability in the Goals 2000: Educate America Act.	Art education is mandated into law through the Goals 2000 Act.
	Technology furthers "the information age" and the development of a global society.	Art education incorporates technology to access and communicate information on a global scale.
2000s		

TABLE 1.1 *(continued)*

TIME	CHILD-CENTERED ORIENTATION IN ART EDUCATION	SUBJECT-CENTERED ORIENTATION IN ART EDUCATION
1870s		
1880s		
1890s		
1900s		
1910s		
1920s	Art is correlated with other subjects to promote experiential learning. Art education focuses on fostering self-expression and learning through experimentation and discovery.	
1930s		
1940s	Art is seen as a developmental activity to promote health and well-being. Experimentation with materials is encouraged for creative self-expression.	
1950s	Art as creative self-expression and experiential learning through manipulation of materials continues.	
1960s	Art as creative self-expression and experiential learning through manipulation of materials continues.	Art education is seen as "a body of knowledge" with discrete subject matter, concepts, and skills. Focus shifts from the art learner to art content. Art education reflects the academic orientation of general education.
1970s	Crafts are revived as an expression of individual creativity and as a protest against mass production and social conformity.	Art education continues to reflect an academic orientation and broadens to include the teaching of art concepts, perceptual skills, and historical content.
1980s	Arts PROPEL presents a studio-centered approach to promote cognitive functioning.	DBAE formalizes "art as a body of knowledge" into the four domains of art criticism, aesthetics, art history, and art production.
1990s	Community-based art education focuses on a studio-centered curriculum based on needs and interests of the child.	Discipline-based approaches offer K–12 sequential instruction in all four domains. Art education emphasizes art content, multicultural involvement, interdisciplinary connections, use of technology, standards, and assessment.
2000s		

- For culture refinement
- To gain access to cultural capital
- For art's sake
- To promote visual literacy
- To develop perceptual skills
- To develop cognitive skills
- To develop psychomotor skills
- To develop social skills
- To develop affective skills
- To promote self-expression
- To develop inquiring minds
- To promote enhanced experiencing of life

These rationales grew from society-, child-, and subject-centered orientations. Sometimes approaches considered to be polar opposites deliver the same message from different ends of a continuum. For example, DBAE places primary importance on the study of art within cultural contexts. As students study the art of others and relate what they are learning to themselves, they progress from the outside in, as diagrammed in Figure 1.2.

FIGURE 1.2
Outside-In Orientation

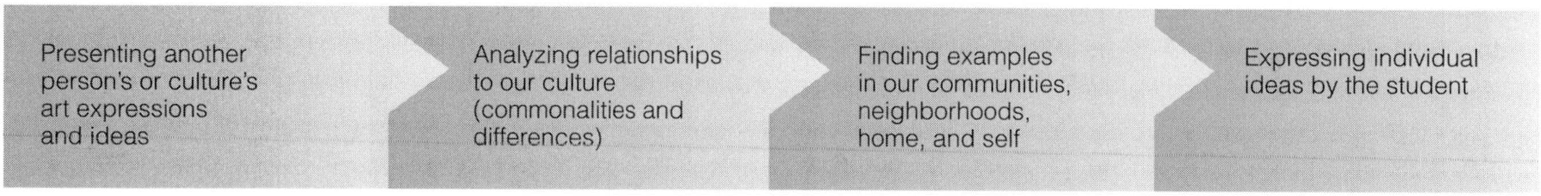

Presenting another person's or culture's art expressions and ideas	Analyzing relationships to our culture (commonalities and differences)	Finding examples in our communities, neighborhoods, home, and self	Expressing individual ideas by the student

Child-centered art education, in contrast, places primary importance on the intrinsic qualities of the learner. Students first look within to express themselves and then discover commonalities with others through shared ideas, experiences, and expressions. They learn from the inside out.

FIGURE 1.3
Inside-Out Orientation

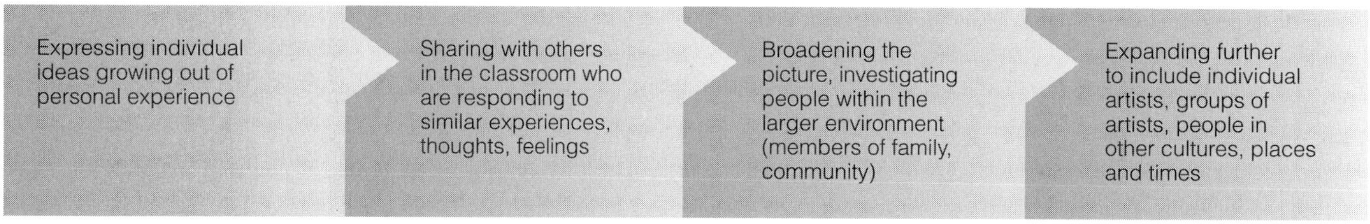

Expressing individual ideas growing out of personal experience	Sharing with others in the classroom who are responding to similar experiences, thoughts, feelings	Broadening the picture, investigating people within the larger environment (members of family, community)	Expanding further to include individual artists, groups of artists, people in other cultures, places and times

One approach begins with the general and progresses toward the particular, and the other proceeds in the opposite way. Although these are significant differences, there is an implied common message: "Art is a visual language that connects human beings, relating the inside to the outside and the outside to the inside."

Understanding the common messages, as well as the differences, is important. As we embark on our study of art education, we must articulate what we believe and define where we stand along the path. If we proclaim ourselves as followers of DBAE, we will move in one direction to deliver our message. If we align with child-centered art educators, we will move in a different direction. Another choice is to consider all of what is being offered and to design our own route selectively. The path presented in this guide is holistic, integrating ideas from multiple points of view. It is based on these beliefs:

1. Art is a visual language through which human beings speak to one another.
2. "Speaking the language" is synonymous with "creating art." Art production is of primary importance and should be emphasized above all else in studio-centered curricular designs.
3. The study of aesthetics, art criticism, and art history develops attitudes, skills, and knowledge that support the ability to "speak" (make) art.

4. Speaking and understanding the language of art involves connecting both the inside to the outside and the outside to the inside.
   a. Every unit of study should offer students opportunities to express their authentic selves in studio experiences intended to promote thinking and creativity.
   b. Every unit of study should include a historical referent to create a connection with the outside.
   c. We can move in either direction, progressing from the inside out or from the outside in to make connections.
5. The domains of aesthetics, art criticism, and art history should be presented in ways that explore "inside" and "outside" issues.
   a. Inside issues

      Aesthetics:

      - What do I like (in terms of art)?
      - How do I assign value to art?
      - Why is art important to me?

      Art criticism:

      - How do I understand and express myself through art?
      - What am I saying through my art?
      - How can I assess my own artwork?

      Art history:

      - How am I connected to others through my art?

   b. Outside issues

      Aesthetics:

      - What is art (as defined by people in different cultures, times, and places)?
      - Why is art valued by others?

      Art criticism:

      - How can I experience and understand the art of others?
      - What are others saying to me through their artwork?
      - How can I assess the art of others?

      Art history:

      - How does humankind express through art?
6. Art touches everyone. It both influences and is influenced by all of life. We can convey the importance of art as an integral aspect of human existence by presenting it within various contexts:
   a. Art as an expression of the authentic self
   b. Art as an expression of one's own culture
   c. Art as a universal expression of humankind
   d. Art as an expression of life in general

These points define a belief system illustrated in Figure 1.4. The model integrates the ideas into a cohesive whole. Notice that *art making* has been placed in the center, signifying its importance as the core of art education. On each side are influences informing art making. These "inside" and "outside" influences have been subdivided into aesthetics, art criticism, and art history to illustrate the supporting roles of these domains. The four additional categories—the authentic self, one's own culture, a global perspective, and life in general—present increasingly expanding contexts in which to explore art. Each outside category is connected to "art making" by double-headed arrows, illustrating that art both impacts and is impacted by everything else. Additionally, the parts of the model are connected by two concentric circles moving in opposite directions. The outside circle suggests that we can move from the outside in, progressing from "life in general" toward "the authentic self". The inside circle implies that we can also move in the opposite direction, progressing from "inside influences" toward "life in general".

FIGURE 1.4
Model of Art Education

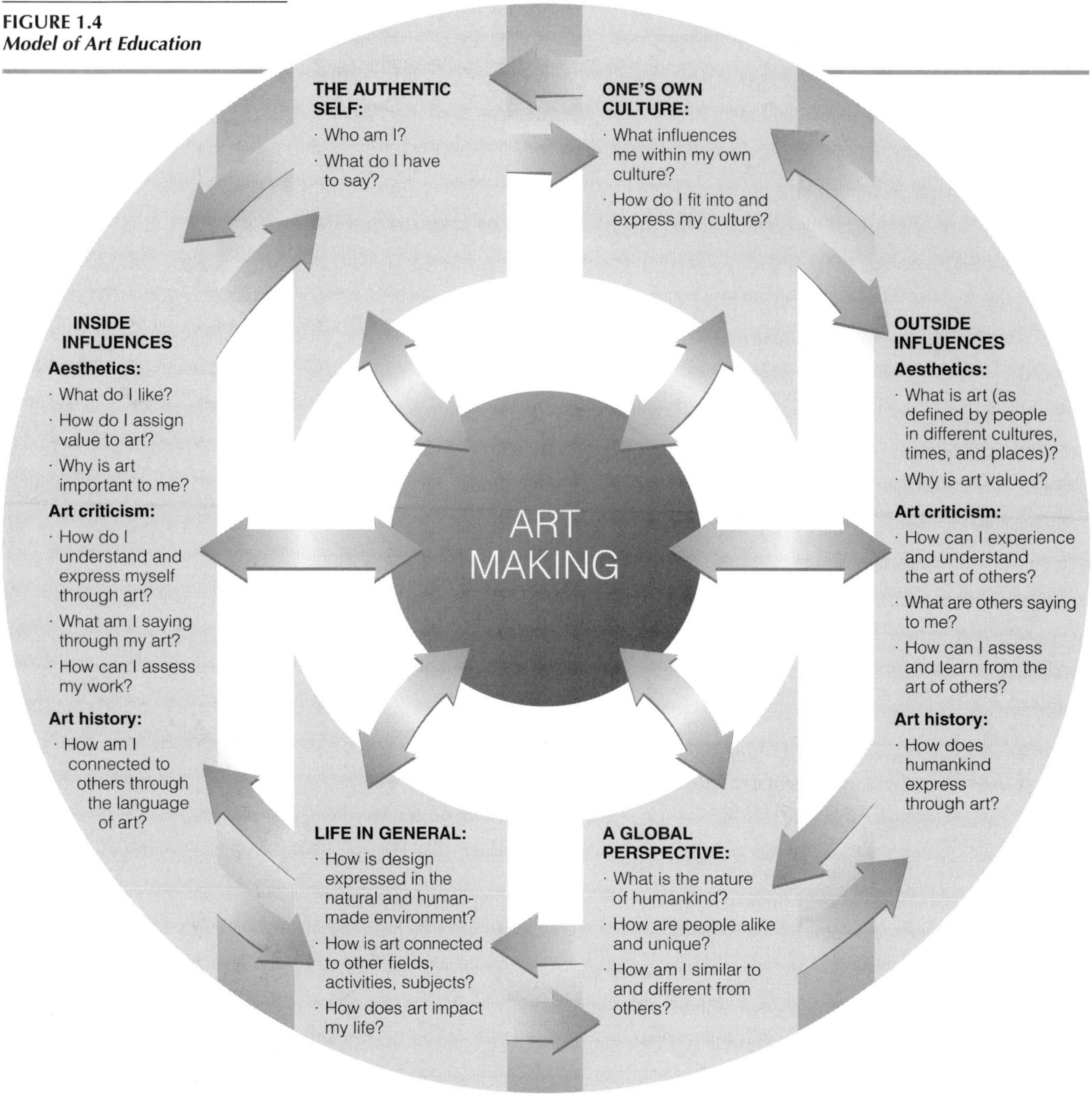

THE AUTHENTIC SELF:
· Who am I?
· What do I have to say?

ONE'S OWN CULTURE:
· What influences me within my own culture?
· How do I fit into and express my culture?

INSIDE INFLUENCES
Aesthetics:
· What do I like?
· How do I assign value to art?
· Why is art important to me?
Art criticism:
· How do I understand and express myself through art?
· What am I saying through my art?
· How can I assess my work?
Art history:
· How am I connected to others through the language of art?

ART MAKING

OUTSIDE INFLUENCES
Aesthetics:
· What is art (as defined by people in different cultures, times, and places)?
· Why is art valued?
Art criticism:
· How can I experience and understand the art of others?
· What are others saying to me?
· How can I assess and learn from the art of others?
Art history:
· How does humankind express through art?

LIFE IN GENERAL:
· How is design expressed in the natural and human-made environment?
· How is art connected to other fields, activities, subjects?
· How does art impact my life?

A GLOBAL PERSPECTIVE:
· What is the nature of humankind?
· How are people alike and unique?
· How am I similar to and different from others?

SUMMARY

The history of art education in America shows the relationships among art education, general education, and the larger society. At any given time in our history we can see a pattern: The rationales for art education, the content of art education, and even the strategies for teaching are a response to historical events and conditions, societal needs and values, and directions of general education.

Two rationales have given rise to two general movements: art to support society and art to enhance the individual child. The society-centered orientation appeared in the 1800s, responding to the needs of a growing nation. Art was seen as a vehicle for promoting societal well-being. Teaching focused on the building of skills through closed-ended instruction. The child-centered orientation began in the 1920s as a reaction against the lack of concern with individual growth and development reflected in the society-centered approach. The child-centered orientation, which grew out of the philosophy of John Dewey and the educational practices of the Progressive Movement, was carried forward by art educators influenced primarily by the writings and teachings of Viktor Lowenfeld. In the child-centered view, art education was seen as a means for promoting growth of physically, mentally, and emotionally healthy individuals. Open-ended and laissez-faire teaching strategies were used, relying heavily on free exploration with materials.

A third broad movement is a subject-centered approach in which art is taught as a curricular discipline. As in previous movements, this one responded to societal needs and perspectives in general education. In the 1960s a back-to-basics movement caused a reevaluation of art education. A shift from child- to subject-centered art education began, and art education was defined as "a body of knowledge." Over the next twenty years, the subject-centered approach was slow to take hold. Not until the 1980s did it emerge as a primary orientation in the form of discipline-based art education. DBAE integrates four domains of art education—art production, art criticism, aesthetics, and art history. It challenged beliefs and practices of child-centered educators and caused considerable controversy in the field. Its advocates supported it because it provided substance and taught students to understand and appreciate art as viewers through experiences in art history, criticism, and aesthetics. Critics argued that it was implemented in ways that de-emphasized art production, stifled creativity, and required students to engage in activities that were often developmentally inappropriate.

The last twenty years of the twentieth century were particularly rich in terms of diversity. Many art educators defined themselves as discipline-based and created their own subject-centered approaches to address criticisms of DBAE. A growing number of art educators embraced an alternative to DBAE in the form of community-based art education (CBAE). This group brought child-centered art education back with renewed strength, developing its curricular structure from the needs, values, interests, and energy of the individual learner. Regardless of where teachers stood philosophically, all were encouraged to move into the twenty-first century providing high quality art education defined by structure and content. This encouragement came in the form of the national Goals 2000: Educate America Act. This law mandated art education in grades K–12. As a result, National Visual Arts Standards were formulated. These stipulated what students should know and be able to do in art on graduation from high school. They reflect the breadth of what is deemed important today: the ability to communicate through the arts, the capacity to reflect on and assess art, knowledge of art within culture and history, and understanding of art's relevance to other subjects within the curriculum.

The vision of art education on which this book is based is holistic, integrating the strengths of various movements, approaches, and individuals. A model for art education illustrates how the subject-centered orientation (with its focus on the world of art outside the individual) and the child-centered orientation (with its focus on the learner) can be brought together in a synergistic whole. The vehicle used to connect the "outside" to the "inside" is art production. The model is studio centered, with aesthetics, art criticism, and art history used to support art making. As you progress through the book, you will discover chapter by chapter how this theoretical model becomes translated into practical application, addressing art in relationship to the authentic self, culture, a global society, and life in general.

WHY TEACH ART?

Scenario

Your principal has just told you that because of budget cuts art (and your position) may be eliminated from the school.

Directions

1. Present a convincing argument that art should stay by listing at least 10 rationales for the teaching of art to all students, 2. Indicate with an asterisk (*) the four rationales you believe are the strongest, and 3. Discuss each of the four in detail in the spaces provided below.

10 Rationales for Teaching Art:

Rationale 1:

WHY TEACH ART? *(continued)*

Rationale 2:

Rationale 3:

Rationale 4:

C H A P T E

EMPHASIZING ART MAKING

Beginning with the premise that art making is central to art education, we turn first to the domain of art production. This chapter presents a view of those who will engage in art-making experiences (the students) and discusses the nature, purpose, and design of different kinds of productive activities. Sections include (1) artistic expression of children, (2) three types of studio activities: closed-ended, open-ended, and laissez-faire, and (3) teaching models to structure studio experiences.

ARTISTIC EXPRESSION OF CHILDREN

To have an art-making experience, we need several components: (1) the art learner, (2) the actions or behaviors of the learner, and (3) the results of those actions—the art expressions. The starting point seems obvious: the students themselves, bringing in their excitement, interests, feelings, and needs. They serve as guides for where to begin in the design of studio activities. Because at this point you may have had limited experience with children, let's turn to someone who has shed light on the subject. Lowenfeld, in *Creative and Mental Growth,* influenced the field with his studies and theories on stages of artistic development and visual and haptic types of expression.

STAGES OF ARTISTIC DEVELOPMENT

In comparing art expressions of learners at different ages, Lowenfeld saw that children draw in predictable ways, going through defined stages, ranging from the free scribbles of 2-year-olds through deliberate mark making of adolescents. These stages are summarized and illustrated in Table 2.1 and Figure 2.1.

As you review Table 2.1, you may have questions, such as these:

- Are the stages universal? Do children everywhere express themselves in these ways?
- Should teachers simply accept artistic expressions of children as typical of a given stage and not interfere?
- Should teachers present skills and information that will carry students from where they are to higher levels of skill and/or understanding?

These are good questions that are not easy to answer. At one time it was generally accepted that all children go through these stages. As interest has increased in multicultural expressions, researchers have found that children in some non-Western cultures do not fit this model of development. In our Western culture, however, you will see drawing after drawing that you can identify as "normal" expression of each stage. It is important to have a stan-

TABLE 2.1
Stages of Artistic Development

STAGE OF DEVELOPMENT	AGE	CHARACTERISTICS OF STAGE
Scribbling Stage	2–4	Children make random marks, feeling the kinesthetic aspect of the experience. Mark making becomes a movement activity that develops motor coordination. As children gain control of their bodies, they move from random scribbles to horizontal and vertical scribbles to circular scribbles.
Preschematic Stage	4–7	Children advance from circular scribbles to their first attempts to represent objects in their environment. People are symbolized by a circular figure with arm and leg lines radiating from the head. Figures or objects float randomly on the page with little regard for size or placement.
Schematic Stage	7–9	Children move from representing objects as more or less circular shapes with appendages to using schemas or formulas. Schemas are conceptual—they represent concepts or ideas of things and people, rather than realistic perceptions of individual objects. (For example, children often draw trees like lollipops regardless of how individual trees are actually perceived.) Children begin to develop ways to organize space. Objects are typically lined up along a ground line; the sky becomes a line across the top of the page; objects are seldom overlapped and space is relatively flat. Drawings and paintings tend to be large, free, and spontaneous. Children are relatively uncritical of their own work and the work of others and they enjoy sharing.
Stage of Dawning Realism (the gang age)	9–12	Children continue to represent objects in schematic form. They become interested in detail and realism. Artwork gradually becomes small and tight. Children are much more aware of themselves and how they are perceived by their peers. They tend to be more inhibited. They become much more critical of themselves and their artwork.
Pseudonaturalistic Stage (the stage of reasoning)	12–14	Children become increasingly aware of surroundings and are concerned with realistic depiction of objects. They develop an interest in portraying depth and correct proportions. Although many children at this stage still represent the environment through schemas, they become increasingly interested in observational drawing (looking at objects and drawing what they see rather than drawing concepts or ideas of imagined objects). Students become even more critical of their work and may be embarrassed to share it.
Period of Decision (adolescent art in high school)	14–17	Mark making moves from an act of natural self-expression to a deliberate attempt to explore art processes and to create art products. Decisions become important as students choose how and to what degree they will involve themselves in making art.

dard for "normal." If you have no standard for normal, you will have trouble recognizing "special." "Special" may be a first grader whose artistic expressions consist primarily of scribbling. "Special" may also be a first grader who overlaps objects and creates foreground, middle ground, and background.

This understanding of what is "normal" and what is "special" brings us to the next issues: Should teachers accept students where they are? Should teachers give students skills and information to accelerate learning into the next stage? During the Progressive Movement there was a hands-off philosophy. Educators were willing to allow abilities of children to develop without much intervention. This laissez-faire approach was considered a healthy counterbalance to the restrictions of closed-ended instruction of earlier times.

Today many art teachers believe that adult intervention is a necessary part of the educational process. When we use language students can understand, present information in small bits through carefully sequenced step-by-step processes, and teach through a variety of experiential activities, students learn

FIGURE 2.1
Drawings Illustrating Stages of Artistic Development

Source: Lowenfeld. © 1982. *Creative and Mental Growth,* 1e. Reprinted by permission of Prentice Hall, Upper Saddle River NJ.

1. Scribbling Stage (2–4 years)

2. Preschematic Stage (4–7 years)

3. Schematic Stage (7–9 years)

4. Age of Dawning Realism (9–12 years)

5. Pseudonaturalistic Stage (12–14 years)

6. Period of Decision (14–17 years)

more at earlier ages. For example, many of you may not have encountered contour drawing until you were in high school. Art teachers now present contour drawing experiences to students in fourth and fifth grade. Most fourth and fifth graders do *conceptual* drawings, using schemas to represent objects. Contour drawing is a *perceptual* activity, involving looking at a specific object and drawing exactly what is seen. Are fourth and fifth graders capable of doing this? Yes. Will it change how they see and draw? Maybe. Will they continue to make schematic drawings? Probably they will, and by providing experiences beyond the schematic mode of representation, you may broaden your students' artistic repertoires and choices for self-expression.

VISUAL AND HAPTIC MODES OF EXPRESSION

In addition to contributing a wealth of information on child art and child-centered art education, Lowenfeld also provided insight into two different modes of artistic expression—visual and haptic. In working with the partially blind, he discovered that some students took in information through what they could see, whereas others took in information through what they could feel. He called those who related primarily through their sense of sight *visual learners* and those who related primarily through their sense of touch, *haptic learners*. Branching out from the partially blind adult to fully sighted adults and children, Lowenfeld continued to test his theory. He found that at about age 12 many children begin to show a preference for how they take in and respond to information. Like any "theory," Lowenfeld's idea has been supported by some and rejected by others. The information in Table 2.2 is offered not as fact but as description of characteristics and behaviors observed by many teachers of art. These categories are not meant to serve as boxes into which to place students and their artistic expressions. Rather, they are presented to heighten your awareness.

Most people are neither exclusively visual nor haptic, but fall somewhere on a continuum between the two polarities. It is important to be sensitive to these two types, to recognize their characteristics, and to provide experiences to accommodate both styles of learning and expression.

TABLE 2.2
Characteristics of Visual and Haptic Types

THE VISUAL TYPE	THE HAPTIC TYPE
• Observes the environment through the sense of sight	• Feels the environment through the sense of touch
• Records what he or she sees from the point of view of an observer	• Interprets what he or she feels from the point of view of a participant
• Sees the whole without an awareness of the details	• Focuses on details, parts, textures
• Progresses from the general to the specific in creating compositions	• Progresses from the parts to the whole in creating compositions
• Is objective and emotionally detached	• Is emotionally involved, often using abstract imagery to suggest feelings
• Uses color objectively	• Uses color subjectively

VISUAL AND HAPTIC TYPES

FRED, an extremely visual student teacher, introduced a lesson to a group of eighth graders using the following strategy: In preparing students to create sculptures from blocks of plaster poured into half-gallon milk containers, he had them fold sheets of paper into four vertical areas and draw what they imagined the sides of their sculptures would look like in each. Tom quietly sat in the back of the room, ripping out sheets of paper from his notebook, folding each into four sections and attempting to draw lines that represented his idea. Clearly he had an idea; he was motivated to try to represent it as he had been told, and he was struggling. At the point at which the wadded failed attempts surrounding his desk were becoming noticeable to other students, he gave up and sat staring into space. After several minutes he came to and realized he was looking into an open cupboard with a bin labeled Plasticine. Quietly he got up, helped himself to some clay, and happily constructed a model of his envisioned sculpture.

The point is this: If we wish to advance our students' artistic expressions beyond where they would be without our intervention, we need to recognize and accept where our students are. Only by starting where students are can we lead them to their next steps. Lowenfeld's studies provide useful information that has helped teachers to recognize where students are artistically along their developmental paths.

THREE TYPES OF PRODUCTIVE ACTIVITIES: CLOSED-ENDED, OPEN-ENDED, AND LAISSEZ-FAIRE

As we reviewed the historical development of art education, we saw that for the most part art production has been central in the teaching of art. The first art activities were *closed-ended,* intended to develop skills in working with tools, materials, and techniques. During the Progressive Movement, the *laissez-faire* approach provided freedom for individual exploration and self-expression. *Open-ended* instruction developed as a balance between the two, offering students broad structure, defined through general criteria, coupled with freedom to interpret in creative ways. The three types can be thought of as points along a continuum, as Figure 2.2 suggests.

Each type of activity has a place in teaching art production and can be used in appropriate or inappropriate ways. Table 2.3 provides guidance in making appropriate use of each.

FIGURE 2.2
Closed-Ended–Open-Ended–Laissez-Faire Continuum

Closed-Ended, Open-Ended, and Laissez-Faire Activities

Closed-ended	**Open-ended:**	**Laissez-faire:**
Provides maximum structure for skill development	Provides a balance of structure and freedom for creative interpretation	Provides maximum freedom for experimentation with media and processes

TABLE 2.3
Analysis of Closed-Ended, Open-Ended, and Laissez-Faire Teaching Activities

	CLOSED-ENDED	OPEN-ENDED	LAISSEZ-FAIRE
Purposes	• To build skills in working with tools, materials, and techniques	• To promote creativity and problem-solving skills • To promote understanding of art concepts • To develop skills in the creation of a work of art	• To motivate students through exploration of media and processes • To encourage self-expression for its own sake • To encourage discovery learning
Characteristics	• There is maximum guidance from the teacher. • The teacher provides an example of what should be done. • Students follow the teacher's step-by-step instructions. • There is only one "right" answer and way to do the assignment.	• The teacher provides broad criteria and some guidance. • The teacher provides several examples of "right" answers. • Students must follow criteria and are allowed freedom for individual interpretation. • The activity may be process or product oriented.	• There is minimum guidance from the teacher. • Examples or criteria may not be needed or provided. • Students have freedom to explore and discover without having to meet preconceived expectations. • The activity is process oriented: exploration of media and processes is valued over making an art object.
Appropriate Uses	• To introduce the use of new tools, materials, or techniques • To teach processes that require specific instruction	• To generate ideas • To learn skills, processes, and concepts necessary for creation of an artwork	• To introduce a new medium or process with which students experiment
Examples of Appropriate Activities	• Draw cubes using the rules of one-point perspective as an introduction to the design of a cityscape. • Throw a 6" cylinder as an introduction to making wheel-thrown pots.	• Create designs illustrating different types of balance. • Create an artwork interpreting a theme explored by other artists.	• Explore the tactile properties of clay as an introduction to creating clay sculpture. • Experiment with color mixing to learn what variations can be made.
Typical Outcomes	• All work looks alike. • Success is determined by how skillful the student is in using particular tools, materials, and processes.	• Each outcome is different. • Products reflect creative thinking as a result of individual interpretation of criteria.	• Although an "artwork" may result, the intention is to explore processes/media. • Success is determined by what the student discovers from the experience while engaging in the activity.
Inappropriate Uses	• Closed-ended activities are inappropriate when used to make final products that are intended to be creative. • Closed-ended activities are inappropriate when there are multiple ways to demonstrate learning of a skill or concept.	• Open-ended activities are inappropriate when specific instruction in using tools and materials is required. • Open-ended activities are inappropriate in assignments that require one "right" answer.	• Laissez-faire activities can be inappropriate to teach skills and to promote creativity. (Skill development often requires instruction from the teacher. Creative behavior requires students to go beyond exploration of media and processes to solve problems.)
Examples of Inappropriate Activities	• Paint a landscape by copying a picture from a nature magazine.	• Use the paper cutter to make as many 3" × 5" cards as possible from a 12" × 18" paper.	• Tell students to be creative! • Invite them to use any materials they want to make a picture for the art show.

As you read the information in Table 2.3, you may have thought, "I would never do anything as stupid as turning the students loose to cut up cards on the paper cutter." Often what is inappropriate may not seem so obvious, as Mandy's piggy bank experience in the Birdwalk below illustrates.

Analyzing Mandy's teaching strategy, we may identify a number of factors that contributed to what Mandy perceived as a "disaster."

- The classroom teacher viewed the purpose of the experience as creating a product. Mandy focused on the process of self-expression. Neither considered how to present activities in age-appropriate ways.
- In Mandy's attempt to turn clones into creative outcomes, she allowed students free rein. Rather than taking a teacher-directive stance, in which she could teach skills in handling a paint brush and applying paint, she took a laissez-faire position.
- Mandy not only overestimated the children's ability to apply paint to a three-dimensional surface, she underestimated the time required to achieve a level of quality she and the classroom teacher had envisioned.

In discussing what Mandy could have done differently, we will address four key issues in the teaching of art: (1) process versus product, (2) age appropriateness, (3) use of productive activities, and (4) sequencing.

PROCESS VERSUS PRODUCT

The process-centered orientation is one in which the experience of making art has intrinsic value, regardless of how the resulting artistic expression looks. The purpose of teaching is to build skills and to foster meaningful self-expression, as a teacher guides students through art-making activities. These activities may result in nothing more than experimentations in mark making, or they may produce powerful pieces that one might label as "works of art." Whether the outcome is short-lived and tossed in the wastebasket when the experience is over or framed and hung on the wall is not important. In the process-oriented approach the quality of the experience and resultant growth or learning are of value. In contrast, the product-oriented approach looks on the object created not simply as the by-product of an experience, but as having worth in and of itself.

PAPIER-MÂCHÉ PIGGY BANKS

MANDY was a recently graduated teacher who was familiar with "bat making." Early in her first year on the job, a first grade teacher came to her with a request. Would she devote an art period to allow children to paint the papier-mâché piggy banks they had made in her room? Reluctantly she agreed. The following week she watched child after child file into her room with identical papier-mâchéd milk cartons with legs. In her mind she saw bats and immediately jumped from the closed-ended products to what she thought would turn clones into individual creative expressions. She said to the students, "Be creative! Do anything you want to make your piggy banks different—stripes, flowers, designs." Then she put out all the colors she had and let them paint. They dove into the colors, mixing reds and blues and yellows and greens. They painted color on top of color, and by the end of the period all had completed their paint jobs. Mandy watched the students file out of the room at the end of the period, each with a dripping wet, muddy, brown pig.

AGE APPROPRIATENESS

In the teaching of art we provide both process- and product-oriented experiences. Students enjoy going beyond the point at which they simply experiment with ideas and media. They like creating and displaying products they view as works of art. However, without engaging in process-oriented experiences in which they learn to generate ideas, use tools, and experiment with techniques, the result might be muddy brown pigs. Muddy brown pigs point to a second issue—age appropriateness. Is it reasonable to expect that first graders have skills to produce well crafted papier-mâché sculptures? Might it be more appropriate to present process-oriented activities that focus on the building of skills rather than on the making of a product? Might a product-oriented papier-mâché experience be more appropriately geared for students in fifth grade? These questions will be answered with more fitting examples of process-oriented experiences at the first grade level and product-oriented experiences at the fifth grade level in discussions that follow.

USE OF PRODUCTIVE ACTIVITIES

The third issue is the use of productive activities. The classroom teacher inappropriately used closed-ended instruction to lead her students through a step-by-step procedure to copy her model. Mandy inappropriately used laissez-faire instruction to encourage students to embellish the clones with creative surfaces. Neither provided a structure that combined teacher-directed instruction with freedom for personal interpretation. The steps that follow illustrate how this product-oriented experience might be redesigned for students at the fifth grade level, integrating closed- and open-ended activities.

1. Provide a variety of materials from which to construct armatures—cans, milk cartons, boxes, paper towel tubes, jars, lids. Show students how to attach forms with tape and glue. Lead them through a short exercise in which they use these processes to attach forms (a closed-ended, process-oriented step).
2. Ask students to discuss how the armature materials might be used to create bodies, legs, eyes, ears, etc. Let students construct piggy (or any preferred animal) bank armatures, using their new skills (an open-ended procedure focused on the final product).
3. Lead students through the papier-mâché process (a closed-ended procedure focused on the final product).
4. During time in which papier-mâché layers are drying, present a painting exercise in which students review and practice painting skills and explore design possibilities (such as pattern and color schemes) to be used in embellishing the sculptures (an open-ended, process-oriented activity).
5. Have students paint their "animal banks" one solid color (a closed-ended experience focused on the final product).
6. Have students embellish the surfaces by painting designs on top of the base color (an open-ended experience focused on the final product).

SEQUENCING

The preceding list illustrates the fourth issue—*sequencing.* "Art" is not created by a single act. It grows from ideas, knowledge, and skills that develop over a period of time. During this period, bit by bit, experiences cause the coming together of behaviors that result in art products. Your ability to sequence activities that result in visual expressions (which may or may not be labeled as

PLANNING VISUALLY

Can you imagine developing a unit similar to the one entitled "The Abstraction of Georgia O'Keeffe" (see p. 47) solely through the process of writing? If you are especially verbal and think linearly, you may be able to do this relatively easily. Most art teachers are visually oriented. They "think" in images. For this reason many make visuals as their primary planning process. Writing simply reflects what they have imagined in concrete form through visuals. Visual planning includes activities such as designing posters to illustrate ideas and procedures, doing demonstrations, selecting and presenting cultural exemplars, exploring media and techniques, and creating examples of assignments. Visual planning should be done along with written planning, prior to the actual teaching of lessons. You can use visual planning as a guide in writing and teaching processes. You also teach your students through the presentation of visual images. The following box lists reasons for making and using visuals.

Why Make Visuals?

- To support unit planning, lesson planning, and teaching
- To learn how to translate what you know as an artist into procedures to teach students
- To see through your students' eyes (as you explore processes from their perspective)
- To discover what will work and what will not
- To provide instruction and sequential steps in teaching studio activities
- To anticipate realistic time allotments for studio work
- To provide examples for visual learners
- To set standards for what you expect
- To model behaviors you want of students

The visuals you show your students for teaching purposes will vary widely. A visual can be a poster, a display, a work of art, a demonstration, or a natural or cultural object. Visuals include what you make, what your students make, and what you present through books, reproductions, slides, videos, and computer generated images. Using visuals in the teaching process is important in all subjects. Using visuals in teaching art is essential. People take in information through what they see, hear, and feel. Of the three modes—visual, auditory, and kinesthetic—the visual mode is dominant. More people learn most easily by seeing rather than by hearing or feeling. By using visuals we support what we tell students, what we ask them to read, and what we present in experiential activities. This section addresses how to design and use visuals to support the teaching/learning process. It includes (1) concept, process, and product visuals; (2) visuals to present cultural exemplars; and (3) technology applications in planning and teaching.

CONCEPT, PROCESS, AND PRODUCT VISUALS

Many of the visuals you will make will be in the form of posters that convey information. What you present can be categorized into three broad areas: information about (1) art concepts, (2) art processes, and (3) art products. This section discusses the purposes, design, and use of these types of visuals.

CONCEPT VISUALS

Concept visuals illustrate ideas. They may convey messages without words, expressing ideas entirely through design and content. Often, however, teachers reinforce ideas by combining simple written text with visual content, as the examples in Figure 3.6 illustrate. Because one concept can pertain to a number of lessons, concept visuals should be general enough to fit many different activities. For example, if you make a visual saying, "Flowers have geometric and organic shapes," you can use the poster only when flowers are the subject matter. If you make visuals illustrating what geometric and organic shapes are, you can use them for many lessons involving shape.

FIGURE 3.6
Concept Visuals Illustrating Types of Shapes

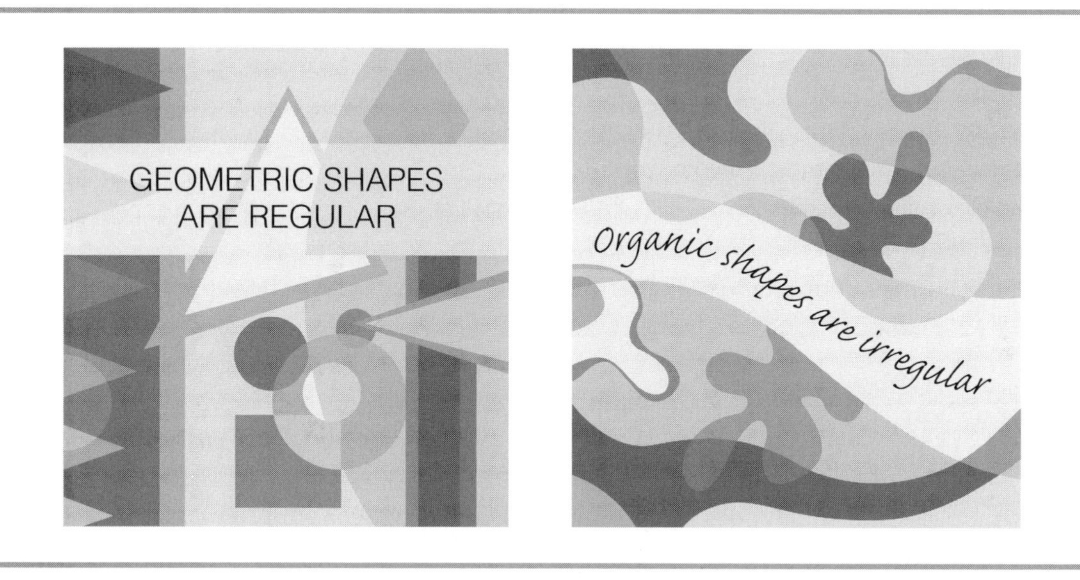

The concept visuals in Figure 3.6 illustrate critical concepts (ideas about how we perceive the visual environment). In addition to illustrating critical concepts, we can also illustrate historical and aesthetic ideas. The fold-out display in Figure 3.7, illustrating multiple examples of O'Keeffe's work, may be thought of as a concept visual because it can be used to present cultural/historical information.

This type of visual can be a valuable teaching tool for a number of reasons:

- It allows students to compare and contrast images.
- Images might be attached with Velcro so that they can be removed for closer inspection.
- It can be set up on a table top or bulletin board as a portable display.

FIGURE 3.7
Concept Visual Illustrating a Cultural Exemplar

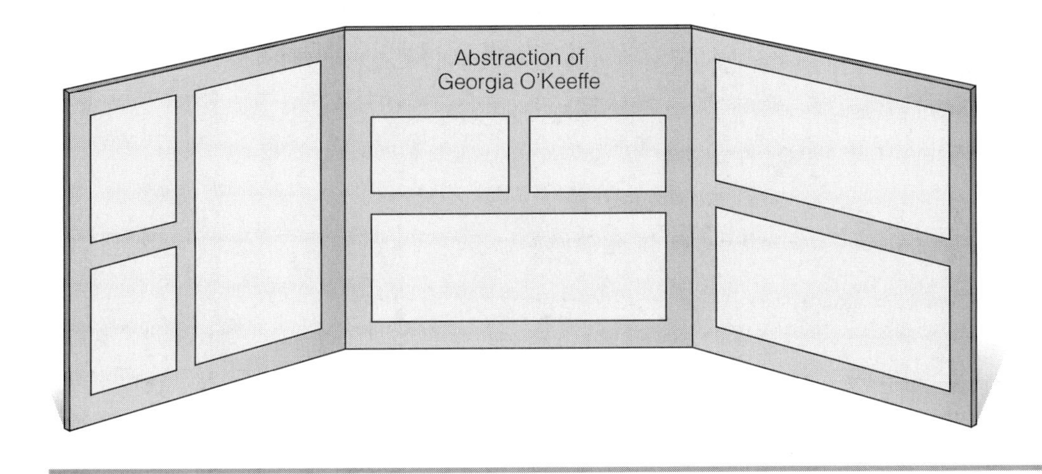

PROCESS VISUALS

There are two types of process visuals, which serve different purposes: (1) One illustrates *use of a particular process*—defining an image in contour line, creating the illusion of depth through value variation or stippling, exploring watercolor techniques, blending with oil pastels, demonstrating ways to abstract an image. (2) The other illustrates a *sequence of steps to complete a procedure* (mixing plaster) *or to fulfill an assignment* (creating a relief print). The first type of visual, shown in Figure 3.8, illustrates three different processes one might use to abstract an image (modifying shapes, simplifying areas, and altering proportions). The second type is exemplified by Figure 3.9, "Progression of Steps in Creating a Design." This visual demonstrates a step-by-step procedure moving from (1) using line to define contours, to (2) adding interest through variation in line, to (3) embellishing through incorporation of pattern. Process visuals can be created in a number of ways: They may simply be a written list of procedures; they may communicate entirely with visual images; they may combine visual and written information. Step-by-step procedures may be illustrated on a single poster or through a sequence of individual posters. Many teachers present separate process visuals lesson-by-lesson as steps within a procedure unfold in a unit of study.

FIGURE 3.8
Processes for Abstracting an Image

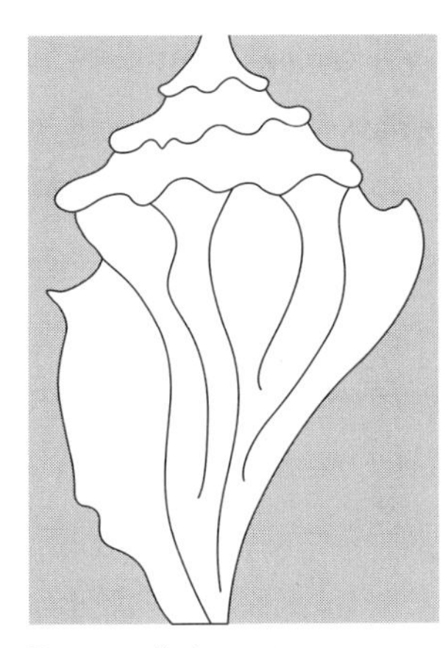

Draw realistic contours.

Modify shapes.

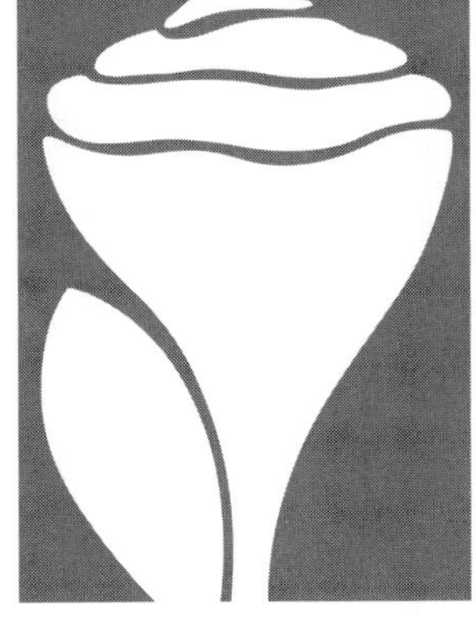

Simplify areas.

Alter proportions.

FIGURE 3.9
Progression of Steps in Creating a Design

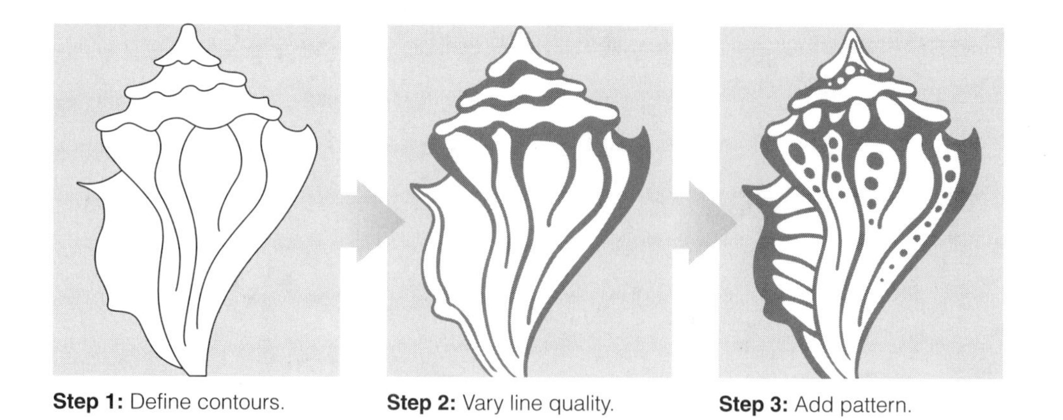

Step 1: Define contours. **Step 2:** Vary line quality. **Step 3:** Add pattern.

PRODUCT VISUALS

One of the ways you will prepare to teach is to do the studio assignments you plan to give to your students. These assignments will be both process- and product-oriented. Regardless of their nature, you should create examples before teaching to work out the best methods of presentation. These teacher examples can be thought of as product visuals. The making of a single example of an art product may teach you what you need to know about designing an assignment. Multiple examples, as displayed in the product poster in Figure 3.10, might serve your students better, however. By making several examples you can illustrate different problem-solving strategies and encourage a class to generate multiple right answers.

FIGURE 3.10
Teacher Examples: Abstract Interpretations of Natural Objects

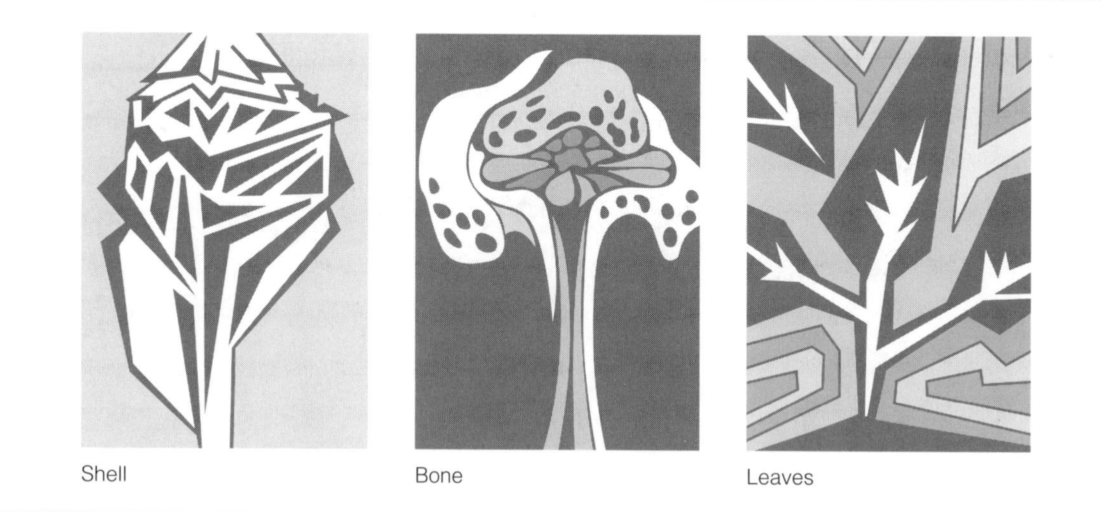

Shell Bone Leaves

Product visuals are made, first, to serve you in your learning process. Second, they are created to share with your students. As examples of creative outcomes (rather than closed-ended processes), they are not meant to be copied, but to inspire authentic self-expression. This is no easy task. Copying can be a perpetual problem. You can cut down on the amount of copying by using these strategies:

- Show multiple examples of an assignment; discuss how each example follows the given criteria; analyze how each piece solves the problem in a unique way.
- Show your teacher example(s) *after* students have begun work on final products.
- Prepare students to work on final products through the presentation of process-oriented activities, rather than through the showing of your example.
- Show ongoing student work throughout the studio experience to exemplify diversity.

You can also diminish the urge to copy (and strengthen your own teaching) by presenting your final product within the context of process visuals supporting its creation, as in the following diagram.

Progressing to a Final Product

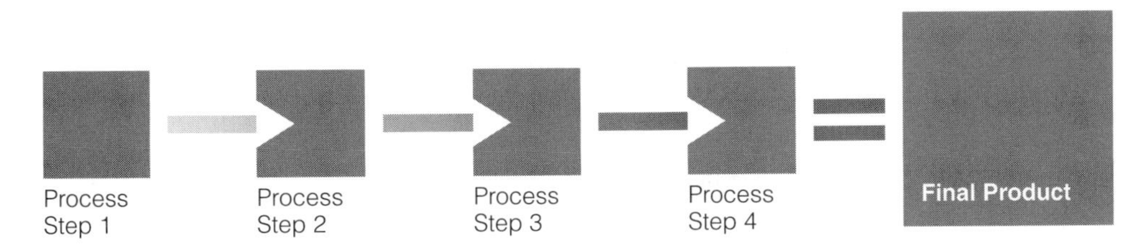

Viewing this diagram, you might assume that as a teacher you should start your visual planning by creating process poster 1 and work in a linear progression toward the creation of the final product. This system may work. It may also inhibit your creativity. This is not necessarily how artists create art. Many artists do not create by consciously stringing together a sequence of thoughts, behaviors, or procedures. They create as a result of being in a creative state, an internal place of feeling, inspiration, insight, spark. What this means for us as teachers/artists or artists/teachers is this: Perhaps the way to proceed is to go with our "artist" natures first, creating a work that has some intrinsic value to us, motivated by something either within or outside ourselves. Then we might look at the product of our "spark" and analyze how we got there. What skills did we have to possess in order to produce the piece? What knowledge or concepts did we employ? What steps in our development led us to the place where we were able to create this? The answers to these questions are the steps we will provide for our students through process-oriented activities. The progression in the following diagram illustrates how to begin with the final product and then work backward, analyzing the steps taken in its creation.

Progressing from a Final Product

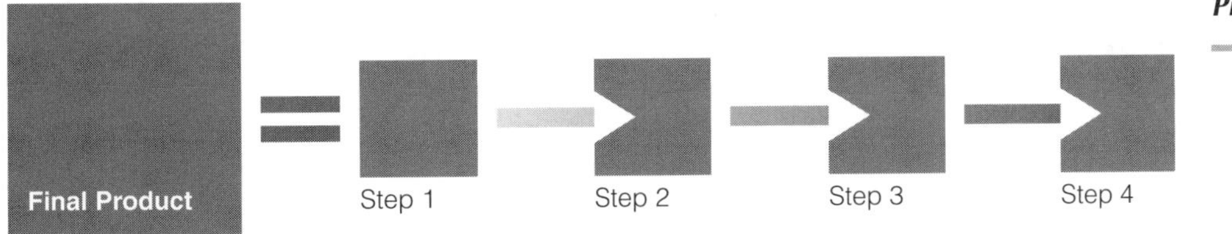

A big difference exists between the processes illustrated in each diagram. The first implies that art making can occur through a linear, logical progression of steps one might employ in solving a math problem. If you proceed in this way, you may create a predictable outcome. If you start from the other direction, allowing for expression to take form in a state where creative spark is more likely to occur, you may produce a much more inventive work.

As you think about whether your visuals are intended to be works of art, a sequence of procedures, or a presentation of a concept or cultural information, consider these words: *communicate, educate, motivate. Communicate* means sharing something with your students. *Educate* means providing new information. *Motivate* means instilling the intent to learn. As you make visuals, ask yourself, "How can I most effectively communicate? Does this communication teach the students something they don't already know? Will this motivate them to meet the desired goals?" The design of a visual is as important as the message it conveys. If lettering is not large enough to be seen from the back of the room, a poster will not communicate. If students are overwhelmed by the number of words on a poster, they will not read it. If the visual image is not interesting, it will not motivate. The following box provides suggestions for designing visuals.

Suggestions for Designing Visuals

- Print, as a general rule.
- Design your letters large and bold. Letters should be at least 2 inches tall and 1/4 inch thick. Use a color that contrasts with the background.
- Check to see that the words can be read from the back of the room. Experiment with several examples to determine what is the best for maximum readability.
- Use as few words as possible. The visual image is what attracts attention.
- Create a focal point. Posters that have an overall sameness tend to blend into the surroundings.
- Keep your designs simple, and limit the amount of information you present in a single poster. For example, make an individual poster for each art element rather than presenting information about all art elements on one poster. A series of posters on a theme can be very effective.
- Use a variety of media and techniques. You can use drawings in magazines and books by enlarging images on a copy machine. Use colored pencils or watercolor washes to add emphasis to black and white. Use an opaque projector to enlarge images from books onto poster board or banner paper. Cut letters and shapes from nonfading colored paper.
- Use a computer to generate words, designs, and print banner-sized visuals.
- Design your posters with the idea that they will be used to enhance the appearance of your room as well as to convey information. You might unify your room environment by using a common color scheme in your posters. Or you might use colors symbolically, for example, illustrating art elements on red and design principles on blue poster boards.
- Present yourself as an artist and teacher as professionally as you can through the visuals you create. Your visuals represent who you are to your students, fellow faculty, administrators, parents, and general public.

In addition to premade visuals, you will make on-the-spot visuals. These are demonstrations and are used to teach processes. They do not take the place of premade visuals but are often used in addition to process posters. There are a number of ways to demonstrate:

- A demonstration method that has become increasingly popular involves the use of the overhead projector. Many art teachers use overheads daily to project objectives and concepts, give instructions, and demonstrate studio processes. Using water-soluble markers, a paint brush, and water, you can actually paint an image on acetate film. Students view an enlargement of the image developing before their very eyes. You can also reproduce images on a copy machine and use a thermofax machine to make transparencies for an overhead projector.
- Some teachers keep easels with large pads of drawing paper in front of the room for demonstration purposes.
- Some use colored chalk especially made for chalkboards to attract attention and teach.
- Some have special demonstration corners or tables—areas in which students gather for a more relaxed, intimate view of "the artist at work."

Additional suggestions for demonstrating effectively are presented in the following box.

Suggestions for Doing Demonstrations

- Vary the ways in which you demonstrate. Work on a table or at an easel. Draw directly on the board. Draw on a large paper taped to the board. Draw on an acetate sheet on an overhead projector.
- Show students how to use processes and techniques, not how to make products or pictures of objects. For example, show students how to achieve a variety of textures, rather than how to draw a tree trunk.
- Demonstrate only as much as is necessary. You do not need to complete what you start.
- Make sure your students can see your demonstration. Draw large, using black magic marker, crayon, or charcoal rather than pencil. Gather the students around you if possible.
- If you feel unsure of your ability to do spontaneous demonstrations, you can use a paper on which you have already drawn lightly in pencil. As you quickly and confidently trace over the lines, you will impress your students with your ability to create art on the spot. You will also save time, because you will not have to think about how or what to illustrate.
- Think out loud as you demonstrate, giving students verbal as well as visual process instructions. Often students can learn more from watching your step-by-step demonstration and hearing your thinking processes than they can from simply viewing a premade example. They can ask questions about what they see or hear at any point in the process.
- Actively involve students in the demonstration process. You might ask them, "Is what I'm doing correct?" or "What should I do next?" One way to enliven a demonstration is to purposefully illustrate how *not* to do something or to leave out important steps. Watching "nonexamples" of what to do can be as informative and possibly much more entertaining than watching "how to do it correctly." You can also invite a student to work with you in demonstrating a process.

VISUALS TO PRESENT CULTURAL EXEMPLARS

In addition to the visuals you make, you will use a wide variety of visuals that already exist. Typical examples are real objects, printed reproductions of objects, slides, and videos. As we move forward in the twenty-first century, we will continue to experience the fruits of new technology. The students may have immediate access to the visual ideas and works of people anywhere on the planet. For purposes of this discussion, we will first address more traditional ways to explore the outside world and then describe ways in which teachers are using technology.

REAL OBJECTS

Sometimes we overlook the obvious. Real objects, whether they are art or simply things in the environment, are more concrete than pictures of objects. If you are teaching paper weaving, bring in an example of a woven fabric. Let your students feel it. Let them see real warp and weft threads. If you are teaching pottery, bring in some ceramic pieces or ask students to bring in examples of clay objects. Let your students know that there is a connection between what they learn and do in your art room and what exists as visual expression in the real world.

REPRODUCTIONS

Reproductions of all sizes—from postcards to door-sized posters—can be useful for a number of reasons:

1. You can keep the lights on when you show reproductions. Students are more likely to pay attention and you can monitor behavior more closely.
2. You can place several prints next to each other and make comparisons.
3. You can use them in experiential activities in which students become actively involved in seeing and learning about art. For example, you might ask a student to identify the focal point in three different prints and then create a design with a focal point using magnetized shapes on the board.

SLIDES AND OVERHEAD TRANSPARENCIES

Commercial slides produced to teach cultural content are plentiful and used by many art educators. Some teachers take their own slides of original art and of reproductions in art books to save on cost. By taking slides themselves, they can be more selective in choosing images to support particular units of study. Another good use of slides is to document studio work. Many teachers motivate and instruct by showing their own and students' work. You might consider doing this to document steps in a studio process, as well as to showcase excellent finished products. An alternative to slides are colored transparencies of artwork. These are becoming increasingly popular in commercially packaged materials and can also be made on color copy machines from reproductions in books and magazines.

BOOKS AND MAGAZINES

Books and magazines can be effectively used as resources conveying ideas and visual content. Many teachers, especially those following a discipline-based approach, use student textbooks or magazines such as *Scholastic Art*, in which they guide students to observe, read about, and discuss visual images. Some teachers show reproductions from books using an opaque projector.

Black and white images may be thermofaxed onto acetate sheets and shown on an overhead projector.

COMMERCIALLY PRODUCED PACKAGES

With the growth of discipline-based art education came an expansion of cultural resources available to art teachers. These materials come in many varieties. Some are packets of posters centering around a specific theme, such as family. Some kits or packages contain posters, videos, slides, and art games to motivate involvement in art history, criticism, and aesthetics. Many DBAE proponents view these as well worth the money. They work as visual packages focusing on a cultural exemplar. Child-centered and studio-centered advocates, who place greater emphasis on art production, have not viewed them so enthusiastically. Some have also viewed them as restrictive because the content is often selected to support a unit of study designed by someone else. Creative art teachers want to make their own decisions regarding whom to choose as exemplary artists, what to include, and how to put the pieces together. Commercially packaged units may or may not fit your student population, your curriculum content, or your particular time frame for teaching. They may do a good job presenting "the outside" (another artist or culture), while neglecting "the inside" (the individual student). In addition, they are expensive. Proceed with caution as you consider spending your art budget to purchase them. As a beginning teacher, you may be better served by building your own collection of visual resources. Some suggestions for how to do this are provided in the box that follows.

Suggestions for Building a Collection of Visual Resources

- Explore museums. Ask what is available as free literature. Visit museum stores. They often sell reproductions, postcards, slides, and books at reasonable prices. Introduce yourself to the museum education director. Find out what kinds of programs are offered to schools and what kinds of pre- and posttour materials are available.
- Look for art calendars and sale books in new and used book stores. (February–March is a good time to find art calendars on sale.)
- Look for old *Smithsonian, National Geographic,* and *Arizona Highways* in addition to other magazines on various subjects (sports, auto, nature, etc.) at rummage sales.
- Look through magazines, finding images you can use to illustrate concepts, processes, or subject matter. Mount, label, laminate, and file these pictures.
- Collect postcards of artwork used as advertising by art galleries.
- Ask the librarian at your school to donate books and magazines to the art room (such as old encyclopedias).
- Attend district, state, and national art conferences. Talk to vendors and sales representatives. Collect brochures and catalogues.
- Organize a filing system. Categories may include art elements, design principles, subject matter, artists, themes, processes, criticism, aesthetics, history, cultures. By using a filing system, you will become aware of what you have and what you need. You may be much more likely to acquire what you want if you have a system for organizing your resources.
- Wherever you go, whatever you see, whatever you read, think with your "teacher mind." You may be amazed at how much you are able to collect by consciously focusing on "visuals."

TECHNOLOGY APPLICATIONS TO PLANNING AND TEACHING

Regardless of whether you choose to purchase commercial packages of visual materials or to create your own, you will use technology. The "information age" has challenged teachers to expand both curriculum content and teaching strategies. We take this opportunity to briefly discuss applications of technology in classroom settings: ways in which teachers are using technology in performing daily routines of classroom management, researching and presenting written information, presenting visual content, and teaching art production.

PERFORMING DAILY ROUTINES OF CLASSROOM MANAGEMENT

Routine management includes such activities as presenting morning announcements, giving instructions, taking attendance, and recording grades. "Smart classrooms," equipped with computers, VCRs, television monitors, and large-screen projection capabilities, can offer teachers and students more efficient and exciting ways of performing mundane tasks and interacting with one another. For example, students may role-play the part of a newscaster, presenting morning announcements over television. By using a computer and a television monitor, teachers can display unit goals, activities, criteria for assignments, process visuals—virtually any information that was once presented on an overhead projector or chalkboard. Some instructors have also replaced roll books and grade sheets with computer printouts.

RESEARCHING AND PRESENTING WRITTEN INFORMATION

Technology has also made acquiring and disseminating information much easier than in the past. "Surfing the Net" has for some replaced reading books. (The fact that the term "school librarian" has been replaced by "media specialist" reflects a shift in consciousness.) Many art educators have found computer technology extremely advantageous in researching information, preparing materials, and teaching. For example, they can

1. Access information from a computer terminal in a classroom or at home
2. Make connections among interrelated areas by visiting different web sites
3. Download content that can be used in written and oral presentations
4. Scan art images into reference materials for students
5. Create computer presentations (such as Power Point) to teach about artists, schools of art, periods in art history, or any other content applicable to art education
6. Teach students how to research and create their own presentations to share with their peers

Certainly one of the pluses of computer technology is the increased accessibility of information. This, however, can also cause a problem. Anyone can create a web site and post information, resulting in a wide range in quality.

Before assuming everything they find is informed and accurate, both teachers and students should check how current information is, credentials of authors, and bibliographical references.

PRESENTING VISUAL CONTENT

The presentation of visual materials often requires the use of technology. Much has changed in this area. The film strips and movies that were once standard audiovisual resources in schools are now almost nonexistent. Students in classrooms today are more likely to view a projection of an artist's studio or a current exhibition in a gallery or museum on the Internet. A teacher, using CD-ROMs and DVDs (digital video discs), can visually transport students to the Louvre. Videotapes on a multitude of artists, cultures, periods in art history, and studio processes are plentiful. Greater technology, however, does not necessarily result in better teaching. As teachers have been introduced to more sophisticated ways of presenting visual information, some have become so enamored of the technology itself that they have lost sight of their educational goals. Responding like children in a candy store, they have gone on and on sharing everything they could find on a topic. We must keep in mind that technology is the *medium*, not the *message*. As you use computers, videotapes, CD-ROMs, slides—any visual device—ask yourself these questions:

1. What is my goal in presenting this information?
2. How much is necessary in order to convey the message?
3. How can I select and integrate only what is necessary to support my goals?

You may find that, as in any presentation, more is not necessarily better, shorter may be more effective than longer, and active participation of students (through discussion, note taking, worksheets) is a key to effectiveness.

TEACHING ART PRODUCTION

One of the most exciting applications of technology is in the area of studio art. Entire curricula have been designed on the high school level in graphic design and computer art. Here, it is especially important that teachers address computer technology as a *tool*. Computers do not think, solve problems, and make "art." People make art through a sequence of steps that involves developing skills in the use of tools, techniques, and processes; generating ideas; experimenting with possibilities; and finally creating visual statements in intentional ways to communicate desired messages. (This is significantly different from simply pushing a button or clicking a mouse to create a symmetrical design and then labeling it "art.") To make art, students must be led to engage in a wide range of art-making behaviors. Whether this is done through the medium of a paint brush, a chisel, or a computer is not the issue. Teaching art through the use of a computer is not so different from teaching art using any other medium. You demonstrate how to achieve effects using software; present process-oriented activities (closed-ended, open-ended, and laissez-faire) to develop skills and knowledge; and give open-ended assignments that allow students to solve visual problems and demonstrate learning in self-expressive ways. The overriding point here is that technology in and of itself is not the substance of a new age, but a vehicle that, integrated wisely into educational practice, holds the potential to deepen understanding of art and expand possibilities for authentic artistic expression.

INTEGRATING VERBAL AND VISUAL PLANNING STRATEGIES

Looking back at the content of this chapter, you may begin to realize how extensive your planning needs to be. Visual planning can be even more time consuming than written planning. For most of us, it is also more fun. Facing the challenge of how to integrate the writing of a unit plan with the making of visuals, you might begin by referring back to the content and processes you had identified using a teaching model.

As you may recall, the unit "The Abstraction of Georgia O'Keeffe" began to take form like this:

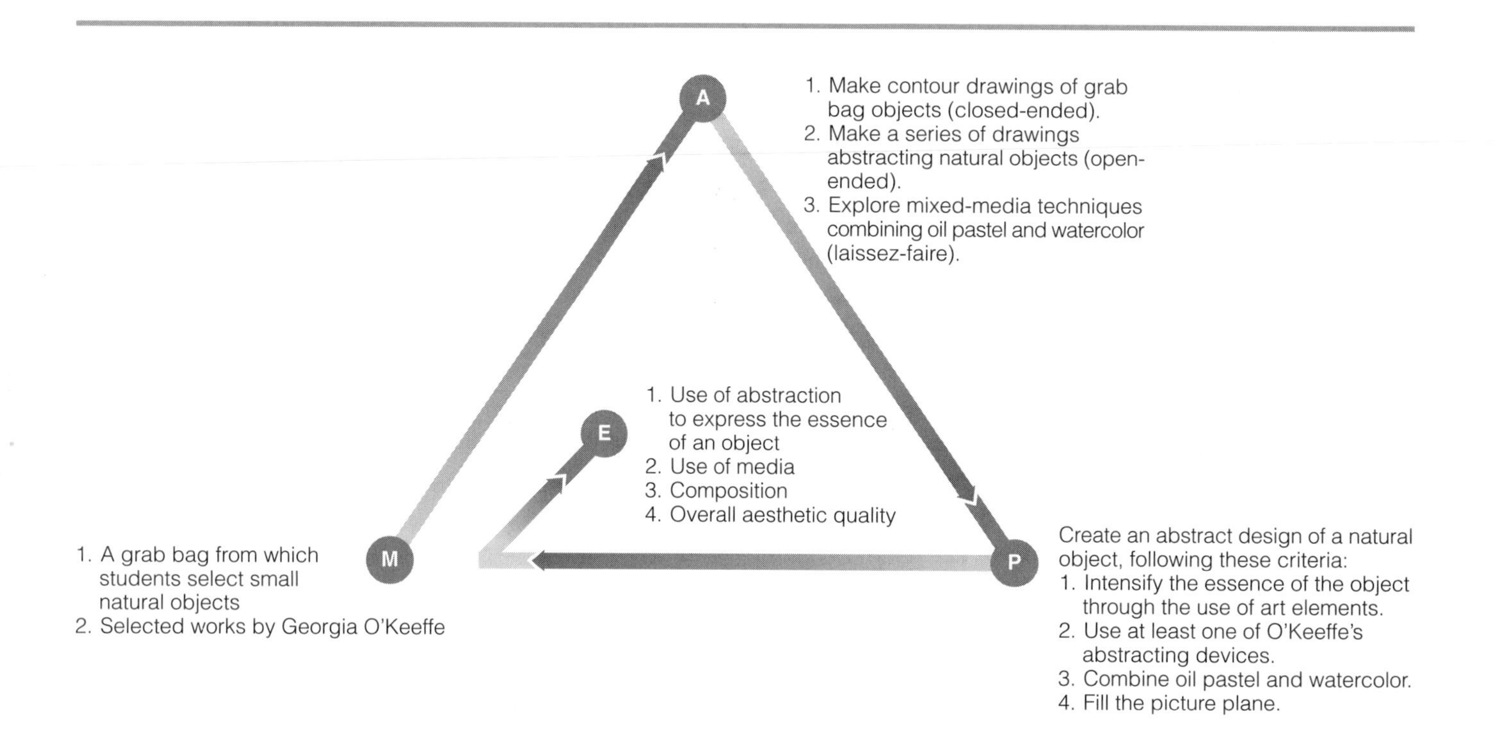

This diagram gives you the information you need to begin planning visually. Starting at the motivation step and working your way around the model, you can determine that you will need to do the following:

1. Collect small natural objects to place in a grab bag.
2. Show representative examples of O'Keeffe's work. This can be done by creating a large poster containing multiple small reproductions or showing large poster size reproductions, transparencies, or slides. You might also excerpt parts from a video, or a CD-ROM, or access images on the Internet.
3. Visually convey what contour drawing is. This might be done through an in-class demonstration and a premade visual comparing correct and incorrect drawing techniques.
4. Visually explain the process of abstracting. Again this may be done through a combination of in-class demonstration and a premade visual.
5. Demonstrate use of media prior to the laissez-faire activity.
6. Create at least one example of the final assignment.
7. Make a poster stating the criteria.

This may look like a lot of work. It is; however, remember the many purposes it serves. It

- Guides you in the writing process
- Prepares you to teach
- Provides the visual information you need as you expand your unit plan into individual lesson plans

Remember also that you will not use all these visuals in the first lesson of the unit. They will be introduced gradually as you progress through the unit. This integration of visual planning and written planning is further demonstrated in the next chapter, dealing with the expansion of a unit plan through individual lesson plans.

SUMMARY

In moving from a teaching model to a fully developed unit of study, you create units in two ways—through what you plan in writing and through what you plan visually. Verbal and visual planning have a synergistic relationship. The written aspect focuses on the design of a unit plan. This framework provides a structure for a sequence of art lessons. It includes these components.

1. The theme provides the foundation that integrates the individual parts of the unit and answers the question "What is my focus?"
2. Goals indicate what students should know and be able to do as a result of learning in the unit. They are statements of outcomes, providing answers to the question "Why am I teaching this?"
3. Concepts pertain to information about art that we present through activities in art production, art criticism, aesthetics, and art history. Concepts address the question "What cognitive information am I presenting?"
4. The cultural exemplar is one or more human-made object(s) presented to illustrate one or more aspect(s) of art. Objects may exemplify processes, media, subject matter, theme, composition, and/or concepts. They serve to link students "inside" expressions to the "outside" art world and answer the question "What can serve to illustrate content, processes, media, and/or concepts explored in studio production?"
5. The scope and sequence of experiences is the content of the unit. It provides a broad outline on which individual lessons will be based and answers the question "What experiences am I providing to lead students to fulfill goals?"
6. The evaluation procedures consist of processes you employ to ascertain your success in planning and teaching and your students' successes in learning. They include assessment of your own preparation, observation of student behaviors, and evaluation of products. These procedures address the question "Was the unit successful in leading students to fulfill goals?"

In addition to using teaching models and the unit-planning continuum to generate ideas for units, you can explore ideas visually. Concept, process, and product visuals are the posters or displays you create to teach concepts about art, to demonstrate studio processes, and to model assignments through your teacher examples. They are extremely important in planning: Through them you not only communicate visually to your students but also teach yourself how to teach. Teaching is not about *telling* students what to do; it is about *showing* them through your example. Presenting cultural exemplars also offers another opportunity to use a wide variety of visuals—postcards, posters, slides, videos, CD–ROMs, the Internet. The expansion of technology has significantly increased our access to visual images and our choices for how to present them.

Visual planning is for many art teachers the primary method for preparing to teach. Because they think visually, they focus first on their visual planning to support them later in writing a unit plan. Where you start your planning doesn't matter. What matters is that whatever method you use works best for you. Planning is a fluid process that may involve moving back and forth from words to images. The goal is to provide a general unit structure solid enough to move into your next steps—the planning of daily lessons and teaching.